Waiting for the Dawn

Translations from the Asian Classics

Waiting for the Dawn:
A Plan for the Prince

Huang Tsung-hsi's

Ming-i tai-fang lu

Wm. Theodore de Bary

Columbia University Press
New York

Columbia University Press
New York   Chichester, West Sussex

Copyright © 1993 Columbia University Press
All rights reserved

Library of Congress Cataloging-in-Publication Data
De Bary, William Theodore, 1918–
    Waiting for the dawn : a plan for the prince :
  Huang Tsung-hsi's Ming-i tai-fang lu / Wm. Theodore de Bary.
        p.   cm. — (Translations from the Asian classics)
    Includes bibliographical references and index.
    ISBN 978-0-231-08097-2 (pbk. : alk. paper)
    1. Huang, Tsung-hsi, 1610–1695 Ming i tai fang lu.   2. China—
Politics and government.   I. Huang, Tsung-hsi, 1610–1695 Ming i
tai fang lu English 1993.   II. Title.   III. Series.
JQ1508.H7883D4   1993
321'.6'0951—dc20   92–32033
                                                        CIP

Printed in the United States of America

Contents

In memory of
Huang Tsung-hsi (1610–1695)

and in tribute to my Chinese mentors over the years:
Liang Fang-chung (1908–1970)
Hu Shih (1891–1962)
Fung Yu-lan (1895–1990)
Ch'ien Mu (1895–1990)
T'ang Chün-i (1909–1978)
Wing-tsit Chan (1901–

Preface

*I*n his own time the standing of Huang Tsung-hsi (1610–95) as a major figure in Chinese thought and scholarship was already established. At least this was so of his work as an intellectual historian, philosopher, classical scholar, critic and man of letters, chronicler of recent military and political history, and indefatigable conserver of the record of Ming Confucian scholarship in literature, history, and thought. Prodigious though his reputation was in these diverse fields, in the arena of political thought Huang's efforts at first gained him little recognition except in the eyes of a few colleagues and students privileged to share in the limited distribution by hand of his *Ming-i tai-fang lu*. Given the radical nature of Huang's ideas, ordinary caution dictated some restraint in circulating, under increasingly entrenched and ever watchful Manchu rule, criticisms of the dynastic system likely to be thought subversive, certain to be provocative, and liable to be suppressed. Only in the last years of the Ch'ing period, with the dynasty in disarray, did portions of Huang's treatise eventually receive first covert and then wider, more open distribution. At this point then, he came to be acclaimed by late nineteenth- and early twentieth-century reformers and revolutionaries as an early champion of native Chinese "democratic" ideas.

My own first interest in Huang, stimulated by the great attention he thus received from modern Chinese (and even Japanese) political thinkers and scholars, was less, at the start, in the claims made for him as a native Chinese democrat (of which I then tended to be skeptical) than in his critique of the dynastic system. In the 1940s the Western scholarly atmosphere was heavy with negative judgments against the Chinese political tradition, which I expected Huang, as a kind of odd man out, backhandedly to confirm. Little did I think that what he had to say, and spoke for, represented an alternative tradition itself.

Yet despite my still quite limited acquaintance with the Chinese historical record (and in those days as a beginning graduate student, with even less of an ability to read it), I nevertheless became aware of how fraught with Western preconceptions and prejudices was the prevailing negative judgment laid against China's Confucian past. Much of it was colored by modern revolutionary doctrines and vitiated by a shallow view of history impatient with anything that seemed to stand in the way of rapid Westernization or that did not yield to instant remedies. Huang had an appeal for me then as someone who might provide a critique of Chinese "despotism" in China's own terms, uncontaminated by European ideological and scholarly preconceptions.

This Huang did provide, and indeed, as I studied his *Ming-i tai-fang lu,* he gave me far more than I had expected. His analysis, though pithy and concise, spanned all Chinese history and drew on the rich resources of a Confucian scholarly tradition I had been little aware of before. Simply to read and translate the work necessitated extensive further study of Chinese intellectual and institutional history, as well as exposure to many long-standing, deep-seated, and intractable problems of Chinese society.

To credit Huang's work with this much breadth and depth is not to say that he was either the consummate scholar or always the most practical of thinkers. Checking out his facts one finds minor errors (as other historians have already noted), and assessing his self-confident, sharply drawn, and very decided opinions about economic and military problems, one realizes that, despite his own "practical" experience in the guerrilla resistance to the Manchus, Huang remained in many ways an armchair philosopher, given (as Confucian scholars often were) to bookish solutions.

Nevertheless, for me Huang proved a great teacher, and he led me to

other great Chinese teachers (as my dedication to this book acknowledges). He compelled me not just to dig deeper into certain discrete
aspects of Chinese history—any page or even paragraph of his could well
serve as pretext for one of today's microscopic Ph.D. dissertations—
but to recognize that there were larger dimensions to his thought than I
could locate and fix in any one work of his or of his Neo-Confucian
predecessors. I was thus launched on what proved to be an extended—
indeed a lifelong—study that became fraught with digressions and
delays. I published one early essay on the subject (to which I shall make
further reference in my introduction), but I felt misgivings over its limitations even then, and had doubts whether its conclusions might not
prove premature. Now, though I regret the disservice done to Huang by
both my earlier presumptions and my later procrastinations, I hope to
make such amends as I can at this late date.

Meanwhile, over the nearly forty years that have intervened, other
scholars in China, Japan, and the West have added considerably to our
knowledge of Huang and the subjects he discussed. I mention here
(and will have occasion to cite later) the important work of Wu Guang
at the Zhejiang Academy of Social Sciences, Ono Kazuko at the Kyoto
University Research Institute of Humanistic Studies, and Lynn Struve
of Indiana University. Still others have written extensively on many aspects of Huang's life and work, but I have kept my focus here on the
Ming-i tai-fang lu itself and have not attempted to cover the larger
ground of Huang's thought and scholarship except as it affords some
important perspective on his political thought. Moreover, in the notes
to the translation, while I have tried where possible to identify names
and technical terms and the sources of Huang's historical references—
citing standard Chinese works and modern studies where relevant to an
understanding of his discussion—I have not attempted an exhaustive
bibliography in each case. Given the broad scope of Huang's discussion, full references in every case would amount virtually to a bibliography of Chinese history as a whole.

If my own perspective has changed over the years since I first began
the reading of Huang's work under the guidance of Professor Wang
Chi-chen, it is attributable not only to the authors and works cited herein but also to discussions I have had with colleagues and students
in conferences and seminars, at Columbia and elsewhere. For this I
am especially grateful to members of my graduate seminar in Neo-
Confucianism, the Regional Seminar on Neo-Confucianism, and the
Society of Senior Scholars at Columbia. I owe a very special debt to two

leading scholars in the field, Professor Yü Ying-shih of Princeton University and the aforementioned Lynn Struve, who have spared time from their own important work to read and comment on the manuscript. I have taken the liberty of incorporating several of their most pertinent observations in the endnotes. For all that, an aging scholar can make more mistakes than even the brightest minds and sharpest eyes can catch up with, and my scholarly benefactors must be exempted from any responsibility for these, as well as exonerated from any errors in those few cases wherein, obdurately, I have held to a somewhat different opinion from theirs.

I am also appreciative of the technical help given me in preparing the manuscript for publication by Dr. Ron-guey Chu, Miwa Kai, Martin Amster, Tsai Heng-ting, and in other ways by my very patient and proficient secretary Marianna Stiles. But as always (or, so as not to exaggerate, at least for the fifty years we have spent together), my greatest debt is to my wife Fanny Brett de Bary for the inspiration, encouragement, and sometimes prodding she has given me, from the earliest beginnings to the long-delayed completion of this work.

Explanatory Note

W hen I began my work on the *Ming-i tai-fang lu,* the standard ro-
manization system for Chinese in scholarly use was Wade-Giles. Since
then the pinyin system has come into official use in the People's Republic and in some Western publications. I have, for the most part, kept
to Wade-Giles, but in the cases of contemporary Chinese scholars and
works published after 1949 in the People's Republic I have followed the
practice there, since their names and titles would be rendered in pinyin
in most bibliographies, catalogs, and other references.

Waiting for the Dawn

*M*ore than forty years ago, when I was completing my initial translation and study of Huang Tsung-hsi's *Ming-i tai-fang lu,* Mao Tse-tung had just completed his takeover of China and inaugurated a new era that would be proclaimed as China's "Liberation" from all bonds and burdens of the past. Soon thereafter, however, I had occasion to preface my first publication on Huang with these words:

> Not too long ago despotism in China was apt to be viewed by Chinese and Westerners alike as a decrepit institution with a long and wearisome past but certainly no future. The old order was crumbling fast, and whatever arose from the ruins of China in the twentieth century could not help being radically new and different. Communism, especially, promised to make a clean break with China's discredited past, vociferously proclaiming its determination to rebuild on the most modern foundations. Yet those who have observed the raising-up of this structure in the first five years of Communist rule are more and more impressed by its similarity to the centralized bureaucratic structures and almost unlimited despotisms of the past. The ques-

tions have had to be reopened, therefore, as to how far China has surmounted certain deep-seated historical tendencies and how far past experience may bear upon the future of the dynasty which Mao Tse-tung has founded. In this light, not only does the new party dictatorship take on unexpected proportions, but the traditional institutions of China emerge from temporary obscurity with a renewed significance for world history, which calls for a re-examination of their most characteristic features.[1]

Today, after the demonstrations and crackdown at T'ien-an men Square in June of 1989, it would take only a few changes in tense to update this judgment and express a widespread feeling among many Chinese scholars that the new regime, as it turned out after 1949, has replicated many of the most repressive features of the old monarchy. Words like "despotism" and "tyranny" may be out of fashion among social scientists, but not among those who still protest the June 4 crackdown and feel strongly about the deprivation of human rights.

We are perhaps most reminded of these features' persistence when reform-minded Chinese today protest against the survival of "feudalism" (*feng-chien*) in the current regime. What they have in mind is its autocratic tendencies, the continued dominance of an entrenched ruling elite, nepotism, ideological conformity, repression, corruption, and so on. In using the word "feudal," they only hoist on its own petard a regime that, in the official ideology (parroted in much recent journalism even in the United States and Europe), has given currency to the term by so stigmatizing the old dynastic system from which China is now supposed to be liberated. Little have its users realized that Marx himself, when he was a London correspondent for the *New York Tribune* in the 1850s, had noted the absence in China of anything like either Western feudalism or capitalism, but had seen the centralized bureaucratic character of dynastic regimes (not decentralized feudalism) as their most salient feature. And in fact for Huang too, as for his contemporary Ku Yen-wu (1613–82),[2] how to understand the true significance of the ancient enfeoffment system (*feng-chien*) remained a key issue. Nevertheless, the view of Huang and Ku that the problems of Ming China were more attributable to the overcentralization of power (rather than the dispersion of power and authority characteristic of Western and Japanese feudalism) is supported by the analysis and conclusions of a modern specialist in Ming economic, fiscal, and military history, Ray Huang. While recognizing the decentralized character of the original Ming fiscal system, Ray Huang concludes his study of sixteenth-century China, and his analysis of many of the same problems Huang Tsung-hsi dealt with, by rejecting the characterization of the Ming regime as "feudal" and attributing its problems to a sluggish, inefficient central bureaucracy, which deprived local officials of the authority to act and "prevented them from improving the quality of their own administration."[3]

It would be unfortunate, however, if, in focusing attention upon the persistent features of Chinese autocracy, the impression were given that all of Chinese history and civilization bears the mark of unrelieved oppression and totalitarian control. This danger besets especially any attempt to characterize Chinese society in general terms, which may highlight only those segments of the traditional order that lie close to the center, contributing to our sense of its massive unity. One example of this is the expression "Confucian state," which points to the historically close association of the leading intellectual tradition with the dominant bureaucracy. This may also have the misleading effect of identifying Confucianism with autocratic institutions it had little part in creating, as well as of emphasizing unduly that teaching's susceptibility to state control. Confucianism was indeed wholly committed to the responsibilities of political leadership, even in the most unpromising circumstances, and it cannot escape entirely the judgment of history upon the imperial institutions its adherents held so long in custody. But we have learned much in recent years about the workings of both the Chinese state and the Confucian mind, about the difficult marriage between the two as they lived through a long and problematic history, and especially about those of the Confucian company who kept their distance from the state and sustained a persistent critique of many features of dynastic rule.

Foreign observers, it is sometimes alleged, have difficulty coming to a balanced estimation of things Chinese, owing to unconscious assumptions of Western superiority, the biases of imperialistic cultural hegemony, or, at the other extreme, overcompensation for the same. Be this as it may, in the years we speak of here—the seventeenth century—there could be no sharper contrast than that between the appreciative, indeed enthusiastic, accounts of China by early Jesuits in the sixteenth and seventeenth centuries and the severe criticism of Chinese institutions by contemporary Confucians of the seventeenth century (or, for that matter, by twentieth-century Chinese scholars and students after the T'ien-an men Square incident, who have despaired over their country's seemingly hopeless bondage to tyranny). If Huang Tsung-hsi can be placed anywhere on this wide spectrum, it would have to be near the latter, negative end—that is, except for two balancing factors: his sharp, unrelenting attack on imperial institutions is informed by an uncommon knowledge of Chinese history and culture, and it is infused by an equally strong determination to see that the Confucian Way should not be lost in the surrounding darkness. His protest breathes the fire of robust indignation, not a sigh of pusillanimous despair or hopeless resignation.

Huang Tsung-hsi needs no introduction to sinologists, who know him already as an outstanding figure in the history of Chinese thought and scholarship. Nevertheless, for the nonsinologist a few remarks about Huang's life and work are called for here.[4] He was the son of a high official of the Ming dynasty, one of the "Six Noble Men" of the Tung-lin reform movement, who died in prison (some eighteen years before the fall of the dynasty) because of his opposition to the powerful eunuch Wei Chung-hsien. Huang himself spent many years in study, partly under an outstanding independent interpreter of the Wang Yang-ming school, Liu Tsung-chou (1578–1645). Although unsuccessful in the civil service examinations, Huang became involved in the politics of the Fu-she Academy at the close of the dynasty. As a supporter of the Ming refugee regime active along the southeast coast of China, he participated in guerrilla resistance to the Manchus for many years and may even have visited Nagasaki on an unsuccessful mission to get Japanese help. He did not return home and settle down to serious intellectual production until 1653, when he started composing a series of political essays for the sake of posterity, not for immediate publication. The *Ming-i tai-fang lu* was the first important outcome of this work, completed in 1663, when Huang was fifty-two.[5] Thereafter, Huang turned from politics and political writing to history, literature, and philosophy, leaving many works of lasting importance, among which his survey of Confucian thought in the Ming period, *Case Studies of Ming Confucians* (the *Ming-ju hsüeh-an*) is the most highly regarded. His reputation as a scholar was well established years before his death, and the Manchu regime attempted to enhance its own prestige by patronizing him, though he declined the formal honors thus proffered to him.

In the history of Chinese thought, Huang has been important less as an original philosopher or as the founder of a new school than as one who combined the broad scholarship characteristic of the Chu Hsi school with the active interest in contemporary affairs shown by the

best of the Wang Yang-ming school (although of course some members
of the latter followed a broad scholarship of their own, while many Chu
Hsi scholars were interested in contemporary affairs). A competent
classical scholar, Huang gave more attention to the study of recent history than did most scholars of his time, whose interests were increasingly in the study of the more distant past. In this sense, *Waiting for the
Dawn* may be considered truly representative of his best work and of
the dominant theme of his learning as a whole: to bring the values of
the classics and the lessons of history to bear on the problems of his
own day.

When Huang compiled his "Plan for the Prince" (see note 8), he selected from among earlier writings of his those that fit into a coherent,
focused whole, while leaving out other essays on closely related themes,
either because they dealt with issues more cultural than political (i.e.,
aimed more at the scholar than the prince) or because they dealt with
highly sensitive questions likely to provoke Manchu reprisal (e.g., the
superiority of Chinese civilization and how best to defend it against bar-
barians). Some of these latter essays he entrusted to his family or followers for the sake of posterity in manuscripts identified as *Remaining
Writings* (*Liu shu*), which subsequently dropped out of sight and only
recently have been recovered, at least in substantial part.[6]

One other short work of Huang's, the *P'o-hsieh lun,* written much
later in life, mostly reaffirms his earlier views.[7] Reference is made to it
here, and to the *Liu shu,* for the purpose of underscoring or clarifying
certain key points. For the most part, however, we can accept the *Tai-
fang lu* itself as representing Huang's major political testament—one
that is meant by him to sum up the essence of Chinese high civilization,
and sharply differentiate genuine Confucian values from debased dynastic traditions. He hoped thereby to preserve these civilized values
through the dark night of barbarian rule but what he achieves is more
than mere conservation of received tradition. In the process Huang
contributes significantly to the reformulation of that legacy and the further development of Confucian thought.

The Aim of Huang Tsung-hsi's Work

No literal translation of the Chinese title *Ming-i tai-fang lu,* by which
Huang's work is best known,[8] can convey its real significance. *Ming-i*
has multiple meanings. Ordinarily, *i* signifies "peace and order," and
therefore *ming-i* literally suggests that the theme of this book is "an ex-

position of [the principles of] good government." But *ming-i* also means "brightness obscured" or "intelligence repressed" and is the title of the thirty-sixth hexagram in the Confucian classic, *Book of Changes* (*I Ching*), originally a divination text, which later attracted much metaphysical and cosmological speculation. The *Ming-i* hexagram is considered to represent a phase in the cosmic cycle, during which the forces of darkness prevail but the virtuous preserve their integrity, hopefully waiting for the power of evil to wane, hence: *Waiting for the Dawn.*

Traditionally, this "waiting" was done by a wise and virtuous minister of state, forced by a weak and unsympathizing ruler to hide his own brilliance and remain upright in obscurity. Chi Tzu, a legendary figure of classical times, exemplified this wisdom and patience during the last reign of the Shang dynasty (traditionally 1766–1122 B.C.). Imprisoned for protesting against the decadent ways of his king, Chi Tzu was freed after the conquest of the Shang by King Wu. He refused to serve under the latter, out of loyalty to the fallen dynasty, but when King Wu visited him to ask his advice in ruling the country, the veteran statesman communicated the political principles contained in the "Great Plan," a section of the *Book of Documents* (Shu ching). Thus, Chi Tzu's knowledge of the ancient ideal of government did not die with him but was preserved and put into practice during the glorious reign of King Wu.[9] Now Huang, during his own "waiting," expectantly prepares a plan for the prince, as Chi Tzu had done.

In his preface to the work, Huang describes himself as living in a period of darkness such as that represented by the *Ming-i* hexagram, and says that he has written down plans for a "Grand System" (*ta-fa*) of governance for the benefit of posterity. He refers to an earlier writer, Wang Mien (1287–1359), who had written such a work in the hope that, if he lived a while longer and by some good fortune met an enlightened prince, that prince could accomplish great things with his plan as a guide. Huang was a veteran of the Ming, living under its conquerors just as Chi Tzu had done during the Shang, so he says, "Though I am old, it may be that I, like Chi Tzu, will be visited by a prince in search of counsel!" The *tai-fang* in the Chinese title, which means "to await a visit," is thus another reference to the Chi Tzu parallel.

Huang's likening of himself to Chi Tzu in this way has given rise to some controversy over the author's real intentions. A friend of Huang's biographer Ch'üan Tsu-wang once pointed out, after reading the *Ming-i tai-fang lu* with Ch'üan, that Huang had put himself in an ambiguous position by this comparison to Chi Tzu. The latter had had no choice but to respond to the request of King Wu for advice, but how could Huang, who remained loyal to the Ming after the Manchu conquest, actually cherish the hope that his counsel might be sought out by some—presumably Manchu—ruler? Much later, the late nineteenth–early twentieth-century scholar Chang Ping-lin, who took issue with Huang on many points, seized upon this reference to Chi Tzu as evidence of Huang's questionable loyalty to the Ming, alleging that he secretly hoped for a "visit" from a Manchu ruler.[10]

Nevertheless, there is good reason to doubt that *Waiting for the Dawn* was written for the Manchus. When Ch'üan's friend first raised this question, he did so not in such a way as to cast doubt on Huang's loyalty but as an example of the kind of careless slip, or lack of precision in expressing himself, of which even a great scholar might occasionally be found guilty.[11] Ch'üan Tsu-wang acknowledged this at the time, yet plainly saw it as casting no reflection on Huang's integrity, which he reaffirmed on the basis of Huang's subsequent admonition to his student Wan Ssu-t'ung against offering any advice of a political nature to the Manchu court,[12] and which is again upheld in Ch'üan's postface to *Waiting for the Dawn*. Moreover, the testimony of Ku Yen-wu, who had read Huang's work shortly after it was written and who, though himself a staunch Ming loyalist, betrayed no doubts on this score in his letter to Huang concerning it, suggests that Huang's contemporaries did not interpret the reference to Chi Tzu as a collaborationist gesture. The anti-Manchu sentiments of the rediscovered *Remaining Writings* confirm this.[13] And of course the most compelling argument against any collaborationist intent on Huang's part is the text itself and its prevailing tone: no one could imagine that Huang's scornful characterization of dynastic rule—so manifest from the very opening lines of the work—was actually addressed to a reigning Manchu emperor.

Of less significance, perhaps, are certain internal evidences of the work. It is not to be expected that *Waiting for the Dawn* would contain any outright declaration of hostility to the Manchus, which would have provoked immediate suppression of both the work and the author. There may indeed have been such passages in Huang's original manuscript, but, as Ch'üan Tsu-wang indicates in his colophon, portions of the work that might give offense never appeared in the published version and some were eventually lost. Still, in the book as we have it, there are hints that the new order he envisioned would not come about under Manchu auspices. In discussing the best location for the imperial capital, for example, Huang argues in favor of Nanking rather than Peking, and in the light of Chinese dynastic tradition a change in the site of the capital was of so momentous a nature as to imply a change of dynasties, especially since Nanking was the original Ming capital.[14] Another possible hint of Huang's attitude is the failure, in the published version of his Plan, to observe the Ch'ing taboo on use of the characters in the personal name of the reigning emperor, Hsüan-yeh,[15] when referring to the Han commentator Cheng Hsüan.[16] In any case, it seems most likely that *Waiting for the Dawn* was meant to preserve the political wisdom of the past, as Huang Tsung-hsi conceived it, and to draw mostly upon the Ming experience (without direct reference to Ch'ing institutions) for the benefit of some well-disposed ruler in the future. As we shall see, this new order was to contrast markedly with dynastic rule as historically known and was certainly not tailored to fit the Ch'ing.[17]

The guidance Huang meant to impart was not simply of a proverbial sort. If his title and preface refer to Chi Tzu and his "Great Plan," it is because he intends it as a definite plan and program, with a structure and organization rare in Confucian writing. It combines theory and practice—not in the Western sense of abstract theorizing, but in stating broad principles first and then working them out in detail based on actual historical practice. It is balanced in its concern for what is central and what is peripheral, for the higher levels of government as for the lower; for economic, political, and military factors as for the moral and intellectual; for both the symbolic and the systemic. Indeed one would look long in Chinese literature, and I think in vain, for anything so carefully articulated as a general program, at once so comprehensive and concise, as this one of Huang's. It may not be equally precise or accurate in all its details but it is, without question, a well-defined plan, not just lofty and loose speculation.

Cycles of Renewal and Prophetic Expectations

A Plan for the Prince was Huang's first important literary effort after he had abandoned active opposition to the Manchus. Considering his past involvement in this struggle and his father's prominence as a Ming official, there was one immediate problem that must have been very much in his mind when he wrote this book (as it was in the minds of other dejected Ming loyalists): What were the real reasons for the Ming defeat by the Manchus? Why did this native Chinese dynasty, which had overthrown the Mongol conquerors of China, succumb to another invasion by foreigners who were far inferior numerically and—so they were regarded—culturally, to the Chinese? Though Huang never specifies this as one of the central problems of his work, in discussing other matters he constantly reverts to it and virtually all modern scholars accept it as such.[18]

One explanation for the downfall of the Ming attributed it to factionalism among the officials and meddling of the schools in politics. This view, which fit the Ch'ing's own interests, particularly exercised Huang, as is shown by his defense of the Tung-lin school in his *Case Studies of Ming Confucians (Ming-ju hsüeh-an)*. But it is clear that, for a writer with as broad an historical perspective as Huang's, the search for an answer to this question would carry him beyond consideration of any single factor in the Ming decline and, indeed, beyond the historical limits of the Ming dynasty itself. Huang's era was not wholly unique in history; such disasters had befallen the Chinese people before.

In the opening lines of his preface Huang muses upon this statement in the book of Mencius: "Periods of order alternate with periods of disorder." How is it, he asks, that since the time of the ancient sage-kings China has never known a period of peace and order but only an unending series of disorders? By this simple quotation and an obvious question Huang sets up the two grand themes that will intertwine through his treatise: the contrast between past and present (a remote past that serves as an ideal standard by which to criticize the present); and the need to analyze and explain the causes of this unrelieved decline and apparently irreversible history, if one is to remedy it. We may note too that while Huang's preface leads off with a quotation from classic scripture, his use of it is not to assert a dogmatic truth but to raise a question for further inquiry and discussion. This too will serve as a keynote of his Plan: the citing of classic teachings in order to raise fundamental questions, to be considered in the light of the actual historic record.

Following Mencius and prompted by early speculation on the meaning of the *Book of Changes,* Confucian scholars had been drawn to cyclical interpretations of human history, which was seen by some as governed by the alternating phases of the cosmic forces Yin and Yang. Among the earlier attempts to work out mathematically the significance of the *Book of Changes* for the future, Huang cites the theory of the fourteenth-century writer Hu Han (1307–81), who at least took into account what seemed to Huang an obvious fact of Chinese history: so far the phase of decline had not yet given way to a more auspicious one. "Since the death of Confucius and throughout the dynasties succeeding the Chou—the Ch'in, Han, Chin, Sui, T'ang, Sung, and so on down for two thousand years—the time has not come for a change."[19] It was on the basis of Hu's prediction of a change at the end of this period (more precisely, 2,160 years) that Huang speculated on the prospects for a Chinese resurgence in the near future. He hoped in vain, but his reasoning at least demonstrates how he approached an explanation of the Ming failure. It was just one in a long series of dynastic failures, all of which, he went on to show, could be explained in much the same terms.

"Whether there is a peace or disorder in the world does not depend on the rise or fall of dynasties but upon the happiness or distress of all the people."[20] Contrary to the conventional view of history, which identifies the interests of the people with those of the dynasty and regards dynastic disorders as a calamity for the people, Huang maintains that the rise and fall of ruling houses ever since the end of the Chou (third century B.C.) has brought no fundamental change in the condition of the Chinese people. Again and again he reiterates this view; Chinese civilization underwent its great crisis with the rise of the Ch'in empire and has never recovered. At one point he indicates that there were two such catastrophes, the first having come with the Ch'in and the second with the Mongol conquest, but he does not elaborate on this point, and nothing he says elsewhere suggests that Mongol rule effected a radical or decisive change in Chinese society.

What Huang probably meant was only that the Mongol conquest gave great further impetus to a process of degeneration set in motion long before. In the course of history less and less had survived of traditions deriving from the ideal society of the distant past, and this steady deterioration, accelerated by the Mongol conquest, probably accounted for the fact that the Ming dynasty suffered from certain evils even more acutely than preceding dynasties. But so far as the basic character of dynastic institutions is concerned, Huang in each case traces their evil origins back to the Ch'in. The weaknesses of the Ming are common to all preceding dynasties, though in differing degree, and it is in this light that he analyzes them. "Unless we take a long-range view and look deep into the heart of the matter, changing everything completely until the ancient order is restored with its land system, enfeoffment system, educational and military systems, then, even though minor changes are made, there will never be an end to the misery of the common man."[21]

At this point Huang places himself in the long line of Neo-Confucians, and particularly those of the early Sung, who saw the institutions attributed to the early sage-kings as the ideal standard by which to judge the present state of affairs. Like them, he takes as his model the enfeoffment system outlined by Mencius and presented in a neat, symmetrical fashion by the classical books of rites, especially the *Rites of Chou (Chou li)*. But, like his predecessors, he must reckon with the vast and profound changes that China had undergone in the intervening centuries and with conditions that seemed to render any such wholesale reform impracticable. And he must reckon too with the failure of these earlier advocates to accomplish their purpose. It was no longer the failure of the Han and T'ang alone to attain the ancient ideal, but that of the Sung itself, and later dynasties, which Huang found hanging oppressively over the landscape of history. Against the long line of Neo-Confucian idealists in the past there were probably arrayed by now at least an equal number of skeptics to declare that return to the classical order was out of the question.

It cannot be said that Huang squarely faced all the obstacles between him and his objective; like many idealists he was more convinced that all other measures had failed than he was prepared to demonstrate that the same difficulties would not stand in the way of his own program. Nevertheless, he was forced to answer the very real question that had confronted the Sung reformers: Should the ancient enfeoffment system be reestablished in every aspect and every detail, or should we merely adapt certain fundamental principles or values embodied in that order, so that the same ends are achieved through different means? Huang's answers are not always consistent, but for the most part he accepts the latter view. When dealing with the problem in its most general terms, he is apt to be carried away by the sweep of his own fervent and oracular rhetoric and to insist, as in the passage just quoted, upon a complete restoration of the early system of government. But when he takes up one by one the specific institutions involved, Huang recognizes immediately that many of the classical prescriptions are inapplicable to his own time. The result is that his "Great Plan" as a whole represents not a duplication of the book of Mencius or the *Rites of Chou,* but a new system of government based on classical principles, yet taking into account historical realities.

What, then, are the principles that Huang seeks to uphold? For him, as for any true Confucian, the most fundamental principles are involved in the conception of rulership, since Confucianism accepts that the key to all social evils, as well as to any hope of improvement, lies in the nature and quality of leadership.

The Prince as Servant[22]

In man's original state, Huang says, there were no rulers. Each man took care of himself and left others alone. To Huang it was essentially the kind of primitive society early Taoists had imagined it to be but not, as they thought, an idyllic existence, since no one promoted the good of all.[23] Then leaders appeared who attempted to remedy this defect, seeking not their own good but the benefit of others. These sage-kings taught men the arts of civilization, saw to it that their people had sufficient land from which to gain sustenance and clothing, established customs and ceremonies that would regulate their social intercourse, maintained schools for their education and moral training, and instituted military service for the common defense. But this was a burdensome task, and few men could be expected to undertake it. A few indeed—sometime paradigms for the Taoists—refused to undertake it, but, as Huang sees it, only because it entailed too great a responsibility and not, as the Taoists would have it, because active government inevitably meant needless interference in the lives of others. This being the case, even those who accepted the office of ruler, like the emperors Yao and Shun, were eager to relinquish it to some worthy successor and had no desire to put such a burden on their own less than worthy sons.

Such, according to Huang, was the concept of rulership in ancient times. In later times, however, and especially with the rise of the Ch'in and Han dynasties, rulership was regarded as a great prize, not as a heavy responsibility. The first Ch'in emperor had no desire to serve others or to share with them, and therefore he abolished the enfeoffment system of the Chou dynasty, which to Huang had represented the natural means of sharing political leadership and property with others, as well as the most effective means of providing for the needs of others through the personal attention of the individual lord to the welfare of his people.

This idea—that the essence of the enfeoffment system is a delegation of power to someone who takes personal responsibility for his people, in contrast to the system of bureaucratic impartiality and impersonality which breeds indifference and irresponsibility—is a consistent theme of Huang's, shown also in his separate essay on the enfeoffment system (*feng-chien*), considered by some to be an unpublished fragment of the *Tai-fang lu*).[24]

To apply the term "feudal" (*feng-chien*) as an epithet for the centralized bureaucracies of the dynastic system, as often is done today, is to use that term in a sense exactly contrary to the meaning of *feng-chien* as "enfeoffment" in the Confucian literature. It is as if the word "paternalism" were being applied to the dynastic system, whereas, in the true Confucian sense of the word "paternal," a genuine fatherly solicitude could only be found in the earlier enfeoffment system overthrown by the Ch'in. At that point, all land was brought under the direct tax control of the emperor, so that he could exploit it for his own ends, through a new system of centrally administered provinces and prefectures. Thenceforth, the ruler's only concern was to keep this vast personal estate intact and prevent it from falling into the hands of others than his own heirs.

Although traditional elements are interwoven in this account of a three-stage transition from a primitive society to a more civilized state and then to a dynastic system, Huang's version is by no means a conventional one. It does not begin, as does the canonical Confucian account in the *Book of Documents* (*Shu ching*),[25] with the myth of the sage-king Yao, who symbolizes the virtues of self-restraint, reverential respect, and paternal affection—virtues that work their charismatic effect on all humanity, unifying them as one loving family. Nor does Huang invoke the other familiar mythic account in the *Record of Rites,* according to which the primitive state of humankind, the primordial age of Grand Unity or Commonality (*Ta-t'ung*) was marked by a sharing of the world by all-under-Heaven in a cooperative community suffused with a totally unselfish spirit. Confucian writers earlier had proclaimed this primordial ideal in clear juxtaposition to claims of sovereign authority based on superior power, established position, or dynastic inheritance. They thereby challenged any pretension to a divine right of kings, stemming from divinized progenitors of the royal house, by upholding an egalitarian ideal of individual merit and shared property that, in effect, desacralized the existing order.

Huang too has in mind to desacralize dynastic rule, but he does so in a more realistic fashion by presupposing a primitive state of society in which it is natural for men to pursue their own self-interest and satisfy their elemental needs. Against this background, as Huang sees it, a more civilized order can come into being only through the superior virtue and voluntary efforts of exceptional leaders, willing to stand forward and offer themselves in service to the common good. Without such self-denying commitment and self-sacrificing dedication, no ruler or dynasty can claim Heaven's mandate or the paternal authority deriving from Heaven. Further, by excoriating the practice of calling the ruler "our Prince and Father," Huang challenges the basis of the whole patrimonial system.

Although we know from the classical writings attributed to Mencius and Hsün Tzu that such a conscious commitment to humane rule and consistent effort on behalf of the common good had early been seen, in the Confucian view, as a sine qua non of all leadership, in the present case we have reason to believe that Huang, when citing the Taoist examples of Hsü Yu and Wu Kuang, echoes as well a work entitled *Po-ya ch'in*[26] by the late Sung writer, Teng Mu (1247–1306).

Teng, a poet and scholar with eclectic interests, who had received Taoist initiation as a *tao-shih,* lived in retirement after the fall of the Sung, refusing to serve the Mongols.[27] His patriotism, noncooperation with the conqueror, and experience under foreign rule as a survivor from a fallen dynasty establish an affinity between him and Huang Tsung-hsi. Through the testing of their most fundamental loyalties and value commitments in the crucible of dynastic upheaval, both arrived at a radical critique of dynastic rule based on higher cultural allegiances. Moreover, in Huang's case the breadth of his scholarship, extending to non-Confucian literature, made him familiar with the Taoist canon (in which Teng's work was preserved, even though it had not been widely circulated or commented upon by scholars), and exposed Huang's mind to fundamental Taoist criticism of the Confucian position. From such philosophical encounters Huang was prepared to take Teng's unconventional views into account in developing his own ideas concerning rulership and governance.

There is a sufficient resemblance between the language and illustrative examples in Teng Mu's discussion of the "Way of the Prince" (or Ruler, *chün-tao*) and Huang's essay on the same subject to warrant the belief that Huang drew in part on Teng Mu's work in respect to the following points: (1) that commonsensical Taoist types, aware of the difficulties of rulership, had refused the throne, and even Confucian sage-kings had accepted this responsibility only with the greatest reluctance, recognizing the heavy burdens it imposed; (2) that rulership was understood to involve service to the people, not domination over them; (3) that the people responded with love for good rulers in return for benefits received; (4) that the task of ruling the empire was too vast for one man alone to fulfill, hence the need for officials to assist him (a view widely shared among Sung and Ming thinkers); (5) that since the establishment of the Ch'in empire, both rulers and officials have been motivated mainly by selfishness and greed, not by self-sacrificing service;

and (6) that people would have been better off if they had just looked out for themselves, without either rulers or officials of the self-seeking or self-important type interfering in their lives.[28]

As they appear in Huang's discussion of the ruler, both the figure of Hsü Yu (with his natural disinclination to take up the burdens of rulership), as well as the idea that in the original state of human life people pursued their own self-interest, are new to Confucian discourse. They stand in marked contrast with the conception of the Grand Commonality in the Confucian classic, *Record of Rites* (*Li chi*),[29] wherein the primitive ideal is communal and a spirit of complete unselfishness prevails. Huang's view is more naturalistic. He neither romanticizes the remote past as an age of perfect love and harmony in which all the world's goods ("all-under-Heaven") are shared (*t'ien-hsia wei-kung*), as it is described in the *Record of Rites* chapter on the "Evolution of Rites" (*Li yün*); nor does he, by contrast, picture the original condition of man as one of constant conflict or as an anarchy of human desires, from which humankind must be delivered by the ruler's formulation of rites or the imposition of law. Rather, with regard to human nature in general, he strikes a realistic balance between such idealism and cynicism.

Huang's appropriation of this conception differs somewhat from Teng's original, however. Teng's position is basically anarchist; he remains pessimistic with regard to the possibilities for basic reform and has no "plan" to offer like Huang's. He is skeptical too that any amount of do-gooding by Confucians can improve upon what individuals would do for themselves. Huang's characterization of the primitive human condition, on the other hand, while allowing for the natural satisfaction of individual desires as preferable to the monopolization of power and wealth by later dynasties, does not preclude a better alternative than either of these: the envisioning of a higher civilizational level, achievable through true Confucian leadership, in which humankind can enjoy a richer, more refined life beyond the primitive level of mere subsistence. Thus his naturalistic characterization of the original state of human existence is essentially neutral, balanced between an optimistic view of human nature (as seen in the Grand Commonality of the "Li Yün") and the view that the brutish state of human nature when left to itself is so ridden by selfish conflict as to require, simply for survival, the intervention of rulers and the imposition of laws to curb man's natural aggressiveness. In neither case of course does Huang see early man as coming together on a "social contract" with the ruler; the initiative remains with the exemplary Noble Man.[30]

Other commentators have seen in Huang's description of the original human condition a new affirmation of the positive value of human desires, reflecting a general reaction in sixteenth- and seventeenth-century China against a puritanical view associated with earlier Neo-Confucianism—a reaction linked to economic and social changes in this period.[31] I have made reference to this same trend elsewhere[32] and will have other occasions to do so in this essay, but here I wish just to note two points. First, insofar as Huang may be thought to derive his view of the original state of nature from Teng Mu, a thirteenth- to fourteenth-century writer, to try to explain it as the product of new trends in the sixteenth and seventeenth centuries could well be an anachronism. Second, and more importantly, though this theory or postulation is new to Confucian thought and is given unusual prominence at the beginning of Huang's work, the idea of a primordial state of natural self-interestedness is not developed by Huang as a main theme even of this initial essay, much less of the work as a whole. In fact nowhere in his Plan does Huang develop or define the idea of individual self-interest except in relation to the nature of the ruler and dynastic rule. There he is quite explicit that in the ruler self-interest must be identified with the public interest and can only be fulfilled by the ruler's subordinating and sacrificing himself to the needs and interests of all-under-Heaven. This ideal of the sage-ruler then stands in contrast to the dynastic ruler's misappropriation of self-interest, turning it into a selfish interest advanced at the expense of others.

Thus, the question of self-interest appears here simply as a foil for Huang's true central thesis: that the cardinal evil to be reckoned with in human society (and real evil it is to Huang) is the entrenched selfishness of the dynastic system, which, as a forcible monopolization of power and wealth, deprives ordinary people of the means of satisfying their natural desires and takes a heavy toll of human life. Indeed the main theme of Huang's work is the contrast between rulership as a public trust and dynastic rule as the embodiment of the selfish desire to own and control everything—employing for this purpose ministers and officials who are treated as one's own servants, soldiers hired to guard one's personal estate, and eunuchs assigned to watch over one's wives and concubines, so that the whole system is made to serve one's self-gratification.

Confucius, Mencius, and Hsün Tzu, as well as many Neo-Confucians, had made similar critiques of rulers who failed to meet the test of responsible rulership, and for like reasons censured their inordinate appetite for power and wealth. Indeed the earlier Neo-Confucian emphasis on curbing desires had been primarily aimed at the ruler and his officials, not the common people. It appealed to the Sung literati's sense of a noble calling, a mission to save suffering humanity, as portrayed in Fan Chung-yen's (989–1052) characterization of the Noble Man (*chün-tzu*) as "first in worrying about the world's worries and last in enjoying its pleasures." This self-sacrificial role of the Noble Man, model for the leadership elite, is reaffirmed here by Huang in his mythic portrayal of the sage-king's self-denying exertions on behalf of humankind, just as earlier Neo-Confucians had upheld the sage as an ideal self-image for both the ruler and themselves, exemplifying the principle of noblesse oblige and calling upon those with access to power and wealth to be strenuously watchful over their own selfish inclinations and desires.[33]

Thus before Huang's time the main thrust of Neo-Confucian self-cultivation for the educated, ruling elite had been directed at the individual ruler or Noble Man. It is true that as Neo-Confucian thought and education reached out to a larger literate audience in the Ming—a "public" comprised in increasing numbers of merchants, artisans, and commoners in general—this elite ideal of noblesse oblige and self-discipline among the ruling class was subject to great strain. It had less and less relevance or plausibility for the commoner, the satisfaction of whose basic appetites and desires was more to the point.[34] Yet this latter view of the legitimacy of human appetites, though certainly shared by Huang and a basic assumption of his whole Plan, is the main point neither of his first chapter nor of the work as a whole, which continues to uphold the austere and demanding leadership ideal among scholar-officials.

Before proceeding further, we should note that the contrast between the naturally self-regarding tendency of the common man and the self-denying heroism of the Noble Man is reinforced by an essay in Huang's *P'o-hsieh lun,* in which he reflects, much later in life, on some of the points made earlier in his Plan. In a discussion of the natural course of either historical development or degeneration, Huang takes issue with the earlier view of Su Hsün (1009–66) that human history naturally tends to move from primitive vigor and simplicity to higher levels of refinement and complexity. Huang argues rather that the normal inclination of people in any age is to revert to this natural condition of ease and simplicity, and it is only the exceptional, self-sacrificing exertions of sage-kings and noble men that sustain civilized society. If, for instance, people really loved the elegance and refinement of the classic rites, the latter would be thriving, yet the opposite is actually the case.[35] This point is reinforced in a surviving, only recently published essay of Huang's contained in his *Liu shu (Remaining Writings)*, which emphasize that the benefits of civilization are hard won and do not accrue to a "natural," laissez-faire, uncultivated state.[36]

Still, the noble calling of rulership is not itself the main point of Huang's first chapter. That only establishes the high ground from which Huang will take aim to shoot down the evils of the dynastic system as a whole. Huang's real argument here, and his most distinctive contribution to Neo-Confucian thought, consists rather in targeting dynastic rule as the prime incarnation of political and economic evil. It is not the individual so much as the institution that is to blame; it is no longer simply the self-cultivation or self-dereliction of the individual ruler that preoccupies Huang as it did so many of his Neo-Confucian predecessors, but the institutionalized greed, selfishness, and irresponsibility of the whole dynastic system. Confronting this monstrous deformity of government, the individual alone is virtually powerless. Indeed, in the final analysis, even of the emperor, his individual heirs, and his family is this true, for eventually they themselves become victims of a cruel system that wreaks havoc impartially on all—and, at the dynasty's end (as Huang reminds his readers at the conclusion of this essay), most brutally upon those who once had been most favored.

As Huang explains the imperial dynastic system set up by the Ch'in, he likens the relationship between ruler and ruled to that between master and servant, or proprietor and tenant. In ancient times the people ("all-under-Heaven") had been masters and proprietors of the land, while the ruler was merely their servant, a temporary occupant of his office. Since the rise of the great empires, however, the emperor had become the master, and the people mere servants or tenants, possessing nothing in their own right. Though the Chinese terms Huang uses here can often mean "host" and "guest," from what Huang tells us of this relationship the analogy of master and servant, or proprietor and tenant, might convey his meaning better than host and guest. In China as elsewhere the host is thought of as under an obligation to entertain and provide for his guests, in which sense it would have exactly the opposite meaning of what Huang intends. In spite of this ambiguity, his characterization of ruler and ruled as master and servant (or "host" and "guest") is what Huang has become famous for, and later writers often cite it as the epitome of his political thought.

As it happened, Huang's choice of terms fit well with liberal democratic discourse from the West when it first reached East Asia through Japan, after which Chinese students and exiles picked up some of the language in which issues of political democracy were first expressed. One major question had to do with disparate concepts of popular sovereignty and traditional monarchy—were they compatible, as in the case of England, or not? In Japan where imperial loyalism was a powerful factor in national politics, an eloquent spokesman for liberal democracy, Yoshino Sakuzō (1878–1933), skirted the issue of sovereignty by emphasizing, in good Confucian language, that, whatever the locus of sovereignty, the needs and interests of the people were paramount. Confucius himself had said that a good ruler took the needs and aspirations of the people to heart, and even the fulfillment of imperial rule, as serving those basic interests of the people, could best be assured, so Yoshino thought, by having an open electoral system for the expression of the people's wishes. Thus, in his formulation even imperial rule "for the people" could best be accomplished through "government by the people," that is, by parliamentary government and universal suffrage, so the question of the locus of sovereignty ("of the people") need not be considered crucial.[37]

Likewise, Chinese reformers in the early twentieth century (still under the Manchus), split between republicans and constitutional monarchists, could recognize a distinction between a doctrine emphasizing the primacy of the people's needs and interests (*min-pen chu-i*; Japanese, *mimpon shūgi*), compatible with constitutional monarchy, and one insisting on the people's sovereignty (*min-chu chu-i*; Japanese, *min-shu shūgi*) as the republicans would have it.

Huang Tsung-hsi did not face the issue in quite these terms, but his recommended solution to the problem of hereditary rule allowed for either of these possibilities. On the one hand, he challenged the whole basis of hereditary rule as historically it had existed, and said the people would be better off without any ruler at all than with the existing system. On the other hand, the system he went on to recommend envisaged the possibility of a sage-ruler, a prince somehow accepted by the people (by means not specified), whose power was so limited by systemic checks and balances as to resemble a constitutional monarchy. Nevertheless, since Huang had expressed himself clearly as believing that "all-under-Heaven" should be "masters" or "proprietors" (*chu*) in the land, his language corresponded closely to that found in modern political discourse to represent democracy as "the sovereignty of the people" (*min-chu chu-i*). Indeed, that Huang went beyond the position expressed simply in terms of government *for* the people (*min-pen chu-i* / *minpon shugi*) is confirmed when Huang again and again, in different contexts, argues that the people (expressed as "all-under-Heaven"), represent Heaven as the ultimate source of authority and it is their needs and wishes that government should serve.

As a concept, the primacy of the people is not new to the Confucian tradition. Mencius had said: "The people are the most important element in the nation; the spirits of the land and grain are next; the prince is the last."[38] Hsün Tzu, the other great exponent of Confucius' teaching in classical times, had used an equally vivid and far more apt analogy than Huang Tsung-hsi: "When the people are satisfied with his government, only then is a prince secure in his position. It is said: 'The prince is the boat, the common people are the water. The water can support the boat or the water can capsize the boat'—this expresses my meaning."[39] Therefore, if Huang had done no more than reiterate the primacy of the people and the consent of the governed as essential to successful rule, one would say that he had not gone much beyond Mencius and Hsün Tzu. His real contribution to Confucian thought lies in the application of this basic principle to political institutions that had undergone substantial changes since the late Chou. Yet as he moved in this direction, and sought to redress an overemphasis in earlier Confucian thought on the power of the individual to deal autonomously with entrenched systemic forces, he also moved into the sphere of laws and institutions previously identified with the Legalists.

Law

The Chinese term *fa* (translated here as "law") has a wide range of meanings: "method," "model," "standard," "regulation," "system," "institution," etc. How to understand it is of prime importance to Huang, and the high priority given to it in his Plan tells us much about his overall aims, especially the centrality to his thinking of the whole question of dynastic rule. For him the basic and most authentic meaning of *fa* is "model" or "system," as a standard set for all time by the ancient sage-kings. In this form, as a projection into a remote, idealized past, *fa* serves Huang as a lofty standard by which to judge existing institutions. At the same time, it is an instantiation or exemplification of how the sage-kings provided for the very real needs of men—typically cited by Huang in the form of the "well-field" system of equal landholding among the peasantry, schools in which to educate them, rites by which to guide their conduct of life, and so on. True law then consisted of basic models set up by the sage-kings, timeless (and in that sense transcendent) but very much of this world and altogether human.

The principal alternative conception of law in actual practice was dynastic law, consisting essentially of the precedents set by the founder or earlier emperors of a ruling house, or regulations defined by dynastic codes. Mostly Huang identifies this kind of law with dynastic institutions that advance or protect the power of rulers, institutions deriving from the first imperial dynasty, the Ch'in, which came to power through the implementation of administrative policies and bureaucratic systems identified with the early Legalist philosophy. In the Confucian mind this was associated with the total organization of power and the use of harsh, punitive law for purposes of the state, not the people. Law in this form expressed the will of an emperor ruling with unlimited powers. Its purpose was to standardize the administration of the country, integrate the activities of the people, and organize all resources under the state. Whereas the Confucian ideal had been a decentralized feudal society, in which the unifying and regulating principle was the personal, moral influence of its rulers, the essence of this new order was its impersonality and its implicit reliance on coercion. For this reason Confucians traditionally held a strong antipathy for law, viewing it as an illegitimate, nonconsensual imposition of the state upon the people. Further, they held it responsible for all the excesses of the Ch'in regime, which had abolished the earlier enfeoffment system. From their point of view, the fewer the laws the better, since ultimately the humane execution of laws and policies depended on the "man"—the moral character of the ruler and his officials.

Huang Tsung-hsi sees the aims and methods of Ch'in rule as perpetuated in substance by all subsequent dynasties. But he refuses to accept the traditional view that there is an inherent antithesis between the rule of law and rule by men. The law of the imperial dynasties is not true law but simply a mass of unilateral dictates enacted for the benefit of the ruling house. True law had been enacted for the benefit of the people by the sage-kings and was embodied in the system of government described in the classics. It consists not in multitudinous statutes, prescribing in detail what men should or should not do and attaching a severe penalty to each infraction, but rather in a simple and general set of institutions which are basic to the proper functioning of government and to the promotion of the general welfare.

By contrasting the former unfavorably with the paradigmatic institutions of sage-kings, Huang accomplishes two things. First he downgrades and desacralizes dynastic law, undercutting any claim of dynastic rulers to rule by Heaven's authority. The purpose here of course was as old as the Confucian concept of the Mandate of Heaven, which held rulers responsible for the welfare of the people and denied the ruler any authority not certified by his fulfillment of this responsibility. Still, it was only a rare Confucian like Chu Hsi who dared to question the validity of dynastic law,[40] and Chu Hsi did not come close to challenging it in as thoroughgoing, radical, and unreserved a manner as Huang Tsung-hsi does in his essay on Law, wherein he not only reasserts the existence of a higher law but goes on to deny dynastic law any legitimacy at all, since it actually obstructs the heroic efforts of Confucian Noble Men to act for people as a whole, rather than for the benefit of the ruling house alone. Here then, we have one measure of Huang's contribution to the further development of Neo-Confucian thought after Chu Hsi.

Second, in place of the dynastic law that he has so devalued, Huang sets up as true law institutions of the sage-kings, which in the canonical literature had always been classified as Rites (in the *Record of Rites, Rites of Chou*, etc.). For Confucians these classic rites had been juxtaposed to Legalist law, whereas "law" for Confucians had been applied mostly to that small area of governmental action wherein coercive, punitive sanctions had to be applied to refractory individuals unreformable by the proper Rites. Even Chu Hsi, though he accepted an enlarged role for law as a necessary evil to be resorted to in degenerate times, still upheld the idea that for Confucians rites should be the first resort and laws the last.[41]

Huang, however, reverses this order, incorporating the paradigmatic institutions of the sage-kings under the general heading of Law, while referring to the rites as just one subset among them. Moreover, among the many topics dealt with in his Plan, Huang devotes no separate essay to the "sacred" subject of Rites, but relegates this matter to just one of several things that the local school superintendent should supervise. Obviously a significant inversion of terms is taking place. Compare this with all the attention given by Chu Hsi to the study and reformulation of Rites, or to the thirty chapters devoted to Rites by the Ming scholar-statesman Ch'iu Chün (1420-95) out of the 160 chapters in his *Supplement to the Extended Meaning of the Great Learning (Ta-hsüeh yen-i-pu)*, and one gets a measure of how far Huang has gone in redefining the problem of government. Indeed what he does here in effect is to accept this enlarged sphere of law, as it has been expanded in the centralized bureaucratic administrations of the imperial dynasties, and instead of attempting actually to reestablish the Chou enfeoffment system (except to a very limited degree in frontier commanderies, as we shall see later), he reconciles himself to the irreversible change that has taken place since the Ch'in and Han, and seeks to convert the existing governmental structure into an instrument for fulfilling the original aims of the sage-kings. In other words, by redirecting the central administrative system so as to serve Confucian purposes, he would invest it with a new constitutional basis that also meets the paradigmatic standards of the sage-kings. Only in such a framework, only with the support of fundamental law properly defined, could good men do their work.

Huang's recognition of the fundamental importance of law differentiates him from most Confucians and is of far-reaching consequence to his political philosophy as a whole. Men of his school, whether in recent times they had followed Chu Hsi or Wang Yang-ming, had most often tended to treat politics as if it involved no more than adherence to certain moral principles and the cultivation of Confucian virtue by the ruler and his officials. There were significant exceptions to this among Neo-Confucian scholars who as practical statesmen or encyclopedists of institutional history gave attention to laws and systems,[42] but the more common view, as noted before, was to see the laws and institutions of a dynasty as largely determined by its founder and held to as unchangeable. All that remained was to ensure proper administration of the established law through sound education of the emperor and selection of upright officials.[43] Huang, however, insists that dynastic law is not only not inviolate but amounts to a positive evil. The net of laws has spread further and further as morbid fears for its own security drive a dynasty to tie tighter the hands of its people and circumscribe further the powers of its officials. So complex and intricate has the net of laws become that it serves only as a refuge for incompetents and clever scoundrels, while able men are deprived by it of any freedom of action. "Unlawful laws," he says, "fetter men hand and foot, and even a man capable of governing well cannot overcome the handicaps of senseless restraint and suspicion." Without proper governance by law, Huang says, there cannot be governance by men.

There is a further significance that attaches to this thought in the

Neo-Confucian context of the late Ming. Scholars and officials schooled in the Four Books would know how Chu Hsi's commentary on the *Great Learning* had put special emphasis on the ruler's self-cultivation as a precondition for the effective governance of men (*hsiu-chi chih-jen*). They would also know that the moral heroism Sung Neo-Confucians had called for in the Noble Man (*chün-tzu*), as the key to human governance and as the highest ideal of the *shih-ta-fu* class, had been exemplified in the Ming by the courage and self-sacrifice of many noble men, among them such Tung-lin leaders as Huang's own father and his teacher Liu Tsung-chou. The latter, in memorials to the emperor, had repeatedly urged him to live up to the high ideals of the sage-kings and to enlist the help of other noble men, dedicated to the highest standards of political morality.[44] Indeed Huang himself had been strongly motivated by such ideals as a young political activist before the fall of the Ming and as a resistance leader afterward. Yet here, after years of unavailing struggle, Huang seems much sobered. He is unready to put his main reliance on such individual heroics, more conscious now of the limits power systems or adverse circumstances put on the effective action of individuals. Thus instead of reiterating Chu Hsi's idea that good governance depends on the self-cultivation of virtuous men, he stresses the prerequisite of proper laws and systems as a condition for effective individual action.

One must be careful not to overdraw this contrast. Chu Hsi himself did not deny the importance of laws and institutions. In fact, as a local official he gave great attention to them. Also, many scholars of his school devoted themselves to the study of institutions in their historical development and current practice, a prime example in the Ming being the above-mentioned Ch'iu Chün. But it is fair to say that the Neo-Confucian experience in Ming politics greatly tempered the earlier optimism, leading Huang Tsung-hsi to strike a new balance between laws and the man. One should not define the issue as a choice between men and laws, but between true law and the unlawful restrictions of the ruler. In place of the existing mass of regulations and punishments a few basic laws must be established. These he conceives as more in the nature of a constitution or system of government than a legal code; they should be laws serving the interests of the people and conforming to moral principles, that can be maintained without resort to force, detailed supplementary legislation, or endless litigation. To define the nature of these institutions is the purpose of his *Plan for the Prince*.[45]

Ministership

One Legalist concept that took hold and persisted at the imperial court long after Legalism itself died out was its view of ministership. Since this philosophy stressed the absolute supremacy of the ruler, it sought to deprive his ministers of any real authority that might limit the power of the throne. Officials were mere servitors, to be rewarded or punished according to their usefulness to the emperor. The early Legalist philosopher, Han Fei Tzu, had put it: "If the ruler does not share the supreme authority with his ministers, the people will regard this as a great blessing." And, again, he advises the ruler, "Search the bosoms of ministers and take away their powers. The sovereign should exercise such powers himself with the speed of lightning and the majesty of thunder."[46]

Such a view of the emperor's ministers and officials made of them mere servants to the throne, dependents of the court rather than advisers having a status and exercising a judgment of their own. Even as high officials they were in a weak position to do more than curry the emperor's favor; much less could they uphold the strong position vis-à-vis the ruler that Mencius had insisted upon for ministers, who, he argued, could serve their proper function as mentors to the throne only on condition that they were treated as virtual coequals of the emperor. Contrary to a widespread view, then and now, that a Confucian minister's primary role was one of personal loyalty and service to the ruler, Mencius defined the relation between prince and minister as one of mutual commitment to right principles of government. Lacking agreement on such basic values, the Noble Man had no choice but to leave a ruler's court.[47] So insistent was Mencius on maintaining the proper dignity of ministers that he urged them to view the prince not with awe but with contempt, and cautioned officials against allowing themselves to be treated as mere playthings or concubines of the ruler.[48]

Much later in Chinese history, following the eclipse of the great families who had shared power at the T'ang court, and after the curbing of regional warlords in the tenth century, a new concentration of power at the Sung court was the cause for much concern among Confucians. Strengthened imperial authority could be used either for good or ill, and a favorable outcome, in the eyes of Confucians, depended heavily on the advice of worthy ministers. In consequence they made a determined effort to enhance the status of ministers at the Sung court, in

order to balance the new imperial power and limit the threat of un-
checked autocracy. The Neo-Confucian philosopher Ch'eng I was a notable proponent of this view and of Mencius' strong advocacy of the
dignity and autonomy of the minister.[49]

Huang Tsung-hsi, both as classicist and as a deep student of dynastic
history, was heir to this tradition. He was, too, aware that the founder of
the Ming dynasty had expurgated the text of *Mencius* to remove such
offending passages, and as a thorough student of the textual record,
Huang no doubt realized that even in the restored version of the *Mencius* text authorized for use in official schools and the civil service examinations in 1415, some commentaries of Chu Hsi and his school sup-
portive of Mencius' views had been softened or suppressed.[50] Such
actions Huang condemned in vivid and sharp language probably un-
matched except by Mencius himself, excoriating the conduct not only
of Ming emperors but also of their acquiescent ministers as mere menial
servants of the court, sycophants and prostitutes.

What particularly exercises Huang is that, in later times, not only
does the ruling house adopt the Legalist view, and its officials cravenly
accept it, but the latter actively promote it. Instead of recognizing that
they are colleagues of the emperor, sharing power with him in order
that they may together serve the interests of the people, their only
thought is to please him and, like courtesans, attempt to anticipate his
every desire. They accept the fact that they, like all else in the land, are
the prince's property, to be disposed of as he pleases. And they take the
lead in deifying the emperor, calling him their "Heavenly Father" and
showing him the same filial devotion owed to one's own father. Thus
they have been unable to provide the prince with what he needs most:
companionship and counsel. "The terms 'prince' and 'minister' derive
from their relation to all-under-Heaven. If I take no responsibility for
all-under-Heaven, I am just another man on the street. If I do have regard for serving all-under-Heaven then I am the prince's mentor and
colleague."[51]

Huang Tsung-hsi does not envision any general return to the ancient
enfeoffment system, which would break up the empire into individual
domains and delegate power to an autonomous nobility. But in the
centralized state he has reconciled himself to, he does wish to maintain
something of the balance or distribution of power characteristic of the
Chou system. In this his aims are similar to those of Mencius, who regarded the minister or official as having status in his own right and en-

titled to a measure of respect from the ruler. He cites Mencius' account of the gradations of power in the Chou kingdom: there was an ordered hierarchy and dispersion of rank descending from the prince down through his officials at court and from the prince down through the en-feoffed nobility in outlying domains. In Huang's time no one had real rank or dignity compared to the emperor, and unless some attempt were made to approximate the ideal of graduated authority, there would never be any curb on the prince's abuse of his powers.

This question had become an especially serious one for the Ming dynasty. Not only had it inherited court traditions of long standing that compelled the minister utterly to abase himself before the throne, but it had developed more and more vicious practices for the degradation and intimidation of officials with any independence of mind. One prac-tice that illustrates this trend is the chastising of ministers at court. In earlier years the flogging of officials was more a formality, intended only to humiliate the offender publicly, than a real corporal punishment. Be-fore the dynasty was a century old, however, flogging had increased so in severity that on one occasion when thirty-five ministers were beaten en masse, though they wore heavy padding under their clothes for pro-tection, many spent months in bed before they recovered. In the period styled, ironically enough, "Correct Virtue" (*Cheng-te,* 1506–22), for the first time officials were flogged naked. In the last year of that reign, those who admonished the emperor against continuing his pleasure-seeking excursions to the south were beaten so unmercifully that many died.[52] Under such circumstances even the ablest of ministers could not be expected to act effectively in the people's interest.

The Office of Prime Minister

The attitude of Ming rulers toward their ministers was demonstrated very early in the dynasty, when its founder abolished the office of prime minister. At that time the official holding this position was accused of plotting against the throne and executed. To prevent anyone in the fu-ture from gaining such dominance in the government that he could seize the throne, Ming T'ai-tsu decided to exercise the functions of the prime minister himself and deal directly with the various ministers in charge of the chief agencies of administration. In this decision Huang Tsung-hsi saw the origin of misgovernment in the Ming.

The office of prime minister was essential for three reasons. First, it gave recognition to the principle that ruling power was not to be held by the emperor alone but was to be shared with others, who themselves should enjoy a status of no mean degree. Second, with the adoption of hereditary succession to the throne by the imperial dynasties, the principle of succession according to personal merit, which had been observed by the sage-kings Yao and Shun, was abandoned. Thereafter, the only check on an incompetent heir to the throne was the prime minister, whose selection was still based on merit. Third, ruling the empire and directing the government was such a burdensome job that the emperor could not possibly discharge this function alone. Failure to appoint a prime minister did not mean that his duties could be dispensed with but only that they fell to others by default, who discharged them in an irregular manner.

In the Ming the functions of the prime minister gradually came to be performed by an inner cabinet of secretaries to the emperor, whose service as close advisers was rendered inevitable by the ruler's inability to cope with the burden of so many executive responsibilities. But from Huang Tsung-hsi's point of view, cabinet secretaries were no substitute for a prime minister. Since no single official had the authority to take positive leadership, power quickly fell into the hands of others close to the emperor with no scholarly or official qualifications whatever—the eunuchs. To remedy this, Huang would have the office of prime minister restored, so that authority and responsibility would be fixed in a single executive. He should take a leading role in conducting the discussion of state business with the emperor and, if necessary, should formulate policy decisions in writing for the emperor. To assist him in these duties he should set up his own administrative offices, which would facilitate a coordination of the regular Six Ministries and ensure that all memorials submitted by the people received consideration, so that free discussion of political questions would be encouraged, while eunuchs would be kept from interfering in the process.

This recommendation is in some contrast to the tendency in Huang's Plan that favors decentralized government, but he also recognizes a prime need to curb imperial power, and simply to disperse power among civil officials would not effectively check the concentration of power in the throne. As a more viable alternative he advocates a stronger, more definite concentration of authority in the prime minister than had generally been the case in Chinese history so as to strengthen the leadership of the Confucian-educated, meritocratic civil administration vis-à-vis the imperial court.

Eunuchs

Of the many topics dealt with in his *Plan for the Prince,* Huang Tsung-hsi leaves until last his discussion of eunuchs in the imperial court, as if to indicate what their relative importance should be in the ideal order. But again and again in his book eunuchs are singled out as responsible for usurpations of power and for many of the worst evils in the Ming dynasty, as well as in previous dynasties. "Throughout the Han, T'ang, and Sung dynasties there was an endless series of disasters brought on by eunuchs, but none so frightful as those of the Ming. During the Han, T'ang, and Sung there were eunuchs who interfered with the government, but no instance of government openly doing the bidding of eunuchs [as in the Ming]."[53]

Among the several reasons given by Huang for the extraordinary power of eunuchs at court, the most basic is the maintaining of a harem for the emperor. If the imperial harem were not so large, obviously there would be less need for eunuchs to attend them, and eunuchs would not be numerous enough to constitute a problem. But akin to his indulgence in women is the ruler's lust for personal power. This had led him to separate the management of his household from the regular civil administration, so that he need not be embarrassed by the intervention of state ministers desirous of curbing wastefulness and debauchery. Left to their own devices, however, eunuchs in the Ming had proceeded to encroach on the powers of the state administration. Behind the scenes they exerted a dominant influence on the emperor, now overburdened with the duties once performed by the prime minister, and because of the complex procedures involved in the drafting of state papers, they were able to intrude their own demands at crucial stages in the process. From this vantage point the eunuchs set up organs of administration paralleling those of the civil bureaucracy, gaining control over a large portion of the imperial revenues, over mining and a host of monopolies that nominally provisioned the palace but actually operated on a much wider scale, over the administration of justice through their own secret service and prison system, and finally over the army itself. Their most potent weapon in accomplishing all this, Huang says, was the argument that the wealth of the empire is the prince's private possession and should be under direct control of the imperial palace. Convincing the emperor that they, rather than the state officials, had his personal interests at heart, and encouraged by the timid servility of civil officials themselves, the eunuchs gained for themselves the powers that should have been exercised by ministers of state, while the latter became virtual palace menials.

One proposal that had been advanced for the curbing of eunuchs was that they should be returned to the control of the state administration by placing them under the prime minister.[54] But Huang considers this inadequate and perhaps dangerous. Palace eunuchs were often drawn, he says, from among criminals punished by castration, and they were too vicious and unscrupulous a lot to be restrained by this means. Indeed, because of their numbers and intimacy with members of the imperial family, they would soon dominate the prime minister himself. This then would defeat a basic purpose of Huang's Plan, which is to lodge responsibility for all governmental operations in properly educated and trained civil officials whose qualification to exercise power and authority is certified by Confucian standards. Elsewhere, as we shall see, he includes among necessary functions to be performed by scholar-officials (*shih*) even military command functions and those of subofficials on the local level. Nothing therefore should be done that would blur the identity and qualifications of the class so entrusted with these responsibilities, as would happen if eunuchs were incorporated into the state administration. For Huang then the only solution is to reduce the need for eunuchs by drastically limiting the number of the emperor's wives and concubines. To those who object that this would limit the number of imperial offspring as well, and thereby seriously jeopardize the dynastic succession, Huang points to the fate of the last emperor of the Northern Sung, whose many sons "served only as so much mincemeat" for their conquerors.

School and State

In China the dynastic state had put a high value on scholarly expertise, and paradoxically the schools had suffered for it. This is because the state's interest in education was closely linked to its recruitment of men with talents useful in government—literary skills, a knowledge of historical precedents, and some competence in the rituals so important to the legitimizing of government. While government schools were maintained in the capital and the principal seats of provincial administration, their main object was to prepare those who passed the district examinations for higher degrees leading to eventual employment in the bureaucracy. Meanwhile, an overwhelming majority of the people went uneducated. Except for the select number who gained admission to official schools and the Imperial College, instruction could be obtained only from private tutors or teachers in private academies whom few could afford. Thus the state's interest in the recruiting of scholars did not have the effect of developing any general system of education.

Even without such universal education or a public school system, however, a degree of uniformity prevailed in education comparable to that achieved by modern states through centralized public school systems. This was because virtually all instruction in China, whether public or private, was oriented toward the civil service examinations. These were the gateway to advancement in government and, in a society which so prized official status, the main road to success, influence, and usually affluence. The government did not need to maintain an extensive school system with a curriculum and texts of its own choosing. Simply by prescribing what was to be called for in the examinations, it could determine what most aspiring students would find it in their interest to learn, whether in or out of state schools.

Against this background we can appreciate why Huang attaches such great importance to educational reform. He wishes to remedy the lack of general education and prevalence of careerism in education by creating a universal public school system with functions much broader than the mere training of officials. In classical times, he attempts to show, schools were centers of all important community and state activities; they had a major role too, he claims, in debating public questions and advising the prince. Ideally, then, schools should serve the people in two ways: providing an education for all and acting as organs for the expression of public opinion. Likewise the prince had two corresponding obligations: to maintain schools for the benefit of all and to give the people a voice in government through the schools. In ancient times "the emperor did not dare to determine right and wrong himself, so he left to the schools the determination of right and wrong." But since the rise of the Ch'in, "right and wrong have been determined entirely by the court. If the emperor favored such and such, everyone hastened to think it right. If he frowned upon such and such, everyone condemned it as wrong."[55]

This argument is suggestive again of Confucian antipathy for Legalist doctrines that had been absorbed into the authoritarian dogma of subsequent dynasties. Han Fei Tzu had said: "Whatever he [the ruler] considers good is to be regarded as good by the officials and people. Whatever he does not consider good is not to be regarded as good by the officials and the people."[56] The Legalist statesman, Li Ssu, who was chiefly responsible for organizing the Ch'in empire, asserted the same principle in suppressing free speech in independent schools:

> At present your Majesty possesses a unified empire and has laid down distinctions of right and wrong, consolidating for himself a single position of eminence. Yet there are those who . . . teach what is not according to the laws. When they hear orders promulgated, they criticize them in the light of their own teachings. . . . To cast disrepute on their ruler they regard as a thing worthy of fame; to hold different views they regard as high conduct. . . . If such conditions are not prohibited, the imperial power will decline.[57]

According to Huang, the prevalence of this view, that the ruler determines what is right and wrong, deprived the schools of one of their most important functions. They could no longer discuss public issues freely, and because the authority of the state was set against the autonomy of the academies, an unnatural separation arose between the two. Thereafter, the schools could not even fulfill the functions remaining to them of training scholars for office, because the true aims of education were lost sight of in the mad scramble for advancement and the desperate endeavor to conform. Thinking men, in their search for true education, turned more and more to the local, quasi-private academies that had become centers of Neo-Confucian thought in the Sung and Ming dynasties. But the independence and heterodox views of these academies brought repeated attempts at suppression by the state. Thus the arbitrary separation of school and state ended in open conflict between them, detrimental to the true interests of both.

Though Huang defends the local academies, which had been so much blamed for the political failure of the Ming, his real purpose is not to assert the claims of independent private schools. These are a recourse only in the absence of true public education, which, according to the Confucians, it is the duty of the ruler to provide. Instead Huang advocates a system of universal public education, maintained by the state but free of all centralized control. There are to be schools from the capital down through every city and town to even the smallest hamlets, but on each level supervision is to be independent of control from above. The principal units of administration, the prefectures and districts, will be presided over by superintendents of education chosen locally, not appointed by the court. These men need never have served as officials before or have qualified for the civil service. Not only should they have complete freedom in ordinary educational matters, including the right to override the provincial education intendants in the appointment of licentiates (those who have achieved the first degree in the prefectural examinations), but their pronouncements on any matter affecting the community should be listened to respectfully by the local magistrates. Similarly, at the capital the libationer (or chancellor) of the Imperial College should lead a discussion each month on important questions, with the emperor and his ministers attending in the role of students.

This arrangement, and the political function it would serve, are of paramount importance to our understanding of Huang's whole Plan. Huang's unhappiness over the "unnatural separation between school and state," and his belief that the semiprivate local academies are no substitute for an adequate system of universal education, are grounded in two corollary assumptions. One is the integration, from earliest times, of political and religious / cultural authority in the ruling power. The other is the parallel and continuing attempt of the Confucians to balance this concentration of power by asserting a moral and intellectual authority of their own in close association with the ruler and on a par with him. A fuller discussion of this matter will be undertaken later, but for present purposes it may suffice to mention that the Neo-Confucian movement, from the Sung onward, had made this an issue in two notable forms.

One of these was the so-called Learning of the Emperors, which, as promoted by Sung Confucians, really meant "what the emperor should learn from his ministers, and how his authority should be shared with them." In the Sung, Yüan, and Ming this function had been served—if at all—by Confucian mentors to the emperor and tutors to the crown prince, and through the institution of "Lectures from the Classics Mat" by leading Confucian scholars who related the principles in the classics to the affairs of state. It is of major significance then for Huang to assert that this function should now be removed from the palace and be conducted on a ground physically and symbolically separate from the halls of power, where imperial prestige and court intrigue dominate the scene. If the "Classics Mat" had represented a strained attempt to create a privileged space at court from which higher principles—transcendent values—could be invoked to admonish the emperor, Huang had decided that the Classics Mat was not enough for the purpose. A separate space, immune to political pressure and free from the overawing effect on the individual of the imperial citadel (the "forbidding" character of the "Forbidden City"), was needed. In the extra-

mural school and especially in the Imperial College, Huang attempted
to stake out a space dedicated to free and open discussion of all public
matters. Moreover, by asking that the crown prince, from the age of
fifteen, attend school regularly at this independent college where he
would be exposed to the views and feelings of others outside the court,
Huang was again acknowledging the inadequacy of that hallowed Neo-
Confucian institution—Confucian tutors giving lectures inside the
palace—to serve the purposes of Mencius, Ch'eng I, and Chu Hsi in
advocating the moral parity of the ruler/minister relation.

Ch'eng I, in the eleventh century, had already complained to the empress dowager that the Confucian mentors to the crown prince had little influence on the formation of his character since they saw him so
infrequently in comparison to the palace women and eunuchs who surrounded the prince almost constantly. Huang Tsung-hsi took up the
same theme:

> When they reach the age of fifteen, the sons of the emperor should
> study at the Imperial College with the sons of the high ministers.
> They should be informed of real conditions among the people and be
> given some experience of difficult labor and hardship. They must not
> be shut off in the palace, where everything they learn comes from
> eunuchs and palace women alone, so that they get false notions of
> their own greatness.[58]

Where court ritual endowed the throne with a sacred inviolability,
and convention shielded the emperor from any challenge to his authority, the ruler had been encouraged to think of his will as absolute. He
ruled as if by divine right. In such circumstances it was difficult for the
Confucian minister to perform the function assigned him by Mencius
of criticizing the status quo or restraining the abuse of power. The personal courage and moral integrity of the Confucian scholar were not
enough. In the absence of any other privileged sanctuary—church,
pulpit, temple, or other religious institution that might afford some im-
munity to the scholar/prophet in his exercise of this critical function—
and, moreover, given the renunciation of such a role by the Buddhists
and Taoists, Huang sought to make the school a kind of secular "sacred
space" for the Confucian *scholar-minister.*

The second consideration underlying this proposal was the need
Huang saw for universal schooling, already a prime issue in the Sung
(and prominently advocated in Chu Hsi's Preface to the *Great Learn-*

ing) as a means of promoting the people's self-development, expanding their human resources and enlarging the number of those who could, in an informed way, participate in the cultural and political life of the society.[59] In this way the Neo-Confucians aimed to share the cultural wealth with larger numbers of people, while still functioning within a single structure of authority, in a society that allowed for no independent institution or countervailing authority outside such a unified structure. A reflection of this is seen in the provision Huang makes in this section of his Plan for the local superintendent of education to exercise many functions that in other societies would be performed by a "church" or other autonomous religious establishment. Thus the superintendent is to have wide authority on the local level over many aspects of community life—public ceremonies, family ritual observances, censorship over publications, and public entertainment. "If in any locality there are unorthodox sacrifices, or if unauthorized clothing is being worn, or if useless things are sold in the market place, or if the dead lie unburied on the ground, or if the actors' songs fill men's ears and the streets are full of vile talk, then the school superintendent is not performing his function properly."[60]

These last stipulations are a reminder that the system Huang proposes, though it stresses decentralization, local autonomy, and a kind of academic freedom, nonetheless assumes the need for a well-defined hierarchy of values and authority. The problem for Huang is to place authority in the hands of those best qualified to exercise it (in his mind the scholar-officials, *shih*), not to encourage unlimited freedom of expression or to make diversity of opinion an end in itself. In the final analysis, he is convinced that the interests and wishes of the people coincide with certain basic values that must be upheld by the *shih*. Huang is a pluralist only in the Mencian sense: he believes in the sharing of power and authority, but he is no relativist when it comes to the question of upholding a definite value structure. In his later years Huang would mellow somewhat in this respect, as his *Case Studies of Ming Confucians* showed a more pluralistic view of truth, but he shares the rationalist bias of the Confucians against all forms of religious superstition and supernaturalism. It is therefore quite possible for him to deny to nonpublic institutions he considers inimical to society the same freedom allowed government schools. Monks and nuns are to be secularized, and temple lands are to be expropriated so that the income from them may be used for the support of poor students.[61]

The Civil Service System

Huang's views on the nature of education are more fully brought out in his essays on the selection of officials through the civil service examinations. It would be difficult to exaggerate the importance of this system, which had been the chief means of recruiting China's ruling class for centuries, and Huang, though he deplores the effect on education of too exclusive a concern with the preparing of candidates for the civil service, nevertheless recognizes what a vital role these examinations play in determining the makeup and outlook of those entrusted with the administration of the empire. The political failure of the Ming dynasty, he feels, is attributable in no small measure to the weaknesses of its civil service system. Indeed, this is one respect in which he finds Ming institutions subject to abuses even more extreme than in previous dynasties.

Huang's criticisms of the Ming system may be summarized under three main points. First, he believes that entrance to the civil service was restricted to only a few, whose qualifications were determined on too narrow a basis. On the other hand, once they had gained admittance, officials were advanced far too rapidly and placed in posts of great responsibility before they had proven their ability or acquired sufficient experience as administrators. This procedure contrasted in his mind with the ancient method outlined in the *Record of Rites* (*Li chi*), which was liberal in admitting young men of talent to government service but strictly regulated their promotion by testing their capabilities while in office. Even in the Han, T'ang, and Sung dynasties, the ancient ideal had been more closely approximated than in the Ming, and advancement was much slower. Therefore, in the system he proposes, Huang would have junior officials serve a sort of internship and be required to pass three successive fitness tests before being assigned to posts as local magistrates.[62]

Repeatedly in his discussion of the handling of officials Huang emphasizes that practical ability is no less important than scholarship, and that advancement should depend on an official's being tested and judged on the basis of the actual conduct of affairs. Knowledge and practice are both necessary. (It is partly for this reason that I have for the most part translated *shih* here as "scholar-official" rather than "literatus" or "scholar" alone.)

Huang's second point concerns the content of the examinations and is related to the first. One of the principal limitations on the selection of candidates was the fact that civil service examinations in the Ming were devoted almost exclusively to writing essays on classical themes. This meant that men who knew nothing else of more practical value might gain admission to the official class through their skill in writing examination essays, while men who had great talents in other fields would have no way to demonstrate them. Huang's remedy for this situation is twofold. He would greatly enlarge the scope of the regular examinations (i.e., the provincial examinations for the *chü-jen* degree and the metropolitan examinations held at the capital for the *chin-shih* degree) by adding three other subjects to the classics. These subject areas were to embrace the more important philosophic writings, including the works of Hsün Tzu (which had not been dignified, as had the book of Mencius, by inclusion in the Four Books), as well as the more prominent Han, T'ang, and Sung philosophers, and even the Taoist works *Lao Tzu* and *Chuang Tzu.* Another subject area would cover the classical historical writings, the voluminous dynastic histories up to the Sung, and the detailed court records of the Ming—truly a formidable array of literature! The last subject area in the examinations was to be concerned with contemporary problems, which, like some of the above topics, had been a part of earlier examinations in the T'ang and Sung dynasties. Ironically enough, these recommendations, which are so much in contrast to the narrow range of the Ming examinations, follow in the main those proposed by Chu Hsi, whose commentaries on the classics were adopted as definitive by the Ming while his views on the content of the examinations were largely ignored. Huang's range of subjects is, in fact, broader still than Chu's.

Another method proposed by Huang for deemphasizing literary skills as a qualification for office is to provide alternatives to the regular examination system, based on other criteria of selection. Among these, he suggests a system of special recommendations, whereby each prefecture would select a man to be examined personally by the prime minister to determine his fitness for office. A second method is for the provincial and district schools to send their best students to the Imperial College, where they would be examined and, upon graduation, be given posts on the same basis as graduates of the metropolitan examinations. Special consideration should also be shown to the sons of high officials in gaining entrance to official schools and the Imperial College, but they should be subject to the same examinations and advancement procedures as other students, so that incompetent ones would not be placed in positions of power through favoritism. Furthermore, promising young men are to be given minor posts in the prefectures and districts, and, after successive fitness tests, those qualified should be sent to the Imperial College or assigned to posts at the capital. A similar system is to be set up for interns serving by temporary appointment under the prime minister, the Six Ministries, the military commanderies, and the provincial governors. If their performance in different posts shows them to be of high caliber, their temporary appointments are to be confirmed and made official. In addition to these types of selection based on administrative ability, men with special knowledge of certain branches of learning are to be sent to court for examination and appointment to the Imperial (Hanlin) Academy. Those who present memorials or books of special value to the throne also should be rewarded with official posts.

Through all these different means Huang hopes to secure civil servants of varied talents or proven competence in office, and in most cases he specifies that they be further examined after taking office. From his insistence that the prime minister and others charged with actual administrative responsibility should be free to select, appoint, and promote their own subordinates, it is also apparent that he wants these officials to obtain assistants who they believe are qualified for particular assignments rather than have them be at the mercy of a Ministry of Personnel so impersonal in its operations that it cannot give adequate consideration to special needs. This is one more evidence of his concern to avoid bureaucratic centralization and to strengthen the hands of individually responsible officials.

Huang's third major criticism of the Ming civil service system has to do with the form in which the examinations were given, as represented by the famous "eight-legged" essays. That this aspect of the selection system was perhaps of the most concern to him is indicated by his treating it first and by his lengthy discussion of its historical origins in pre-Ming times. This is one case in which Huang makes us well aware that he is dealing with a question which has been the center of political and intellectual controversy for centuries. Reform of the examination system, in order to place greater emphasis on an understanding of the classics, had been one of the chief aims of the early Neo-Confucian leaders in the Sung dynasty.[63] Huang's discussion of the problem focuses on the most ambitious attempt in the Sung to make this ideal a reality: the examinations instituted by Wang An-shih on the "general sense" of the classics.

Before Wang's time the examinations for the prized *chin-shih* degree had placed the greatest stress on skill in the composition of prose and poetry, while the examinations dealing with the classics were in disrepute. The reason for this was that in the T'ang dynasty, which instituted the types of examinations inherited by the Sung, the tests for the classics degree (*ming-ching*) had degenerated into a mere exercise in memorization of the classics and their commentaries and, therefore, were not considered as much of a demonstration of the candidate's intellectual attainments as the *chin-shih* examination. Wang An-shih (and others before him in the late T'ang and Sung, as Huang is careful to point out) wished to restore the classics to their rightful importance, but also to dispense with memorization of these texts and the commentaries, by requiring instead that the candidates show an understanding of the general purport of the classics. Wang therefore revised the *chin-shih* examination along these lines, but in doing so he found it necessary for the efficient and impartial administration of this vast examination system to introduce a large measure of standardization. His problem, which was a perennial one in the history of the Chinese examinations, is similar to the problem of American college instructors today in using objective-type and essay-type questions on examinations. The old classics examination was of the objective type, consisting mainly of completion-questions that required the candidate to finish a quotation or fill in specific details from the texts cited. Here only a precise answer would suffice, not an interpretive one, and consequently the student was forced to memorize texts. But if this approach were abandoned and interpretive essay questions adopted, the problem immediately arose in judging the answers of such a large number of candidates: "What form of essay and what interpretation of the classics is to be considered acceptable?" It was easy enough to dispense with the standard commentaries, but only if some other authoritative interpretation of the classics were set up as a criterion for judgment. Wang An-shih settled this by prescribing both the form of the essay and his own interpretation of key classics, which were disseminated for the guidance of all candidates. In the Ming dynasty essentially the same procedure was followed. Chu Hsi's commentaries on the Four Books were established as the authoritative interpretation, and the "eight-legged" essay as the prescribed form.

Huang for his part would require that the candidate demonstrate a knowledge not only of the original classic texts themselves and of Chu Hsi's version of the Four Books but also of the Han commentaries, T'ang subcommentaries, and alternative interpretations in still other commentaries. And just as he stresses in general the need for integrating one's knowledge and experience to make it truly one's own, so Huang specifies in this case that the candidate should offer his own interpretation of a question after he has noted the views of other authorities. By employing this method, Huang would have candidates master both the letter and the spirit of the classics, and, by extending the examination system to include other subjects of practical value to an administrator, he would secure officials who are men of practical ability as well as men of learning and character.

Subofficials

Men of character and ability—this was the ideal of the Confucian scholar-official, who alone could be entrusted with political power. Yet in the Ming dynasty, Huang tells us, the functions that should have been reserved to men of this class were increasingly usurped by a new type of petty bureaucrat. For this development Wang An-shih was again largely responsible. During his regime in the Sung dynasty, Wang had abolished the system by which many minor governmental functions, particularly on the local level, had been performed by drafting the services of persons in the locality, supposedly on a rotating basis to distribute the burden. These functions included such duties as those of tax collectors, custodians of official property, policemen, messengers, porters, and the like. For various reasons the most burdensome duties, or those involving the greatest financial liability, had come to be borne by those who could least afford to meet the expense or labor involved. To remedy this, Wang put these services on a paid basis, the expense of which was met by a money-tax graduated to put the greatest burden on rich landlords and merchants. Though abandoned by Ssu-ma Kuang, this system was later restored and kept in modified form by the Ming dynasty.

According to Huang, once these minor functionaries obtained permanent paid positions, they tended to become a class by themselves with vested interests and considerable power over the ordinary business of government. Those most successful even obtained positions on higher levels of administration, which should have been reserved for regular civil officials. Many succeeded in making their jobs a family possession, turning them over to their sons when they retired. On the local level they were able, through their identification with the state bureaucracy, to oppress the people with impunity. In the agencies of provincial and central administration they became masters of bureaucratic red tape and legalistic procedure, though actually they had little or no classical education to qualify them for the exercise of such power.

Huang would eliminate this class entirely by restoring the system of draft services at the lowest local level and by placing properly trained civil officials in the more important posts these subofficials had usurped. In effect, he would incorporate the miscellaneous draft services into the old *li-chia* (or *pao-chia*) system, whereby they would be rotated regularly among the households of a locality. He believed that the local citizenry, particularly the responsible leaders of each 100-family unit, would refrain from oppressing their neighbors because they themselves might suffer in turn when their neighbors took over the same posts. The people of a locality would trust one of their own number as they never could an outsider who was a hireling of the state.[64] The higher positions of fixed responsibility, whether at court or in the provinces he would assign to graduates of the regular civil service system or men obtained through the other methods of selection he proposes. This fits in with his plan to make officials serve internships in subordinate positions before being placed in more important posts. It would also strip the Ministry of Personnel, which, he says, had control over the appointment and promotion of subofficials, of its power over the subbureaucracy and thus serve his overall aim of strengthening the position of responsible officials by allowing them to select, train, and control their own assistants.

Some recent studies have suggested that during late imperial times the Chinese governmental apparatus, instead of growing with the increasing population and complexity of economic life, actually was stretched much thinner.[65] This is certainly not Huang's perception of the problem. He might agree that the employment of properly accredited officials was unduly limited; hence in his discussion of the civil service system Huang complains that access to its ranks was too restricted, while on the other hand advancement of those admitted was too rapid, perhaps owing to an actual dearth of certified scholar-officials to serve higher-level functions. But the main thrust of his argument is that, instead of the empire being underadministered, it is poorly administered by a swollen subbureaucracy with neither the proper humanistic education and truly professional commitment of the Confucian-minded scholar-official, nor the kind of close rapport with people on the local level that ensures a proper degree of local autonomy.

The problem then is not a vacuum in administration, for on the local level there is a sense of chronic grievance and strong resistance to the interference of subofficials representing the higher administration of the empire.[66] Rather, as Huang perceives the problem, instead of an attenuation of control there is, between local consensual leadership and accredited state officials, an area that is filled by intrusive, mercenary, and nepotistic subofficials who constitute a vested interest of their own, to the detriment of both the people and the state.

To correct this situation Huang would do away with the corrupt infrastructure of subofficialdom, extend the area of autonomous local control, and above this enhance the effective administration of certified state officials who likewise would be given greater freedom of action from centralized control. This is in keeping with his consistent emphasis on curbing central powers, dispersing authority in a structured way by strengthening the position of scholar-officials as a class of dedicated professional administrators, and, last, by encouraging local autonomy and consensual self-government on the lower level.

What warrants this redistribution of power, in Huang's mind, is his conviction that good government can only be assured by a properly educated, suitably certified, meritocratic elite who have earned their positions by dedicated service that has met the test of repeated fitness reviews.[67] Others may perceive the *shih* or *shih-ta-fu* class in terms less idealistic than Huang's, most often in terms of economic or social class interest, but for him there can be no doubt that, for all the evils and systemic weaknesses he has perceived in the Ming dynasty, and for all the contempt he has shown for "vulgar Confucians" who have prostituted themselves in the service of that dynasty, the question of qualified leadership is still inescapable. In that sense, we can see that he still carries the torch of Sung, Yüan, and Ming Neo-Confucians who believe in the indispensable role of the scholar-official as Noble Man (*chün-tzu*).

Land Reform

Relation of Land Tenure to Taxation

Perhaps nothing was of such vital concern to both the government and the people of China as the land tax, which for centuries had provided the state bureaucracy with its life's blood in revenue and, in the process, had often deprived the peasantry of the life-sustaining fruits of their own labor. For this very reason it was also a matter of concern to Huang's Neo-Confucian predecessors, who generally regarded oppressive land taxes as just one more manifestation of the failure of later dynasties to rule according to the precepts of the sage-kings. But Huang's predecessor in the Sung, Su Hsün, upon examining this question, concluded that tax rates in later times actually compared favorably with those of the classical age, and that the real difficulty of the peasants arose from their having to pay high rents along with land taxes, which had not been the case before the abolition of the enfeoffment system by the Ch'in. Huang's conclusion is substantially the same, but he takes issue with Su at many points along the line of his argument and is especially at pains to show why the tax rates of later times were not really as low as they might appear to be.[68]

During the Han dynasty (202 B.C.–A.D. 220) the land tax in grain had been based for the most part on a rate of one part in fifteen, or one-in-thirty, of the estimated yield. This was regarded by some persons as extremely low in comparison with the rate of one-in-ten, which was said to have prevailed in ancient times, and, therefore, if the tax were subsequently raised to one-in-ten, it was no more than could be expected in view of the ancient practice. Huang insists, however, that the Han tax rates are actually not comparable to those of ancient times, since they are based on a different system of land tenure. Under the sage-kings there was no private ownership of land; all land was shared in common, and the king, who distributed it through the well-field system, saw that everyone had enough to meet his needs. The tribute that they rendered to the ruler in return for the land given them was therefore not comparable to taxes paid on private holdings in later times. After the enfeoffment system was abolished, the people no longer were granted land but had to obtain it for themselves through purchase or the payment of rent. It was unreasonable, under this private property system (which no longer assured the cultivator of a fair share of land), to expect him to pay as much to the ruler when he received nothing in return. Moreover, under the ancient system, tribute was determined in accordance with the quality of the land held by the grantee, and instead of a general tax rate for all, it was graduated so that those on poorer land paid less in tribute. The rate of one-in-ten, then, was actually what those holding the best land paid, while others paid much less.[69]

After the abolition of the well-field system and the adoption of private landholding, the Han imposed a general tax rate on all land. In this situation a rate of one part in thirty, says Huang, was fair enough—what even those holding the poorest land could afford. But a rate of one-in-ten was oppressive for two reasons: it could no longer be justified as a return on land granted the cultivator (but was in addition to what he had to pay to purchase or rent his land), and it represented a tax on all holdings, which only those best off could afford. Since those on poorer land lived close to the subsistence level, the same amount of tax would work a much greater hardship on them.

In this way Huang asserts that there is a fundamental relationship between the system of land tenure and what constitutes a fair tax. For land purchased and held privately, he regards a rate of one part in thirty or one-in-twenty as reasonable. For land provided by the government at no cost, however, a rate of one-in-ten is allowable. But Huang is not so optimistic as are some advocates of the well-field system that its restoration alone will solve the tax problem. Throughout Chinese history he sees a tendency for taxes to proliferate and increase, often in hidden forms, as each dynasty conceives urgent needs for additional revenue. Special taxes imposed in times of crisis are rarely abolished when the crisis has passed. Tax reforms designed to consolidate existing taxes do not, in effect, reduce the burden on the people but merely clear the way for imposing still further levies. So downtrodden have the people become, generation after generation, that they themselves no longer have any conception of what a just tax is; in Huang's day, he says, they consider a three-tenths tax light and only a rate of five- or six-tenths is thought of as heavy.[70]

Thus it is essential, in Huang's view, to attack the problem from two sides: to redistribute the land so that all have a means of livelihood and to reform the administration of taxes so that those who obtain their own land will not lose it by falling heavily into debt.

Land Redistribution and the Well-Field System

Ever since the establishment of private landholding in the Ch'in and Han, the concentration of landownership in the hands of a few had been a recurrent problem, to which two main solutions were proposed by scholars and officials attempting to deal with it. The first was to restore the well-field system that supposedly had prevailed in earlier times. This would have involved the abolition of private property, the expropriation of all land, its redistribution by the state in accordance with the "nine-squares" formula of equalized plots, and thereafter a permanent prohibition on the purchase or sale of land. Some who accepted this as the ideal, like the leading Han Confucian, Tung Chung-shu, nevertheless conceded that conditions had so changed as to render a full return to the well-field system impracticable. As the next best so-lution, they proposed a simple limitation on the amount of land an indi-vidual could hold, the excess being distributed among those in need, with private ownership retained. As early as 7 B.C. a decree was promul-gated embodying this latter proposal, but owing to powerful opposition at court it was never carried into effect.

Huang Tsung-hsi believes that this type of simple limitation on land-ownership does not in itself put land into the hands of landless peas-ants. Moreover, any expropriation of privately owned land for distribu-tion to the poor is certain to provoke opposition and could only be effected by the use of force. Any such resort to force is what Mencius called "doing an injustice," in keeping with the Confucian doctrine that coercion cannot be employed even for a good end. Hence Huang rules it out. For essentially the same reason, he rejects the notion of others who had urged that restoration of the well-field system be held up until just after a period of chaos and bloodshed, when the population would be sufficiently reduced so that there would be enough land to go around. If restoration of the well-fields is truly desirable and practica-ble, Huang maintains, it need not wait until some dire calamity pro-duces such a "favorable situation."

The question then becomes: "Is the well-field system truly practica-ble?" Su Hsün (1009–66) had said that it was not. The advocates of this system in his time had given a rather literal, fundamentalist reading to the *Rites of Chou (Chou li)* as a guide to reestablishment of the ancient order, and this text gave detailed specifications for the types of rivers and highways, canals and roads, ditches and lanes, and trenches and pathways that were to be maintained in connection with the division of land into well-fields. Su thought this beyond all hope of accomplishing. Only by "driving all men under Heaven, exhausting all revenues, and spending all efforts in this direction alone for several hundred years, without doing anything else, could one hope to see the empire con-verted into well-fields."[71] Therefore, like Tung Chung-shu, he recon-ciled himself to private landownership but with an upper limit on any-one's holdings.

Huang is glad enough to credit Su Hsün with having presented "most fully the reasons why well-fields could not be restored," but he insists that the difficulties Su regards as so formidable are only minor details which in no way vitally affect the system and would take care of themselves once the well-fields were restored. On the other hand, he credits two later writers in the Ming, among them Hu Han,[72] with having most cogently argued in favor of the system, but declares that they failed to present a practical method for achieving this aim. His own contribution, Huang believes, is precisely in offering such a method. Hu Han had recommended that well-fields be adopted in one district, after which, if successful, they might be extended to the whole empire. But Huang finds that the essential principle of the well-field system has already been embodied and tested in the military farm system instituted at the inception of the Ming dynasty. Each soldier-cultivator received fifty acres (*mou*) of land, which was to provide for his needs and make it unnecessary for the government to pay or supply him from its own revenues. Huang is convinced that the same system could be extended to the empire as a whole. Basing his calculations on statistics for the late sixteenth century, which were available to him in an official compilation, the *Collected Statutes of the Ming* (*Ming hui-tien*), he first asserts that military farmland already constitutes one-tenth of the total cultivated lands of the empire, and concludes that what has already proved successful on such a large scale could easily be extended to the other nine-tenths. Then he shows that the total land under cultivation, when divided among the total number of households in the empire, would provide fifty *mou* for each with enough left over so that the private lands of the well-to-do need not be expropriated.

This seems almost too easy for words since it rests on a—perhaps deceptively—simple arithmetical calculation and on statistics the reliability of which is open to question. Be this as it may, however, the underlying implication of Huang's proposal is that the land needed for redistribution as subsistence plots would come mainly from the reassignment of official lands and large estates created for members of the imperial family or others favored by the throne, and need not seriously affect private landholding (the "lands of the well-to-do," *fu-min*). In other words, it would fit in with Huang's overall objective of eliminating the private estates of the imperial house (*chuang-t'ien*) and official lands (*kuan-t'ien*), but it would not abolish private property altogether.[73] Hence his lower tax rate on land already in private hands (i.e., already paid for), in contradistinction to the higher rate on plots given to peasants from official lands and imperial estates, in return for which they might be expected to pay somewhat more.[74]

But Huang still has at least one obvious objection to deal with . The military farm system was not actually a proved success, since great numbers of the soldier-cultivators had abandoned their land and deserted from the army. This Huang explains as due not to any inherent defect in the land system but rather to military maladministration and simple homesickness among the deserters. The able-bodied soldiers were not allowed sufficient time to cultivate their farms, which consequently did not produce enough. On top of this, they were taxed at an excessive rate and were subject to the "squeezing" of rapacious military over-lords. Such factors would not operate, Huang assumes, on civilian farms.

Huang's high estimation of the military farms gains some support from at least one modern historian of the Ming who tends to agree that as a system it worked reasonably well and only later abuses of the system rendered it nonviable.[75] Even so, one wonders at the ease with which Huang confidently asserts that what had worked for a time in roughly one-tenth of the cultivable land could certainly be made to work in the country as a whole. In view of the short-lived earlier attempts to estab-lish and maintain a fixed system of equal landholding under Wang Mang in the first century A.D. and again under the early T'ang in the seventh century (neither of which he comments on), one suspects that Huang, like many a Confucian scholar before him, underestimated the problem of moving from a rationally appealing model to a functionally workable system.

A simple arithmetical calculation based on figures in the *Collected Statutes of the Ming* (leaving aside modern doubts that the Ming "ever" produced a set of consistent land data throughout its history),[76] would not seem sufficient to dispose of the enormous practical difficulties in implementing (and no doubt enforcing) such an ideal plan. Nor could these difficulties simply be equated with the trivial details Huang so easily dismisses in Su Hsün. The historical difficulty of redistributing land and then holding to a fixed system of landholding leaves one with doubts that the problem could have been susceptible to such a simple solution. Thus one cannot help but smile at the relative ease with which Huang claims that, where others earlier have failed, he has found a practical method for dealing with the land problem. What he has done really is only to argue that the military farms have never had a fair test, and that theoretically, once delivered from the burdens and abuses of the military system, the farms should work. This is not the same thing as having a well-tested model.

It does, however, tell us something about what Huang really has in mind when he talks about "restoring the well-fields." It is primarily a way of providing the minimum of land needed for the subsistence of each household, by taking land away from imperial estates and official lands, and reassigning them to peasants. In this respect it would fulfill Mencius' idea that no one should be without the physical means of sustaining one's existence—to Mencius a sine qua non of any attempt to educate and civilize them. But it is not necessarily predicated on a completely egalitarian ideal, any more than was Mencius' system of landholding, which allowed for differences in land held by different orders in the hierarchy of the enfeoffment system. No complete social or economic leveling is implied, nor even a completely communal society, since both Mencius and Huang, by assigning a minimum of subsistence land to each household, thereby confirm the individual family as the irreducible unit of economic organization rather than imagining a system of jointly owned and cooperatively worked land.

Tax Reform

There are three chief tax evils that Huang would correct: the constant accumulation of taxes through the centuries, the payment of taxes in money rather than in kind, and the imposition of a uniform tax rate on all land regardless of the quality of the soil. In discussing the first two evils, he provides a review of the major tax developments in Chinese history, which indicates that he has drawn upon such sources as the economic treatises of the dynastic histories and such encyclopedic works on the history of Chinese social institutions as the *T'ung tien* of Tu Yu; the *Wen-hsien t'ung-k'ao* of Ma Tuan-lin; its continuation by the Ming scholar Wang Ch'i; the *Ming hui-tien,* the *T'u-shu pien* of Chang Huang, etc. To these he adds firsthand observations on contemporary developments.[77] Here only the high points of his analysis can be touched upon.

In ancient times the only tax was on land, payable in kind. By the early T'ang dynasty (A.D. 624), the land tax in grain had been supplemented by a tax on households, payable in cloth, and a labor tax on adult males. By the middle of the T'ang, however, the collection of these separate taxes had become complicated by the difficulty of maintaining up-to-date and uniform land registers, so they were combined into one system, the Twice-a-year tax, payable in cash and grain in the summer and fall. Thus the household and labor taxes were incorporated into the land tax. But by the Sung dynasty (960–1279) new taxes were imposed on adult males and households, without the people realizing (says Huang) that in effect they were being charged twice for the same items.

During the Ming dynasty another tax reform movement, which came

to be known as the "Single-whip" method,[78] had the effect of con-
solidating a variety of taxes into the land tax, increasingly commuted to
payment in silver so as to simplify collections. Subsequently, the process
of adding new taxes began again. Separate charges were made for miscellaneous labor services, and then, toward the end of the dynasty, special taxes were imposed in order to supply new troops raised to fight the
Japanese in Korea and the Manchus in the north. A year before the fall
of the Ming dynasty, these new pay-and-rations taxes, centrally assessed
for national defense, were added to existing collections. Thus, according to Huang's analysis, the effect of these reforms to simplify tax collections had only been constantly to increase the amount of the basic
tax without putting a stop to the further proliferation of taxes. To correct this, he would repeal all such increases since ancient times and return to a basic land tax calculated at a rate of 5 per cent for private landholding and one-tenth for land distributed on the model of the military
farm system.[79] The only other tax he would permit is one on households for the maintenance of a militia system he later proposes.

The crucial question then arises: Would such a low tax rate meet the
needs of government? Huang's answer is revealing. Without attempting to estimate the legitimate expenses of government, even under his own plan, to see whether or not they would be provided for, he is
content merely to show that the benevolent governments of ancient
times got along with much less. Under the ancient enfeoffment system,
according to the Confucian texts, a much greater share of the tax proceeds was applied to the expenses of local government than to those of
the court. Now, he implies, even though the central government has
taken over many of the functions of the former feudal lords and is entitled to a larger proportionate share, still the overall cost of government
should not have increased. China has changed, he seems to admit, but
China, as he sees it, has not grown. The increasing cost of government is
due not to expanded functions of state but to political degeneration,
manifesting itself in waste and inefficiency.[80]

Throughout Chinese history taxes had been paid for the most part in
grain or cloth. Only with the adoption of the Twice-a-year tax in the
T'ang dynasty did payment in copper cash become a common practice
in commutation of taxes in kind. And only with the Single-whip tax did
payment in silver become mandatory. A famous essayist of the T'ang
dynasty, Lu Chih, had complained that people lost heavily in converting
their produce into copper cash for the payment of taxes. "He thought
that was bad!" exclaims Huang. "How much worse it is that all taxes

should have to be paid in silver!" In earlier times money payment had in certain instances been authorized where it was a convenience to the people and where the rate of exchange for goods was favorable to the producer. But in the Ming dynasty the people often lost heavily when forced to convert their grain or cloth into silver at disadvantageous rates, and often a bountiful harvest would be of no benefit to the peasantry, since the value of their goods would drop sharply in relation to the silver they were forced to pay in taxes. Therefore it is essential to return to the ancient system of accepting in taxes whatever the land itself produces rather than ask the people to pay what they can obtain only with difficulty.

Finally, Huang attacks the practice of fixing a uniform tax rate for all land regardless of quality, as tended to be the case with the Single-whip method. Land values actually vary as much as twenty to one, and a tax that is equitable when applied to productive land may be ruinous when exacted from poor land. If an adjustment were made for unproductive soil, it might be allowed to lie fallow for a year or two and thus be gradually restored in fertility, but under existing conditions the peasant is forced to work it continually in order to meet his taxes. Consequently, Huang recommends the restoration of a practice once tried by Wang An-shih, whereby the size of a Chinese acre (*mou*) varied for tax purposes according to the productivity of the soil. This was called the system of "square fields" and provided for five different land classifications. In this way a uniform rate might be retained, but the taxable acreage, as the basis of the assessment, would vary so that the burden would be equally borne. Ultimately, this should result in an increase of tax revenue as the poorer land, allowed to lie fallow, gradually improved in quality and produced more.

Other Reforms

The full scope of Huang's reform program cannot be adequately presented here, but it is worth indicating at least that he had a wide awareness of the other economic and social factors directly affecting the exercise of political power. The maintenance of a sound monetary system is one such problem that he analyzes in detail, showing that the state had in the past failed to appreciate the importance of a stable and convenient medium of exchange to the economy as a whole and instead had shortsightedly manipulated or controlled the currency to its own immediate advantage. He therefore urges the adoption of a sound system of paper money and copper cash (which we recognize as essentially modern) and the abolition of gold and silver as circulating media.

A considerable part of *A Plan for the Prince* is devoted to questions of military organization, for Huang realizes that some of the basic weaknesses of the Ming dynasty are attributable to an unsound defense system, which had disastrous repercussions on the political and economic life of the nation. His fundamental thesis is that military power should not be left to a separate class of professional soldiers or allowed to fall into the hands of eunuchs, but that army organization and service should be integrated into the regular pattern of civil life and administration. At the same time, Huang recommends the creation of autonomous commanderies—virtual feudal states—on the borders of China, which would serve as buffers against China's traditional enemies on her northern and western frontiers and thus eliminate the need for sending the home militia on campaigns in remote regions. The commanderies would also serve as counterweights to the court itself, constituting centers of power beyond the reach of those at court who seek to monopolize such power for themselves.[81]

Huang prefaces his proposal for border commanderies by acknowledging that the enfeoffment system of the Chou, to which he pays as much lip service as most Neo-Confucians, is something of the remote past and to attempt its literal restoration would be impractical. Semiautonomous border commanderies would fulfill something of the same purpose of decentralization, however, while the strengthening of independent military initiatives on the frontier would actually serve the defense purposes of the center. In other words, the commanderies would be satellites surrounding China proper, but the center would still hold. That this is the residual meaning for Huang of restoring the "enfeoffment system" (*feng-chien*), and not any reestablishment of autonomous feudal domains or patriarchal communities, is confirmed by Huang's much later discussion of "*feng-chien*" in his *P'o-hsieh lun*.[82] Thus he concedes what is already implicit in the other administrative, fiscal, and military measures he has recommended: the continuance of the centralized system of prefectures and districts in China proper itself.

From this we see that the significance of the Chou ideal for him is really as a general principle for the sharing and dispersal of power; it is a model of the delegation of authority and vesting of power in semiindependent units or bodies, which Huang proceeds to implement in forms more reflective of recent historical experience. But it is also a model that remains suggestive of a unified order—with graduated ranks, delegated authority, and power dispersed throughout the structure, yet still related to a single center. It is not a plurality of independent states that join together in a federal union. The idea is not unity out of plurality (*E pluribus unum*) but one sharing with many.[83]

Similarly with respect to the other prime symbol of Chou "feudalism," the well-field system. As we have seen, for Huang it represents essentially a distribution of land to ensure the minimum subsistence for each peasant household in individually held lots. It is not thought of as joint property, communal land, or a clan community. And Huang would make the same adaptation of the well-field's equal landholding principle as Wang An-shih did in his "square fields" taxation system— well short of restoring either the well-fields or the enfeoffment system.

General Discussion

In Huang's discussion of political principles and Chinese institutions, certain underlying themes appear. Certainly one of the most evident is his emphasis on government being conducted in the interests of the people, not of their rulers. And if having the people's interests at heart sufficed to make a thinker "democratic," then Huang would doubtless be among the first to qualify, for his analysis and condemnation of Chinese despotism, which had reached its peak in the Ming dynasty, are probably a more thoroughgoing and outspoken defense of the people's interests than any that has come down to us in Chinese literature. Nevertheless, we have reason to be uneasy with one modern appraisal of Huang Tsung-hsi, which links him to John Locke and John Stuart Mill and concludes: "All three are democrats, believing as they do that the state is created for man, not man for the state."[84] There is indeed this much of a resemblance between the three, and yet in making such a comparison we do well to remember that Western democracy has drawn on a variety of elements in the recent, as well as the remote, past. Identifying it too exclusively with Locke and Mill, with their strong emphasis on the primacy of human society and individual liberty vis-à-vis the state, not only oversimplifies the Western case but sets up too limited a frame for useful comparison with China.

No less important to the rise of Western political democracy has been the development of constitutionalism, marked by a concern for the primacy of law over the state and for independent bodies to check the arbitrary exercise of state power. Broadly speaking, constitutionalism has been less than fully optimistic about the inherent goodness of human nature when simply left to itself, and more disposed to believe that human liberties can be guaranteed only by the acceptance of certain constraints, especially legal restraints that would curb the more aggressive, power-seeking, and self-aggrandizing aspects of human behavior. Among the thinkers of the eighteenth-century Enlightenment, Montesquieu, with his "Spirit of Laws" is probably the most representative figure in this alternative tradition, which has seen a proper defining and balancing of state power as necessary to the protection of social and individual rights.[85] This view has deep roots in Roman law and medieval canon law, while in the English "constitutional" tradition, it goes back at least to the Magna Carta and the barons of Runnymeade defending their rights versus the king.

China has known no exact counterpart to Locke or Mill, asserting the priority of human society and prime value of the individual vis-à-vis the state; much less has it any equivalent to the barons of Runnymeade or a charter limiting the royal power as in the Magna Carta. Still, we must consider both points of reference if we are to judge how close Huang Tsung-hsi may come to expressing any of these values in Chinese terms.

For even though Confucianism exhibits nothing like the radical individualism of the modern West, it does express a deep concern for the self-development of the individual in nurturing social contexts, and Huang Tsung-hsi was, to a significant degree, heir to a main Neo-Confucian current, coming down from the Ch'eng brothers and Chu Hsi to Wang Yang-ming, which emphasized this liberal view of the self and its irreducible value vis-à-vis the state and society. For this very reason, it catches our attention when we see Huang, at the outset of his Plan, juxtaposing the legitimate self-interest of the individual to the inordinate selfishness and self-indulgence of the ruler, while also showing how the excessive demands of the latter deprive the former of his natural birthright and livelihood.

Similarly, when we find Huang making a distinction between unlawful laws and lawful ones, we can understand it as having more than one significance. First of all, it asserts a new concept of Law as higher than the state, challenging the sacredness of dynastic law (i.e., the precedents set by the founding father of the dynasty and the legal codes of his successors) on the ground that they serve only a private house, not all-under-Heaven. Law, properly speaking, should at a minimum protect the self-interest of the many from the selfishness of the powerful few.

Second, by explicitly denying the right of the ruler to treat "all-under-Heaven" as his private property, to be disposed of as he will, Huang implies that the people themselves should have—not property rights in the Western sense—but freedom from the threat of confiscatory taxation or expropriation by the state in respect to the land individual households acquire (though under Mencius' well-field system, which he endorses, it would presumably be a right to hold and use, not to sell). Third, by subjecting the ruler to a higher law conceived in the interests of "all-under-Heaven," Huang puts his reliance on a constitutional limitation of the ruler's power, rather than continuing to put faith, as earlier Neo-Confucians had, in the ruler's ability to match the virtue of the sage-king and thereby rectify the evils of human society.

Further, the same principle applies to the *shih* as professed Confucian Noble Man, but somewhat in reverse for Huang, inasmuch as he sees the latter, in contrast to the ruler, as essentially powerless. Law in this case is needed to strengthen the Noble Man's position and protect him, in his role as public servant, from the arbitrariness of the ruler. In this way Huang drew from the Neo-Confucians' unhappy Ming experience a new lesson concerning the individual's need for law and the importance of law for the curbing of imperial power. Prior to this, in the Sung, Yüan, and Ming, Neo-Confucians had put their hope in persuading rulers to perform as sage-kings by listening to the advice of wise mentors. From this hope sprang their strenuous efforts to elevate and reinforce the position of the Confucian minister.[86] As Huang, however, reviewed the results of this effort over several centuries, he could no longer believe that the individual heroism and dedication of the Noble Man, as minister, was sufficient to cope with the inordinate power of the ruler or the latter's indisposition to accept the self-discipline that goes with sage-kingship. Something more would be needed by way of a supporting infrastructure such as, in the West, Montesquieu had identified with the *"corps intermediaires"* between the state and society at large.

It is not, certainly, that Huang believed any the less in the noble calling of the Confucian scholar-official, but only that this lofty vocation needed support and structural reinforcement at every level. Accordingly, in the recommendations of his Plan, Huang calls repeatedly for strengthening the status and identity of the scholar-official class (*shih*) and expanding both their numbers and functions—giving them an increased role in civil government generally, but especially an enhanced status for the prime minister, as leader of the *shih*, and thus in a position to balance the power of the emperor.[87] Further, he would have a more active involvement of the *shih* in military affairs; firm control over eunuchs, who had gained such dominance in the Ming; and, above all, greater independence and authority in education, from the lowest level of society to the very top.

Recent commentators, especially in the People's Republic and Japan, have noted Huang's clear commitment to the leadership of the *shih,* and often have evaluated it, pro and con, in "class" terms based on the presumed self-interest of the *shih,* whether as landed gentry—in an ambivalent relation to the state above and the peasantry below—or perhaps even as increasing collaborators of a growing merchant class.[88] Huang himself expresses deep concern for the oppressed peasantry, some sympathy for merchants, mild disdain for the rich (whatever their "class" status), utter contempt for "vulgar Confucians" who debase their calling, and only relentless hostility to the dynastic state. In these terms, what comes through clearly is his commitment to government for the people and to the curtailing of imperial power.

One may still question, however, in what way this enhanced status of the scholar-official serves Huang's aim of establishing the people as masters in the land—whether this translates into "government by the people," or anything very closely resembling representative democracy as known in the modern West, with institutions designed to provide people with the means of freely expressing their will and in some way controlling the conduct of government. He advocates government "by the people" only in the sense that, with Mencius, he justifies the overthrowing of tyrannical rulers and also in the sense that, ideally, those he would entrust with political power will be sensitive to the desires of the people and speak for them. But like Mencius too, he takes for granted that political leadership requires literary education, testing and training —all activities that require some freedom from the hard labor of the peasant, some leisure for the cultural pursuits essential to civilized rule. To the extent that they lack these, most peasants are unprepared to make political judgments. For this very reason then both Huang and Mencius emphasize that those to whom such leisure and education are vouchsafed must accept a heavy responsibility as custodians of the people's welfare: learning cannot be indulged in simply for one's own self-enjoyment. The educationally privileged incur the burdens of noblesse oblige.

This natural assumption of leadership responsibility on the part of the *shih*—of both their right and duty to speak for the people—is not, of course, something Huang draws simply from a direct reading of Mencius alone. It is an assumption just as natural to his Neo-Confucian predecessors (followers of Mencius too) from the Sung onward, and it was powerfully reaffirmed by his immediate predecessors in the Tung-lin movement.[89] Thus, given this as a long-established, axiomatic principle of the educated class, one can perhaps understand why Huang only reiterates the need for the *shih* to live up to their own best professions, instead of having recourse to forms of representative government, including legislative bodies, elections, referendums, political parties, and the like, in order to convey the wishes of the people.

It is true, however, that the institutions Huang does recommend would fulfill some of the same functions as do the organs of representative government in Western democracies. Especially as embodied in his proposal for a strong prime minister and for ministers who are servants of the people and cannot be arbitrarily overruled by the ruler, this constitutional order would have certain resemblances to the present British system of government. Moreover, in the great importance that he attaches to schools, going far beyond their immediate educative functions and setting them up as centers for the expression of public opinion, Huang intends that they should perform much the same purpose as political parties or parliaments.[90] Indeed, considering the whole trend of Chinese political history, it is quite natural that he should think of them in this light. What were called "factions" at the Chinese court represented the nearest thing to the political parties of the West, and, insofar as these factions were alignments based on political principles rather than mere cliques held together by personal loyalties, they tended to become identified with certain schools, as in the late Ming dynasty. Unquestionably, Huang's conception of the high place of schools in the political sphere is inspired by the attacks that had been made in his time on precisely this role of the schools as organs of political expression.

A more fundamental reason, perhaps, why schools should seem to Huang the most suitable representatives of public opinion may be found in the traditional structure of Chinese society itself. In the absence of a strong middle class, which in the West has usually provided the basis for an effective party system, it was more natural to turn for this purpose to some institution indispensably bound up with the scholar-official class, for whom the state had an inescapable need in its recruitment of officials for the carrying out of bureaucratic functions. Other than this there was no real ground for political parties to stand on, no organized class or group for them to represent. Nor were there, beneath the ruling bureaucracy and its territorial agents, any corporate institutions or voluntary associations with sufficient economic power, social position, and established political rights to make themselves a force to be reckoned with. There was only the mass of common people, for the most part peasants, inarticulate and unaccustomed to political action except in the form of violent revolt. In such a situation the schools alone provided some mechanism for the expression of—not public, perhaps, but at least informed—opinion, since schools were indispensable to the ruling class itself. Though there had been attempts to make them, too, subservient to the ruling power, this very suppression testified to the fact that schools were potentially dangerous centers of opposition in a state that placed such a premium on learning. Even in modern times this has continued to be so, for with the imposition of one- party rule during most of the twentieth century in China, schools and research institutes have remained the most articulate centers of political discussion in mainland China.

If, therefore, we appreciate the forces with which Huang had to contend, and the limited institutional resources available to cope with them, it is not surprising that he should have proposed different means of achieving some of the same ends as Western democratic institutions. But having made allowances for the historical situation, there are still some deep-seated differences between Huang Tsung-hsi and Western proponents of "government by the people." In spite of his emphasis on law and a quasi-constitutional order, the prime minister to whom he would grant great powers and the ministers whom he calls servants of the people are still to be appointed by the ruler, not elected. Similarly, although he denies that "the principle of monarchy is inescapable," his denial implies only that a tyrant may be overthrown; he does not specify how else the ruler may be chosen except that somehow it should be done through a consensual process.

Earlier Confucian thought is much concerned with the question of whether the Confucian minister should accept or decline the ruler's invitation to serve, whether he should "advance to or withdraw from" office.[91] But in any case the ruler is always presumed to be there, in place, either respectfully inviting or imperiously commanding such service on the part of the Confucian. There is discussion too of how justified anyone was, earlier in history, who overthrew a reigning ruler or ruling dynasty. Thus the possibility was recognized of a change of rulers and dynasties, and with it the consequent problem of whether or not Confucians could accept the change and be willing to serve a new ruler or dynasty. Huang Tsung-hsi, though unwilling to serve the Manchus, was compelled to accept such change as an historical fact, and would have accepted even more readily a change that would dispense with hereditary rule altogether.[92] But the thought does not apparently occur to him, anymore than to earlier Confucians, that Confucian activists themselves might band together, install a new ruler, and institute a new order.

In the paradigmatic cases cited by Huang of rulership being offered to sagely or worthy men, who prove unwilling or reluctant to serve, nothing is revealed as to who it is that makes the offer, or by what consensual process the invitation is initiated. (Parenthetically, we might note that Huang's contemporary, Lü Liu-liang, who also deplores dynastic rule and lineal succession, speaks of Confucian ministers as the ones who should offer the throne to a worthy person, but Lü too fails to specify the process of selection.)[93] In the somewhat similar cases of education officials being locally chosen and conducting some autonomous direction of affairs, Huang is likewise reticent concerning the consensual mechanisms to be used in making the choice, though in local situations some natural community leadership is presumed to exist, probably based on family, lineage, gentry, or guild organizations. Yet, however practicable these means might be on the local level, it leaves one without any clear picture of how the consensual process would work on the intermediate or higher levels of government.

In part, Huang's reticence may be attributable to the deference he must show to one of his prime authorities in the past, Mencius, for the latter had said that the deposing of an unworthy or incompetent ruler was a family matter for "ministers of the royal blood" to decide. It was, then, up to the leadership of the ruling house to meet this responsibility, not for ordinary ministers, who are left simply to decide whether they will stay with the ruler or leave.[94]

This passage in *Mencius* being well known to Neo-Confucian readers of the Four Books with Chu Hsi's commentaries, and Mencius in particular having such high standing among them (as certainly he did for Huang), the latter were bound to be inhibited in any attempt to redefine the question on a basis different from Mencius—that is, in suggesting that it should be addressed by others than the royal family or in a manner other than by outright revolt.

A more general reason for this reticence, however, may lie in the Confucian's characteristic aversion, seen already in the Master himself, to address the problem of power. So committed were Confucians to the idea that real power consisted in moral and intellectual virtue, in the inner power of charismatic leadership, and so juxtaposed was this in their minds to rule by force or other coercive means, that Confucians felt a reluctance to discuss how power should be gained or organized until after someone else had seized it. Never, throughout the long history of Chinese dynastic history and upheaval, had a Confucian leader promoted military or political action by a Confucian party to seize power and found a new regime (with the possible exception of Wang Mang at the end of the Former Han, who was not, in any case, considered by Confucians to be an appropriate model). Given this moralistic outlook and normally reserved manner, Confucians simply waited for the founder of a dynasty or ruler to come to them, rather than seem to be taking any initiative themselves in grasping for power.

Lenin is said to have attributed the success of the Bolsheviks to the fact that they "found power lying in the gutter." Huang Tsung-hsi, for his part, is critical of most Confucians for leaving power to the "generals." And his experience of the failed resistance to the Manchus must have left him with strong feelings of both frustration and the powerlessness of the Confucians. Whether from such feelings, or from a begrudging acknowledgment that dynastic history, realistically read, allowed little immediate hope for the establishment of a radically different system, Huang seems to have reconciled himself, like so many Confucians before him, to waiting for an enlightened ruler to appear, rather than trying to rally other Confucians and engage them in setting up a new, nondynastic regime.

Thus, though we have no reason to believe that representative government and electoral processes would be incompatible with Huang's consensual, meritocratic, and fiduciary conception of government, these would, in the circumstances of seventeenth-century China and in view of past Confucian experience, be unlikely vehicles for the realization of his ideal plan. Such being the case, the enlightened prince, and ideally a sage-ruler, however chosen or installed, remains for Huang an almost necessary figure.

True, when Huang invokes the symbolism of the *Book of Changes,* as he does by reference to the *ming-i* hexagram in his preface to the work, we are reminded that Confucianism, under this aspect, is not always to be taken literally as political program or ideology but more as an ethico-religious system. Just prior to writing his Plan, Huang had been immersed in a study of the *Book of Changes* and its "emblems and numbers," and it was this kind of hopeful speculation that encouraged him, against the near despair of the failed resistance movement, to believe that all might not be lost if only his ideas could be bequeathed to posterity. The *Book of Changes* offer the Confucian Noble Man prudential wisdom as a guide to his personal conduct of life, in situations that may require of him an attitude of religious resignation, a patient acceptance and endurance of momentary adversity, while not giving up hope for the future. In this respect then, Huang pictures himself in a human situation of almost universal significance, to be understood in symbolic rather than literal terms.

It remains true, however, that the enlightened ruler, besides being an archetypal symbol of religious hope, is also a key figure in Huang's plan of meritocratic, constitutional government. Otherwise, there would be no point to his opening argument concerning the true nature of rulership, the ruler's proper collegial relation to his ministers, his need for a prime minister, and the importance of the ruler deferring to the leading scholar who is to lead the discussion of public issues in the Imperial College (understood here as the highest institution of learning, *t'ai-hsüeh*, in the land).

Hence it is to the prince and the scholar-official that Huang addresses this book, not to multitudes of common people among whom he would sow the seeds of a grass-roots democracy. Reform must necessarily start from above, because, in the given circumstances (which had prevailed from time immemorial), there was no infrastructure through which it could come up from below (unless one counts the very uncertain route for the submission of memorials to the throne, which are essentially petitions for the emperor to act, not manifestos for concerted action by others).[95]

At this point I should acknowledge that my views in the matter have changed somewhat over the years. In an essay on this subject written nearly forty years ago, I may have leaned over backward in trying to disassociate myself from a view that equated Huang Tsung-hsi—too facilely I thought—with Western democratic values and processes. Much concerned with identifying certain basic Confucian assumptions that would distinguish Huang's thought from Western conceptions, I explained the need for reform to come from the top down in these terms:

> For any true follower of Confucius good government works from the top downward. The sage-king is the sum of virtue, from whom all goodness radiates down upon the people. It is the moral authority and example of the Prince which rectifies all evils and maintains order in society. . . . .

Huang Tsung-hsi would not have it any other way. Such limitations as he would place on the Prince's sovereignty are truly in the nature of moral restraints. They are not intended to make him less of a king but help him to be a king.[96]

This characterization, I would say now, leaned too heavily on a stereotypical view of both Confucianism and Neo-Confucianism and did not sufficiently take into account the evolution and significant modification of Neo-Confucian thought up to Huang Tsung-hsi's time. In particular, as I have since explained in *The Trouble with Confucianism,* my earlier view failed to register both the seriousness of the Neo-Confucians' efforts to turn Sung, Yüan, and Ming emperors into sage-kings—serious even though failed efforts—or the extent to which some Neo-Confucian scholars had come to recognize the need for institutional reforms that would offset the overconcentration of power and misuse of authority at the top and center.

Peter Bol, considering the possibilities for finding some near equivalent of a civil society in imperial China, has noted the relatively independent growth in the Sung of a Confucian intellectual movement among the *shih* class, which strongly resisted pressures for conformity from above and subordination to the official culture of the civil service examination system. Bol emphasizes the autonomy this Neo-Confucian "civil culture" was able to maintain vis-à-vis the Chinese state system: "the real legacy of the Sung dynasty was the independence of civil culture from government both institutionally and intellectually."[97]

Huang Tsung-hsi, himself a strong partisan of the *shih,* was heir to this same civil culture, but he became convinced that the *shih* could not develop and fulfill their proper leadership role if all they had was a free-standing "civil *culture,*" unincorporated into a "civil *society*" that provided the supporting infrastructure necessary for coping effectively with the dynastic state. For him the autonomous culture (*wen*) of the Sung literati (to which he fully subscribed as an undiminished champion of the *shih*) was insufficient without the support of proper laws and institutions that went beyond the limited foothold the literati had managed to establish as a countervailing force in the Sung court.

In this changed perspective, I would now credit Huang with, first, building more on this later experience and scholarship, and second, making a significant further advance in articulating what had been learned from it, especially from the dismal Ming record. Since Huang was in other respects deeply loyal to certain central values in both Ming and Neo-Confucian culture, his revisionist views on the political record cannot be discounted either as the product just of one man's personal alienation or as a reflection of some general cultural disorientation in the wake of the Ming collapse. Indeed it is far more appropriate to see Huang's Plan as reaffirming the essence of Confucian political tradition, than to let it be confused with the fate of dynastic rule.[98] Yet, if there is something of continuity and growth here, simply to treat it as a recasting of classical stereotypes, as I mistakenly tended to do earlier, is not satisfactory either.

Thus when I went on to say, in that same essay, that the importance of ministers and officials for Huang is that "they are not simply co-administrators of the realm but colleagues and moral preceptors who will help the Prince to be a real king," I was putting things in the wrong order. It was, of course, important to Huang that the ruler be surrounded by men of wisdom and strength of character, rather than by eunuchs and other servile types, but I misrepresented Huang's priorities by seeming to minimize the function of scholar-officials as coadministrators in comparison to their unquestionably important role as moral counselors. That latter role had already been stressed by any number of Neo-Confucians from Ch'eng I, Chu Hsi, and Chen Te-hsiu in the Sung, on down to Hsü Heng in the Yüan, and among many in the Ming, Huang's own teacher Liu Tsung-chou (1578–1645), all of whom had done their best to institutionalize this mentoring function in lectures from the Classics Mat or as censors, but to little practical avail.[99] Consequently, it is of some significance when Huang wants to go further and establish a leading scholar-official (*shih*) as prime minister. As such, this person could indeed serve as a genuine coadministrator because concrete steps would have been taken to strengthen his executive role and insulate its public functions from the covert interference of the inner court—especially by having him lead the open discussion of state matters at court and by giving him a strong role in the decision-making process.

It is also from this perspective that I would now attach a different significance to Huang's proposals for the strengthening of the educational system and of the educated scholar-official's role in government. Successive Neo-Confucians earlier had insisted on the need to expand education as a prerequisite to more informed participation by the people in government. The failure of these efforts (as well as of formal gestures in the direction of a universal school system by Khubilai Khan in the Yüan and Ming T'ai-tsu later) provide a background for this renewed advocacy by Huang Tsung-hsi.

Chu Hsi, as noted earlier, had drawn special attention to the need for expanded education on every level of society. In his preface to the *Great Learning,* which all educated persons encountered as the first item in standard editions of the Four Books, Chu had even spoken of the need for the institution of schools in every village and town (not just for training or tutoring in the home, or lecturing in regional academies). Chu too, besides hoping thereby to contribute to the general uplift of the people, which he thought of as "renewing the people," no doubt also believed that this education would strengthen the ranks of the *shih-ta-fu* as a meritocratic leadership elite. But even so, Chu does not come close to Huang in articulating and defining the specifically political (and not just the cultural) role of the schools, to establishing their autonomy at every level, and to asserting the importance of having educated leadership in every sphere of governmental activity.

For these reasons, as well as because Huang is far more pointed than his predecessors in asserting, by his special attention to law (*fa*), the necessary form in which to institutionalize these Confucian values, it seems to me clear that Huang's Plan goes far toward drawing up a real system, a kind of Confucian constitution, in a way that no one before him had tried to do. Yet it is no less true that he does so by building on lessons learned from the earlier—mostly unhappy—experience of Neo-Confucian scholar-officials, especially late Ming writers whose reform proposals anticipated many of Huang's.[100]

The shift in the late Ming from a heavy emphasis on the moralization of politics—the appeal to individual conscience and self-discipline, summed up in Chu Hsi's phrase "self-cultivation for the governance of men" (*hsiu-chi chih-jen*)—to a greater emphasis on specific instrumentalities and institutions of practical benefit to human society, is often expressed in terms of "practical efforts for the ordering of the world" (*ching-shih chih yung*). As a general trend this was concerned with concrete programs, methods, and systems for ordering human efforts, and Huang's attempt to incorporate Confucian values and implement reforms in specific institutions both fits in with this larger trend and renders it more plausible for us to think of his Plan as indeed aimed at the framing of a new constitutional order.

A measure of the distance Neo-Confucian thought has traveled between the thirteenth and seventeenth centuries may be found by comparing Huang's approach to systematic, programmatic reform with the typical earlier Neo-Confucian approach of the leading scholar-statesman Chen Te-hsiu. As a powerful advocate of Chu Hsi's teaching in the late Southern Sung period, Chen is well known for his *Extended Meaning of the Great Learning,* a guide to rulership, and for his *Classic of the Mind-and-Heart* (*Hsin ching*), an anthology for the ruler's self-cultivation in the vein of the [Sage] "Emperor's and King's Learning of the Mind-and-Heart" (*ti-wang chih hsin-hsüeh*).[101] But in a separate preface to an edition of the *Rites of Chou* (*Chou li*), Chen addressed the central question facing so many Sung Neo-Confucian reformers: Is it really possible to resurrect the model institutions prescribed in the *Rites of Chou?*

Chen's answer is yes, but the indispensable prerequisite is for this "bible" of Neo-Confucian reformers to be read, understood, and interpreted by someone who grasps the true intentions of the Duke of Chou, presumed to be the author of these Rites. "Only if one has the mind-and-heart of the Duke of Chou can one carry out the Rites of Chou. Without such a mind, the attempt to carry them out will be countereffective." Likewise, Chen says one cannot properly discuss or explain the Rites unless one "has the learning of the Duke of Chou." In the present age, however, the key to understanding the mind and learning of the Duke of Chou, says Chen, may be found in the teachings of the Sung masters, the Ch'eng brothers, and Chang Tsai. The essential and primary task, then, is to inculcate the ruler with this learning and "mind-and-heart," in order to overcome his ignorant and self-indulgent ways.[102]

Huang Tsung-hsi, out of the Wang Yang-ming school, is hardly an opponent of the Learning of the Mind-and-Heart (*hsin-hsüeh*), but his whole approach to radical reform on the model of the *Chou li* is based on the development of a systematic institutional plan, which, far from being predicated on converting and reforming the mind of the emperor, attacks from the outset the primacy and ultimate authority of the ruler. True, Huang looks for a prince to adopt his Plan, but the Plan itself, if it speaks to the "mind of the ruler" at all, subjects it to the most severe critique as (in its dynastic incarnation) the quintessence of selfishness, which only fundamental institutional changes can curb and rectify. Obviously there is a continuity in the focus on selfishness by both writers, but Huang's diagnosis and prescription in terms of institutions goes well beyond Chen Te-hsiu's personal approach to the ruler.

As a proposal that emerges from the late Ming Neo-Confucian experience, and at the same time differs in form from most Western constitutions, it may be fair to call Huang's Plan a kind of Confucian constitutionalism, perhaps most distinguishable from the Western type in that, while both are predicated on the consent of the governed, the contractual element so prominent in Western parliamentary systems (a document ratified by elected representatives and implemented through electoral processes) is largely absent here. On this point too we recall that, in Huang's mythic account of the origin of rulership, he does not speak of the people as coming together and establishing a ruling order where before there was none. Instead he pictures a state of affairs in which individuals were going about their own business, taking care of themselves, and it was only when a sage-king stood forth and showed, by his own self-sacrificing efforts, how a better order of things could be managed, that civilization came into being. Thereafter, it was a question of whether other high-minded Noble Men could be persuaded to emulate this self-denying role, not whether any contractual agreement, ratified by the people and binding on both parties, would be arrived at.

Thus we may call it a *Confucian* constitutionalism insofar as it depends on the vocation of the Noble Man and the esprit de corps of the *shih,* but it is a constitution nonetheless insofar as Huang will no longer rely simply on the good intentions and exemplary character of the ruler, but insists on institutionalized limits to the exercise of the ruler's power. When he condemns those who "think that the prince shares the world with one [the minister] so that it can be governed, and that he entrusts one with its people so that they can be shepherded, thus regarding the world and its people as personal property in the prince's pouch," Huang clearly denies legitimacy to even a benevolent ruler who might assume that governance was something for him to delegate to ministers as he chose, rather than an inherently corporate, nondiscretionary, and Heaven-ordained sharing of responsibility, to be embodied in the basic structure of government.

Inasmuch as this is a product of Chinese historical experience, and of a particular class of *shih* in the late Ming, it is best to think of it as a collective, Confucian product and not simply as the creation of a single (perhaps idiosyncratic) genius. Nevertheless, there is still reason to credit Huang himself with making a special contribution to the devising of this new institutional order, for who before him had put together such a unified, systematic document that addressed both fundamental issues and concrete proposals? Who before Huang had thought to make the proposal—shocking to the more conventionally minded— that the emperor and his ministers should sit periodically as students at the Imperial College and listen while the libationer (i.e., rector or chancellor) conducted a discussion of current issues among the scholars in attendance?[103] Who had both symbolically and practically asserted the higher intellectual and moral authority of the scholarly community, in a way that so dramatically challenged imperial claims to ultimate authority? And who before Huang had thought to generalize this deference to "public opinion" as a pattern to be followed on all levels of education and administration?

Plainly my use of the term "public opinion" cannot refer to the people or popular opinion as a whole, inasmuch as the great mass of the populace would have been unable to participate significantly in the process of generating and expressing opinion or forming any general consensus (there being few media of communication or discussion available outside of literati circles). "Public" then refers here to opinion generated both within the government and autonomously outside the state apparatus, and to discussion that addresses issues of concern to "all-under-Heaven" (i.e., issues affecting society as a whole and not the interests of the state or dynasty alone).

Literati and scholar-officials called such discussion *chiang-hsüeh* (literally, "the discussion of learning"). It was mainly carried on in Ming academies, *shu-yüan* (literally, "libraries"), considered "private" schools to the extent that support for them had to come from within local scholarly communities without whose collegial solidarity it would have been impossible to carry on open discussion.[104] Thus it was in a scholarly and academic—that is, mostly elite—setting that this kind of public forum was conducted, by a class who thought of themselves as dedicated to public service. True, in many mid-Ming academies philosophical discussion had become so focused on issues of human nature and the mind that Tung-lin reformers, who felt the urgent need for political action, dismissed it as just so much empty talk. Yet if they often regarded the prevailing *chiang-hsüeh* as airy and impractical, their purpose was to direct this discussion to more immediate questions of public importance, and it was to this experience that Huang referred when he spoke of establishing this "public" function in a system of government schools, with the libationer leading a discussion (*chiang-hsüeh*) open to any and all issues.[105]

In my earlier essay I tended to underscore—perhaps unduly—the comparatively limited scope and elite character of this process, in contrast to the more populist character of the Western democratic process. "There is no place here for mass meetings, monster rallies or clambakes," I said. "Not through talking with the people and soliciting their support, but through consultation with the wise and virtuous in an aristocracy of merit, is the government to achieve its objective of ruling in the interests of all." [106] By this I meant to avoid any simple equation of Huang's proposals with Western parliamentary or electoral systems, but I had in mind also the importance of respecting the authentic character of Huang's thought by not sloughing off or distorting any of its characteristic Confucian emphases.

More recently, I have had occasion to point to these same features as a distinct limitation of Confucian discourse: its being carried out in relative isolation from the people as a whole was a severe handicap when Confucian statesmen had to confront national crises in the nineteenth century, without any effective means of rallying support except among the literati (if indeed they could do even that).

But there is another way of looking at the matter—from the standpoint of the resources Huang and even much later reformers had to draw upon in trying to generate something like open discussion of public issues. Huang's aim to create a public space for the airing of important matters is made unambiguously clear when he asserts, in the opening lines of his essay on Schools, that the Son-of-Heaven in ancient times did not try to decide "right and wrong" for himself but left this to be publicly aired and decided by the schools (*kung ch'i shih-fei yü hsüeh-hsiao*).

The fact that he uses the language of the Confucian academy—"the discussion of learning" (*chiang-hsüeh*) and "public discussion" (*kung-i*)—to describe the essential function to be carried on in this public space, rather than the language of teaching, instructing, or indoctrinating, tells us that he is drawing on the one tradition and institution available as a working example—the academy—and trying to incorporate its characteristic activity in a fully recognized constitutional body. Moreover, he is broadening its application—its public dimension—by stipulating that the scholar (*ju*) chosen to head the prefectural and district schools may be anyone with the requisite personal qualifications, even a commoner, and need not be someone accredited through the civil service exams, but could be quite unconnected to the state.

Much as Huang defended the intellectual autonomy of the "private" academies themselves, his aim to establish this open discussion as a public function both at court (where he specifies that the discussion of state matters should be thoroughly aired by the prime minister and his ministers, who are to be scholar-officials), and also in state-supported schools, has much to say about his constitutional intentions. It was to be

a well-defined, state-supported, fully accredited, and legal function of a
duly constituted order, and yet as independent as it was possible for
him to make it in a society that lacked a middle class, popular press,
church, legal profession, or other supporting infrastructure independent of the state.

In this important respect I also did Huang less than full justice when
I said in the same earlier essay that we should "not make the mistake of
interpreting Huang's reliance upon law and a well-defined system of
government as placing him in a class with advocates of constitutional
government in the West." The point, as I would now see it, is not whether to "classify" Huang with the latter, but whether any of his distinctive
Confucian concerns or commitments necessarily disqualify him from
being recognized as an advocate of a constitutional order—one suited
indeed to the conditions he faced—that would provide for a public
space or sphere sorely lacking in traditional China.

I do not now think they should. If, for instance, the sharing, distribution, or decentralization of power has often been the aim of constitutional movements, as I said earlier, the fixing of considerable power in
the hands of men of strong character and ability, and allowing them
broad freedom of action (largely unconstrained by regulations of a
central authority), should not be seen as necessarily antithetical to a
constitutional order—as long as the respective spheres of authority and
responsibility are properly defined. Nor do I believe that Huang was so
concerned with preserving Confucian harmony that he would con-
strain dissent in the discussion of major issues. True, his Plan does call
for the local education officers to censor certain books and activities
considered dangerous to the public moral health, and in this respect
Huang, like most Confucians, would be considered conservative and
strait-laced by modern standards but by no means repressive of all
nonconformity. Indeed his views in later life grew considerably more
tolerant.

If, as I would now grant, Huang can reasonably qualify as a constitu-
tionalist, albeit a Confucian one, judgments may still differ as to how
appropriate it is for him, as an advocate of a public space or sphere, to
invest so heavily in the *shih* (scholar-official or literati) class, as the principal custodians of such a sphere. Among social and economic historians, opinions vary widely as to just what the special economic and social self-interest of this class was, or in what way that special interest
might have operated to condition, qualify, or distort the outcome of the
reforms Huang Tsung-hsi or other members of that class proposed.

In economic terms, Huang's most important recommendation had to do with the well-field system and a tax program compatible with it. From his discussion of this in the Plan, he seems, like Lü Liu-liang, to have been primarily interested in seeing that every peasant household had land enough to provide for its livelihood. For this purpose it seems to have sufficed for Huang that one could ascertain, from figures available in the *Ming hui-tien,* that enough land was indeed available for redistribution so as to assure the feasibility of a minimum of individual landholding on at least a subsistence basis. Other aspects of Mencius' well-fields as a communal land system Huang easily dismissed as inconsequential, and so too did he slight the communal aspect when he failed to include in his Plan any reference to the community compact organization (*hsiang-yüeh*), which had been of considerable importance to both Chu Hsi and Wang Yang-ming and was a significant part of the Neo-Confucian program exported to Korea and Vietnam. True, Huang in his later discussion of taxes in the *P'o-hsieh lun* does speak of the well-field as a unit of tax collection (corresponding to its tribute-rendering function under Mencius' conception of the enfeoffment system), but that is far short of what Chu Hsi and Wang Yang-ming sought through the community compact.[108] (In this respect, one might see Huang's emphasis on individual landholding as differing from that of Ho Hsin-yin a century earlier, whose aim was to promote the communal benefits of clan or lineage organization as a way to build a kind of social infrastructure.)[109]

I forbear from considering whether and how these two rather different approaches to land organization—"private" or communal—might be thought to reflect any particular class interest (considering that their proponents were all *shih-ta-fu*). Rather I will now take a great leap forward to the present era and regime, which first saw land reform in the late 1940s and early 1950s give land to individual proprietors, then in the fifties saw a new system withdraw it in favor of a massive shift to communes, and thereafter in the late seventies and eighties witnessed a substantial reversion to individual (family) management of land. All this was under the auspices of a new elite leadership, avowedly classless but actually drawn heavily from families with a social background similar to the traditional elite—similar except for the great difference in ideology and in their lack of one of the old elite's most defining characteristics: its classical training and traditional scholarly or literary credentials. In other words, I am suggesting by this rough analogy that whatever the ideological rhetoric in which either the class character of this leadership or the proposals themselves are clothed, what in fact we are dealing with here is a limited number of real options—defined by historical, geographical, and economic givens that persist through political upheavals and yield only slowly to long-term cumulative change. Persistent enough are these so as to be resistant even to technological change. Even today the processes of modernization have not yet altered the basic pattern in which the great majority of the population (engaged in relatively small-scale, family-managed agriculture and industrial or craft production) are largely governed by a self-perpetuating managerial elite, and Chinese society is still without the benefit of any independent infrastructure or autonomous public sphere whereby the supreme authority of the one-party state could be effectively challenged or its concentration of power held in some check.

It is true that elsewhere in East Asia, Eastern Europe, and the Soviet Union new steps are now being taken in the direction of electoral democracy, which, if successful, may in the longer run have some beneficial influence upon the People's Republic of China as well. On the other hand, despite significant advances toward representative democracy in Taiwan and South Korea, there are authoritarian countertendencies in the People's Republic and some in Singapore that invoke a conservative version of Confucian tradition as an antidote to liberal influences from the West (as I have explained further in *The Trouble with Confucianism*).

This may leave the prospects for liberal democracy (and especially of pluralistic, multiparty, electoral democracy) still uncertain, with powerful inertial forces in Mainland China tending to sustain the present system for the foreseeable future. In these circumstances, if freedom of public discourse and electoral processes are not a likely prospect in the near term, the present regime still has need of educated men to serve the managerial elite, as well as to provide essential services in support of the modernization program to which it is still committed. Can this be done without depending on schools, technical institutes, research centers, and scholarly academies, roughly the modern equivalent of Huang's schools and academies? If not, then is it unrealistic to think that such institutions, given the autonomy needed effectively to do their work, might not be able to serve as a kind of intermediate level or stage for the gradual expansion of a more liberal constitutional order? Given both China's past history and the present obstacles to rapid and substantial political changes, it would seem that to define a protected role for schools and academies, to promote the expansion of education, and along with this the means of publication and the circulation of ideas, are not unlikely first steps which might be taken on the way to such a new order.

In this perspective then, Huang's proposals have some continuing relevance and should be recognized as a contribution to a liberal Confucian tradition that not only offers more hope for the future but also is more representative of Confucian humanism in its historical development than the authoritarian versions of Confucianism being promoted by some regimes today. In this light too, with these authoritarian versions placing so much stress on "harmony" as the supreme Confucian virtue, I would regret it if my own earlier discussion of the matter might lend any support at all to such a conformist interpretation. Confucius' "harmony without conformity" (*ho erh pu t'ung, Analects* 13:26) is a motto much truer to the authentic tradition, as Huang would certainly agree.[110]

Recent Appraisals

Though Huang Tsung-hsi anticipated some of the more important economic and social reforms undertaken in modern China, it was for his political thought that Huang became an important figure in the reform and revolutionary movements of the last century. Liang Ch'i-ch'ao, probably the most influential writer of this period, acknowledges the relevance to his own time of proposals by Huang such as land equalization, currency, and military reform, and the transfer of the capital to Nanking. But it is not to these ideas that Liang refers when he relates that Huang's writings proved "a powerful tonic for students in the 1890's" or when he says, "My own political activities can be said to have been influenced very early and very deeply by this book."[111] Rather it was Huang's political principles asserted in *A Plan for the Prince* that make him appear to Liang as an early champion of democracy, a native authority from whom reformers could obtain sanction for the democratic ideas and institutions they wished to import from the West. For this reason, Liang tells us, he and his colleagues exhumed Huang's book, which had been lost sight of during the eighteenth and early nineteenth centuries, and used it as a vehicle for spreading "democratic ideas" during the Kuang-hsü period (1875–1908).[112] When Liang and T'an Ssu-t'ung were "advocating popular sovereignty and republicanism, they printed abridged portions of *A Plan for the Prince* in several tens of thousands of copies and circulated it secretly, so that it had a most powerful effect on thought in the late Ch'ing dynasty."[113] Another contemporary source, setting forth the intellectual origins of the Chinese revolution, pictures Huang as the direct progenitor of the democratic and nationalist movement in modern times. "Viewed in proper historical perspective, the Chinese National Revolution was but the logical continuation of the struggle started by adherents of the late Ming Dynasty against the Manchu conquerors." Not only was Huang Tsung-hsi the most important philosopher of this "anti-imperialist" group, but, realizing that armed opposition to the Manchus was doomed to failure, he "conceived the plan of reorganizing the secret societies in China on a revolutionary nationalistic basis."[114]

From this idolization of Huang as the Chinese patriarch of the revolutionary movement, at least one monarchist in the last years of the Ch'ing, Li Tzu-jan, sharply dissented, accusing Huang of abandoning the constant human relations of ruler/minister, parent/child, etc., and, in his discussion of law, inviting complete lawlessness and anarchy. His detailed critique of Huang's chief political essays, published in 1909, has some interest as an expression of conservative thought identifying Confucianism with the established monarchy, but it is more of a challenge to Li's contemporary antagonists than to Huang himself, and since Li seems unaware of, and does not come to terms with, Lü Liu-liang's orthodox Neo-Confucian critique of dynastic rule, so parallel to Huang's, Li's discussion falls short of going to the heart of the issues even from a Confucian standpoint.[115]

Another more trenchant critique of Huang came from the leading scholar and thinker Chang Ping-lin (1868–1936). In a long essay, "Against Huang," he analyzes the political aspects of *A Plan for the Prince* and opposes, in particular, his ideas concerning the nature of law, the prime ministership, and the schools. Though much of his criticism is abusive and unjust, inspired by what seems a deep-seated personal animosity toward his political opponents, at times it serves as an illuminating commentary on the uses to which Huang's ideas were put by modern apostles of democracy and nationalism. In opposition, for instance, to the intensely active student movement of his time (some of whose champions found in Huang a justification for the intervention of students in politics),[116] Chang excoriates the notion that the opinions of immature and meddlesome students can be taken as representing the will of the people as a whole.[117]

Chang also deplores the way in which Huang is acclaimed as an exemplar of the doctrine of constitutional government. "Today people who talk about making the government over anew, all base their ideas on Huang Tsung-hsi."[118] Huang he dismisses as an insincere and inept proponent of government based on law. The excessive power granted the prime minister by Huang and his undermining of the civil service system demonstrate that his form of government would be dominated by individual political leaders, not governed by law. In this respect, Chang finds that Huang's proposals would indeed open the door to some of the worst features of the so-called constitutional democracies of the West, where the English cabinet is a rubber stamp for the prime minister, and the American president is a powerful demagogue whose followers will stop at nothing to get themselves and their party leaders elected.[119] "Today everyone talks about government according to law, but . . . among the Western powers today there is none which truly governs according to law. What Tsung-hsi advocates is what the Western world practices; they praise government according to law but stumble around because they overrate human intelligence."[120]

In spite of the lengths to which Chang carries his polemic, identifying Huang with all that is worst in the Western democracies where others had identified him with all that is best, Chang nevertheless exposes certain issues that separate Huang's view of government by law and this doctrine as professed by modern proponents of political democracy. Subsequent criticism of Huang's work has not failed to observe this. One contemporary authority on Chinese political thought, Hsiao Kung-ch'üan, has revealed his doubts over the enthusiasm that was expressed for Huang as a champion of democracy and nationalism just a few decades earlier. Huang, he readily admits, was a stout foe of absolutism and would most likely have stood in the democratic camp had he been born in the nineteenth century. But, as it was, Huang failed to transcend the traditional limits of monarchism and was therefore simply "following in the ruts that Mencius had already worn in the road."[121]

Recent Marxist critics, though their evaluation of him is couched in the same stereotypical terms of seventeenth-century China as a "feudal society," have had as much difficulty as other writers in coming to agreement on his political significance. One such critic, for instance, classes Huang with Ku Yen-wu and Wang Fu-chih as a last-ditch defender of the crumbling feudal aristocracy, which sought to recoup something from its defeat by the Manchus and maintain the power of the landlord class through a "self-salvation" movement. This, according to T'an P'i-mo, necessitated analyzing the causes of their previous

failure and initiating reform measures that would stave off peasant revolt and complete collapse. Thus Huang's emphasis upon the "people"
is no more than an attempt to placate the peasants and keep them from
throwing off the domination of "feudal" landlords. From this standpoint all of Huang's proposed reforms partake of this apparently
meliorative but actually conservative character: land reform is merely
an enticement to keep peasants on the land; tax reform is intended to
head off the revolt of the peasants against excessive taxes; the abolition
of gold and silver as money is designed to restore a natural barter economy, which will likewise keep the people on the land. And of course the
schools, as well as the border commandery system, are to serve as in-
struments of class domination by the feudal aristocracy. [122]

On the other hand, the well-known historian Hou Wai-lu, [123] who
accepted this same pseudo-Marxist (but more correctly Stalinist or
Maoist) view of Chinese society at that time as essentially feudalistic, [124]
came to precisely the opposite opinion concerning Huang. Centuries
ahead of his time in his thinking, Huang, says Hou, had liberated himself from the shackles of "medieval dogma" and anticipated most of the
important developments in modern thought and social reform. His revolutionary doctrines were expressed, it is true, in traditional terms, but
this was characteristic also of the heralds of the modern age in the West.
In fact, for Hou, Huang is more truly an apostle of democracy than its
Western advocates, because he sees the necessity for economic equality
as well as for government in the interests of the people. [125] His modern
outlook is therefore most clearly apparent in the economic reforms he
calls for: land reform to give the peasants the means of production, as
was then being done (in 1946–47), says Hou, in the countries of Eastern
Europe; [126] currency reform, to abolish the "feudalistic" money system
and provide a circulating medium that would stimulate economic activity and development; and tax reforms to eliminate gross inequalities
in the distribution of the tax burden. [127] Politically, Huang stands out in
Hou's mind for his attack on the "feudalistic" nature of the court bureaucracy, for his advocacy of a modern cabinet system giving extensive
power to a prime minister chosen on a merit basis, and for his cham-
pioning of free speech in the schools. [128] In short, Huang is "antifeudal," "enlightened," and, above all, "scientific" in his approach to the
intellectual and social problems of his day. [129]

Among the more recent variations on this theme is one that distinguishes between *shih* or *shih-ta-fu* on the basis of whether they are in or
out of office. Those not in the government but active as scholar-gentry

on their own home ground (*ti-chu chieh-chi tsai-yeh p'ai*), according to this view, are moved to criticize the government because, as landlords feeling the pressure of peasant discontent and anxious to protect their own local interest, they seek to redirect this pressure toward the central bureaucracy, advocating reform, especially the reduction of taxes and redistribution of official lands, that would relieve some of the burden on the peasants but leave the scholar-gentry essentially intact. Huang Tsung-hsi is sometimes "classed" among this group, and the reforms in his Plan are then viewed more or less favorably as "progressive" for his time inasmuch as they attack the main citadel of "bureaucratic feudalism."[130]

One can neither deny nor discount such "class" interests as factors in the thinking of Confucian scholars like Huang, when evidence can be adduced to link together the economic circumstances, social involvements and personal outlook of late Ming or early Ching figures, while still taking into account the variegations of reformist thought in the seventeenth century. But Ono Kazuko's studies of the Tung-lin movement and the social background of its leaders (of which Huang's father was one) show the difficulty of identifying them with any single economic class; many Tung-lin scholars were not well off, experienced hard times themselves, and would not necessarily identify themselves with even the well-to-do, much less the very rich. Rather, an image of the *shih* as a cultural elite whose highest values placed them beyond considerations of economic self-interest receives strong, if indirect, confirmation (and indeed stronger for being indirect) from recent studies of the role of women in *shih ta-fu* households, whose prudent and frugal management of family affairs, often in straitened circumstances, enabled them to triumph over adversity and even made it possible for their husbands and sons to devote themselves to scholarship and the higher life of the mind, eschewing all thought of money, personal gain, or appointment to office, rather than compromise their high moral standards.[131]

Nor should we overlook the evidence, so strong in Huang's work, that he himself defined the educated elite (*shih*) primarily in terms of their commitment to the task of cultural and political leadership. As *chün-tzu* and *ming-shih* (reputable scholars), they would be expected to hold themselves to a demanding standard, to accept a higher responsibility for the general welfare of all-under-Heaven than for any sectional interest. Even after witnessing the seemingly vain sacrifice of such noble men as his own father and his teacher Liu Tsung-chou toward the end of the Ming, Huang is still not ready to forswear the high ideal of dedi-

cated, self-sacrificing service that had marked the *shih* as Noble Men
from the time of Fan Chung-yen (989–1052) on. It is such shared ideals
and standards that Huang so naturally invokes when he speaks of
choosing senior scholars of good repute to serve as chancellor of the
Imperial College, educational intendant in the province or prefecture,
or school superintendent in the districts, as if a consensus could easily
be reached on the basis of these shared values among educated men,
without Huang's having to spell out the process by which the choice
would be made.

Thus Huang's conception of the *shih,* as it is revealed at crucial junc-
tures in the laying out of his Plan, lends itself readily to John Dardess's
view of the "Confucian profession" in his *Confucianism and Autocracy.*
Dardess proposes "for purposes of historical analysis the legitimacy of
the idea of a 'self-sufficient' Confucian community whose ties to office-
holding or landholding, though important, were marginal rather than
central to its composition and outlook. This means that when the activities or opinions of the Confucian elites are taken up for study and
scrutiny, one may legitimately expect to discern lying behind them a
strictly professional interest, and not necessarily an interest that must
somehow be tied to economic or bureaucratic or other extraneous considerations."[132]

Historically speaking, of course, this "self-sufficiency of the Confucian community" was difficult to sustain, and Dardess himself notes
that "the observance or non-observance of professional ethics constituted the principal focus of conflict within the broad ranks of Confucianism."[133] Thus a measure of ambiguity attaches to the practical implementation of such lofty professions. To the extent that Huang would
entrust a large role to the *shih* as trustees of public discourse and
spokesmen for "public opinion," the question would remain as to how
fairly they served this role or how often their professed impartiality
might be compromised by rationalizations advancing their own interests. This proved to be a problem for the Confucian scholar-official.
Given this self-definition in strongly moral terms and its highlighting of
the issue of personal integrity versus self-interest, he carried the burden
of suspicion that, despite all outward professions to the contrary, he was
acting out of ulterior motives rather than in the public interest. Ad
hominem attacks and character assassination by innuendo, frequently
countered by undue defensiveness and self-serving protestations, often
obscured real policy issues.

Among recent writers a variant type of "class" analysis has seen the sixteenth and seventeenth centuries as witnessing the rise of a capitalist or quasi-capitalist development, often spoken of as the "sprouts of capitalism."[134] In these terms Huang, because of the encouragement he would give to trade and manufacturing and his espousal of a new currency based on the use of paper money and cash, is sometimes classed as a spokesman for a supposedly burgeoning capitalist trend. Nevertheless, since the "feudal" state in the end proved stronger than the incipient capitalist class and resisted the democratic trend associated with it, reformers like Huang, though seen as "progressive" for that day, turn out to have been premature or stillborn, heralds of a day that had not yet come.[135]

A somewhat eclectic mix of these views, more scholarly and less doctrinaire, may be found in the work of the research group at the Zhejiang Academy of Social Sciences, responsible for producing a definitive edition of Huang's writings. In the introduction to a new edition of the *Ming-i tai-fang lu* in 1985, they took advantage of the freedom allowed regional centers after the Cultural Revolution to promote the achievements of historical and cultural leaders in their home territory. In this introduction they give a generally appreciative account of Huang's work. Endorsing his critique of "feudal" dynastic rule, "feudal bureaucracy," "feudal law," and the "feudal military and tax systems,"[136] they acclaim Huang as an advocate of democracy and credit him, in his discussion of schools, with proposing something like the parliamentary systems in capitalist nations today.[137] In his economic proposals they see him as advocating the essential elements of a capitalist economy freed from bureaucratic controls—freedom of trade, a viable currency, and so on.[138] In his political reforms they see Huang as building on the efforts of the Tung-lin and Fu-she academies, but going beyond them to break through the "feudal" ethic implicit in the ruler/minister relation to become a true forerunner of a modern "enlightenment."[139]

In sum, though still handicapped by having to employ an obsolete and seriously distorted nineteenth-century "Marxist" terminology, the editors wish to identify themselves with Huang Tsung-hsi (along with his contemporaries T'ang Chen, Ku Yen-wu, and Wang Fu-chih) as spokesmen for an "enlightenment" that, even if it does not run exactly parallel with the Enlightenment in the eighteenth-century West, deserves to be recognized as a substantial development in Chinese thought and scholarship in the late Ming–early Ch'ing period—one that needs to be reclaimed after the wholesale repudiation and destruction of traditional culture during the Great Proletarian Cultural Revolution.[140] The same sentiments, with minor reservations, prevailed at a large international conference held under the Zhejiang Academy's auspices in Hangzhou in 1986.[141]

In this respect, one can also see a certain thread of continuity from the writings of late nineteenth-century reformers like Liang Ch'i-ch'ao, through such diverse scholars as Hu Shih and Hou Wai-lu in the mid-twentieth century, to those writing on the subject in the post-Mao era. Among the latter, too numerous to be dealt with individually here, one detects a general consensus favorable to Huang and running along the same lines as we find expressed by the Zhejiang Academy group. One can easily dismiss this dwelling upon an eighteenth-century Enlightenment (or even the desire of contemporary scholars to link up with late nineteenth- and early twentieth- century reformers, rather than with a Leninist-Stalinist-Maoist line and lineage)—discount it as wishful thinking or as a sentimental hankering for better days in the past. Yet it is not unreasonable that Chinese scholars today, instead of conjuring up still another revolutionary illusion for the future or grasping at some panacea from abroad, should want to be done with the Cultural Revolution's violent rejection of all past culture and seek to reclaim elements from a neglected tradition such as Huang represents. Reviewing and reevaluating alternatives not availed of earlier (as today they are reconsidering Sun Yat-sen and turn-of-the-century reformers like Liang Ch'i-ch'ao and T'an Ssu-t'ung), these scholars not unnaturally turn to the seventeenth-century Chinese thinkers whose writings encouraged these later reformers with the thought that Chinese tradition, instead of being wholly decadent or retrograde, could be as self-critical and potentially self-renewing as it was in the work of Huang Tsung-hsi.[142]

Yet it would be a mistake to think of this as purely a Chinese problem—a question simply of how modern China relates to its political past. By the time late nineteenth-century reformers and early twentieth-century revolutionaries rediscovered Huang Tsung-hsi, they were already heavily involved with the Japanese on many levels—the Japanese as aggressors in the Sino-Japanese War of 1894; Japan as a potential model for constitutional government; the Japanese as teachers of Chinese students abroad who soon would become political activists; the Japanese as supporters of Chinese reformers, and so on. For their part the Japanese were highly conscious of their close, interdependent relation with the Chinese—not only in political, economic, and military terms but, just as importantly, in their long-standing cultural relationship. Educated Japanese always had one eye on Chinese history and culture. Even when, after 1853, they turned to the West, what they learned from the West was translated mostly into political language borrowed from the Chinese, and what many overseas Chinese students learned from the Japanese about the West was couched in the same terms or in neologisms coined by the Japanese in Chinese characters.

When Chinese expatriates (escaped leaders of the failed reform movement of 1898 like Liang Ch'i-ch'ao, or the exiled revolutionary leader Sun Yat-sen) brought with them new political tracts claiming Huang Tsung-hsi as a native champion of democracy in the seventeenth century, it had real meaning for Japanese scholars and writers strongly conscious of their long-standing ambivalent relationship to the Chinese —their shared Confucian culture, as well as significant differences in the historical development of each. But they were aware too of the modern problem they faced together: how to relate these past traditions to the challenges of the modern West.

As we have seen, when Japanese advocates of liberal democracy in the early decades of this century, working to expand the political ground afforded them by the Meiji constitution, faced the question of popular sovereignty versus imperial rule, they skirted the issue by making the distinction noted earlier between *minpon shugi* (roughly "government for the people"), a doctrine compatible with constitutional monarchy, and *minshu shugi* (government of and by the people), which asserted popular as opposed to imperial sovereignty and republicanism over monarchism. Such language, current in the years when expatriate Chinese were active politically in Japan and when Japanese China scholars were in touch with these modern movements, entered naturally into the discourse surrounding the rediscovered Huang Tsung-hsi and his significance for the understanding of China, past and present. As a result, few scholars, whether Japanese or Chinese, then or now, have failed to make reference to these categories when discussing Huang's *Ming-i tai-fang lu.*

Moreover, Huang's work itself assumed great importance in analyses of the "China problem." Naitō Konan (1866–1934), a dominant figure in Japanese sinology in the first quarter of this century, acknowledged what a formative influence the *Ming-i tai-fang lu* was in shaping his view of China's past and in recommending a kind of federal, republican system for modern China.[143] And with few exceptions, Japanese scholars of Chinese history, politics, and thought have continued to treat the *Ming-i tai-fang lu* as a major landmark in the history of Chinese political thought.[144] Whether or not they have gone along with the claim made by Liang Ch'i-ch'ao and others that Huang stood as "China's Rousseau"[145] (and most of them have reservations on this score), they have usually made prominent reference to this comparison, perhaps discounting any easy equation of Huang's ideas with Rousseau's, but not denying Huang as important a place in Chinese thought as Rousseau has held in that of the West.[146]

With the importance thus attached to Huang and the *Ming-i tai-fang lu* in Japan, scholars have sustained a lively discourse on the subject during years when, on the mainland, Maoist ideology and the Cultural Revolution have stalled or inhibited free scholarly dialogue, and when useful research on Huang has focused more on the factual and textual side than the interpretive. Given the extensive literature produced in this process, it would be difficult, within a brief compass, to give an adequate account and evaluation of the individual contributions to this discussion, but the following composite account may serve our purpose here.

On the question of Huang as a "democrat," there seems to be a rough consensus that he does bespeak a kind of democratic thought, with strong emphasis on Huang as a champion of government for the people, but with less agreement on whether he advocated anything like government by or of the people,[147] and likewise whether he went so far as to advocate the overthrow of the monarchy or whether instead he accepted the inevitability of some monarchical system.[148] There is not much doubt that Huang, like Mencius, justified the revolutionary overthrow of unworthy rulers and dynasties; the question is with what would he replace them. On the whole, it is accepted that Huang advocated some type of constitutional order, with a modest part for the ruler, a strong executive role for the prime minister, and, an important parliamentary function for the schools. Several writers emphasize the importance to Huang of limits on the ruler and a system of checks and balances that approximates modern constitutional systems.[149]

A key factor in all these judgments is the value assigned to the class of educated scholar-officials who are given a central position in Huang's Plan. Because of Huang's great stress on the importance of "all-under-Heaven" as "masters" in the land rather than as tenants, clients, or guests, as well as of his persistent emphasis on strengthening the position of the *shih,* both in central and local government, Yamanoi Yū, a leading Japanese specialist on Ming-Ch'ing thought and on Huang Tsung-hsi in particular, has combined these two elements in his characterization of Huang's view as "elite democracy" or "democracy by the elite" (*shi minshu shugi* or *shitaifu minshu shugi,* substituting the Chinese term *shih-ta-fu* for what Huang usually refers to simply as *shih*).[150]

By now there seems to be a general recognition of the key role of the *shih* or *shih-ta-fu* in Huang's Plan. Opinions differ, however, on whether this elite should be understood as representing local landowning gentry, a rising merchant or incipient capitalist class, some alliance of all these classes with each other (particularly in the Kiangnan region)[151] or with collaborators in the bureaucracy, etc. Such estimates vary with historical judgments (or simply assumptions?) made about the relative status and rising or declining position of such groups in a changing historical situation. But no one, to my knowledge, has been willing to claim that any of these groups or classes achieved the independent power or assertive role of the middle class in the nineteenth-century West.

Conclusion

If writers differ on the role of the *shih* depending on their own reading of the historical, contextual evidence, the text of the *Ming-i tai-fang lu* itself offers little help either in arbitrating among such claims, or in providing conclusive support for any one of them. Whatever the alleged economic interests that Huang's proposals might be thought to serve, his own references to the *shih* make it clear that he thinks of them neither as landlords nor merchants but as scholar-officials: educated men who should have a strong commitment to public service, and whose cultural attainments as literati should be balanced by practical experience in government. Above all, they should be Confucian scholars of whom some sense of a vocation to leadership or dedication to civilized values could be expected, something beyond the self-interest that, in Huang's eyes, naturally and legitimately motivates those primarily concerned with property management or mercantile enterprise. Huang's primary commitment to the *shih*'s upholding of cultural values is suggested by his repeated recommendation that a "reputable scholar" (*ming-shih* or *ming-ju*) be entrusted with the function of leading the discussion of public questions in the schools, whether on the local level or at the capital.

In the recruitment and promotion of officials a prime criterion should also be practical ability and experience in the handling of affairs. Interestingly, there is no reference here specifically to business enterprise, financial know-how, or practical experience in the management of property, and Huang implicitly downgrades such skills when, in effect, he would put more specialized subofficials out of business and replace them with broadly educated scholar-officials, even on the local level.

Nevertheless, he does recommend the direct advancement to probationary service at court of persons recognized as having specialized knowledge in such fields as calendrical science, music, astronomy, firearms, and water control. And in his complaint that scholar-officials are woefully deficient in military leadership capabilities, we see that the special importance Huang attaches to the practical abilities of the scholar-official, far from being a tribute to their demonstrated fitness, arises instead from a desperate awareness of their deficiencies in regard to the kind of effective leadership Huang looks for in the civil service.

Since, however, Huang assigns such an enlarged role and enhanced status to the *shih,* after he has already emphasized the need for "all-under-Heaven" to be masters in their own house, the question becomes whether, and how, in serving "all-under-Heaven" or "the people under Heaven" (*t'ien-hsia chih jen*), the scholar-official may actually represent the common people (*min*). Put another way, if in Yamanoi's terms Huang is proposing "democracy of the elite" (*shitaifu minshu shugi*), how does the elite (*shih-ta-fu*) relate to the *demos* as *min*? This is not at all clear in Huang's Plan. That the scholar-official should serve "all-under-Heaven" is plain enough, but this is akin to serving "the public good" in the sense proposed earlier, as an abstract ideal; it implies nothing specifically about how the common people (*min*) would themselves participate in the process, make their own wishes known, or in sum, be self-governing.

From this standpoint, though Huang has made a definite advance over Mencius and Hsün Tzu in articulating a constitutional order with checks and balances appropriate to a mature centralized bureaucratic system (such as neither Mencius nor Hsün Tzu knew), and has defined a kind of public sphere or civil society that might mitigate the authoritarianism and offset the concentration of power in the late imperial system, we are still left uncertain as to whether the custodians of that public sphere, as a scholarly elite, could not still become isolated from the common people, serving more their own sectional interests than the general welfare.

From hindsight a modern observer may be mindful of how easily ruling elites have convinced themselves that they knew what the people wanted or needed better than the people did themselves, as did Communist elites later, who, often idealistically and quite conscientiously, lent their services to a "dictatorship of the people's democracy" that made up its own mind about what was best for the people. In this heightened perspective we can still appreciate Huang's achievement in recognizing the need for a constitutional order and a public sphere as a check on the ruler, and yet also be conscious of the ambiguity that attaches to the strengthening of the Confucian scholar-official's ambivalent status between the ruler and the common people. With no middle class to support him, with little of a popular press, without a consensus-making infrastructure (other than the schools and academies of the *shih*), and without a defined electoral process for expressing the wishes of the common people, the public service of the scholar-official, even when conscientiously rendered as a Noble Man, leaves him in an exposed and precarious position between ruler and ruled—caught in the middle, so to speak, of a public sphere that is meant to serve the general welfare (*t'ien-hsia*) but stands in a dubious and insecure relation to both ruler and common people (*min*).

To pose the question in these terms is not to suggest that a perfect solution to the problem has ever been at hand. Modern electoral processes in themselves, being subject to some pressures and manipulation, are not as such any guarantee of effective representative government, though in East Asia they have already proven superior to "people's democracies" led by a one-party dictatorship and controlled by "democratic" centralism (which, in the words of one-time People's Republic of China President Liu Shao-ch'i, could dispense with elections as "needless formalities"). Even in modern democracies, something like Huang's parliament of scholars, if carried on in autonomous schools and conducted in the open manner he suggests, could serve a function in helping to offset other concentrations of power; still more could they serve such a purpose in entrenched authoritarian regimes, which, though unlikely to accept multiparty politics, might be disposed to allow a measure of freedom to scholars and scientists upon whom they depend for technical expertise.[152] In this latter case, however, the scholars and scientists would still, and somehow, have to be, as Huang insisted, persons of conscience, people liberally educated to meet their public responsibilities.

Whether or not I am right in thinking that Huang's Plan still has relevance to the persistent problems of contemporary China, it seems clear that, in the light of recent scholarship in both China and Japan, his stature has been confirmed as a major figure in the overall development of Chinese political thought.[153] Some writers emphasize Huang's debt to his immediate scholarly forebears, as do Ono Kazuko and Lynn Struve especially.[154] I myself have been more inclined than I was earlier to see in Huang's Plan the product of a significant long-term development of Neo-Confucian thought and scholarship, neither just a retread or recycling of Mencius, on the one hand, nor a work of genius sui generis, on the other—a star that suddenly shot across the seventeenth-century firmament and disappeared into the night of Manchu rule. Huang and his work, while owing much to the classical masters and sharing much also with his own age, stand out as a singular synthesis of Confucian thought with the thinking that emerged from the Chinese experience under late imperial, Legalist-type, dynastic institutions. This in turn served as the basis in his thought for a new Confucian constitutionalism, a major advance over the dynasty- and ruler-centered thinking that had undergone much further development after Confucius and Mencius. Likewise, from the Neo-Confucian experience Huang drew both on the intellectual breadth and encyclopedic scholarship of the Chu Hsi school, and on the freshness and vitality of thought stimulated by Wang Yang-ming. Indeed it is unlikely that he could have commanded such a range of institutional issues as he did in his Plan had it not been for the monumental histories and encyclopedic compilations of Neo-Confucian scholars of more than one school in the Sung, Yüan, and Ming periods, from which he quotes so freely.[155] Nor could he have been so incisive about key issues, had he not learned much from the "utilitarian" thinkers of the Sung (Li Kou, Yeh Shih, and Ch'ien Liang)[156] as well as from the actual experience of the Tung-lin and Fu-she movements in the late Ming.[157]

No one is more conscious than Huang of his indebtedness to earlier writers, some famous and others comparatively obscure, who had wrestled with the same problems. In certain cases, indeed, it is quite apparent that his solution for a given problem was anticipated by others. It is also true that other men of his own time shared Huang's views. They were by no means generally accepted, and yet, among men with an intellectual inheritance similar to his, the same Confucian ideals inspired identical sentiments in regard to the critical questions of the day.[158] Among them Ku Yen-wu is an outstanding example. He says, in his letter to Huang after reading *A Plan for the Prince,* that his own views are in agreement with "six- or seven-tenths" of what is set forth therein. A reading of Ku's essays on "Commanderies and Prefectures" (*Chün-*

hsien lun) and "Taxes in Money" (*Ch'ien-liang lun*), as well as relevant passages in his great work *Jih chih lu,* confirms that his views were close to Huang's on many major issues.[159] Other contemporaries, such as Lü Liu-liang (1620–83)[160] and T'ang Chen (1620–1704),[161] are likewise outstanding exponents of the people's welfare against despotic rulers and oppressive institutions.

Elsewhere I have discussed at some length the views of Lü Liu-liang, who, though of a different philosophical orientation, shared many of Huang's basic views concerning dynastic rule. Enough work has been done too on other scholars of the period to show that Huang was not alone. Indeed one cannot dwell on the singular accomplishment of Huang's *Tai-fang lu* without acknowledging that it is the product both of a rich tradition and a striking efflorescence in the seventeenth century that is itself the culmination of a substantial scholarly development. Scholars are justified in claiming much for both Huang and his age in this respect, and even though this same line of development was not sustained to the same degree thereafter, it need not, on that account, be seen as any less of an achievement.

In that perspective then, one can still say that Huang's work is the most eloquent and comprehensive statement of its kind in Chinese political literature.[162] It draws together the ideas that others, in the past or present, had expressed in scattered or unsystematic form, and, while his discussion of certain problems is sometimes less exhaustive than the treatment of them by others (here the comparison to Ku Yen-wu is particularly apt), the balance that Huang achieves between general principles and their historical application adds considerably to the force of his presentation. It is for this reason, perhaps more than any other, that *A Plan for the Prince* has proved the most enduring and influential Confucian critique of Chinese despotism through the ages, as well as the most powerful affirmation of a liberal Confucian political vision in premodern times.

Translation of the
Ming-i tai-fang lu

Preface of Huang Tsung-hsi

I have often wondered about Mencius' saying that "periods of order alternate with periods of disorder."[1] How is it that since the Three Dynasties[2] there has been no order but only disorder?

According to the "Twelve Cycles" of Hu Han,[3] from 477 B.C. to the present there has been one long cycle of disorder, but twenty years from now a period of Great Prosperity[4] is to begin, inaugurating an era of order. Thus hope is not lost for a revival of the glories of the Three Dynasties.

In summer of last year, 1662, I set about itemizing the essentials of a grand system of governance, but before I had finished more than a few chapters, a fire occurred and I ceased work on it. This year when I returned home from Lan-shui,[5] and was putting in order the papers that had survived [the fire?], the manuscript proved not to have been lost from my belongings while being carried overland and by boat. My son urged me to finish it and so in the tenth month, while rain beat at the windows, I set to work writing. Heaving a sigh, I said, "Long ago Wang Mien[6] wrote a book of one *chüan* on the model of the *Rites of Chou*

[*Chou li*],[7] saying to himself, 'If I live a while longer and by chance meet an enlightened ruler, with this book it would not be difficult to accomplish what I Yin[8] and Lü Shang[9] did.' But he died without having had an opportunity to try it out. I have not seen his book and cannot tell whether or not his ideas might have brought peace and order. But since the cycle of disorder has still not come to an end, how could an era of prosperity have been brought about then?

Old though I am, it may be that I, like Chi Tzu,[10] could still be visited [by a prince in search of wisdom].[11] "Dawn is just breaking and the light is still quite faint,"[12] but how could I, on this account, keep my opinions to myself?

In the year 1663
The Old Man from Li-chou[13]

On the Prince[1]

*I*n the beginning of human life each man lived for himself and looked
to his own interests. There was such a thing as the common benefit, yet
no one seems to have promoted it; and there was common harm, yet no
one seems to have eliminated it. Then someone came forth who did not
think of benefit in terms of his own benefit but sought to benefit all-
under-Heaven, and who did not think of harm in terms of harm to himself, but sought to spare all-under-Heaven from harm. Thus his labors
were thousands of times greater than the labors of ordinary men. Now
to work a thousand or ten thousand times harder without benefiting
oneself is certainly not what most people in the world desire. Therefore
in those early times some men worthy of ruling, after considering it,
refused to become princes—Hsü Yu and Wu Kuang were such.[2] Others undertook it and then quit—Yao and Shun,[3] for instance. Still others, like Yü[4] became princes against their own will and later were unable to quit. How could men of old have been any different? To love
ease and dislike strenuous labor has always been the natural inclination
of man.

However, with those who later became princes it was different. They believed that since they held the power over benefit and harm, there was nothing wrong in taking for themselves all the benefits and imposing on others all the harm. They made it so that no man dared to live for himself or look to his own interests. Thus the prince's great self-interest took the place of the common good of all-under- Heaven. At first the prince felt some qualms about it, but his conscience eased with time. He looked upon the world as an enormous estate to be handed on down to his descendants, for their perpetual pleasure and well-being. When Han Kao-ti asked [his father], "Considering the estate I have acquired, which of us, Elder Brother or myself, has done better for himself?"[5] in these words he betrayed his overweening selfishness.

This can only be explained as follows: In ancient times all-under-Heaven were considered the master,[6] and the prince was the tenant. The prince spent his whole life working for all-under-Heaven. Now the prince is master, and all-under-Heaven are tenants. That no one can find peace and happiness anywhere is all on account of the prince. In order to get whatever he wants, he maims and slaughters all-under-Heaven and breaks up their families—all for the aggrandizement of one man's fortune. Without the least feeling of pity, the prince says, "I'm just establishing an estate for my descendants." Yet when he has established it, the prince still extracts the very marrow from people's bones, and takes away their sons and daughters to serve his own debauchery. It seems entirely proper to him. It is, he says, the interest on his estate. Thus he who does the greatest harm in the world is none other than the prince. If there had been no rulers, each man would have provided for himself and looked to his own interests. How could the institution of rulership have turned out like this?

In ancient times men loved to support their prince, likened him to a father, compared him to Heaven, and truly this was not going too far. Now men hate their prince, look on him as a "mortal foe,"[7] call him "just another guy."[8] And this is perfectly natural. But petty scholars have pedantically insisted that "the duty of the subject to his prince is utterly inescapable,"[9] so much so that even tyrants like Chieh and Chou should not have been executed by T'ang and Wu.[10] And they have irresponsibly passed on unfounded stories about Po I and Shu Ch'i.[11] As if the flesh and blood of the myriads of families destroyed by such tyrants were no different from the "carcasses of dead rats."[12] Could it be that Heaven and Earth, in their all-encompassing care, favor one man and one family among millions of men and myriads of families?

Thus indeed King Wu was a sage, and the words of Mencius are the words of a sage.[13] The princes of later times, wishing to use vacuous comparisons of themselves to "Father" and "Heaven" so as to prevent others from coveting the imperial estate, and finding that the words of Mencius did not serve their purpose, have gone so far as to disestablish him [from the curriculum].[14] Now did not all of this originate with petty scholars?

If it were possible for latter-day princes to preserve such an estate and hand it down in perpetuity, such selfishness would not be hard to understand. But once it comes to be looked upon as a personal estate, who does not desire such an estate as much as the prince? Even if the prince could "tie his fortune down and lock it up tight,"[15] still the cleverness of one man is no match for the greed of all. At most it can be kept in the family for a few generations, and sometimes it is lost in one's own lifetime, unless indeed the life's blood spilled is that of one's own offspring.

In the past men have prayed that they "might never again be born into a royal family."[16] (Ming) I-tsung cried to his daughter, "Why were you ever born into my house?"[17] How bitter these words! Reflecting upon his [the Ming founder's] accession to power, upon his ambition to own the whole world, who would not be disillusioned and wish he had desisted?

Therefore, if the position of the prince were understood as in the time of T'ang and Yü,[18] everyone would pass the job on to someone else, and men like Hsü Yu and Wu Kuang would not be rare. The position of prince not being clearly understood, every man in the marketplace covets it, which is why through all subsequent generations no one has heard of another Hsü Yu or Wu Kuang.

It is not easy to make plain the position of the prince, but any fool can see that a brief moment of excessive pleasure is not worth an eternity of sorrows.

On Ministership

Suppose there is someone who, in serving the prince, "sees [what to do] without being shown and hears without being told."[1] Could he be called a [true] minister? I say no. Suppose that he sacrifices his life in the service of his prince. Could he then be called a [true] minister? I say no. "To see without being shown and hear without being told" is "to serve [one's prince] as one's father."[2] To sacrifice one's life is the ultimate in selflessness. If these are not enough to fulfill this duty, then what should one do to fulfill the Way of the Minister?

The reason for ministership lies in the fact that the world is too big for one man to govern so governance must be shared with colleagues. Therefore, when one goes forth to serve, it is for all-under-Heaven and not for the prince; it is for all the people and not for one family. When one acts for the sake of all-under-Heaven and its people, then one cannot agree to do anything contrary to the Way even if the prince explicitly constrains one to do so—how much less could one do it without being shown or told! And if it were not in keeping with the true Way, one should not even present oneself to the court—much less sacrifice one's life for the ruler. To act solely for the prince and his dynasty, and attempt to anticipate the prince's unexpressed whims or cravings—this is to have the mind of a eunuch or palace maid. "When the prince brings death and destruction upon himself, if one follows and does the same, this is to serve him as a mistress or some such intimate would."[3] That is the difference between one who is a true minister and one who is not.

But those who act as ministers today, not understanding this principle, think that ministership is instituted for the sake of the prince. They think that the prince shares the world with one so that it can be governed, and that he entrusts one with its people so that they can be shepherded, thus regarding the world and its people as personal property in the prince's pouch [to be disposed of as he wills].

Today only if the toil and trouble everywhere and the strain on the people are grievous enough to endanger one's prince, do ministers feel compelled to discuss the proper means for governing and leading the people. As long as these do not affect the dynasty's existence, widespread toil, trouble, and strain are regarded as trifling problems, even by supposedly true ministers. But was this the way ministers served in ancient times, or was it another way?

Whether there is peace or disorder in the world does not depend on the rise or fall of dynasties, but upon the happiness or distress of the people. That is why the fall of Chieh and Chou were occasions for peace and order; why, too, the rise of the Ch'in regime and of the Mongols[4] were nevertheless occasions for disorder; and why the rise and fall of Chin, Sung, Ch'i, and Liang[5] had nothing to do with the stability or instability of the times.

If those who act as ministers ignore the "plight of the people,"[6] then even if they should succeed in assisting their prince's rise to power or follow him to final ruin, they would still be in violation of the true Way of the Minister. For governing the world is like the hauling of great logs. The men in front call out, "Heave!," those behind, "Ho!"[7] The prince and his ministers should be log-haulers working together.[8] If some, instead of holding tightly to the ropes with feet firmly set on the ground, amuse themselves by cavorting around in front, the others behind will think it the thing to do and the business of hauling logs will be neglected.

Alas, the arrogant princes of later times have only indulged themselves and have not undertaken to serve the world and its people. From the countryside they seek out only such people as will be servile errand-boys. Thus from the countryside those alone respond who are of the servile errand-boy type; once spared for a while from cold and hunger, they feel eternally grateful for his Majesty's kind understanding. Such people will not care whether they are treated by the prince with due respect [lit., according to the proper rites governing such a relation] and will think it no more than proper to be relegated to a servant's status. In the first years of the Wan-li period (1573–1620) Chang Chü-cheng was treated by Emperor Shen-tsung[9] with more respect than most ministers are shown, but it was not one-hundredth of what was shown to the counselors[10] of ancient times. At the time people were shocked because of Chü-cheng's acceptance of ritual respect that seemed inappropriate to a subject. His fault, on the contrary, lay in being unable to maintain his self-respect as a counselor, so that he had to take orders from servant-people.[11] Yet he was blamed for exactly the opposite. Why so? Because people's minds had been saturated for so long by vulgar notions about what a minister was—notions that had become accepted as standard. How much less did they realize that prince and minister differ in name only, and are in substance the same?

It may be asked, is not the term "minister" always equated with that of "child?"[12] I say no. Father and child share the same vital spirit [psychophysical force, *ch'i*]. The child derives his own body from his father's body. Though a filial child is a different person bodily, if he can draw closer each day to his father in vital spirit, then in time there will be a perfect communion between them. An unfilial child, after deriving his body from his father's, drifts farther and farther from his parent, so that in time they cease to be kindred in vital spirit. The terms "prince" and "minister" derive from their relation to all-under-Heaven. If I take no responsibility for all-under-Heaven, then I am just another man on the street.[13] If I come to serve him without regard for serving all-under-Heaven, then I am merely the prince's menial servant or concubine. If, on the other hand, I have regard for serving the people, then I am the prince's mentor and colleague. Thus with regard to ministership the designation may change.[14] With father and child, however, there can be no such change.

*U*ntil the end of the Three Dynasties there was Law. Since the Three Dynasties there has been no Law. Why do I say this? Because the Two Emperors and Three Kings[1] knew that all-under-Heaven could not do without sustenance and therefore gave them fields to cultivate. They knew that all-under-Heaven could not go without clothes and therefore gave them land on which to grow mulberry and hemp. They knew also that all-under-Heaven could not go untaught, so they set up schools, established the marriage ceremony to guard against promiscuity, and instituted military service to guard against disorders. This constituted Law until the end of the Three Dynasties. It was never laid down solely for the benefit of the ruler himself.

Later rulers, once they had won the world, feared only that their dynasty's lifespan might not be long and that their descendants would be unable to preserve it. They set up laws in fear for what might happen, to prevent its coming to pass. However, what they called "Law" represented laws for the sake of one family and not laws for the sake of all-under-Heaven.

Thus the Ch'in abolished feudal fiefs and set up commanderies (*chün*) and prefectures (*hsien*) with the thought that this system would better serve their own interest.[2] The Han gave domains to members of the royal house, thinking to have them stand as a buffer around their empire.[3] The Sung abolished the regional commanderies because commanderies were not to their own advantage.[4] Such being their laws and systems, how could they have manifested the slightest trace of consideration for all-under-Heaven? Indeed, could we call these "Law" at all?[5]

The "Law of the Three Dynasties" safeguarded the world for the sake of all-under-Heaven."[6] The prince did not try to seize all the wealth of the land, high or low, nor was he fearful that the power to punish and reward might fall into others' hands. High esteem was not reserved to those at court; nor were those in the countryside necessarily held in low esteem. Only later was this kind of Law criticized for its looseness, but at that time the people were not envious of those in high place, nor did they despise humble status. The looser the law was, the fewer the disturbances that arose. It was what might be called "Law without laws." The laws of later times have "safeguarded the world as if it were something in the [prince's] treasure-chest."[7] It is not desired that anything beneficial should be left to those below, but rather that all blessings be gathered up for those on high. If [the prince] employs a man, he is immediately afraid that the man will act in his own interest, and so another man is employed to keep a check on the other's selfishness. If one measure is adopted, there are immediate fears of its being abused or evaded, and so another measure must be adopted to guard against abuses or evasions. All men know where the treasure-chest lies, and so the prince is constantly fretting and fidgeting out of anxiety for its security. Consequently, the laws have to be made tight, and as they become tighter they become the very source of disorder. These are what one calls "un-Lawful laws."

Some say that each dynasty has its own laws and that succeeding generations of the royal house have a filial duty to follow the ancestral laws. Now "un-Lawful laws" are originally instituted because the first prince of a line is unable to curb his own selfish desires. Later princes, out of the same inability, may break down these laws. The breaking down may in itself do harm to all-under-Heaven, yet this does not mean that the original enactment of the laws did no such harm. Yet some still insist that we get involved in this kind of legalistic muck, just to gain a little reputation for upholding the regulations[8]—all of which is just the "secondhand drivel" of vulgar Confucians.[9]

It has been argued that order and disorder in the world are unrelated to the maintenance or absence of Law. Now as to this, among the major changes from the past to the present are one complete upheaval, which came with the Ch'in dynasty, and another with the Yüan dynasty. Following these two upheavals nothing at all survived of the sympathetic, benevolent, and constructive government of the early sage-kings. So, unless we take a long-range view and look deep into the matter, tracing back through each of these changes until the original order is restored with its land system, enfeoffment system, school, and military service systems, then even though some minor changes are made, there will never be an end to the misery of the common people.

Should it be said that "There is only governance by men, not governance by law,"[10] my reply is that only if there is governance by law can there be governance by men. Since un-Lawful laws fetter men hand and foot, even a man capable of governing cannot overcome inhibiting restraints and suspicions. When there is something to be done, men do no more than their share, content themselves with the easiest slapdash methods, and can accomplish nothing that goes beyond a circumscribed sphere. If the Law of the early kings were still in effect, there would be a spirit among men that went beyond the letter of the law. If men were of the right kind, all of their intentions could be realized; and even if they were not of this kind, they could not slash deep or do widespread damage, thus harming the people instead [of benefiting them].[11] Therefore I say that only when we have governance by law can we have governance by men.[12]

Establishing
a Prime Minister[1]

The origin of misrule under the Ming lay in the abolition of the prime
ministership by [the founder] Kao Huang-ti.[2]

The original reason for having princes was that they might govern all-
under-Heaven, and since all-under-Heaven could not be governed by
one man alone, officials were created for the purpose of governing.
Thus officials shared the function of the prince.

Mencius said, "The Son of Heaven constituted one rank, the Duke
one, the Marquis one, and Viscounts and Barons each one of equal
rank—five ranks in all. The Prince constituted one rank, the Chief
Minister one, the Great Officers one, the Scholars of the Highest Class
one, those of the Middle Class one, and those of the Lowest Class one—
six ranks in all."[3] In terms of external relationships,[4] the Son of Heaven
was removed from a duke to the same degree that duke, marquis, earl,
and viscount and baron were in turn removed from each other. As to
internal relationships,[5] the prince was removed from the chief minister
to the same degree as the chief minister, "great officers," and scholars
were in turn removed from each other. Rank did not extend to the Son
of Heaven alone and then stop, with no further degrees of rank.

In ancient times during the regencies of I Yin and the Duke of Chou,[6] these men, in serving as prime ministers, acted for the emperor, and it was no different from the great officers' acting for the chief ministers, or the scholars acting for the great officers. In later times princes were arrogant and ministers servile, so that for the first time the rank of emperor fell out of line with those of the chief ministers, great officers, and scholars. Because of this, petty scholars regard the matter of regency as something that need not be seriously considered[7] and go so far as to insist on the immediate accession of a new ruler upon the death of the old, thus permitting the son to neglect to honor his father's memory by the customary mourning, and to engage directly in "governmental and military affairs."[8] That the prince and ministers have thereby fulfilled their duties is questionable; that the son has prematurely disposed of his obligation to his father is quite clear. If the country should, unfortunately, have no prince of age to rule, power was entrusted to the empress dowager. Then the prime minister would let the government fall apart rather than take a strong hand in things, which might arouse suspicion that he intended to usurp the throne; thus he became the laughing stock of history. And did this not result from looking upon the emperor's position as too exalted?

In ancient times the prince treated his ministers with such courtesy that when a minister bowed to the emperor, the emperor always bowed in return.[9] After the Ch'in and Han this practice was abandoned and forgotten, but still when the prime minister presented himself to the emperor the emperor rose from the throne or, if he were riding, descended from his carriage.[10] When the prime ministership was abolished, there was no longer anyone to whom respect was shown by the emperor. Thus it came to be thought that the Hundred Offices[11] were created just for the service of the prince. If a man could serve the prince personally, the prince respected him; if he could not, the prince treated him as of no account. The reason for having officials being thus corrupted, how could the reason for having princes be understood?

In ancient times the succession passed, not from father to son, but from one worthy man to another. It was thought that the emperor's position could be held or relinquished by anyone, as was the prime minister's. Later the emperor passed his position to his son, but the prime minister did not. Then, even though the sons of emperors were not all worthy to rule, they could still depend on the succession of worthy prime ministers to make up for their own deficiencies. Thus the idea of succession by a worthy man was not yet entirely lost to the emperors. But after the prime ministership was abolished, the moment an emperor was succeeded by an unworthy son there was no worthy person at all to whom one could turn for help. Then how could even the idea of dynastic succession be maintained?

It may be argued that in recent times matters of state have been discussed in cabinet,[12] which actually amounted to having prime ministers—even though nominally there were no prime ministers. But this is not so. The job of those who handled matters in the cabinet has been to draft comments of approval and disapproval[13] [on memorials] just like court clerks.[14] Their function was inconsequential enough to begin with, yet worse still the substance of the endorsement came from those closest to the emperor,[15] and was then merely written up in proper form. Could you say that they had real power?

I believe that those with the actual power of prime ministers today are the palace menials. Final authority always rests with someone, and the palace menials, seeing the executive functions of the prime minister fall to the ground, undischarged by anyone, have seized the opportunity to establish numerous regulations, extend the scope of their control, and take over from the prime minister the power of life and death, as well as the power to award and confiscate, until one by one all these powers have come into their own hands. In the cabinets of the Ming, capable men were only given crumbs [by the eunuchs] while incapable ones were treated with derision and scorn. This sort of thing became common knowledge to everyone and was even written up in the dynastic histories, so that it has come to be accepted by all as the role of prime ministers. Therefore, what gave the real powers of the prime minister to palace menials was the mistake made in abolishing the prime ministership.

The best that could be done by the worthy men in these cabinets was to talk about "following the ancestral example." This was not because the ancestral example was always worthy to be followed, but because no one took the position of these men seriously, so they were forced to use the prestige of the royal ancestors as a means of restraining their rulers and thwarting the palace menials. But the conduct of the royal ancestors was not always what it should have been, and the craftier of the palace menials could find a precedent for each of their own bad practices, saying they were "following the ancestral example." So the argument about following ancestral law became absurd. If the prime ministership had not been abolished, the practices of wise kings and ancient sages could have been used to mold the character of the ruler. The ruler would have had something to fear and respect, and he would not have dared to flout it.

One man should serve as prime minister, but there should be no fixed number of vice-premiers.[16] Each day in the side-chamber state matters should be discussed, with the emperor seated facing south, and the prime minister, six ministers of state, and censors seated in order facing east and west. All those who participate in these deliberations should be scholar-officials (*shih*). The presentation of all memorials to the emperor should be handled by the supervising secretaries of the Six Offices of Scrutiny.[17] They should explain matters to the prime minister, and the prime minister should explain them to the emperor. After consultation between them as to approval or disapproval of these memorials, the emperor should endorse them in red;[18] or, if he is unable to go through them all, the prime minister should endorse them, after which they should go to the Six Ministries for execution. There is no need to present them again to the throne. To have each item circulated in the cabinet for final drafting, reviewed once more by the throne, and then sent down to the proper yamen was frequently the practice in the past, and it resulted in final authority resting with the palace menials.

The prime minister should set up a Hall of State Affairs[19] and put new *chin-shih* graduates in charge or use [Hanlin] probationers.[20] When Chang Yüeh[21] became prime minister during the T'ang dynasty, he set up five offices behind the Administration Chamber. The first was called the Personnel Office (*li fang*); the second, the Control Office (*shu-ch'i fang*);[22] the third, the War Office (*ping fang*);[23] the fourth, the Revenue Office (*hu fang*);[24] and the fifth, the Justice and Rites Office (*hsing-li fang*).[25] The handling of all affairs was done through these different departments. This is an example of how it should be done. Those from all over the land wishing to present memorials on matters pro and con, and all Hanlin probationers, should assemble there, so that no matter fails to come to the government's attention.

Schools

*S*chools are for the training of scholar-officials. But the sage-kings of old did not think this their sole purpose. Only if the schools produced all the instrumentalities for governing all-under-Heaven would they fulfill their purpose in being created. The functions of the College of the Son of Heaven[1] went beyond even the organizing of the court,[2] issuing decrees, honoring retired officials and caring for the orphaned,[3] reporting on those captured or killed in punitive expeditions,[4] conferring with generals and officers on the occasion of great military reviews,[5] meeting with officials and people during great judicial proceedings, and making offerings to the first ancestors at great sacrifices.[6] Indeed, schools were meant to imbue all men, from the highest at court to the humblest in country villages, with the broad and magnanimous spirit of the Classics. What the Son of Heaven thought right was not necessarily right; what he thought wrong was not necessarily wrong. And thus even the Son of Heaven did not dare to decide right and wrong for himself, but shared with the schools the determination of right and wrong. Therefore, although the training of scholar-officials was one of the functions of schools, they were not established for this alone.

Since the Three Dynasties right and wrong in the world have been determined entirely by the court. If the Son of Heaven favored such and such, everyone hastened to think it right. If he frowned upon such and such, everyone condemned it as wrong. The "keeping of public records and making of annual reports,"[7] state finances, military and judicial affairs—all have been left to petty subofficials. Rarely, indeed, has anyone escaped the evil tendencies of the times; consequently, people are apt to think the schools of no consequence in meeting the urgent needs of the day. Moreover, the so-called schools have merely joined in the mad scramble for office through the examination system, and students have allowed themselves to become infatuated with ideas of wealth and noble rank. Finally, because of the seductive influence of the court, there has been a complete change in the qualifications of schoolmen. Furthermore, those scholars with real ability and learning have often come from the countryside, having nothing to do with the schools from start to finish. So, in the end, the schools have failed even in the one function of training scholar-officials.

Consequently, the place of the schools has been taken by the academies.[8] What the academies have thought wrong, the court considered right and gave its favor to. What the academies have considered right, the court thought must be wrong and therefore frowned upon. When the [alleged] "false learning" [of Chu Hsi] was proscribed [in the Sung][9] and the academies were suppressed [in the Ming],[10] the court was determined to maintain its supremacy by asserting its authority. Those who refused to serve the court were punished, on the charge that "they sought to lead scholar-officials throughout the land into defiance of the court."[11] This all started with the separation of the court and the schools, and ended with the court and schools in open conflict. Not only are the schools unable to train scholar-officials, but they do scholars actual harm. Why, then, should we maintain schools at all, simply to perpetuate the name?

During the Eastern Han (A.D. 25–220), "30,000 scholars at the Imperial College engaged in outspoken discussion of important issues without fear of those in power, and the highest officials were anxious to avoid their censure."[12] During the Northern Sung (960–1127) students knelt at the palace gate and "beat the drum," pleading for the reinstatement of Li Kang.[13] In only these [two instances] have the schools come close to the lingering spirit of the Three Dynasties. If those at court had taken as right and wrong what the men of the schools held right and wrong, the brigands and traitors would have trembled before rectitude and purity. The prince would have been safe and the land secure. Nevertheless, some people now look upon that activity of the schools as a sign of decadence in those times. They do not realize that what actually brought the downfall of the state was precisely the destruction of the schools through the arrest of the party men [at the end of the Latter Han], and the banishment of Ch'en and Ou [during the Southern Sung].[14] Yet they condemn the men of the schools for it!

Alas, Heaven gave birth to the people and entrusted their care and education to the prince. When the ancient system of land tenure was abolished,[15] people bought their own land and took care of themselves, yet he imposed taxes just to harass them. When the school system was abandoned, people became ignorant and lost all education, but the prince led them still further astray with temptations of power and privilege. This, indeed, was the height of inhumanity, but still he made people call him by what is now just an empty name, "The Prince our Father, the Prince our Father." As if anyone really believed it!

The prefectural and district school superintendent (*hsüeh-kuan*) should not be appointed [by the court]. Instead, each prefecture and district should, after open public discussion, ask a reputable scholar to take charge. Anyone, from commoners to retired prime ministers, should be eligible for the position, regardless of whether he has held office before. If even the slightest suspicion attaches to the incumbent with regard to his public reputation, the students should rise up as a group and have him replaced, saying, "He is not fit to be our teacher."

Under the school superintendent there should be teachers of the Five Classics and teachers for each of the following: military tactics, astronomy, medicine, and archery. These appointments should all be made by the school superintendent himself. The youngsters of each district should pack up the necessary provisions and proceed to school. In populous towns and villages far from the city, wherever there are large numbers of scholars, a classics teacher should also be appointed, and wherever there are ten or more young boys among the people, longtime licentiates not holding office should act as elementary teachers. Thus, in the prefectures and districts there would be no students without worthy teachers. And students [i.e., licentiates] who have completed their education and training should be either serving in the Six Departments [of local administration],[16] or charged with educational duties. Thus, too, no worthy person should be without useful employment.

Outside the official schools, all of the larger temples, monasteries, and nunneries, in both city and country, should be converted into academies with classics teachers in charge, while the smaller ones should be converted into elementary schools, with elementary teachers in charge. Students should be apportioned to each of these for the purpose of receiving instruction. The property of the temples should belong to the school and be used for the support of poor students. Disciples of either Buddhism or Taoism should be classified into two groups: those of learning and character, who should be sent back to school; and the rest, who should be returned to their proper occupations.

The libationer [rector][17] of the Imperial College[18] should be chosen from among the great scholars of the day. He should be equal in importance to the prime minister, or else be a retired prime minister himself. On the first day of each month the Son of Heaven should visit the Imperial College, attended by the prime minister, six ministers, and censors. The libationer should face south and conduct the discussion, while the Son of Heaven too sits among the ranks of the students. If there is anything wrong with the administration of the country, the libationer should speak out without reserve.

When they reach the age of fifteen, the sons of the emperor should study at the Imperial College with the sons of the high ministers.[19] They should be informed of real conditions among the people and be given some experience of difficult labor and hardship. They must not be shut off in the palace, where everything they learn comes from eunuchs and palace women alone, so that they get false notions of their own greatness.

In the various prefectures and districts, on the first and fifteenth of each month, there should be a great assembly of the local elite, licentiates, and certified students in the locality, at which the school superintendent should lead the discussion. The prefectural and district magistrates should sit with the students, facing north and bowing twice. Then the teacher and his pupils should bring up issues and discuss them together. Those [officials] who excuse themselves on the pretext of official business and fail to attend should be punished. If minor malpractices appear in the administration of a prefectural or district magistrate, it should be the school's duty to correct them. If there are serious malpractices, the members of the school should beat the drums and announce it to the people.

In out-of-the-way prefectures or minor districts where it may not be possible readily to find a reputable scholar to act as school superintendent, and where a prefectural or district magistrate may be more learned than the available scholars, it is permissible to have the former sit facing south and lead the discussion at the semimonthly meetings.

But if the magistrate is a young man without solid learning and he arrogantly attempts to put himself above the older scholars, the scholars and students should protest and drive him out.

A reputable scholar should also be chosen to act as provincial education intendant,[20] but the school superintendent should not be subordinate to him. In learning, character, reputation, and rank, they should be regarded as fellow teachers of one another. Every three years the school superintendent should send his brightest students to the education intendant, who should examine them and give them the title of licentiate.[21] The licentiate should be sent again to the intendant for examination and be assigned to the Ministry of Rites. (A separate examiner need not be sent for this purpose.) If a scholar is left off the list of successful candidates, but has consistently shown himself to be someone of learning and good character, the school superintendent may inform the intendant of the fact and have his name entered on the list. The dismissal of a licentiate should be determined by the school superintendent on the basis of his overall record, and the intendant should have no say in the matter.

Students of calendrical science, when they have become proficient in reckoning seasons and the phases of the moon, should be made licentiates. The most able of them should be included on the list of those to be examined by the Ministry of Rites and then appointed to the Imperial Directorate of Astronomy.[22]

Students of medicine should be sent to the provincial education intendant for examination and appointment as licentiates; only then should they be allowed to practice. At the end of each year, statistics should be compiled as to the number of dead and living, cured and uncured, among their patients. The figures should be recorded in books and the practitioners classed in three grades: the lowest, to be barred from practice; the middle group, to continue their practice as usual; and the highest, to be sent to the Ministry of Rites for examination, after which they should enter the Imperial Academy of Medicine[23] and be given official positions.

When community wine-drinking ceremonies[24] are held, all the officials and scholars of a prefecture or district should be brought together. All scholars seventy or older whose character is above reproach, and all commoners eighty or older who have never been guilty of a criminal offense, should sit according to age facing south. The school superintendent and the prefectural or district magistrates should face north, honoring their elders and seeking their counsel.

The question of enshrining worthy personages and famous officials of a locality should not be decided on the basis of the position they held or the descendants they had. If their excellence is said to have been in achievement and character, the dynastic histories should be examined for evidence of it; if in letters, the available writings of the nominee should be investigated; if it is the "learning of principle" (*li-hsüeh*),[25] their words and actions should be taken as the basis for judgment. All other men, whether they have won their places because of some slight repute in their own locality, because of the fame of their examination essays, because of their phrase-by-phrase exegesis of the classics, or because of glory reflected upon them by others—all these should be cast out.

All books written by natives of the prefectures and districts, whether they are published works or manuscripts in private collections, should be sought out and bought up. Three copies should be made of each book: one to go to the Imperial Repository (*pi-fu*), one to the Imperial College, and one to the local school. As for the collected works of contemporary writers, if they are "classical-style" prose not faithful to a genuine tradition, recorded conversations with no distinctive insights, memorials of no practical benefit, or narratives of no use to historians, they should not be circulated or printed. As for eight-legged examination essays, novels, popular songs, things written for social occasions or ghost writings, the blocks for those already printed should be turned in and burned. If "scholars" compile selections from examination essays or essay exercises prepared under private auspices[26] in order to swindle and delude those in the market for books, then the men involved, if still licentiates, should be dismissed; or if they have been appointed to posts in the meantime, they should be discharged; or if they have already been retired from service, they should be deprived of their credentials as former officials.

All festive and mourning ceremonies among the people should be conducted according to the "Family Rituals" of Chu Hsi.[27] But since the common people may not be familiar with the ceremonial details themselves, regulations for mourning clothes, the dimensions of tablets to the dead, the style of dress and headwear, and arrangements of shrine furnishings should all be prescribed by the school superintendent for the information of tradesmen in the market who produce such items. Outside the cities, in remote places, the elementary teachers should adopt the same usage in order to correct undesirable practices.

All adornments and inscriptions to be put on famous sites, as well as on tombs and shrines to the honored dead, should be the business of the school superintendent. Everywhere illicit shrines should be destroyed, keeping only the altars to Gods of the Soil and Grain,[28] where tablets should be erected and sacrificed to. If in any area there are unorthodox sacrifices, or if unauthorized clothing is being worn, or if useless things are sold in the marketplace, or if the dead lie unburied on the ground, or if actors' songs fill men's ears and the streets are full of vile talk, then the school superintendent is not performing his function properly.

The Selection
of Scholar-Officials (Part 1)

The evils in the selection of scholar-officials are at their worst in the present examination system. Out of concern over this the Emperor I-tsung (r. 1628–44) instituted the *pa-kung,*[1] the *pao-chü* ("Guaranteed Recommendation"),[2] *chun-kung, t'e-shou,*[3] *chi-fen*[4] and *huan-shou*[5] systems, hoping thus to obtain scholars outside the regular system. But today the examination for the *pa-kung* is still a matter of interpreting the classics, and it is not conducted by a special examiner sent from the Hanlin Academy[6] but is left to the provincial education intendant, so that it is not taken as seriously as the provincial examinations. As for the "Guaranteed Recommendation" (*pao-chü*) system, the claim is made that it selects men according to their reputation, but no one knows today what a man's reputation rests upon; under the circumstances, bribery and favoritism inevitably have some part in it. Moreover, when the candidates come with their certificates to the Ministry of Personnel, they are examined only on one question of interpretation (*i*)[7] and one dissertation (*lun*),[8] so that it is of even less consequence than the provincial examination. Under the *chun-kung* system candidates are chosen from the supplementary lists for the provincial examinations,[9] and under the *t'e-shou* from the supplementary list of the metropolitan examinations; but the supplementary lists consist of those who have failed, and if we hold the failures in such high esteem as this, what is to be done for those who pass the examinations? As for the *chi-fen* system, it will remain corrupt at the roots unless we do away with the purchase of appointments. The *huan-shou* is used to give preferment to members of the royal family, but should not education be given them before official honors?

None of these six systems gets beyond the interpretation of the Classics. It is hoped that these men will be superior to those chosen through the regular examinations, but these systems are actually less exacting than the regular examinations, so it only results in confusion and is of no advantage in the present situation.

During the T'ang dynasty, *chin-shih* candidates[10] were examined in the composition of poetry (*shih*),[11] and in poetic expositions (*fu*),[12] while the *ming-ching*[13] examinations consisted of a written examination on the meaning of the Classics (*mo-i*).[14]

In the first part of the Sung dynasty, scholars[15] were examined on the composition of poetry (*shih*), of poetic expositions (*fu*), and of dissertations (*lun*)—one of each. There were five problem-solving essays (*ts'e*),[16] ten quotation questions (*t'ieh*)[17] on the *Analects,* and ten written questions (*mo-i*) concerning passages in either the Spring and Autumn Annals or the Record of Rites (*Li chi*). In the examinations on Nine Classics,[18] Five Classics,[19] Three Books of Rites,[20] Three Commentaries[21] [on the Spring and Autumn Annals], or Intensive Study[22]—regardless of the types instituted, they were all like [the T'ang example above] in being written examinations on the meaning of the Classics (*mo-i*).[23]

When Wang An-shih[24] introduced his reforms, he abolished the writing of poetry (*shih*) and of poetic expositions (*fu*), as well as quotation questions (*t'ieh-ching*) and written questions on the meaning of the Classics (*mo-i*). Standard texts were drawn up covering the general sense of the Classics by the Imperial Grand Secretariat, and promulgated for all to follow,[25] so that everyone had to have an understanding of the Classics in general and write in good literary style in order to qualify. This was not simply like the written examination (*mo-i*) for the *ming-ching* degree, in which nothing more was asked for than a rough understanding of selected passages.[26]

However, this type of examination did not originate with Wang An-shih. As early as the T'ang period (618–907), Liu Mien[27] made the proposal that "those who understand the Six Classics and comprehend the Way of the Early Kings be considered in the upper class, while those with distinction in the reproduction of the commentaries [from memory] were to be put in a lower class." Ch'üan Te-yü[28] objected to this, saying that "examinations on the basis of the various commentaries still can be used to check on the candidates' knowledge; without them personal prejudice would affect the judgment of the examining officials, so that one would neither get rid of the abuse nor serve the original purpose—in the end nothing whatever would be accomplished by it." Later on, Sung Ch'i[29] and Wang Kuei[30] successively wrote memorials favoring nothing but examinations on the general meaning without requiring memorization work, but this was not put into effect at the time. Not until Wang An-shih's day was this done.

Therefore, today's examination essays are a debased form[31] of the quotation (*t'ieh-shu*) and written examinations (*mo-i*) in the Classics, and their weaknesses today were thoroughly discussed by Ch'üan Te-yü in his time. If we continue them without change, everyone will turn to plagiarism, there will be a steady decline into superficiality, and the day will never come again when real talent appears among men. If, on the other hand, interpretation of the Classics is abolished altogether, I fear lest scholars abandon the Classics and study them no more, and also lest the Way of the Early Kings come to seem more and more impracticable, like a useless tool.

I say that the old style of written examination on the meaning of the Classics (*mo-i*) should be restored, so that classical interpretation is all done by writing out [the Han and T'ang] commentaries and those in the Great Compendia.[32] After listing one by one what is said by the various Han and Sung scholars, the candidate should conclude with his own opinion, there being no necessity for blind acceptance of one authority's word. Through the first part those who are ignorant [of the classics and commentaries] will be failed, and through the second part those who show themselves to be dull in reasoning. This is the way to correct such superficiality.

Some may say that the *ming-ching* examination was considered of lesser consequence in the T'ang period because its criterion was skill in memorization. Could we now, they might say, esteem what the T'ang looked down upon? In reply to this, I ask if anyone writes today's examination essays without memorizing other examination essays?[33] It is a question of memorizing in either case, and obviously it is better to memorize the learned ideas of early scholars than the secondhand drivel of today.

One cannot say that to follow this system is all-sufficient as a means of obtaining scholar-officials, but if scholars are encouraged to be balanced and solid, then men will appear who understand the Classics and have studied the Ancient Way. In the past was the use of *shih* and *fu* poetry in examinations sufficient for the obtaining of scholar-officials? Yet at least one had to reason carefully and write verse with the proper rhyme. It was nothing like the present examination essays, which can be written by any ignorant or insubstantial person.

The Selection
of Scholar-Officials (Part 2)

*I*n ancient times the selection of scholar-officials was liberal, but the employment of them was strict. Today the selection of scholar-officials is strict, but the employment of them is liberal. Under the old system of "district recommendation and village selection,"[1] a man of ability did not have to fear that he would go unrecognized. Later on, in the T'ang and Sung, several types of examination were instituted, and if a man did not succeed in one, he could turn around and take another. Thus the system of selection was liberal.

According to the Royal Institutes of the *Record of Rites,*[2] [districts] examined talented students (*hsiu-shih*) and sent them up to the Minister of Instruction (*ssu-t'u*), where they were called "Select Scholars" (*hsüan-shih*). The Minister of Education examined the most talented of the Select Scholars and sent them up to the Imperial College where they were classed as "Eminent Scholars" (*chün-shih*). The Grand Director of Music (*ta-yüeh cheng*)[3] examined the most talented of the "Accomplished Scholars" (*tsao-shih*)[4] and sent them up to the Minister of War (*ssu-ma*), where they were called "Presented Scholars" (*chin-shih*). The

Minister of War examined the most worthy of the Presented Scholars and had their names presented to the king before making a final decision on their qualifications. Only when a final decision had been made were they given official posts. Only after serving in office were their official ranks determined. And only after their ranks were determined did they receive official stipends.[5] In his lifetime each man had to pass these seven processes: four preparatory to entering office and three after taking office. Only then was he given a stipend.

In the T'ang a scholar who passed the examinations did not immediately doff his plain clothes [and assume office]. He was examined again by the Ministry of Personnel. Han Yü[6] was examined three times by the Ministry of Personnel without passing, and remained a commoner for ten years.[7] In the Sung dynasty men sometimes entered official service directly after passing examinations but served only in such minor capacities as assistant magistrate (*chu-pu*), sheriff (*hsien-wei*), clerk (*ling-shih*), and office manager (*lu-shih*).[8] Only if their names were at the top of the list did they obtain positions as assistant district and departmental magistrates.[9] Thus the employment of them was strict. The selection of official- scholars being liberal, talent was not wasted. The employment of them being strict, men could not advance through mere luck.

But today this is not so. There is only one way to become an official: through the examination system. Even if there were scholars like the great men of old, such as Ch'ü Yüan,[10] Ssu-ma Ch'ien,[11] Ssu-ma Hsiang-ju,[12] Tung Chung-shu,[13] and Yang Hsiung,[14] they would have no other way than this to get chosen for office.[15] Would not this system of selection be called too strict? However, should candidates one day succeed, the topmost are placed among the Imperial attendants and the lowest given posts in the prefectures and districts. Even those who fail [the metropolitan examinations], and yet have been sent up from the provinces,[16] are given official posts without having to take examinations again the rest of their lives. Would not this system of employment be called too liberal? Because the system of selection is too confined, many great men live to old age and die in obscurity. Because the system of employment is too liberal, frequently the right man cannot be found among the many holding official rank.

The common man, seeing only that in the past two hundred years a few men of character and achievement have appeared among those chosen, concludes that the examination system is good enough and there is no need to look elsewhere. He does not realize that among the hundreds and thousands taken in by the examination system, some men of character and achievement would inevitably find their way in. This means that men of character and achievement may find their way through the examination system, but the examination system does not find them. If we had scholars draw lots and chose them according to the length of the lot drawn, in the course of several hundred years men of character and achievement would naturally appear among those so chosen. But would we call this a good way to choose officials?

After all, the men of today who have character and ability are a far cry from those of the Han and T'ang dynasties. Today we have only mediocre and shallow men cluttering up the world. But it is surely not because Heaven has ceased to produce men of talent, is it? The system of selection is wrong.

Therefore, I would broaden the system for selecting scholar-officials, and choose men [not only] through the regular examinations [but also] through special recommendations, through the Imperial College, through the appointment of high officials' sons, through [a merit system for] junior officials in prefectures and districts, through special appointments, through specialized learning, and through the presentation of memorials. And the strictness in the employment of these men might be correspondingly elaborated upon.

The Regular Examination System (k'o-chü)

The examinations should be modeled on the proposals of Chu Hsi.[17] In the first session (*ch'ang*),[18] the *Book of Changes, Book of Odes,* and *Book of Documents* should constitute one subject, and candidates should be tested on them every first and seventh year [in the twelve-year cycle]. The three books of rites and the Rites of the Elder Tai[19] should constitute another subject, and candidates should be examined on them every fourth year. The Three Commentaries on the Spring and Autumn Annals (*Tso chuan, Kung-yang chuan,* and *Ku-liang chuan*) should be the subject of an examination every tenth year. Each examination on interpretation of these Classics should have *two questions;* a question on the Four Books should be included with each one of the Classics. In answering questions of interpretation (*i*), one should first list what is said in the [Han] commentaries and [T'ang] subcommentaries on the subject and what is said by later scholars. Only after this has been done should one offer one's own opinion in conclusion. Those who do not list what the various commentators say, or list some but not all and simply put in their own ideas instead, should be failed even if they have a general understanding of it. If those in charge of the examinations should make up themes that are not based on passages in the Classics, but are pieced together from different texts, or if they should consider mourning customs, mourning dress and taboos as unfit subjects for examination, they should be penalized.

In the second session the Six Sung Masters: Chou [Tun-i], Ch'eng [Hao], Ch'eng [I], Chang [Tsai], Chu [Hsi], and Lu [Hsiang-shan] should constitute one subject; the military classics by Sun [Wu] and Wu [Ch'i] another; Hsün Tzu, Tung Chung-shu, Yang Hsiung, and Wen Chung Tzu a third; and Kuan Tzu, Han Fei Tzu, Lao Tzu, and Chuang Tzu a fourth subject. In the different years [i.e., the first, fourth, seventh, and tenth], one from each of these groups should be the subject of an examination dissertation.

In the third session the Chronicles of Tso Ch'iu-ming (*Tso- chuan*), Discourses of the States (*Kuo-yü*), and Three Histories (*Shih chi, Ch'ien Han shu, Hou Han-shu*) should constitute one subject; the History of the Three Kingdoms (*San-kuo chih*), of Chin (*Chin shu*), and of the Northern and Southern Dynasties (*Nan-pei shih*) another subject; the New and Old Histories of the T'ang (*Hsin, Chiu T'ang shu*) and the Five Dynasties (*Wu-tai shih*) another subject; and the History of the Sung, together with the Court Records of the Ming Dynasty (*Ming shih-lu*) a fourth subject.[20] In each of the different examination years, two questions should be asked involving dissertations on these histories. When answering, the candidates must concern themselves with the facts and distinguish the moral issues involved. If their factual presentation is not complete, or if they bring in extraneous matters so that the main issue is not fully dealt with, they should not be passed.

In the fourth session three questions should be asked about current problems.

In the eighth month of every fourth year, as indicated above, the licentiates (*po-shih ti-tzu yüan*) should assemble in the provincial capital for examination. A limit should not be set upon the number to be graduated;[21] the limit should be the number qualified. A reputable scholar should be asked to serve as the examining official, without regard for whether he is a commoner or in office or not. The provincial education intendant should be in general charge.

The following year metropolitan examinations should be held, with the Classics, Masters (*tzu*) and Histories as subjects in the different years corresponding to the [subjects given in the previous year's] provincial examinations. The Minister of Rites should take charge of the metropolitan examinations, and the prime minister should have the say in assigning graduates to minor offices in the Six Ministries and various yamen, where they could supervise the keeping of records. The most capable of them should then be chosen to serve close to the Son of Heaven in the same capacity as the imperial attendants[22] of the past. Only when they have successfully passed the three-year review should they be sent out as prefectural and district magistrates. From among these again the best should be chosen to become secretaries[23] of the various ministries. But those who fail to pass this scrutiny should revert to the status of licentiates (*ti-tzu yüan*) and take the provincial examinations again before being readmitted to the metropolitan examinations.

Special Recommendations (chien-chü). Each year every prefecture should select one man to be placed among those in attendance on the emperor. The prime minister can then consult him on problems facing the nation, observe what he has to say, and have the ministers and other leading officials cross-examine and debate with him, just as was done in the "Debate on Salt and Iron between the Worthies and Scholars" of the Han dynasty.[24] Any candidate who can justify his point of view should be given an official post commensurate with his abilities; or else be given duties on a trial basis, and if he is seen to be competent, appointed to an office.

If anyone so recommended proves to be of mediocre ability, cunningly making capital of other's ideas, those who have recommended him should be punished and the man himself dismissed. If, however, he proves to be of fine character, like Wu Yü-pi[25] and Ch'en Hsien-chang,[26] then he should not be left to advance in routine fashion, and those who have recommended him should receive imperial awards.

The Imperial College (T'ai-hsüeh). Each year the provincial and district schools should take students with scholarly attainments, rate them as to ability, character, and learning, and send them up to the Imperial College. The number of names should not be limited; the only limit should be a dearth of qualified men. The Imperial College should take and examine them, whereupon those should be dismissed whose actual talent and learning do not measure up to the rating given them. All students in the College should be examined at regular intervals for several years and divided into three classes: the highest, to be variously assigned by the prime minister as assistants to the imperial attendants, like the graduates of the regular [metropolitan] examinations; the middle group, to be exempt from the provincial examinations and directly enter the metropolitan examination hall; the lowest, to be dismissed and sent back to their hometowns.

Privileged Sons (Jen-tzu). When the sons of men holding the sixth rank or higher reach the age of fifteen, they should be admitted to provincial or prefectural schools and be listed as licentiates. If they are unsuccessful after fifteen years of instruction, they should leave school. When the sons of officials holding the third rank or higher reach the age of fifteen, they should enter the Imperial College, and if they are unsuccessful after fifteen years of instruction, they should leave school.

Today the sons of high officials are examined along with the sons of ordinary people. If the education intendant accedes to requests [that special consideration be shown them], they are launched on their careers by questionable means. If he does not accede to such requests, due consideration cannot be shown to sons of the elite. If the sons of high officials are given appointments without considering whether they are capable or not, the capable ones are involved in the usual slow process of advancement, while the incapable ones are placed in positions of power over the people, doing the people harm and doing the men themselves no real favor.

Junior Officials in Prefectures and Districts (Chün-hsien tso). Each prefecture and district is to establish six sections. The provincial education intendant should then examine students and assign the best of them to duties as follows: in the Revenue Section, supervising the collection of taxes; in the Rites Section, supervising sacrificial ceremonies, wine-drinking rites (*hsiang-yin-chiu*), and festive and solemn occasions among high and low; in the Military Section, being in charge of militia drawn from the various households, defending towns, and apprehending criminals; in the Works Section, supervising prefectural and district projects; in the Legal Section, handling judicial and penal matters; and in the Personnel Section, handling the appointment and payment of officials in the various departments. Should they pass three reviews successfully, they should be sent to the Imperial College. Those who prove of outstanding ability should be assigned to the Six Ministries and various yamen as secretaries. The appointment of stipendiaries (*lin-sheng*)[27] should be abolished altogether.

Special Appointments (p'i-chao). The prime minister, the six ministers, the military commanders, and the provincial governors should all be allowed to appoint their own subordinate officials and try them in different capacities as did the "acting officials"[28] of earlier times; then notify the throne of those who have demonstrated exceptional ability and make their appointments official.

Specialized Learning (chüeh-hsüeh). These may be in such fields as calendrical science, music, astronomy, divination, firearms, and water control. The prefectures and districts should send the scholars to court, where the results of their work may be tested. If they prove to have made an original contribution, make them probationers [of the Hanlin Academy]. If not, dismiss them and send them home.

Presentation of Memorials (shang-shu). This may be of two kinds. First, when the country suffers from a crisis or grave plot and no one at court dares speak out, someone outside the court may speak up, as did Liu Fen[29] during the T'ang dynasty and Ch'en Liang[30] during the Sung. If so, he should be given the function of censor. But if another man puts him up to it in order to stir up trouble in the government, as was the case during the Eastern Han when Lao Hsiu[31] made accusations against the party men and had them arrested, he should be condemned and beheaded.

Second, when a man presents something he has written for imperial perusal, or someone else presents it for him, it should be studied carefully and, if found worthy to be preserved for future generations, then the writer should be advanced in government service along with the graduates of the regular metropolitan examinations. If, however, there is nothing new in what he writes and he has just put together something from old books, confusing what is wrong with what is right, as in the present day Chao I-Kuang has done in the *Shuo-wen ch'ang-chien*[32] and Liu Chen has done in the *Shih ta-pien*,[33] then even if his work is voluminous, his writings should be rejected and sent back.

Choosing a Capital

*I*t may be asked, "Why did the Northern Capital[1] fall so quickly?[2] What was the reason for it?"

I say it may have fallen for more than one reason, but since a mistake was made in the original establishment of the capital, there was no hope of saving it. In every age crises develop in the normal course of a reign. During the rebellion of An Lu-shan, the Emperor Hsüan-tsung of the T'ang "visited" [i.e., a euphemism for "sought refuge in"] Szechuan;[3] during the trouble with the T'u-fan, the Emperor Tai-tsung "visited" in Shan;[4] during the turmoil caused by Chu Tz'u, the Emperor Te-tsung "visited" Feng-t'ien.[5] The capital at K'ai-feng [during the Sung dynasty] was centrally located with roads going in all directions, so if it was necessary to move in case of emergency, escape was not blocked.

But [at the end of the Ming] when the brigand Li besieged the capital and I-tsung[6] wished to go South, he found himself isolated and cut off in the North, without any means of communication. At that time he was unable to get out, and even if he might have gotten out there was no assurance of his reaching the South. Unable to do anything else, he gave up his life for the honor of the dynasty.[7] If the capital had not been at Peking, why could he not have done what the three T'ang emperors did?

It may be asked, "Since the Yung-lo emperor established the capital at Peking, fourteen generations have passed; so how can its loss in the last reign be grounds for arguing that its original establishment there was a mistake?"

My reply is this: in ancient times rulers were concerned about governing the world successfully, and not concerned about losing it. The Ming capital at Peking lasted not much more than two hundred years, and yet Ying-tsung had to go "hunting" at T'u-mu;[8] Wu-tsung was trapped in Yang-ho;[9] the capital was besieged in the first year of the Ching-t'ai era (1450)[10] and again in the 28th year of Chia-ching (1549);[11] the Wall was broken through by men of the borderlands in the 43rd year of Chia-ching (1564);[12] and during the Ch'ung-chen period (1628–44) the capital was threatened year in and year out. The morale of everyone, high and low, was disturbed over the danger of enemy attack, and the court was always concerned over possible loss of the country. Under such circumstances how could one expect any notable achievements in the fields of rites, music, government, or education? The energies of the people south of the Yangtse were exhausted transporting grain northward, and the wealth of the "Treasury"[13] was expended on canal building.[14] All this the harm done by having the capital at Peking!

It may be asked, "If a [true] king should arise, where should he reestablish the capital?" The answer is Chin-ling [Nanking]. Yet it may be objected that, according to the ancients, Kuan-chung [the Sian region][15] was the best location of all and Nanking was not even considered. Why is this? My reply is that times are different. During the Ch'in and Han dynasties Kuan-chung was the center of all culture, the best-developed farming region, and the most prolific in men of genius. The Wu-Ch'u region[16] had just rid itself of the epithet "barbarian land," and was of a crude culture. Therefore, no case could have been made out for the superiority of Nanking. Today Kuan-chung is far short of producing men of genius the way the Wu-K'uai region does, and has been for some time; it has experienced the ceaseless ravages of marauders, and of its hamlets and villages not two or three stand where ten once did. The rehabilitation of life and culture would take a long time.

But the Southeast supplies the whole country with grain and cloth, and so the Wu-K'uai region[17] has become to the country what storehouses and strongboxes are to the rich man. Today the man of wealth will be certain to guard his storehouses and strongboxes himself, leaving to servants the care of his gate and courtyard. To disregard Nanking, by failing to make it the capital, is like leaving it to servants to look after one's storehouses and strongboxes. To make Peking the capital, as in the past, is like trying to guard the outer gate oneself. Is it conceivable that in ruling the whole land we should not show as much wisdom as the man of wealth?

Frontier Commanderies[1]

*T*he enfeoffment system is now a thing of the distant past. In the present time and under present circumstances we should reestablish a system of commanderies.

In T'ang times, it is said, commanderies brought on the fall of the dynasty, and the average man has become so accustomed to this idea that he thinks of commanderies as an invitation to disaster. But if we look into the heart of the matter, this is not so. When T'ai-tsung established the commanderies (*chieh-tu*)[2] they were all set up on the borders of the empire and were limited to only a few in number. Each commandery had 100,000 troops,[3] which is sufficient to crush any invasion or rebellion. Consequently, although An Lu-shan[4] and Chu Tz'u[5] both rose up by putting certain commanderies to their own uses, in suppressing these rebellions use was made of other commanderies.[6]

Later these commanderies were broken up into many smaller ones, weak forces with only a few troops. The troops of the commanderies were no longer strong enough to hold each other in check. So in the end Huang Ch'ao[7] and Chu Wen[8] destroyed the dynasty without hindrance. Therefore, the fall of the T'ang was really due to the weakness of the commanderies, not to their strength.

The trouble with the enfeoffment system was that the strong devoured the weak, and there were areas in which the authority of the emperor did not apply. The trouble with the prefectural and district system is that there is no end to the ravages suffered by the border regions. If we wish to eliminate the defects of both and blend the two together, a system of frontier commanderies is perhaps the solution.

Commanderies should be established in Liao-tung, Chi-chou, Hsüan-fu, Ta-t'ung, Yü-lin, Ning-hsia, Kansu, Ku-yüan and Yen-sui.[9] Beyond, in Yünnan and Kueichou,[10] the same pattern should be followed. Prefectures and districts in the vicinity should be apportioned and assigned to the different commanderies to insure that their supply of money, provisions, men, and horses is sufficient to maintain stability and to ward off attacks from without. Each commandery should be allowed to collect land taxes and commercial duties in order to meet military needs. The application of governmental policies need not be in conformity with the central administration. In selecting their subordinates, commanders should be allowed to make their own choices and then merely notify the court. Each year a tribute-bearing mission should be sent to court, and every three years a personal visit be made to the court by commanders.[11] If, at the end of the commander's term, it is found that his soldiers and people live in harmony and the border regions are tranquil, he might be permitted to transmit his post to his heirs.[12]

If all this is done, five things will be gained by it: In recent times each border region has had a supreme commander (*tsung-tu*),[13] a grand coordinator (*hsün-fu*),[14] a regional commander (*tsung-ping*),[15] a main commander (*pen-ping*),[16] and in times of trouble a military commissioner (*ching-lüeh*).[17] No one of them has had full control. Those who were capable got tied up in red tape; those who were incapable found it easy to make excuses, to stall as long as they could, and to conceal the gravity of things in reports and memorials sent to the throne. It was simply a matter of time until they brought things to utter ruin. If we unify command and make one man solely responsible, his deliberations will naturally be thorough and his plans for defense and offense effective, for each commander would want to think of the future of his heirs. This is the first thing to be gained.

Often when the nation has had a crisis, the resources of the whole country were not enough to meet the needs of the one region [affected].

Now under the new system the resources of a region would alone supply the needs of that region. This is the second thing.

Hitherto, the home troops[18] of a commandery were frequently inferior to troops brought in from other garrisons,[19] and disorders broke out with the transfer of troops. Examples of this are the Chieftain She[20] during the T'ien-ch'i period (1621–28) and the siege of Lai-chou[21] during the Ch'ung-chen period (1628–44). Under the new system the troops of one region would be used in that region alone. This is the third thing.

When the training and supplying of troops is all handled from the capital, a disturbance in one region often agitates many regions. But if each region has its own area of jurisdiction, troops and supplies need not be brought in from outside. Then when peace is disturbed in one region, others may remain undisturbed. This is the fourth thing.

If there are powerful forces on the borders, those at court[22] naturally look upon them with a healthy respect. "When there are tigers and wildcats loose in the mountains, people do not dare to go and pick greens."[23] This is the fifth thing.

Land System (Part 1)

*I*n ancient times Yü classified all land and fixed taxes accordingly.[1] Later the *Offices of Chou (Chou kuan)*[2] speaks of dividing up the imperial domain and laying out the countryside in towns and villages.[3] Thus, what was fixed upon in Hsia times no longer served as an adequate standard in the Chou dynasty. In those days the ruler of each state considered the fertility of the soil within its borders, increases or decreases in the population, and changes in the general conditions of life as if they were matters affecting his own household. After the well-fields were broken up,[4] the Han dynasty first taxed at the rate of one part in fifteen[5] and then at the rate of one-in-thirty during the reigns of Wen and Ching [181–144 B.C.].[6] During the reign of Kuang-wu [A.D. 25–57], the system was at first one-in-ten and later on one-in-thirty again.[7] Now the land under cultivation at this time was very extensive, and it was not possible to make precise evaluations of each holding. Taking a rough average of the quality of the land as a whole, they wanted to spare the people on poor land from any suffering. For these reasons, all land in the "Nine Provinces" was combined under one general rate, and the poorest land served as the standard for taxation. If those on the poorest land did not suffer, then peaceful conditions would prevail throughout the land. Thus the ruler thought that one could do without precise classification of lands, and so without the business of "classifying land" or "laying out the countryside."[8]

Now the tax rate of one part in thirty is a rate designed for the poorest land. During the great days of the Three Dynasties there were nine classes of taxation; it was not possible to take the worst land as the general standard. The Han alone, it might seem, succeeded in doing what the Three Dynasties were unable to do. But how could the Han be thought to have surpassed the Three Dynasties in virtue? The old well-fields took care of the people, and these lands were lands given by the government to the people. In the Ch'in and after, land was owned by the people themselves. Once rulers no longer had the means to take care of the people, the people had to take care of themselves. In addition, they became subject to taxes. In comparison to the earlier system the [Han] tax rate of one part in thirty could hardly be called low.[9]

In later times men could not fathom the whole truth of the matter. They thought that a tax rate of one-for-ten[10] had obtained under the earlier system, and that the "reduced" taxes of the Han were not such as could be universally and permanently kept in effect. It was necessary, they thought, to make taxes accord with the old system. But if the lands throughout the "Nine Provinces" were not granted by the ruler and the tax was one-for-ten, then it amounted to taking the best land as the standard.[11] And if the best land serves as the standard, how could the common people escape suffering?

Emperor Wu of the Han [140–87 B.C.] found his revenues insufficient and was brought to such measures as the selling of rank,[12] imposing fines in lieu of punishment,[13] the taxing of liquor,[14] capital levies[15] and monopolies over salt and iron.[16] He left no stone unturned trying to raise money, yet did not dare in the end to increase land taxes. Could it be that [his fiscal experts] Tung-kuo Hsien-yang, K'ung Chin, and Sang Hung-yang did not fully consider the possibility?[17] Thus to make the tax rate one-in-ten, even though it be called the "old system," is far indeed from being in accord with the old system. Moreover, in time of war, they could not keep to the rate of one-in-ten. The people were taxed, not according to the yield of their land, but according to the expenses of government. Thus taxes were fixed according to the needs of the government in an emergency, and later rulers automatically continued them. If a later ruler found himself in dire straits, he instituted new taxes to meet the expenses of government in that crisis, and later rulers likewise continued them. So alas, we see that taxes have increased day after day, and in each successive era people have been worse off than ever before.

Some scholars have said that if the well-fields are not restored, humane government cannot be achieved and the common people will become poorer and poorer. None of them realizes that since the people of the Wei and Chin dynasties were worse off than the people of the Han dynasty, and the people of the T'ang and Sung dynasties worse off than those of the Wei and Chin, the people's suffering does not come simply from failure to restore the well-fields alone.

Today the tax resources of the empire lie in Kiangnan.[18] In the time of the house of Ch'ien,[19] taxes in Kiangnan became heavy, but they were not revised downwards in the Sung. In the time of Chang Shih-ch'eng,[20] they became even heavier, but they were not scaled down in the Ming dynasty. Consequently, the tax on one *mou* of land rose from three pecks (*tou*) to seven. And besides the tax of seven pecks there were arbitrary impositions to meet losses incurred through transport and storage. Supposing that one year's harvest did not exceed one picul of rice—even if the whole of it went to the government, it would not be enough. The reason for this lies in the perpetuation of measures hastily adopted in times of crisis.

If a true king should arise, I believe he should revise the taxes of the empire, and when he does so, he must take the poorest land as the standard. Only then will taxes be in accord with the old system.

It may be objected that a tax of one part in thirty is insufficient for government expenses. Now in ancient times, the Son of Heaven collected revenue from his domain of a thousand *li* and used only one-tenth of the tribute collected by his vassals.[21] Today, out of prefectural and district taxes, local officials may use only one-tenth and the remaining nine-tenths is sent to the capital. Those who collected only one-tenth in ancient times still found it sufficient for their needs. How much less should those who collect nine-tenths need to worry about not having enough!

Land System (Part 2)

*A*fter the abolition of the well-fields, Tung Chung-shu proposed a limitation on the amount of land a man could hold.[1] Shih Tan[2] and K'ung Kuang[3] supported the same principle, and it was decreed that no one could hold more than thirty *ch'ing* [about 340 acres],[4] and that after a grace period of three years the land of those who violated this decree was to be confiscated. Their intentions were good, but whereas in ancient times the wise ruler granted land so as to provide for the people, today people own their own land and if an attempt is made to deprive them of it by decree—it is [what Mencius] called "doing even one act that is not right"[5] and should not be done.

Some people say that "If we seize the lands of the well-to-do, disorders will result; then, if we wish to restore the well-fields, it can be done by taking advantage of the strife and bloodshed, when the population is small in relation to the vastness of the land. What a pity, therefore, that it was not done when it might have been: when Han Kao-tsu destroyed the Ch'in dynasty [206 B.C.] or Kuang-wu assumed the throne of Han [A.D. 25]."[6]

Now the early kings instituted the well-fields in order to provide for the livelihood of the people, in order to make them prosper and multiply. But now these people seem to regard the massacre of the people as something fortunate, because this makes it possible for them to advance their own projects. But what if, after turning the land into well-fields, the people should thrive and multiply and thus create difficulties for the system—would they regard it as a misfortune?

Among the scholars of later times, none presented so fully as did Su Hsün[7] the reasons why well-fields could not possibly be restored, and none so cogently as did Hu Han[8] and Fang Hsiao-ju[9] the reasons why well-fields should be restored. Su Hsün believed that without several hundred years of exhausting labor, it would be impossible to establish a system of rivers and highways, canals and roads, waterways and roadways, ditches and lanes, and trenches and pathways.[10] Now if we actually grant land to the people, [they themselves would see to it that] all routes were kept open for traffic and all irrigation works kept in repair. So why need we get bogged down in the secondary details of the system? All the things Su Hsün worried about were in no way vital to the well-field system.

Hu Han and Fang Hsiao-ju said well-fields should be restored, but were unable to specify an effective method for restoring them. Through a consideration of the military farms,[11] however, I have learned how the well-fields may be restored—in just the same way as the military farms were set up in [Ming] garrisons and stations. These days scholars admit, when it comes to military farms, that to operate them is quite feasible, but when it is a question of well-fields they say it cannot be done. They don't even know that two fives make ten!

[In the Ming military farms] each soldier was allotted fifty *mou*[12] which is equivalent to one hundred *mou* in ancient times.[13] Is it not, then, just the same as the hundred *mou* allotted to each man in Chou times?[14] The regular grain tax on fifty *mou* of land was twelve piculs, which the soldier-cultivator was permitted to use for his own needs; an additional tax of twelve piculs went to the officers and men of the local garrison for pay and supplies.[15] Thus, actually, the tax is just twelve piculs, and this amounts to two pecks (*tou*), four pints (*sheng*) per *mou,* just the same as under the tribute system used in the central districts during the Chou dynasty.[16]

The total area of military farm land at present is 64,424,300 *mou.*[17] In the sixth year of Wan-li [1578], the total land actually under cultivation was 701,397,628 *mou.* If we find the ratio between them, military farm land is seen to occupy one-tenth of the total. [Since all military farm land is government land distributed to cultivators], that part of the total in which land distribution has not been effected is only nine-tenths. To apply to these nine-tenths of the land what is already true of one-tenth would not seem a difficult thing to do.[18]

All land is either official or private. Official land cannot be bought and owned by an individual. Within the area organized into prefectures and districts, official land occupies three-tenths of the total. Now if we take the total land under cultivation and average it out, with a total of 10,621,436 households in the land,[19] each household would receive fifty *mou* and there would still be 170,325,828 *mou* left over. If the well-to-do were allowed to occupy this remainder, no one need feel that he did not have enough. So why should there be any fuss over property limitations and land equalization, or should one needlessly make a big thing out of causing the well-to-do to suffer?[20]

From the successful operation of military farms, I know that well-fields can definitely be reestablished. Yet, it may be argued, "If the military farms are just like the well-fields, then the soldiers on the military farms should daily thrive and multiply. Why is it that there is instead constant attrition [in numbers]?"

There are four answers to this. The military farms are not worked by natives of the region, and even the granting of land to them is insufficient to dispel their homesickness. This is the first reason. Furthermore, the young and able-bodied are made to stand guard at the fortress-cities, while the old and weak must work the military farms.[21] Now if the working of the military farms is left to the old and weak, how much of a harvest can we hope to reap? Moreover, seeing that those soldiers who do not work the farms are never without enough to eat, what reason have the old and weak to take up the burden of so much toil? This is the second reason. In ancient times the tax was one part in ten. Today it is two pecks (*tou*) and four pints (*sheng*) per *mou*. Estimating the crop from one *mou* at no more than one picul, then it is actually a tax of one part in four.[22] This is the third reason. Again, the collection of taxes is left in the hands of military authorities, and the civil administration has nothing to do with it. So if the military governor wants to squeeze the settlers, there is no limit to what he can do. This is the fourth reason. Why be so surprised at the attrition!

Land System (Part 3)

*I*t may be asked, "We have heard what you have to say about the possibility of restoring the well-fields. Now what must be done about the fixing of taxes if all is to turn out well?"

The people have long suffered bitterly from oppressive taxes: from the evil of taxes that have piled up without ever being repealed, from the evil of having to pay in taxes what they do not themselves produce, and from the evil of not having land classifications.

Now what is meant by the evil of taxes that have piled up without ever being repealed? The taxes of the Three Dynasties, the *kung, chu,* and *ch'e,*[1] only taxed the land and nothing else. In the Wei and Chin the term "household tax" (*hu-tiao*) was added.[2] If one had land one paid taxes in grain, and if one had a household he paid taxes in cloth. Thus, in addition to the land tax there was a household tax.

In the beginning of the T'ang dynasty was established the system of land, household, and service taxes.[3] "For all land there was a land tax (*tsu*), for every household there was a household tax (*tiao*), for every person there was a service tax (*yung*)."[4] The land tax was paid in grain, the service tax in silk gauze, the household tax in silk cloth, silk floss, linen, or hemp. Thus, in addition to the household tax, there was a personal [service] tax.

Yang Yen[5] changed this and established the Twice-a-year tax system.[6] Men were not taxed according to age and fitness, but only according to wealth. Although the terms "land tax," "service tax" and "household tax" completely disappeared, actually the service and household taxes were incorporated into the land tax. This was continued into the Sung dynasty without the service and household taxes ever being deducted or eliminated from the land tax, but in addition new taxes on adult males and families were levied, payable in money and rice.[7] The people of later times accepted this without questioning, calling the Twice-a-year tax the land tax, and calling the new taxes on adult males and families (ting-shen) the "service and household" taxes (yung-tiao), without realizing that these taxes were being collected twice. If the terms "service tax" and "household tax" had not been eliminated, this could never have come about. Thus Yang Yen's work was of some benefit for a short time and of great harm for a long time thereafter.

In the Ming, besides the Twice-a-year tax and the taxes on adult males and families, there were the labor and silver services,[8] which had to be met once every ten years. At the end of the Chia-ching period (1522–66) the "Single-whip"[9] method was introduced throughout all prefectures, subprefectures, and districts. In the ten-year period the summer and fall (Twice-a-year) taxes, the tax proceeds reserved for the locality as well as the amount collected for transport to the state,[10] the equal corvée (chün-yao),[11] the li-chia labor duty,[12] the local tribute (t'u-kung),[13] and silver surcharges to meet expenses incidental to the hiring and conscripting of labor[14]—all were collected under one heading. What had been paid in one year out of every ten was spread over the ten-year period, so that the year in which the aforementioned exactions had previously been due was just the same as any other year. Thus the labor and silver services were combined into the Twice-a-year tax.

A little later, in the year during which the li-chia labor tax had been due, the institution of the Miscellaneous Services (tsa-i)[15] again brought back the old confusion of taxes. But, again, people in later times accepted this without questioning and called the "Single-whip" the Twice-a-Year tax, while the Miscellaneous Services were regarded as the service customarily due once every ten years, not realizing that the same service taxes were being collected twice. If the terms "labor service" and "silver service" had not been eliminated, this could

never have come about. So the "Single-whip" system was of some benefit for a short time and of great harm for a long time thereafter.

During the Wan-li period [1573–1619], the old levy for army pay
and rations (*hsiang*) amounted to five million taels.[16] In the last year of
that period the new levies for army pay and rations (*hsin-hsiang*) added
the amount of nine million taels.[17] During the Ch'ung-chen period
[1628–44], the increased levy for militia pay and rations (*lien-hsiang*)
amounted to 7,300,000 taels.[18] When Ni Yüan-lu[19] was president of the
Ministry of Revenue, he combined the three pay-and-ration levies, and
the New Rations as well as the Militia Rations levies were incorporated
into the Twice-a-Year tax. To this day it is thought of as a natural part of
the Twice-a-Year tax. How are people to know that this is what brought
the dynasty to ruin? If the terms "New Rations" and "Militia Rations"
had been retained, it is quite possible that people would have noticed
the names and considered their meaning. This is all the fault of Yüan-
lu's ignorance and ineptitude.

Alas, with the piling up of taxes like this, it is small wonder that the
people can hardly eke out a living. If we want to fix taxes anew, we must
return to the state of affairs prior to these accumulations and fix that as
the system. If land is granted to the people, one part in ten should be the
tax rate. Where land is not granted, one part in twenty should be the
rate. Taxes based on the number of individuals in the household should
be used for the raising and supplying of troops.[20] In this way the needs
of the state would be adequately met, and there would be no need for
taking up oppressive taxes.

What is meant by the evil of having to pay in taxes what one does not
oneself produce? In ancient times men paid tribute according to the
yield of the land they held. Even the feudal lords were spared forcible
exaction of that which the land did not produce—how much less
would the common people have had to suffer it! Therefore taxes were
paid in grain, which the land itself produced, or in cloth, which the people themselves made. The paying of taxes in money was adopted later as
a convenience to the people. In lieu of a piece of cloth worth a thousand
cash, the tax collector would accept nine hundred cash; in lieu of one
worth six hundred, five hundred cash was accepted in payment. Compared to the current market rate, the rate for tax purposes was lower.
Thus the paying of taxes in money was simply a convenient substitute
for paying in cloth.

The paying of land taxes in grain, however, was never changed during the Han and T'ang dynasties. When Yang Yen combined the tax on

able-bodied members of a household with the land tax, the paying of an equivalent in money for cloth thereupon became utterly confused with the grain tax, until eventually no one realized that money taxes were not supposed to be paid on land.

In the Sung dynasty, during the second year of Lung-hsing [1164], it was proclaimed that, owing to the impassability of the water routes in Wen-chou, T'ai-chou, Ch'u-chou, and Hui-chou,[21] the two taxes on grain and cloth could be paid in silver, according to a system of conversion.[22] Now at that time the price of silver was low, and permission to pay silver for produce and cloth was granted to the people as an option. Moreover, in the Hsi-ning period [1068–1078], of the total collected through the Twice-a-year tax, the tax in silver was only 60,137 *liang*,[23] and when grain was cheap, the ever-normal granaries[24] made a practice of buying grain, so that even though some taxes were paid in silver, the people still did not suffer any great distress.

In the Ming dynasty, except for the rice tribute all taxes were paid in silver;[25] not only was the cash equivalent of cloth paid in silver, but even the grain taxes, which throughout history had never been paid in any equivalent—this and all else were paid in silver. Not only was grain unacceptable in the payment of taxes, but even the payment of copper cash in lieu of silver was not allowed. Lu Chih [during the T'ang dynasty] had said of the payment of taxes in cash: "What must be paid is not what one produces, and what one produces is not what must be paid."[26] He thought that was bad; how much worse is it that all taxes should have to be paid in silver!

If silver is scarce in the country, in a bad year the land will not produce enough to pay taxes; and in a good year what the land produces might be enough to pay taxes, but when converted into silver, it is still insufficient for taxes. Does this not make every year a bad one for the people? Heaven gives the people a good year, and yet those who rule rob them of it. It is as if those who ruled the world treated its people as enemies!

When the sage kings ruled the world, taxes were always in keeping with what the land was good for. If the land produced grain, it was taxed in grain. If it produced mulberry or hemp, it was taxed in silk or hemp cloth. No matter what the variety of goods, taxes were collected in whatever was produced, so that the common man hardly ever suffered great distress.

What is meant by the evil of not having land classifications? According to the Ta Ssu-t'u section of the *Chou li* "a family lot on land suscepti-

ble of continuous cultivation consisted of 100 *mou.* A lot of land requiring one fallow year consisted of two hundred *mou.* If still another fallow
year were required, the family lot consisted of three hundred *mou.*"27
Thus besides establishing the nine classes of land for tax purposes, the
early kings also made more detailed subclasses.

Today land values vary exceedingly, sometimes more than twenty to
one. And by putting all land in the same category for purposes of local
tax administration,28 on some barren land a yearly tax has to be paid
though the crop return is nil, or is sometimes paid on land cultivated
year after year so that the harvest drawn is not enough to pay for oxen
and seed. The common man simply accepts it as poor land, but if it had
been worked according to the old system of resting it for a year or two,
who knows but what it might never have become barren? Since there is
no letup in the government's tax demands, even the man who wishes to
let his land lie fallow finds it difficult to do so. No wonder the strength
of the soil is exhausted day by day! We see farms of 100 *mou* which are
not as good as others occupying a few tenths that much land. This is the
damage done by lack of fallow periods.

Now we should measure the land in the empire, and in the best of it,
according to the system of square fields,29 240 *pu* should constitute one
mou; and in the medium grade land, 480 *pu* should constitute one *mou;*
and in the worst, 720 *pu* should make one *mou.* There should also be
intermediate categories, with 360 and 600 *pu* constituting a *mou,* dividing the whole into five classes.

When the lots are listed in the land register,30 each lot should be
standardized at one *mou,* without bothering about odd leftovers. If several *mou* are found in one spot, there is nothing to prevent them being
made into several lots; if one *mou* is broken up in different spots, there
is nothing to prevent its being made into one lot. If the land is classified,
not according to the amount of tax paid on it31 but according to its
capacity, then those lands that are now unequal will be made equal.
Thus the medium- and low-quality land can be worked in rotation, so as
to bring in what the high-grade land would yield. If, however, the available manpower is enough for all the land to be cultivated, there is no
harm if the yield from the two or three *mou* lots is not exactly equivalent
to that from the one *mou* lots of high-grade land.32

Military System (Part 1)

*D*uring the Ming the military system assumed three different forms when the original forces of the garrisons and stations[1] were changed into mercenaries,[2] and then during the Ch'ung-chen (1628–44) and Hung-kuang (1645) periods when the mercenaries were changed into the personal armies of the generals.[3]

The trouble that developed in the garrisons-and-stations system was that officers and men totaling 3,138,300,[4] all became dependent on the people for food. Leaving out the 300,000 Northwest border troops,[5] to repel invasions and quell internal disorders necessitated the raising of additional troops for the support of the regulars. To make separate classes of soldiers and cultivators [in the garrisons and stations][6] is bad enough, but further to make separate classes of [hereditary] soldiers and [hired] troops[7] amounts to making the people of one country support enough armies for two countries.

The trouble with the mercenaries was shown on the outbreak of the Eastern Incident,[8] when at a cost of several million taels for family subsistence allotments, active duty pay and rations, and horses and arms, more than 100,000 troops were raised who were not worth 30,000 regular troops and stirred up great trouble in the land.

The trouble with the personal armies of the generals was that the commanders held on to their troops in order to protect their own interests and did business with the enemy. Killing and looting went unpunished, and when the government called upon them they would not make a move. Such were these men that they did not hesitate to lead the troops against the very people who had paid and fed them. Was not the fall of the Ming due to these three things?[9]

It may perhaps be argued, "The changing of the garrisons and stations into the mercenaries was done because it could not be helped. The changing of the mercenaries into the personal armies of the generals was dictated by the course of events and was not [meant to be] a permanent system.

"The original system of garrisons and stations was not in itself bad. The troops of a commandery were adequate for the defense of its territory, and the land given each soldier-cultivator was adequate to meet his needs. The garrisons and stations went hand-in-hand with the military farms. Later, with losses and desertions from the ranks of solder-cultivators, there was no one to cultivate the land, and so the military farms did not produce enough food. When reinforcements came in from other garrisons, there was a great number of men who ate but did not grow food, creating a still greater shortage in the food supply of the military farms. Therefore the supply was augmented by grain taxes on civilians, by revenues from the salt monopoly, and even by part of the grain sent to the capital. Only then did the system of garrisons and stations begin to fall apart.

"After the capital was established at Peking, the grain transported there was four million piculs yearly.[10] There were twelve army commanders in charge of 140 garrisons, with 126,800 banner troops, alternately assigned to grain transport duty each year,[11] drawing regular monthly pay and rations as well as travel pay and rations.[12] Since each man got food enough for two men, each year it amounted to having 253,600 soldiers who ate but did not grow food. So another reason for the breakup of the garrisons-and-stations system was the business of transport escorts.

"The garrisons and stations in the regions of Chung-tu,[13] Ta-ning,[14] Shantung, and Honan sent alternate groups to the capital for periodic defense duty.[15] The spring group went in the third month and returned in the eighth. The fall group went in the ninth month and returned in the second. They drew regular monthly pay and rations plus travel pay and rations. Since each man drew enough food for two men, each year it amounted to having more than 200,000 who ate without growing food. So another reason for the breakup of the garrisons-and-stations system was the business of periodic defense duty.

"If one border region had a disturbance, then the troops of several other border regions were called in. Those responding to the call ate the 'new rations'[16] of the border region to which they came, and their families subsisted on the 'old rations' of their respective border regions. If the troops did not return, these regions had to raise replacements, and for each replacement another new ration had to be supplied. Thus for each soldier [actually available] three rations had to be supplied. When this happened the system of garrisons and stations became so broken-down that it could no longer be sustained.

"All of these are later corruptions of the system. It is not to be supposed that the original system itself was like this."

But it may be answered that these later corruptions are really the product of the inherent unsoundness of the system, and the unsoundness of the system lies in the marked separation between the soldiers and the common people (*min*).

The prime strength of manhood does not last for more than thirty years, and if seventy years is the average life span, then forty years are taken up by immaturity, old age, and infirmity. If a soldier is unable to return to civilian life, then his service in the ranks will include forty years during which he is aged or infirm. And if this is the case, how can the loss and desertion of troops be avoided?

The longing for home—who does not feel it? Today the ranks are filled up by exiled criminals,[17] some from as far away as ten thousand *li* and the nearest a thousand *li* or more. Being unaccustomed to the region to which they are sent, eight or nine out of ten die or desert. And if this is the case, how can the loss of troops be avoided?

For more than two hundred years while the capital has been at Peking, the wealth of the land has all been sent to the capital. Was it not, indeed, the army that exhausted the people's resources in the Southeast?

Or perhaps it may be said, "A great proportion of the people in the region of the capital served in the army,[18] and they were being supplied with rations according to the number of mouths to feed in their families. 'Therefore when a year of famine struck the land, the people of the capital region still suffered no lack.' It was clearly seen how disadvantageous this was for the country as a whole, but nothing could be done about it."

If this is so, the [military service] is not just supporting soldiers but supporting common people. If common people do not work the soil but count on the government to support them, who is supposed to work the land? What crime did the people of the Southeast commit [that they should have to work while others do not]? If the supplying of troops with food cannot be accomplished without furnishing food to common people, how could such a system be called sound?

I believe that troops should be drawn from the [adult] population, and subsistence for these troops should be drawn from the households. When soldiers are to be trained, two men should be drawn from every fifty persons in the [adult] population. When soldiers are to be sent on active duty, one man should be drawn from every fifty persons. As to the households providing subsistence, every ten households should provide for one soldier on active duty. Troops in training would have to furnish their own subsistence.

In the sixth year of Wan-li [1578], for example, the population and number of households was as follows:[19] population, 60,692,856, from which could have been drawn 1,213,857 soldiers; households, 10,621,436, which could have supported 1,062,143 soldiers. Now if one man is drawn from every fifty persons, such service is not a heavy burden. If every ten households have to provide subsistence for one soldier, the expense is not a great problem. And if there are more than 1,200,000 soldiers in the land, that is no small number.

Within the capital district 200,000 men should rotate on garrison duty, but not at a distance greater than a thousand *li* from their homes. If Chin-ling [Nanking] is made the capital, garrison duty should be limited to men in the districts and prefectures under direct jurisdiction of Chin-ling, and other provinces should not have to contribute. The population of Chin-ling is 10,502,651,[20] which would provide 210,500 of the finest troops. One hundred thousand of these should guard the various districts, and 100,000 should be put in the capital garrison. The following year those who had served in the defense of the districts should enter the capital garrison, and those who had served in the garrison should be sent back to defend the outlying districts. The next year after that those who had been in training in the meantime would be called up to active duty, while those on active duty would be paid off and sent home, subject only to training duty and no more.

Now if one man is drawn from every fifty persons, and he serves one term of active duty every four years, and if every man is on call for thirty years, entering the ranks at twenty and leaving at fifty, he will have only seven terms of periodic service and would not be sent more than a thousand *li* away. Such being the case, military service would not be hard to bear. If the state does not have to meet the expense of providing subsistence for the troops, the country will prosper. If there are, in the ranks of our armies, no aged or unfit, then our armies will be strong. Every ruler wishes his country to prosper and his armies to be strong, but there has been too great a separation between soldier and commoner. Since the T'ang and Sung dynasties, despite the comparative superiority of one system to another, in the evils suffered on account of their armies all were just as bad as the Ming.

Military System (Part 2)

When the nation was at peace, if a military man who had risen to a high command called upon a civil official, even though the latter was greatly inferior to him in rank, he had to wear "the traditional uniform, with a sword hanging at his left side, a bow and quiver at his right, and with warrior's cap, trousers, and boots on."[1] When he entered the hall to make obeisance, he had to identify himself on a calling card as "Your Honor's Running Dog." And when he withdrew, he had to go along with the civil officials' slaves or servants.

But later, when war came [with the Manchus], someone said to the emperor, "Today we do not honor our military officers. Therefore we do not distinguish ourselves in war." By this I-tsung was persuaded to give exclusive authority to the high military commanders and no longer allowed supervision by civil officials.[2] It was not more than two or three years before the military officers amassed large forces to use for their own purposes. In plain sight of each other, they and the enemy went about their business of pillaging the countryside. When the brigand Li Tzu-ch'eng attacked the capital, the garrison commanders in the "immediate vicinity"[3] and on out to Ch'ing and Ch'i[4] were encamped en masse around the city.[5] In order to keep their support the emperor made these men dukes and marquises,[6] but in the end they would not shoot an arrow in his defense. Alas, this was the result of I-tsung's giving such importance to the military.

Yet does this mean that the military are not to be given such importance? In my opinion I-tsung, instead of attaching too much importance to the military, attached too little. What is important in the military is generalship. When T'ang of Shang subdued Chieh of Hsia, I Yin was his general; when Wu Wang overthrew the Shang, the Duke of Chou was his general.[7] When the Chin created the Six Armies, their generals were drawn from among the Six Ministers.[8] Although this system was not preserved in the Ming dynasty, and military men were used exclusively as regional commanders, nevertheless the actual direction was in the hands of the provincial governors, the governors-general and military commissioners[9]—so these officials were the real generals, while the regional commanders were just subordinate officers. They had the title of general without the real power. And if this was bad, how much worse would it have been to give them the real power!

To protect the nation and its sacred shrines is the business of gentlemen (*chün-tzu*). To obey commands and exert themselves physically is the business of ordinary men. In the security of the nation and the preserving of its sacred shrines intact, what is more important than generalship? If ordinary men can be deemed worthy of it, what greater honor can we bestow on gentlemen? Today the most important matters are entrusted to the least of men. Is this treating the military as important or as unimportant?

Such being the case, the men who followed I-tsung in death were all civil officials.[10] At that time, if they had been given a brigade and had joined in a death struggle with the brigands, there might still have been some hope of saving the situation. At least they would not have had to commit [useless] suicide the day the capital was taken. Those who held out for the right cause in the country districts were all civil officials and scholars.[11] If at that time they had been given the means to do something, who knows but what they might have won instead of lost? Need they "have come to driving helpless civilians out to fight"[12] and having them slaughtered?

At that time the military men who were given high commands were mere upstarts, like clouds raised by a whirlwind. They had not in the past dared to strike a blow against the enemy, and when the crisis came they rode with the tide, changing flags and "using their sharp swords on nothing but the carcasses of the helpless."[13] It was what Pao Yung called "using one's men to advance one's own fortunes."[14] From this we can see that it was no mistake to have treated these men as underlings in time of peace.

It may be asked, "If that is so, were not P'eng Yüeh[15] and Ch'ing P'u[16] good generals in ancient times?" My reply to this is that P'eng Yüeh and Ch'ing P'u were not made generals by Han Kao-tsu. They owed nothing to him, yet he owed much to them.[17] The case is like one who eats aconite and hellebore[18] to cure disease. If people, seeing that P'eng Yüeh and Ch'ing P'u were accomplished in war, want to make generals of military men, it is as if someone, seeing that aconite and hellebore cure diseases, want to eat them as regular food. These brutish rascals profit from the world's misfortunes and subvert the natural order. How can we give them power and "let them do as they please with the keys to our fortress"?[19]

"But Shu-sun T'ung[20] spoke only of using warriors who cut down generals to capture the enemy flag. He did not recommend using scholars.[21] Why is that?"

At that time Han Kao-tsu had already made Han Hsin[22] his general. The type of man recommended by Shu-sun T'ung was the soldier who fought the enemy at the risk of his life, who matched brute strength with brute strength. Who would call this type a "general"?

"But do we not value the man who is stout and unafraid to die, who is adept at sword and spear?"

The qualities of stoutness, fearlessness, and adeptness with sword and spear are to men what sharpness and fine temper are to arms and armor. The bow must not be sticky with lacquer; the straight and curved sections of a lance must be in proportion; armor must have tough plates and strong thongs binding them together.[23] Men must be stout, unafraid to die, and adept with sword and spear. The principle is the same in each case. The sharpness and fine temper of weapons is put to use by men. The stoutness, fearlessness, and fighting skill of men is put to use by generals. If, now, we made generals of stout, fearless, and skilled fighters, it would be just like expecting fine, sharp weapons to fight by themselves, without men to wield them.

Military System (Part 3)

*B*eginning with the T'ang and Sung dynasties, civil and military officials were differentiated along two separate paths.[1] Nevertheless, in fill-
ing official posts, whether in the Chief Military Commission or in provincial government and army commands, civil officials were intermixed
with military. Only in the Ming were the two definitely separated and
not mixed.[2] Though the provincial governors and governors-general
were civil officials involved in military affairs, their authority was confined to administration and logistics, and they had no direct control
over the soldiers.[3] Thus the men who led the troops were not allowed to
control supplies, and those who controlled supplies were not allowed to
lead troops. Those who ran the administrative system were not allowed
to command armies, and those who commanded armies were not allowed to run the administrative system. It was thought that this would
make one act as a check on the other, and make it impossible for anyone
to revolt against the state.

Now in this world there are revolt-proof men, but there is no such
thing as a revolt-proof system. The scholar-officials spoken of by Tu

Mu[4] as virtuous and capable, well-informed and learned, were revolt-proof men; but the rough and brutish type of rascal is ignorant of rites and rightness, delights in plundering, and cares not whom he serves. In time of peace such men obeyed our directives and could be ordered about with a mere gesture or written notice. But in time of danger they held on to their troops in order to enhance their own position. Those who were supposed to supervise them naturally adapted themselves to the latter's every whim. If we survey the history of the Ch'ung-chen period [1628–44], can we find one governor-general or provincial governor who did not hasten to do the bidding of the big military men? At that time, the system [of divided authority] was certainly there, but it was never proof against a revolt.

Under the Ming military system, at the capital were established the Chief Military Commission (*tu-tu-fu*) and the Imperial Guards (*chin-i-wei*). Throughout the country there were twenty-one regional commands (*tu-ssu*), 493 garrisons, and 359 [independent] stations (*so*).[5] The peacetime military organization consisted of chief commissioners of the right and left (*tso-yu tu-tu*), regional commissioners (*tu chih-hui-shih*), deputies (*t'ung-chih*), and assistant secretaries (*ch'ien-shih*) attached to each,[6] commanders of a thousand households, commanders of a hundred households, and military judges (*chen-fu*).[7] In operational command of the troops were the regional commanders (*tsung-ping*), vice-generals (*fu-chiang*), assistant regional commanders (*tsan-chiang*), brigade commanders (*yu-chi*), company commanders (*ch'ien-tsung*) and squad leaders (*pa-tsung*).[8]

All the peacetime positions and ranks should be abolished and only the troop commands and capital garrisons retained. The head of the Ministry of War should serve concurrently as commanding general [of the capital garrison], the vice-ministers as vice-generals, and the subordinate officials of the ministry variously assigned as assistant regional commanders and brigade commanders. On the occasion of a campaign, generals should be sent out by the central government. A vice-minister should be given the seal of command in the field and direct all military operations, with subordinate officials of the Ministry of War assigned to him just the same as in the case of the capital garrison. In case provincial governors serve as generals and are given command in the field, their aides, commissioners, and vice-commissioners should be made vice-generals and the prefects made assistant-commissioners. If in the ranks there are any men who show a capacity for daring and resourceful generalship, they may be used along with the others, as was the case in recent years with men like Shen Hsi-i,[9] Wan Piao,[10] Yü Ta-yu,[11] and Ch'i Chi-kuang.[12] They should be used either at the capital in the Ministry of War or in the field as provincial governors.

Since Confucian scholars have long been unused to serving as generals, in military affairs they have taken the attitude that a job either required a show of brute strength and should be entrusted to someone of the "strongman" type, or else required craft and cunning and should be entrusted to scholars of the "schemer" type. Now to take up arms, wield a sword, and thrust a spear is the work of soldiers, not of generals. Even though a man may be known for his great strength, ten men can always overcome him. When the war crisis arose, any man from country or town who was a little stronger than other men would be treated by those in authority as something of a marvel; but it usually turned out that he was not worth one ordinary soldier. Since the Wan-li period [1573–1619] our generals have tried to conceal their defeats while exaggerating their achievements. There was no length to which they would not go in order to deceive their "Prince-and-Father." These men could really be called "schemers," but their schemes were successful only when practiced on their "Prince-and-Father," never when practiced on the enemy. From this it is clear that what has brought us to defeat and ruin today is not the lack of brute strength or careful scheming.

If soldier and scholar are brought together in one profession, the scholar would realize that military classics and battle tactics do not lie outside his province; studying them, he would learn that they are not completely impractical subjects. The military man would learn that personal concern for the ruler and love of the people are the basis of military service, and that crudeness and violence are not to be mistaken for ability. If this is done, all men would be revolt-proof.

Finance (Part 1)

*I*f a sage-king of the future wishes his kingdom to be peaceful and prosperous, must he not abolish [the use of] gold and silver?

In ancient times taxes were considered high or low in relation to the increase or decrease in the value of grain and cloth. Instances of this are the taxes to the government, which consisted of "a grain tax and a cloth tax,"[1] as well as market transactions among the people, for the Odes speak of taking grain to seek divination[2] and Mencius talks of "the exchange of the products of specialized labor, with men growing surplus grain and women making surplus cloth."[3] At that time, gold and silver were not considered any different from pearls and jade, being used for presents or ornaments and nothing more.

In the period just after the Three Dynasties, grain and cloth were still used as media of exchange, but cash was used to balance them[4] so that cash was inversely proportionate to grain and cloth in value. In the time of Emperor Chang of the Han [A.D. 76–88] the price of grain and cloth was high and Chang Lin [n.d.] said "this was due to there being too much cash. It should be decreed," he said, "that all taxes be in cloth, that all market transactions use cloth, and that the flow of money be stopped; then everything would be cheap again."[5] In the time of Emperor Ming of the Wei [227–239] cash was abolished and grain was used.[6] Huan Hsüan, who served as chief of state under the Chin dynasty [265–419], also wanted to abolish copper cash.[7] K'ung Lin-chih said, "The early kings established a medium of exchange in itself useless, so as to circulate goods of real utility. This was why cash took the place of shells. Grain and cloth originally served as food and clothing. When diverted to use as a medium of exchange, they were worn out in the hands of the merchants and partly lost in the process of being cut up to make change. The drawbacks in this were clear from very early times."[8] Yet, while the early kings used cash along with grain and cloth, they still did not intend that cash should have special importance.

In the beginning of the Liang dynasty [502–556], money alone was used in the capital and the regions of San-wu,[9] Ching,[10] Ying,[11] Chiang,[12] Hsiang,[13] Liang,[14] and I.[15] All the other provinces and districts used grain and cloth in addition. Throughout the regions of Chiao and Kuang[16] gold and silver were the only media of exchange. Ch'en [557–588] used money together with tin [money], iron [money][17], grain, and cloth. In Lingnan [Canton], for the most part salt, rice, and cloth were the media of exchange, and not money.[18] During the Northern Ch'i [550–577] north of Chi-chou[19] money was not circulated at all, the medium of exchange being silk and cotton cloth alone.[20] In the Later Chou dynasty [557–581] the districts west of the Yellow River sometimes used the gold and silver currency of the Western regions,[21] and this practice was not forbidden by the government.[22]

During the T'ang dynasty in many places people used cloth as a medium of exchange; in few places was cash used. In Lingnan before the Ta-li period [766] there was a variety of media in addition to copper cash, including gold, silver, cinnabar, and ivory. In the twentieth year of Chen-yüan [804], it was decreed that in market transactions such media as silk gauze (*ling lo*), silk and cotton cloth (*chüan pu*), and various other goods should be used along with money.[23] The Emperor Hsien-tsung [806–820] declared that wherever silver mines existed, there must also be copper mines; but since silver was useless to men, it was ordered that anyone who mined even one tael of it north of Wu-ling[24] should be banished to other provinces and the officials of the area punished.[25] In the sixth year of Yüan-ho [811], when ten strings of cash or more were required for a transaction, part of the amount could be paid in cloth.[26] In the third year of T'ai-ho [829] gold and silver were permitted for the adornment of Buddha figures, but copper was prohibited for such use.[27] The following year, in transactions involving one hundred strings of cash or more, half of the amount had to consist of grain or cloth.[28] Judging from all this, we may say that during and before the T'ang dynasty gold and silver were not used at all, whether in the payment of taxes or in market transactions, except in Chiao and Kuang. This can be clearly proven from the foregoing.

In the Sung dynasty, during the twelfth year of Yüan-feng[29] when Ts'ai Ching (1046–1126) was at the head of the government, those who refused to accept currency composed partly of tin in all transactions normally involving the use of gold, silver, silk, silk cloth, and so forth, were punishable by law. It would seem that by this time there was definitely some use of gold and silver.[30]

However, by a decree of the Ch'ung-ho period [1118] [actually in 1159], it was commanded that all officials be allowed to keep only 20,000 *kuan* of copper cash on hand, and the common people half that amount.[31] Anything over this limit was to be exchanged within two years for such things as gold and silver. Thus, as a medium of exchange among the people, cash was still important.

Beginning with the Shao-hsing period [1131–63] the annual quota for gold was only 128 ounces with no fixed quota for silver; seven-tenths of this went to the Imperial Treasury and three-tenths to the state administration.[32] Thus, in taxes to the throne, silver and gold had not yet become standard, nor did they meet the expenses of the state administration.

But when the Yüan dynasty rose up in the North, the copper cash system was abandoned.[33] Therefore, gold and silver became the reserve, and paper notes the circulating, media of exchange,[34] and both were kept in balance with each other,[35] so that eventually gold and silver became universal currency.

In the beginning of the Ming dynasty gold and silver were once prohibited as media of exchange, but it was permitted to exchange gold and silver for paper money through the government.[36] This amounted to swindling the people and taking away their wealth. Who could have confidence in it? Consequently, today silver alone is permitted to be used in paying taxes and in market transactions, and it has become the greatest evil in the land.

For silver and paper money go hand-in-hand. If the supply of silver is strained, paper money should be used to ease the strain. For this reason the tax system of the Yüan dynasty permitted payment in paper money but not in silver. However, today, since paper money is not used at all, and cash is used only in small transactions (not being acceptable for the payment of taxes), all the many functions of money must be fulfilled by one medium of exchange. Therefore, silver resources are greatly strained.

The Yüan dynasty, moreover, had maintained the various [economic control] supervisorates (*t'i-chü ssu*),[37] established the gold-panning industry,[38] opened up gold and silver mines, and permitted the common people in each circuit (*lu*) to extract and refine precious metals, so that a large amount of gold and silver came into the hands of the people. Today the mines are closed up.[39] Occasionally they have been opened for the extraction of ore, but then only as a monopoly under the control of palace eunuchs.[40] Everything has gone to the Imperial Treasury and nothing to the people. Consequently, silver resources are greatly strained.

For over two hundred years the gold and silver of the land has been sent off to Yenching [Peking], like a flood of water plunging through a ravine. In time of peace, 20 or 30 percent of this found its way back to the people through merchants and officials, but since the great crisis arose, all the gold and silver of the capital has been drained out to the regions beyond our borders. Moreover, rich merchants and venal officials from North to South, through the power of their wealth, gathered up all the gold and silver in the land and took it away. This being the case, how could we expect that any of the silver would find its way back to the people?

Now when silver is scarce yet taxes remain as before and trade goes on as before, there is a feverish demand for silver. But where is it to come from?

Consequently, land values have dropped to less than 10 percent of what they were in other times. Has the soil perhaps been exhausted? No, it is because taxes cannot be paid. The price of goods has likewise dropped to less than 10 percent of former times. Is there perhaps a superabundance of goods? No, it is because there is no money in the markets.

In the world today the people who toss and turn in a sea of misery receive no benefit even from times of peace and years of plenty, and so such things as encouraging agriculture and reclaiming wastelands are fruitless. In my opinion nothing can be done unless gold and silver are abolished.

Abolition of gold and silver would have seven advantages. First, things like grain and silk are within the reach of the common people so that each household would easily have enough. Second, if cash is coined to supply all needs and the coining goes on unceasingly, there will be no shortage of the medium of exchange. Third, if there is no hoarding of gold and silver, there will be no households that are extremely rich or extremely poor. Fourth, it is not easy to carry cash around, and people would find it difficult to pick up and leave their hometowns. Fifth, it would be difficult for officials to hide their ill-gotten wealth. Sixth, thieves and burglars would have heavy loads to carry and could easily be traced. Seventh, the interchange of cash and paper money would be facilitated.

However, the law must be made severe enough to work. Those who illegally mine gold and silver should be punished with death, and those who circulate gold and silver as means of exchange should be punished as if they were counterfeiters.

Finance (Part 2)

*T*he use of cash currency is supposed to bring benefits. But we can obtain long-term benefits only if we are willing to forgo benefits of the moment. To spend three or four cash and make ten cash in profit, or to use a few inches of paper in place of gold and silver, are of benefit for the moment. To enable the entire country to have the continued use of millions, and to have this money circulate to meet all needs, are of long-term benefit. The latter-day rulers of the land have generally had their eyes set on the former and have neglected the latter, thereby prejudicing from the start the success of their policies.

The Ming dynasty tried to maintain a cash system, but did not succeed for several reasons. In the first place, they were stingy with copper and niggardly about the quality of the workmanship.[1] Since the cash was thin and of poor quality, there was an abundance of counterfeits. A second reason was that the system was never stable, since denominations varied from two or three, to five and ten cash.[2] Third, the restrictions on the use of copper were not strictly enforced, and some of it was diverted to the making of household utensils.[3] Fourth, every reign had a different issue with different stamps on it.[4] These four defects had also been found in previous systems.[5]

A fifth defect was the simultaneous use of gold and silver [besides cash], so that the rate of exchange could not be kept uniform.[6] A sixth was the difference between the payment of salaries and rewards, and the payment of taxes.[7] The government made payment to the people in cash, but the people could not make payment to the government in cash. In the past there were [only] four things that impaired the currency. Today[8] there are six. And so the cash currency of today is useful only in small transactions. No benefit accrues from its use either to the public or to the individual. To maintain cash currency on this basis is the same as not using it at all.

We must abolish gold and silver and make copper the standard of value for all goods. In the capital and each of the provinces an official should be charged with casting of coins. Wherever there are copper mines the official should open them up and work them. Household utensils and images or ornaments in temples should all be melted down and the copper turned in to treasury offices. A thousand cash should have a standard weight of six catties and four ounces.[9] Each copper should weigh one-tenth of an ounce. The workmanship should be of fine quality and a uniform casting should be used which need not bear the reign name. Aside from the payment of land taxes in grain or cloth, all taxes and revenue from salt and liquors should be paid in cash. If these things were done, I do not believe there need be any fear of the [cash] system not working.

The Ming dynasty also tried to institute a system of paper money but could not make it work.[10] In the Ch'ung-chen period [1628–44] a licentiate from T'ung-ch'eng named Chiang Ch'en[11] said: "It is feasible to operate a system of paper money. If in one year 30,000,000 *kuan* of paper notes could be printed, with one *kuan*[12] equal to one tael of silver,[13] in a year 30,000,000 taels of silver could be obtained." A vice president of the Ministries of Revenue and Works, Wang Ao-yung,[14] espoused this idea and said: "If 30,000,000 is printed, 50,000,000[15] taels of silver could be obtained, and since the amount brought in is so great, silver would be as cheap as dirt." So the emperor established a Paper Currency Office in the Imperial Treasury, which printed money night and day. Then the government rounded up merchants and called upon them to sell it [float the issue], but no one was willing to do so. The Grand Secretary Chiang Te-ching[16] remarked, "Exchange an ounce of silver for a piece of paper? Not even a fool would do it!" The emperor countered by citing the paper money system instituted by Kao Huang-ti (the first emperor of the Ming, T'ai-tsu).[17] Te-ching replied, "Kao Huang-ti 'ruled as if in accordance with the divine way of Heaven,'[18] yet he applied the use of paper money only to rewards, gifts, and salaries, and nothing else. He certainly did not use it to pay his troops."

The use of paper money started with the "flying money"[19] of the T'ang dynasty, which was like the commercial tender (*hui-p'iao*)[20] of the present time. Not until the Sung dynasty was it adopted officially.[21] But the reason why the Sung could do this lay in its having a limit[22] on each issue, which was backed by a reserve of 360,000 strings of cash[23] and also supported by other items such as salt and liquor. When the people wanted paper money, cash was paid into the Treasury. If they wanted cash, paper money was paid into the Treasury. If they wanted salt or liquor, paper money was paid into the monopoly administration. Therefore, having paper money in one's hand was the same as having cash. One reason why it was essential to place a limit on each issue was so that the actual cash reserve of the issuing authority would correspond to the amount of paper money issued.[24] If there were no limit, successive printings would be uncontrolled. Another reason was so that after each issue of so much paper money, so much could be withdrawn from the circulation with the next issue. Thus counterfeits could be easily detected. Without limited issues, the amount withdrawn or issued could not be kept track of.

Such was the Currency Stabilization System[25] of the Sung dynasty. The reason why the Yüan dynasty system worked was that it provided for the establishment of official treasuries in the various circuits (*lu*) and maintained the stability of paper currency through the purchase and sale of gold and silver.[26] In the Ming dynasty the Paper Currency Office of the Imperial Treasury did no more than withdraw old notes.[27] The Currency Stabilization System was completely neglected. No wonder that it failed to work!

The ministers of I-tsung who spoke of the benefits of paper money did not understand everything affecting its success or failure. They saw only that a slip of paper could just in itself be used for gold and silver. They took into consideration only the measures of printing money, not the measures for keeping it in circulation. The issuing authorities had no cash reserves; how could the people have any confidence in the money? Therefore, to say at that time that a paper system was workable, was like seeing a crossbow and expecting to find roast pigeon in front of you.[28]

But if we limit the accumulation of cash and paper money; if we make five years the term of one issue, and withdraw old notes and burn them; if the currency is used by officials and common people alike, in customs offices for the payment of commercial duties and at salt factories in exchange for salt certificates,[29] then what fear need there be of its not working?

Again, if we abolish gold and silver, then instead of being inconvenienced by having to carry grain or cloth or coin for long distances, paper notes just a few inches in size could be carried around. The notes would be exchangeable wherever one went, and in all official business as well as commercial trade it would become indispensable.

Te-ching failed to state that paper money and cash currency are inseparably interrelated. Instead he talked about "ruling with divine power" and not using paper money to pay troops. Why did he not make a thorough study of its successful use in the Sung and Yüan dynasties?

Finance (Part 3)

*I*t is not enough for the ruler to lighten the tax burden; he must further eliminate certain customs, superstitions, and extravagances before the people can be made to prosper.

What do I mean by "customs"? Since the ancient rites of celebration and mourning[1] were abandoned, popular customs have taken their place. For weddings there are the marriage baskets,[2] the dowry,[3] and the feast. For funerals there is the dressing of the corpse and placing of it in a coffin,[4] the holding of a sacrifice,[5] the Buddhist ritual, the feast, and effigies buried with the dead.[6] The rich take these opportunities to vie in the display of their wealth, and the poor do their best to imitate the rich.

What do I mean by "superstition"? Buddhism and the magic rites.[7] In the case of Buddhism there are temples and chapels, Buddhist vestments and food, Buddhist clerics and assistants. All the devices and paraphernalia that are needed for the maintenance of Buddhism must be provided without exception, so that Buddhism consequently cuts deep into the productivity of the people. In the case of a magic cult,

paper prayer money,[8] incense, and candles are required for the performance of their rites, as well as animals to be sacrificed. Singing and
dancing, too, are required for the performance of magic rites. All
the things needed for the incantations and ceremonies in behalf of the
dead[9] must be provided without exception, and so consequently the
magic rites consume much of what the people produce.

What do I mean by "extravagances"? The worst of these are entertainers,[10] wine shops, and fine silk factories.[11] The cost of entertainers
consumes in one night the resources of the man of moderate means.
The expense of wine shops is such that one party consumes a whole
year's worth of food. One suit of clothes bought at a fine silk factory
costs enough to clothe ten men.

Therefore, to remedy these evils at the root and base[12] it is first necessary that all celebrations and mourning ceremonies among the people
be conducted according to the "Rites";[13] that Buddhism and magic
rites be driven out; and that my recommendations concerning education be put into practice.[14] To remedy the evil outgrowths[15] there must
be a prohibition on entertainers, on wining and dining, and on everything except the simplest clothing. In the markets and stores of our
cities today, nine places out of ten deal in Buddhist goods, or in goods
used for magic rites, or in theatrical entertainment, or in clever contri-
vances and fancy accessories. Since none of them really satisfies a need
of the people, to eliminate them all should be one way of remedying
things.

The way of the ancient sage-kings was "to uphold essentials and
eliminate nonessentials."[16] The "scholars" of recent times have not recognized this and talk of commerce and industry as nonessentials, which
they foolishly propose to eliminate. Now industry was certainly something that the sage-kings wanted to develop,[17] and they also wanted
merchants to be plying the roads,[18] because both industry and commerce are essential.

*W*here there was one subofficial in ancient times, today there are two. In ancient times the custodians, scribes, aides, and orderlies[2] kept the official records and made the annual reports;[3] runners and flunkies' jobs were filled by men procured in the locality. When Wang An-shih changed the rotational draft services (*ch'ai-i*) into hired services (*ku-i*),[4] runners and flunkies became subofficials. Therefore, if we wish to eradicate the evil of having runners and flunkies as subofficials,[5] we must restore the draft services. And if we wish to avoid the evil of having subofficials keep the official records and make the annual reports, we must employ scholar-officials (*shih*) for this purpose.

What do I mean by restoring the draft services? During the Sung dynasty among the various types of draft service were the supply master (*ya-ch'ien*),[6] runner (*san-ts'ung*),[7] warrant-bearer (*ch'eng-fu*),[8] archer (*kung-shou*), porter (*shou-li*), elder (*ch'i-chang*), chief of households (*hu-chang*),[9] and policeman (*chuang-ting*).[10] The supply master (*ya-ch'ien*) was put in charge of official property,[11] like the storekeeper (*k'u-tzu*) and transporter (*chieh-hu*)[12] of today. The chief of households was in charge of tax collection, like the precinct and village headmen (*fang li chang*)[13] of today. The elder, archer, and policeman were used for the apprehension of thieves and bandits, as the bowman (*kung-ping*) and thief-catchers (*pu-tao*)[14] are today. The warrant-bearer, porter, and runner served as yamen runners, like the police-runner, fast carriers, and messengers of today. The storekeeper, transporter, and district or village leader of today are all draft services. The bowman, thief-catchers, police-runners (*tsao-li*), fast carriers (*k'uai-shou*), and messengers (*ch'eng-ch'ai*)[15] are hired services.[16] I believe that each district or village headman (*fang-li chang*), after his year of labor service, should provide yet another man the following year to perform these miscellaneous services.[17]

There are three reasons why subofficials have no qualms about wrongdoing. The first is that, having the power of the government to back them up, they find that none of the local citizenry dares to give them trouble. Should their jobs be put on a draft service basis, they would realize that if they make trouble for someone this year, that person might well make trouble for them the next year. The second reason is that under the present system state officials and peasants constitute two separate classes of people and do not share the same interests. With draft service, however, the functionaries and people are on intimate terms with each other, and the people have nothing to fear from them. The third reason is that a man in a government post for a long time entrenches himself in it and is virtually impregnable. Men on draft service are unfamiliar with the tricks of professional bureaucracy, and do not dare to tamper with the law. Therefore, even if the district or village headman (*fang-li chang*) colludes with the government, the local populace does not think of him as working completely against their interests. That is the difference between draft and hired services.

To rule the land well one must take into account the inherent tendencies of any particular system. If it is basically unsound and subject to abuse, then no matter what prohibitions one enforces, there are always some evils or abuses that cannot be stamped out. If, however, it is basically sound and not subject to abuse, the stamping out of abuses is accomplished without the need for prohibitions. The draft service system cannot be considered inherently subject to abuse.

It may be protested, "From the time that Wang An-shih changed the system until the end of the Sung dynasty, attempts were made to restore the earlier system,[18] but without success. Was this not because the people were dissatisfied with the draft service system?"

The evils of the draft service system were limited to the supply master (*ya-ch'ien*).[19] Consequently, Wang An-shih corrected this by making them hired officials. Today, however, the storekeeper (*k'u-tzu*) and transporter (*chieh-hu*) [who correspond to the earlier *ya-ch'ien*] have had to be made draft services again. Why, then, cannot those paid jobs, which were not subject to any evils or abuse in the first place, be made draft services again?

During the Sung people wished to restore the draft services, because they thought the expense of hiring was a great hardship.[20] I think the expense of hiring scholar-officials is a small hardship, while having subofficials is a great hardship.

What do I mean by employing scholar-officials? Minor posts in the Six Ministries, the departments (*yüan*), and the courts (*ssu*) should be filled first of all from among the metropolitan graduates who are serving government internships,[21] next by men appointed as the sons of privileged officials, and next by members of the Imperial College who have qualified to serve in the government. When their terms of office are completed, they should be made magistrates in the provinces and districts or continue on in the various ministries and departments.[22] Those who prove incompetent should be dismissed from office.

In the prefectures and districts six sections should be established and staffed with licentiates from the local schools who have qualified for government stipends.[23] When their terms of office are completed, they should be sent up to the Imperial College or assigned directly to posts in the various offices of the Six Ministries, departments, and courts. Those who prove incompetent should not be eligible for official posts for the rest of their lives. The posts of registrar, record keeper, and clerk[24] in the prefectures, and the posts of assistant magistrate, deputy assistant, and warden[25] in the districts, should all be abolished. It should be the same in provincial administration as in the prefectures and districts.

It would be impossible to list all the evils attributable to the subofficials, but the most important of them are four in number. First, the subofficialdom is staffed with riff-raff, men who are feverishly seeking personal gain. When they are put in positions where it is possible to profit for themselves, there is no limit to what they may do. In order to serve their own ends they devise all sorts of legal snares. The legal code in effect today is entirely their creation. Indeed, the empire is governed by the laws of the subofficials, not by the laws of the Court.

Second, not only is the subofficialdom in the hands of unscrupulous ne'er-do-wells, but the assistant magistrates' posts have become a re-ward for service as a subofficial. Scholars look upon such posts as some-thing beneath them and are ashamed to be put in a class with their hold-ers. In ordinary times there are great numbers of scholars, but since the way to official preferment is open only to a few, many capable men die in obscurity. It is not as it was in the time of Confucius and Mencius, when even such posts as storekeeper, field-watcher, gate-keeper, and night watchman were all filled by scholars (*shih-jen*).[26]

Third, the assistant magistrates of the various yamen cannot be ap-pointed by the heads of the yamen. Each of them must be selected by the Ministry of Personnel, and since the ministry does not even know most of the candidates' names, how can we expect it to know anything of their qualifications? Therefore, the Selection Board [i.e., the Minis-try of Personnel] has become nothing but a Lottery Board.[27] It is the laughing stock of all time!

Fourth, the succession[28] to key posts held by subofficials at the capi-tal is worth several thousand taels. Fathers leave their jobs to their sons, elder brothers to younger brothers. If a man gets involved in a violation of the law, he simply turns his job over to another—either his son or younger brother, or a protégé who takes up his master's mantle. And so "today this country, which no longer has an enfeoffment system, nev-ertheless has an enfeoffed subofficialdom."[29]

If we should employ scholars in all such minor posts, everything would be changed, and these evils would be eradicated.[30] What are to-day the staff supervisors[31] of the various yamen, and the assistant mag-istrates of the prefectures and districts, were in Han times classed as section clerks.[32] Their superiors were all permitted to make their own appointments. Thus, they were the subofficials of ancient times. Later on, such appointments were handled by the Ministry of Personnel.[33] Their superiors still, however, appointed their own departmental em-ployees to serve as subofficials. This continued down to the present, when the term "section clerk" was lost, while the true status of the sub-official was also lost. Consequently, the subofficials of today duplicate the section clerks. In my system the section clerks would be restored to their proper status, and the redundancy of the subofficials would sim-ply be eliminated.[34]

Eunuchs (Part 1)

*T*hroughout the Han, T'ang, and Sung dynasties there was an endless series of disasters brought on by eunuchs,[1] but none of these was so frightful as the disasters of the Ming dynasty. During the Han, T'ang, and Sung, there were instances of eunuchs interfering with the government, but no instance of the government openly doing the bidding of eunuchs. In recent times the prime minister and the six ministries have been the nominal organs of administration. But the approval or disapproval of memorials has been determined first by private consultation and only then put into writing;[2] the taxes collected in the empire have gone first of all to the palace storehouses[3] and after this to the State Treasury of the Ministry of Revenue;[4] penal matters have been handled first by the Eastern Yard[5] and only after this by the law courts.[6] There has been nothing in the government of which the same was not true. Consequently, the prime minister and six ministries have been nothing but functionaries carrying out the will of the eunuchs.

Since rulers have come to consider the world their own private property,[7] they have looked upon as their own holdings whatever was held in the State Treasury, and have thought of the army as their own personal bodyguard. Yet this was no more than typical of latter-day kings. In recent times, however, the control of all clothing, food, horses and cattle, arms and armor, music and ceremonial, precious goods and fine handicrafts has been concentrated within a few miles of the Forbidden City;[8] even the yamen established by the state administration, together with all the wealth supplied by them, were thought of as not sufficiently the ruler's personal property, and so a fuss was raised and a fight put up for these things too.[9] This confining of the ruler's realm to within a few miles of the Forbidden City was all done by the eunuchs.

In the Han, T'ang, and Sung dynasties eunuchs could only get what they wanted by taking advantage of a ruler's weaknesses. In Ming times, however, the whole system of control was already established; the eunuchs simply held fast to the strings and kept one another in power. Though I-tsung was a wise king and at first distrusted the eunuchs, in the end he could not get rid of them.[10] Even in the last hours of his life he could not see his ministers of state.[11] Never before were the consequences so disastrous.

A ruler's eunuchs should be his slaves; his ministers should be his friends and teachers. What is desired in slaves is obedience to one's desires; what is desired in friends and teachers is moral virtue. The anticipation and satisfaction of his every whim is what a ruler prizes in a slave. But if a teacher and friend caters to his ruler's whims he is toadying. The pointing out of mistakes is what a ruler should prize in a teacher and friend. But if a slave points out his ruler's mistakes, it is impudence.

Since eunuchs became ministers of the imperial household[12] and scholar-officials became ministers of state, the eunuchs served their lord as slaves would, and whenever ministers of state opposed the emperor's misguided desires, the eunuchs would say, "Are they not subjects of the emperor like everyone else? How can they be so disrespectful?" The emperor, too, having come to accept the conduct of slaves as befitting conduct for ministers, treated the eunuchs as it suited his fancy, and they acquiesced in it. But when he treated his scholars and high officials in this way, they did not acquiesce in it. So he said, "Are they not my subjects just like everyone else? How can some of them be respectful and others not? It seems as if the household ministers really love me, while the state ministers only love themselves!" Thereupon, those who served as ministers took this as an indication of what pleased the emperor and what displeased him. As a result, they abandoned the true way of teacher and friend, hastening to adopt the manners and appearance of slaves.

When people had grown accustomed to such conduct over a long period of time, petty Confucians lost any understanding of high principles and fell in with this attitude, saying, "The Prince, our Father, is Heaven itself!" Therefore, when memorials were presented during the Ming, a man who knew quite well what was right and wrong, nevertheless did not dare to state clearly what was right and wrong. Instead he pointed out minor mistakes and ignored great errors, or concentrated his attention on modern usage and overlooked ancient precedent. He thought this the only proper way to serve his ruler. How was he to know that in these later times the character and thinking of men had been utterly reduced to servile depravity—all the work of eunuchs! Under such circumstances, what else can one expect but disastrous consequences?

Eunuchs (Part 2)

*E*veryone has known for thousands of years that eunuchs are like poison and wild beasts. Why is it, then, that rulers so often end up with broken bodies and battered heads on account of eunuchs? Can it be that there is no system by which to control eunuchs? No, it is simply due to the excessive desires of rulers themselves.

Originally, rulership was conferred by the Decree of Heaven, and men accepted it with the greatest reluctance. Men like Hsü Yu and Wu Kuang, in fact, actually demonstrated that they regarded the world as a ball and chain by brushing aside the offer of rulership and having nothing to do with it. Who, then, would have supposed that later rulers would look upon the world as a means of their own gratification? Having built themselves splendid palaces, there was nothing for it but to fill them with women. Having acquired so many women, there was nothing for it but to have eunuchs to guard them. One thing just followed another.

This being the case, who can blame[1] rulers of more recent times for what they have done. But Cheng Hsüan,[2] in commenting on the *Rites of Chou* (*Chou li*), said that kings had eighty-one imperial concubines in nine nights, twenty-seven wives of the third rank in three nights, nine wives of the second rank in one night, three wives of the first rank in one night, and the empress in one night.[3] This makes it appear that the sage-kings of old were no different from the rulers of later times. If Cheng Hsüan is correct, the *Rites of Chou* would be a book that encourages wantonness. But Mencius said that "having hundreds of women in attendance was something I would not want even if I could get it."[4] At that time the rulers of the states of Ch'i, Liang, Chin, and Ch'u were all[5] given to such excess and extravagances,[6] but neither the Eastern nor Western Chou indulged in it. If what Cheng Hsüan spoke of had been the practice instituted by the Duke of Chou, Mencius would have accepted it without question. Since he spoke of not wanting it even if he were in a position to get it, it would amount to saying that the Duke of Chou was wrong.[7]

If, as Cheng Hsüan says, a ruler had one hundred and twenty women in the palace and female attendants in addition, the number of eunuchs needed to guard and serve them would run into the thousands. Some scholars of later times have claimed that assigning eunuchs to the prime minister[8] was the system by which the *Offices of Chou* [i.e., *Rites of Chou*] so wisely provided for the control of eunuchs.[9] Now men who have been punished with castration[10] have no respect for propriety or rectitude, and are well known for their cruelty and violence. What logic is there in collecting these cruel and violent men by the thousands, and by the device of placing them under the prime minister, hand them the keys to the palace?

From the earliest times to the present, no one has cared about whether eunuchs can contribute to governance, but only about how to prevent eunuchs from making trouble. Yet when a ruler has a great multitude of eunuchs, even though they have not yet made trouble, they are like a fire hidden under a pile of kindling wood.

I believe that a ruler should dispose of all but his Three Palaces.[11] If he does this, no more than several tens of eunuchs will be enough to serve their needs. An opponent of this may express fear that the ruler's progeny would not be numerous enough. But what in the world can be possessed forever? If I felt myself unequal to ruling the world and wished to spare myself the task, how much more would I not wish to spare my descendants? This anxious concern lest rulership of the land fall to others than one's own descendants is an attitude common to rich men. Yao and Shun had children, but did not leave them the throne.[12] Emperor Hui-tsung of the Sung dynasty certainly had a great many sons, but they served only as so much mincemeat for the men of Chin.[13]

Letter from Ku Yen-wu
to Huang Tsung-hsi[1] Concerning
the Ming-i tai-fang lu

W hile on a visit to Wu-lin[2] in the year 1661, I thought of crossing the O River[3] to the East in order to pay my respects to you. But I kept putting it off and nothing came of it. During the fifteen years since I came to the North, I have visited extensively through the rivers and mountains and toured the borders of the empire. Though I have thus learned a little about the relics of the past, I have lived a solitary life apart from my friends, much like an addled old Northerner.[4] Now I am over sixty[5] and still have accomplished nothing. What shall I do! What shall I do!

To my own way of thinking I have, since middle age, done nothing else but follow in the path of earlier scholars, "making notes on textual matters"[6] and composing verse on the breeze and moonlight. As the years and months have gone by, I have delved into the secrets of the past and present. Only so have I learned that "the sea comes last, and the river first";[7] that to make a mountain requires many baskets of earth.[8] Gradually, too, I have glimpsed the meaning of the Sages' Six Classics, the causes of order and disorder in the nation, and the basic factors in the livelihood of the people. Yet I regret that I have not had the benefit of your criticism.

Recently I visited Chi-men[9] and met your disciples there.[10] From them I learned that all has been well with you. They took the opportunity to show me your great work, the [*Ming-i*] *Tai-fang lu*. I read it several times and realized, as a result, that the world is never without true men, that the evils of a hundred kings can be repaired and the glories of the Three Dynasties in time revived. In the affairs of the world, the right man to deal with a situation may never be faced with it, and yet when the situation arises the right man cannot perhaps be found. Therefore, the superior man of old wrote with a view to posterity, so that when a worthy king appeared in later times he could learn from it. Thus "when a series of changes has run its course, another change ensues. When it obtains free course, it will continue long."[11] "When sages rise up again, they will not change my words."[12] Of this I can feel confident now.

I have put some of my ideas into a book entitled *What I Have Learned from Day to Day* (*Jih chih lu*), and now I congratulate myself that the opinions expressed therein agree with six- or seven-tenths of what you have said [in the *Ming-i tai-fang lu*]. There is just one thing: your proposal about location of the capital.[13] It should certainly be in the Kuan-chung region.[14] Mo-ling [Nanking] is only suited to serve a minor state. Unless one has had firsthand knowledge of these places, one cannot know this.[15]

However, I constantly revise my own work, and have had to refrain from printing what might give offense. The only things published to date are eight books of the *Jih chih lu* and an essay on money-taxes in two parts,[16] the manuscript for which I wrote several years ago. I submit them now to your esteemed judgment. If I may presume to take a humble place among your colleagues, please do me the favor of criticizing it, and do not hesitate to write me at length about it. Do so for the sake of bringing light to my ignorant mind, of leaving an endowment to later generations, and of benefiting all mankind. That is indeed my fervent prayer.

Respectfully,
Your junior colleague,[17] Ku Yen-wu

Ch'üan Tsu-wang
Colophon to the Ming-i tai-fang lu[1]

*T*he *Ming-i tai-fang lu,* in one book, was written by the Honored Master,[2] Huang T'ai-ch'ung[3] of Yao-chiang.[4] His contemporary Ku T'ing-lin sent him a letter acclaiming such genius, which might have served a king well. Had it been used, the glories of the Three Dynasties could have been revived.

This was written in the year 1663. Huang was not yet sixty,[5] but he signed the preface "The Old man from Li-chou." Wan Hsi-kuo[6] told me that until 1662 the Honored Master had not lost hope for [the Prince of] Lu.[7] And when news of his death came from the Far South,[8] for the first time he felt that the tide had run out and a pall of gloom was descending. As a scholar of the Ming he had nothing left to live for.[9] This book appeared as a consequence, which explains why he called himself "Old Man."

The original book was more extensive than the present one. Because of numerous objectionable passages, it did not appear in its entirety, and now even the printing blocks previously cut have been destroyed by fire. The Honored Master's writings once amounted to several car-loads, but nine-tenths of them have been lost or scattered—a tragic loss indeed!

[signed] Ch'üan Tsu-wang[10]

Notes

References in the notes for Chinese and Japanese sources are to chapter (chüan) and page except where otherwise specified; references to Western language sources are to volume number and page except where otherwise specified. See the bibliography for complete citations.

Introduction

1. W. T. de Bary, "Chinese Despotism and the Confucian Ideal," in J. K. Fairbank, ed., *Chinese Thought and Institutions* (Chicago: University of Chicago Press, 1958), p. 163.

2. See Arthur W. Hummel, ed., *Eminent Chinese of the Ch'ing Period (1644–1912)*, pp. 421–26; and Ku Yen-wu, *T'ing-lin wen-chi*, in *T'ing-lin i-shu*, Sui-ch'u t'ang ed. 1:7a–12b, Feng-chien lun 1–9.

3. See Ray Huang, *Taxation and Government Finance in Sixteenth-Century Ming China*, pp. 310–11, 321.

4. For a standard biography see Hummel, *Eminent Chinese*, pp. 351–54; for further information on Huang's life and work see Lynn Struve, "Huang Zongxi [Tsung-hsi] in Context: A Reappraisal of His Major Writings," pp. 477–502, and Struve, "The Early Ch'ing Legacy of Huang Tsung-hsi: A Reexamination," pp. 83–121. See also W. T. de Bary, "Plan for the Prince," Ph.D. diss., Columbia Univer-

sity, 1953 (Ann Arbor, Mich.: University Microfilms, 1953), pp. 1–50; and Ono Kazuko, *Kō Sōgi* (Tokyo: Jimbutsu Ōraisha, 1967), which gives an extensive biographical account in historical context, and more on Huang's early, pre-MITFL life in "Kō Sōgi no zen hansei: toku ni *Min-i taihō roku* no seiritsu katei to shite," pp. 135–98.

5. Wu Guang (Wu Kuang), *Huang Tsung-hsi chu-tso hui-k'ao* (hereafter, *Chu-tso*), pp. 2–5.

6. This has been principally the work of Wu Guang at the Zhejiang Academy of Social Sciences, abetted by the efforts of the Japanese scholar Ono Kazuko. See Shen Shanhong and Wu Guang, eds. *Huang Zhongxi quanji* (hereafter *Quanji*) 1:416–48, and Wu Guang, *Chu-tso*, pp. 1–9; also Ono Kazuko, "Ryūsho no shisō," in Iwami Hiroshi and Taniguchi Kikuo, eds., *Minmatsu Shinsho no kenkyū,* pp. 503–45, and " 'Fu Zōshō kyūzō Kō Rishū sensei *Ryū sho*' ni tsuite."

7. See *Quanji* 1:191–206.

8. Huang's original title was simply *Tai-fang lu* (Record of waiting for a visit). To this was later prefixed (by Ch'üan Tsu-wang) *Ming-i* (see Wu, *Chu-tso,* pp. 4–5). Since all published editions use the amended title, that is used here except in the text where for convenience it is sometimes shortened to *Tai-fang lu,* or in English to "Plan," and in the notes it is abbreviated MITFL.

9. Cf. James Legge, *The Chinese Classics* 3:269, 278, 320ff., and Legge, *Yi-king,* pp. 269, 242, 311.

10. Chang Ping-lin, *T'ai-yen wen-lu* 1:116b. Liang Ch'i-ch'ao attempted to defend Huang from this charge by claiming that the death of the first Manchu emperor and the immaturity of his heir had in 1662 encouraged Ming adherents to believe that the new dynasty would soon collapse (*Chung-kuo chin san-pai nien hsüeh-shu shih* 17:48). The reference in Huang's preface to Hu Han's prediction of a new cycle, which was about to usher in a Golden Age, lends some credence to this view. However, Ch'üan Tsu-wang, who had studied Huang's writings carefully and was acquainted with members of Huang's family, asserts that Huang wrote this book precisely because he had given up hope for the Ming cause and could do nothing else to perpetuate the best traditions of that dynasty.

11. Ch'üan Tsu-wang, *Chi-ch'i t'ing chi* (in *Kuo-hsüeh chi-pen ts'ung-shu* ed., hereafter cited as KHCPTS), ch. 22, p. 267.

12. *Chi-ch'i t'ing chi* and *Wai-pien,* ch. 44, p. 1331.

13. See Wu, *Chu-tso,* pp. 4–5.

14. It is true that the Ming capital had later been changed from Nanking to Peking, but this was done by a virtual usurper of the throne, Yung-lo.

15. Reign title: K'ang-hsi (1662–1722).

16. During the Ch'ing dynasty, the name of the Han commentator Cheng Hsüan was rendered Cheng Yüan because of the taboo in force during the long reign of K'ang-hsi and the great awe in which he was held thereafter. Huang's preface is dated the second year of the K'ang-hsi reign, though much of the work was written in the preceding reign. In the absence of an original manuscript one cannot be sure whence arose the nonobservance of the taboo, whether from Huang or the later editors of the earliest extant printed edition, but the latter would seem more likely

to observe the taboo than Huang and therefore less likely to have initiated this departure from it. Cf. *Tz'u-hai, tzu* 284c, no. 7; and *Chou li* 1:1a, in *Sung-pen shih-san ching chu-su fu chiao-k'an chi* (hereafter cited as SSCCS, *Mai-wang hsien kuan* ed., 1887).

17. On this point, cf. Hou Wai-lu, *Chin-tai Chung-kuo ssu-hsiang hsüeh-shuo shih* 2:116–77; and Koh Byong-ik, "Huang Tsung-hsi's Expectation of the Coming of a New Era," in *Journal of Humanities and Social Sciences* 30 (Seoul: Korean Research Center, June 1969): 61.

On this matter Professor Yü Ying-shih has offered the following observations and evidence, pertinent enough to warrant my quoting him as follows:

> The late Ch'en Yin-k'o points out in his monumental study of the Ming-Ch'ing transition, [that] since Huang explicitly referred to himself as Chi Tzu, the "prince" whose "visit" he was "waiting for" can only be identified with the reigning emperor of the new dynasty, namely K'ang-hsi. (See Ch'en's *Liu Ju-shih pieh-chuan,* Shanghai: Ku-chi ch'u-pan she, 1980, vol. 3, p. 844.) Given Huang's profound knowledge of Chinese classics and history, the suggestion that Huang's use of the Chi Tzu analogy was a "careless slip" is rather unconvincing. Second, the most recent discovery of Huang's draft letter to Hsü Ch'ien-hsüeh throws a completely new light on his attitude toward Emperor K'ang-hsi. The letter, in Huang's own hand writing, was written sometime in late 1685 or early 1686 when Hsu was promoted to the sub-chancellorship of the Grand Secretariat. In this letter Huang referrd to K'ang-hsi once as "Sage-emperor" (*Sheng-chu*) and twice as "His Majesty" (*Huang-shang*) and specifically praised the latter's "spirit of benevolence" (*jen-feng*). Moreover, even though it was only a first draft with many changes to be transcribed into a formal letter, he nevertheless took great care in each case, to write "Sage-emperor" and "His Majesty" in an elevated form. In light of this previously unpublished material, we must reconsider Huang's relationship with the Ch'ing court. During his lifetime his friend-turned-enemy Lü Liu-liang had already openly accused Huang of compromising his integrity by seeking favors for his two sons from a high-ranking official (i.e., T'ang Pin) in charge of provincial examinations (in 1681). (See Lü's "Letter to Wei Fang-kung" in *Lü's Wan-ts'un wen-chi,* Taipei: Commercial Press reprint, 1973, *chüan* 2:12b.) Now this charge is also substantiated by the newly-discovered draft letter in which he requested Hsü Ch'ien-hsüeh to write a letter of introduction to a local official on behalf, this time, of his grandson who was about to participate in district examinations. (See Huang's hand written draft in *Huang Tsung-hsi Nan-lei tsa-chu kao chen-chi,* ed. by Wu Kuang, Chekiang Ku-chi ch'u-pan-she, 1987, pp. 159–161; for a printed version, see pp. 278–280.)
>
> I don't think that on the basis of this new evidence alone we can argue for "any collaborationist intent on Huang's part" as far as the writing of *Waiting for the Dawn* was concerned. When Huang was writing this treatise in the early 1660's, it was very unlikely that he had a "Manchu prince" in mind. However, in the next two decades of his life, Huang's anti-Manchuism seems to have been gradually subsiding. It seems reasonable to suggest that by the 1680s he

probably would not have minded if Emperor K'ang-hsi turned out to be the "prince" seriously interested in his *Plan*. Ironically, in the first half of his draft letter to Hsü Ch'ien-hsüeh what he was doing was exactly contrary to his earlier admonition to Wan Ssu-t'ung of what not to do: "offering advice of a political nature to the Manchu court." (letter to author from Professor Yü)

A similar conclusion is arrived at by Ono Kazuko in a forthcoming article, "Son Bun ga Minakata Kumagusu ni okutta 'Genkun Genshin' ni tsuite" to appear in *Son Bun kenkyū*.

Speaking for myself, I would agree with Professor Yü's judgment above that "when Huang was writing this treatise in the early 1660s, it was very unlikely that he would have had a Manchu prince in mind," but also "that by the 1680s he would not have minded if Emperor K'ang-hsi turned out to be the 'prince' seriously interested in his Plan." Huang's loyalty to the Ming was not so much to the dynasty as such (since he was severely critical of it) as to the values of Chinese civilization he had fought to defend. It is believable that by the 1680s Huang might have looked on the K'ang-hsi emperor as having come to accept many of these values, but hardly credible that he could have done so in the first two years of the latter's reign, much less in the 1650s when the first drafts of his Plan were written.

18. See, for example, *Quanji* 1:6–7; Ono Kazuko, *Kō Sōgi*, pp. 206–07; Yamanoi Yū, *Min Shin shisōshi no kenkyū*, pp. 276–77, and *Kō Sōgi*, p. 126.

19. Hu Han, *Hu Chung-tzu chi* (*Ts'ung-shu chi-ch'eng* ed., hereafter cited as TSCC), ch. 1, p. 2. For a detailed study of Huang's use of Hu Han's theories, and his calculations based on Shao Yung and the *Book of Changes*, see Koh Byong-ik, "Huang's Expectation," pp. 43–74.

20. *Ming-i tai-fang lu* (hereafter MITFL), *Erh-lao ko* ed., p. 4b, lines 9–10; *Quanji* 1:5. In this case "all the people" is my translation for *wan-min* in the original. As a general rule I translate the related and somewhat overlapping Chinese terms as follows: *min* ("common people"); *t'ien-hsia* ("all-under-Heaven"); *t'ien-hsia chih jen* ("Heaven's people)." For a discussion of Huang's use of *t'ien-hsia* see Shimada Kenji, *Chūgoku kakumei senkusha tachi*, p. 130n1, and the discussion by Zhou Chizhi in Wu Guang, ed., *Huang Zongxi lun*, p. 317.

21. MITFL, p. 7b, lines 3–5; *Quanji* 1:7.

22. Topics discussed in this section generally follow Huang's order of presentation in the original. Exceptions to this are the inclusion of his ideas on eunuchs (actually found at the end of the work) with other topics on the central administration; of his view on subofficials (next to last in the original) with those on the civil service generally; and of his discussion of border commanderies and the location of the capital (found in the middle of the work), placed here at the end along with his observations on military affairs.

23. Lin Mou-sheng misses this fundamental distinction between Taoist romanticism and Confucian idealism when he states: "Rousseau, father of modern liberalism, Marx, father of modern communism, and Proudhon, father of modern anarchism—all great revolutionary philosophers—assume the primitive state to be the utopian existence. So does Huang" (*Men and Ideas*, p. 196).

24. See Huang, "Feng-chien," in *Quanji* 1:418–20.

25. See W. T. de Bary, Wing-tsit Chan, and Burton Watson, eds., *Sources of Chinese Tradition* 1: 8–9.

26. Teng Mu, *Po-ya ch'in,* in *Chih-pu-tsu chai ts'ung-shu* ed.

27. See Teng Shih, "Teng Mu-hsin *Po-ya ch'in* chi pa," in *Kuo-ts'ui hsüeh-pao,* wen pien 36, p. 6ab; Satō Shinji, "*Hakugakin* no shisō to *Min-i taihō roku,*" pp. 80–94.

28. Satō, "*Hakugakin,*" pp. 89b–90b. See also Mizoguchi Yūzō, *Chūgoku zenkindai shisō no kussetsu to tenkai,* p. 266.

29. See de Bary, Chan, and Watson, eds., *Sources of Chinese Tradition* 1: 175–76.

30. Lin Ch'i-yen's view that Huang saw rulership as created by society in response to historical needs is not, in my opinion, consistent with a careful reading of Huang's account. If, as Lin suggests, Huang accepted a Taoist view as the only naturalistic and realistic one, people would have felt no need to "contract" for rulership of the kind Lin speaks of, nor would Huang have proposed a more Confucian solution. See Lin Ch'i-yen, "Yüan-yüan," pp. 34–35.

31. See Mizoguchi Yūzō, *Zenkindai,* pp. 4–11; and in relation to Huang's sixteenth-century predecessor Wang Ken, see the article by Monika Übelhör in Wu Guang, ed., *Huang Zongxi lun,* pp. 303–309.

32. See W. T. de Bary, *Neo-Confucian Orthodoxy and Learning of the Mind-and-Heart,* pp. 81–82, 124, and de Bary, *The Message of the Mind in Neo-Confucianism,* pp. 11–12, 21–22, 131.

33. See W. T. de Bary, *Learning for One's Self* (New York: Columbia University Press, 1991), pp. 8–10, 29–34, 37–41, 360–61.

34. See de Bary, *Neo-Confucian Orthodoxy,* pp. 81–82, 124, and de Bary, *Message of the Mind,* pp. 11–12, 21–22, 131.

35. Huang, "P'o-hsieh lun," in *Quanji* 1:416–18.

36. See Ono Kazuko, "Ryūsho no shisō," pp. 517–22, 538–39.

37. See Ryūsaku Tsunoda, W. T. de Bary, and Donald Keene, eds., *Sources of Japanese Tradition,* 2 vols. (New York: Columbia University Press, 1958) 2: 217–38.

38. *Mencius* 7B:14, in James Legge, trans., *The Chinese Classics* (all subsequent quotations in English from *Mencius* are from this edition).

39. H. H. Dubs, *The Works of Hsüntze,* p. 125.

40. See W. T. de Bary, *East Asian Civilizations: A Dialogue in Five Stages,* pp. 50–51.

41. See W. T. de Bary and John Chaffee, eds., *Neo-Confucian Education,* pp. 14, 268–71, 515–16.

42. See W. T. de Bary, "Chen Te-hsiu and Statecraft," in Robert Hymes and Conrad Schirokauer, eds., *Ordering the World: Approaches to State and Society in Sung China* (Berkeley: University of California Press, 1992); also Hung-lam Chu, "Ch'iu Chün's *Ta-hsüeh yen-i pu* and Its Influence in the Sixteenth and Seventeenth Centuries," pp. 1–32.

43. Not all Confucians took this view, however. Fang Hsiao-ju (1357–1402) takes essentially the same position as Huang in his essay on government administration (*kuan-cheng*). Cf. *Hsün-chih-chai chi* (Ssu-pu ts'ung-k'an, hereafter SPTK, 1st ser.) 3:9b.

44. *Liu Tzu ch'üan-shu* 15:5a–6b Tse-nan chih i . . . shu. See also Frederic Wakeman, "The Price of Autonomy," pp. 35–70.

45. Ono Kazuko, in "Tōrinha to sono seiji shisō," *Tōhō gakuhō* 28 (1958): 262–82, links Tung-lin efforts in the late Ming to institutionalize rulership, establish legal checks on the exercise of imperial power, and organize scholarly associations (especially academies) to promote open discussion of public issues, as leading the way for the next generation more fully to articulate these "progressive ideas," most notably by Huang Tsung-hsi in his *Ming-i tai-fang-lu.*

46. W. K. Liao, *Complete Works of Han Fei Tzu* 1:57, 61. Theoretically for Han Fei Tzu the ruler too was supposed to accept and subject himself to sovereign law, but practically (as the Legalist-minded prime minister of the Ch'in dynasty, Li Ssu, put it), the first emperor of the Ch'in had secured for himself, by Legalist means, a position of sole and indisputable supremacy. See de Bary, Chan, and Burton, eds., *Sources of Chinese Tradition* 1: 140–41.

47. See *Mencius* 2B:2, 5, 14; 4B:3; 5B:9.

48. See W. T. de Bary, *The Trouble with Confucianism,* pp. 15–16.

49. See *Honan Ch'eng shih ts'ui-yen,* in Zhonghua shuju ed. of Ch'eng Hao and Ch'eng I, *Erh Ch'eng i-shu,* pp. 1242–52, and in *Erh hsien-sheng yü* 5:77, *Erh Ch'eng chi* (Beijing, 1981). Also *Chin-ssu lu* 7 (Wing-tsit Chan, *Reflections on Things at Hand,* hereafter *Things at Hand* [New York: Columbia University Press, 1967], pp. 183–201).

50. See *Meng Tzu* 5B:9, in Ssu-k'u ch'üan-shu chen-pen ed. (hereafter SKCSCP) of *Meng Tzu chi-chu ta-ch'üan* 10:33a–34b (205/756); Sano Kōji, "*Min-i taihō roku* ni okeru eki-sei kakumei shisō," p. 138b; and Shimada Kenji, *Shushigaku to Yōmeigaku,* pp. 63–66; and Huang's reference to the suppression of the *Mencius* in the Plan, sec. 1, p. 3.

51. MITFL. p. 5b, line 11; 6a, lines 1–2; *Quanji* 1:5.

52. *Ming shih* 95:1a, 3a (Zhonghua shuju ed.). References to other dynastic histories are to the [*Ch'in-ting*] *Erh-shih-ssu shih* (*Han-fen lou* facsimile reprint of the Palace ed. of 1739: Shanghai, 1916). Because of the frequent references to the *Ming shih,* they are rendered as in the now more generally available 1974 Zhonghua ed. Cf. also Ch'en Teng-yüan, "Shu *Ming-i tai-fang lu* hou," p. 277.

53. MITFL, p. 47b, line 7; *Quanji* 1:44.

54. Ku Yen-wu was one who subscribed to this view. Cf. *Jih chih lu,* KHCPTS, ch. 5, p. 28; ch. 9, p. 33.

55. MITFL, p. 10b, line 10, and p. 11a, line 2; *Quanji* 1:10.

56. Liao, *Han Fei Tzu,* p. 65. This is essentially a restatement of the view advanced at an earlier time by Mo-tzu: "What the superior thinks to be right all shall think to be right; what the superior thinks to be wrong all shall think to be wrong." Yi-pao Mei, *The Ethical and Political Works of Motse,* p. 56; and Burton Watson, trans., *Mo Tzu* (New York: Columbia University Press, 1963), p. 35.

57. Derk Bodde, *China's First Unifier,* p. 82.

58. See translation, under "Schools."

59. This larger educational aim is discussed in relation to Huang by Sano Kōji in "Eki-sei kakumei," p. 131ab.

60. MITFL, p. 15a, lines 3–6.

61. If we are to judge from his earlier and later prefaces to the *Ming-ju hsüeh-an*, Huang's conception of orthodoxy changed later in life, and he would presumably have allowed Buddhism and Taoism a greater measure of toleration.

62. In his essay on schools Huang reveals that he has a special grudge against conceited young magistrates who fail to show sufficient respect to local civilians older and wiser than they.

63. See W. T. de Bary, "A Reappraisal of Neo-Confucianism," in Arthur F. Wright, ed., *Studies in Chinese Thought* (Chicago: University of Chicago Press, 1953), pp. 88ff.

64. Among recent social historians this is a disputed point, and the evidence varies in individual cases, as well as in time and place. Reciprocity among local gentry could yield different results, whether as to mutual restraint or mutual collusion, in the scale of demands made by local leaders upon the peasantry. In reviewing Japanese scholarly discussion of the matter, Mori Masao tends to the conclusion that, for the most part, gentry (*shih-ta-fu*) resident in their home localities shared the concerns of the local population more than did bureaucrats in towns and cities, and for this reason the former were more trusted and respected than the latter. See Mori Masao, "The Gentry in the Ming Period—An Outline of the Relations Between the *Shih-ta-fu* and Local Society," in *Acta Asiatica* 38 (Tokyo: Tōhō Gakkai, 1980): 43–47.

65. See especially G. William Skinner, *The City in Late Imperial China* (Stanford: Stanford University Press, 1977), pp. 23–26. On subofficialdom in general, the classic work is Wada Sei, *Shina chihō jichi hattatsushi* (Tokyo: Chūka minkoku hōsei kenkyūkai, 1939; reprint, Tokyo: Kyūko shoin, 1975). For the Sung see James T. C. Liu, "Sung Views on the Control of Government Clerks," *Journal of Economic and Social History of the Orient* 10, no. 2 (1967): 3; and Brian McKnight, *Village and Bureaucracy in Southern Sung China.* For the Ming, see Leif Littrup, *Sub-bureaucratic Government in China in Ming Times;* and Albert Chan, *The Glory and Fall of the Ming Dynasty,* pp. 305–10.

66. Chen Te-hsiu (1178–1235) in the late Sung is particularly exercised on this score, perceiving the problem as a prefectural administrator sympathetic to the grievances of local villagers. See de Bary, "Chen Te-hsiu and Statecraft," in Hymes and Schirokauer, eds., *Ordering the World.*

67. Cf. Littrup, *Sub-bureaucratic Government,* p. 192, with respect to the functions of subbureaucratic government and the inability to create local organizations to perform them. He says: "[For] these or similar offical sub-bureaucratic government organizations [to] have functioned for a long time, they would have needed an effective leadership. The 'elite' could, on the basis of official positions, degrees and property, have provided such leadership, but the government was apparently not prepared to assume such official leadership, either because it was not able to or did not want to do so."

68. In only one instance does he cite Su specifically, but the issue he raises had been discussed earlier in Su's essay on "The Land System" (*Chia-yu chi* 5:7a–9b, SPTK, 1st ser.), and Huang undoubtedly had this in mind when he wrote.

69. In *A Plan for the Prince* this argument is presented in an extremely elliptical manner (see "Land System," parts 1 and 2). An essay on taxes in Huang's *P'o-hsieh lun* (1:6b), written much later as a postscript to the present one, clarifies his position somewhat.

70. This assertion is made in the *P'o-hsieh lun*, ch. 1, p. 6b. Huang's thesis concerning the proliferation and steady augmentation of taxes is fundamentally challenged by Ray Huang in *Taxation and Finance* (see especially pp. 315–16).

71. Su, *Chia-yu chi* 5:8b.

72. Hu Han's essay on the well-field system, *Ching-mou* (*Hu Chung-tzu chi*, TSCC 1:7–11), anticipates many of the points made here by Huang, who was obviously much indebted to his work, and suggests a solution similar to Huang's based on earlier statistics for the Sung dynasty.

73. See Liang Fang-chung, *The Single-Whip Method of Taxation in China*, p. 2; Littrup, *Sub-bureaucratic Government*, pp. 41–42.

74. Huang held firmly to this basic distinction throughout his life, reaffirming it in his *P'o-hsieh lun* written thirty years later. See *Quanji* 1:203–304, and also *Meng Tzu shih shuo* (*Quanji* 1:1.60–61).

75. See Chan, *Ming Dynasty*, pp. 40–44, 245–49.

76. Ray Huang, *Taxation and Finance*, p. 313.

77. Huang's work has been cited as an important source for the study of Chinese tax history by some modern writers. Cf. Wu Chao-hsin, *Chung-kuo shui-chih shih* (History of Chinese tax systems) 2:141; Takashima Katsumi, ed., *Shina zeisei no enkaku* (The development of Chinese tax systems), p. 155.

78. See Liang Fang-chung, *The Single-Whip Method of Taxation*, pp. 23–64; Littrup, *Sub-bureaucratic Government*, pp. 91–99, 130–51.

79. In other words, on land granted the cultivator by the government an additional 5 per cent could be charged as rent. According to Liang Fang-chung (*The Single-Whip Method of Taxation*, pp. 3, 138), the rate of taxation was customarily heavier on government land than on private land, as if it were in lieu of rent leased from the government rather than privately owned. See also Littrup, *Sub-bureaucratic Government*, pp. 41–42.

80. Although Ray Huang does not agree that tax revenues increased as much as Huang Tsung-hsi claims, he concludes in *Taxation and Finance* that the functions of the state had, indeed, not grown and that the problems of the government were, as Tsung-hsi had said, more due to waste, inefficiency, and poor planning than to an actual increase in government services. Contrary to Huang Tsung-hsi, however, Ray Huang believes that there had actually been growth in the economy and there should have been an increase or improvement in government services to support that growth (Ray Huang, *Taxation and Finance*, pp. 306–23).

81. Naitō Torajirō (Konan) saw this as a key feature of Huang's Plan. See his *Shina ron*, pp. 113–14.

82. See *Quanji* 1:419.

83. See the discussion of Satō Shinji, "*Min-i taihō roku* no kihon shisō," *Akademia* 30 (1960): 19.

84. Lin Mou-sheng, *Men and Ideas*, p. 199.

85. See Charles Taylor, "Modes of Civil Society," in *Public Culture: The Bulletin of the Center for Transnational Cultural Studies* 3, no. 1 (Philadelphia: University of Pennsylvania, Fall 1990): 95–118.

86. Ono Kazuko, "Tōrinha to sono seiji shisō," pp. 266–82, particularly emphasizes the combination of legal restraints on the ruler and the institutionalization of public discussion in academies as an attempt by Tung-lin scholars to subject dynastic rule in the late Ming to a higher constitutional law.

87. Yamanoi Yū, *Kō Sōgi,* pp. 73–76. In discussing the role of the prime minister and other reforms to curb the ruler in the MITFL, Yamanoi repeatedly uses the word "check" in transliteration. I believe he is right in this, as I came to recognize subsequent to my discounting of this aspect in my earlier essay, "Chinese Despotism," p. 197. On this point see also Mizoguchi, *Zenkindai,* pp. 267–68, and Li Jinquan (in Wu Guang, ed., *Huang Zongxi lun,* p. 328).

88. See Ono Kazuko, "Tōrinha to sono seiji shisō," p. 268.

89. Among recent attempts in the People's Republic of China to evaluate Huang's economic views in other than simple class terms, see Qin Peikeng, "Huang Lizhou jingji sixiang gouzhen," pp. 68–71 and note 29; and Ye Shichang, "Guan yu Huang Zongxi te gongshang jie ben lun," pp. 108–10.

90. Luo Huaching, "Gong chi shifei," pp. 55–58.

91. See *Chin-ssu lu* 7 (Chan, *Things at Hand,* pp. 182–201).

92. On this point see the extended discussion of Sano Kōji, "Eki-sei kakumei," pp. 129–42; also Satō Shinji, "*Min-i taihō roku* no kihon shisō," *Akademia* 30 (1961), Nagoya, Nanzan daigaku, p. 18.

93. Lü Liu-liang, *Ssu-shu chiang-i* 6:10ab, commenting on *Analects* 3:19; de Bary, *Learning for One's Self,* p. 328.

94. *Mencius* 5B:9.

95. On the general lack of such an infrastructure to support public services, see Ray Huang, *Taxation and Finance,* pp. 314, 317–18.

96. de Bary, "Chinese Despotism," p. 195.

97. Peter Bol, "Sung Civil Culture and the Examination System" (Paper presented to the European-American Symposium on State and Society in East Asia, Paris, May 29–31, 1991).

98. This important point is underscored by Ono Kazuko in "Ryūsho no shisō," p. 540. In a personal communication Professor Yü Ying-shih emphasizes what a longstanding tradition this was in Confucian thought:

> The idea of the school as an organ of public criticism . . . is deeply rooted in classical Confucian tradition. . . . According to the *Tso chuan* (Duke Hsiang, year 31) the wise statesman Tzu-ch'an of Cheng refused to take any action against village schools where his policies were harshly criticized. When Confucius heard of this, he said: "Looking at the matter from this, when men say that Tzu-ch'an was not benevolent (*jen*), I do not believe it." (See James Legge, tr., *The Ch'un Tsew with the Tso Chuan,* pp. 565–566.) I believe Huang's conception of "schools" is developed out of this classical model. More recently, I discovered that before Huang, Su Shih of Northern Sung had already proposed to revive this classical tradition by transforming local

schools into "organs of political expression." Since it was one of Su Shih's best-known writings and received critical attention from Chu Hsi (see *Chu Tzu yü-lei,* Peking: Chung-hua shu-chü punctuated edition, 1956, vol.8, p. 3115), we have good reason to assume that Huang must have been aware of it. In any case, this seems to me to be an excellent piece of evidence for the argument that *Waiting for the Dawn* is "a product of a significant long-term development of Neo-Confucian thought and scholarship." In modern times, I may also add, Hu Shih was particularly fascinated by Su Shih's essay and recognized it as "a very odd piece of writing." (See *Hu Shih te jih-chi,* "Hu Shih's Diary," Taipei: Yuan-liu Ch'u-pan kung-ssu, 1990, vol. 17, February 28, 1952 entry, unpaginated).

This additional evidence, underscoring the traditional precedents for the idea that ruler's should listen to the views of schoolmen, helps to clarify more precisely Huang's own contribution, which was not as the originator of the idea but as one who carried it a step further, seeking to incorporate it in a larger structure of laws or constitutional order. This would leave less to the discretion or good intentions of the benevolent monarch, as to whether he would personally heed such opinions, and rely more on systemic means for the active promotion of "public opinion" on successive levels of education and administration, through a structured process encouraging and protecting the exercise of such expression.

99. Liu Tsung-chou emphasized the ruler's need to share power with his ministers on the traditional assumption that the ruler and minister can agree on fundamental principles—the Mencian view, confirmed by Chu Hsi. Huang reaffirms this in his discussion of ministership, but goes beyond it to institutionalize dissent in the schools. See *Liu Tzu ch'üan-shu* 15:2b–7a; and also Zhong Erju, "Lun *Mingyi daifang lu* te zhexue sixiang," pp. 6–10.

100. See Struve, "Huang Zongxi in Context," pp. 475–79; Ono "Tōrinha to sono seiji shisō," pp. 249–82; "Minmatsu no kessha ni kansuru ichi kosatsu—toku ni Fusha ni tsuite," in *Shirin* 45, no. 2 (1962): 37–67; and "Tōrintō kō: Kaibu Ri Sansai wo megutte," *Tōhō gakuhō* 52 (1980): 563–94.

101. See de Bary, *Neo-Confucian Orthodoxy,* pp. 91–98.

102. Chen Te-hsiu's preface to the *Rites of Chou,* revised by Wang Yü-chih (active late twelfth–early thirteenth centuries), in *Choh-li ting-i* 1:1a (T'ung chih t'ang ed.), and Chen, *Hsi-shan wen-chi* 29:509–10 (KHCPTS ed). See Yves Hervouet, *A Sung Bibliography* (Hong Kong: Chinese University Press, 1978), pp. 29–30.

103. There is sometimes a tendency to equate the "progressive" thinking of seventeenth-century Enlightenment scholars as if they fell into a uniform emerging pattern, as when T'ang Chen's discussion of the education of the crown prince is likened to Huang's proposal for the court and the heir apparent to attend the discussion at the Imperial College. T'ang Chen would subject the heir apparent to a rigorous experience of life and work among the peasants, which may have the same value as later Maoist policies for the reeducation of intellectuals in the countryside, but has the opposite effect from establishing an autonomous public space for intellectuals, as Huang would have it. See Xiong Yüezhi, "Lun Huang Zongxi, Tang Zhen fantui fengjian zhuanzhi zhuyi te minzhu sixiang," pp. 27–31.

104. For the less favorable connotation attaching to *chiang-hsüeh* (even as it may be used by the same author) to mean "vapid, groundless, pedantic discussion," see Yamanoi, *Min Shin,* p. 271, and my own discussion of Huang's contemporary Lü Liu-liang in *Learning for One's Self,* pp. 278–82.

105. On this question in the late Ming see Ono, "Tōrinha to sono seiji shisō," pp. 266–67, and Mizoguchi, *Zenkindai,* pp. 14–16.

106. De Bary, "Chinese Despotism," p. 196.

107. See de Bary, *East Asian Civilizations,* pp. 84–92; and de Bary, *The Trouble with Confucianism,* pp. 87–103.

108. See Huang, "Fu-shui," in *Quanji* 1:202–203.

109. See W. T. de Bary, "Individualism and Humanitarianism," in de Bary, ed., *Self and Society in Ming Thought,* pp. 183–87; Ronald Dimberg, *The Sage and Society* (Honolulu: University of Hawaii Press, 1974), pp. 73–91, 134–38; and Joanna Handlin, *Action in Late Ming Thought: The Reorientation of Lü K'un,* pp. 27, 35, 47, and 217.

110. De Bary, "Chinese Despotism" p. 197. In a review of my book *The Liberal Tradition in China* (Hong Kong: Chinese University of Hong Kong Press, 1982), Frederick Mote drew attention to the disparity between the views I expressed there and those found in my earlier essay cited above. The disparity is palpable enough, and I can only regret that in my Ch'ien Mu Public Lectures, brief and general as they had to be for that purpose, I could not explain fully the reasons behind my change in views. I have tried to do so in respect to some of these issues in three subsequent works—*The Message of the Mind in Neo-Confucianism, Learning for One's Self,* and *The Trouble with Confucianism*—but this is my first opportunity to explain more fully why I have come to an enlarged appreciation of Huang Tsung-hsi as compared to the views expressed in my earlier essay, which, ironically, Professor Mote found more to his liking. I only hope that I have now responded, if not to his satisfaction, at least to the extent I am able, to the questions Professor Mote raised in this connection in *Ming Studies* 19 (Fall 1984): 17–25, and in his Surrejoinder in *Ming Studies* 21 (Spring 1986): 94.

111. Liang Ch'i-ch'ao, *Chin san-pai nien hsüeh-shu shih* 17:47.

112. Ibid. According to L. C. Goodrich, *The Literary Inquisition of Ch'ien-lung,* Huang's *Ming-i tai-fang lu* does not appear on any of the extant lists of proscribed books. See also Shimada, *Senkusha tachi,* p. 162; Yamonoi Yū (*Kō Sōgi,* pp. 286–87) believes that the MITFL was not widely known or read before the late Ch'ing and thus escaped being formally proscribed (as were some of Huang's other writings). Thus inhibition or circumspection (self-censorship, if you will), owing to the adverse climate of the times, rather than actual proscription, seems to explain why the work had so little effect on any continuing developments of Ch'ing thought. See also Xie Gang, "Mingyi daifang lu yu Chingchu wenci yu," pp. 71–84, and Xiong Yüezhi, "Lun Huang Zongxi, Tang Zhen," pp. 27–31.

113. Liang Ch'i-ch'ao, *Ch'ing-tai hsüeh-shu k'ai-lun,* pp. 32, 141.

114. T'ang Leang-li, *The Inner History of the Chinese Revolution,* p. 2. Needless to say, the role of Huang as the ideological and organizational genius of the anti-imperialist struggle is a mythical creation, by which T'ang, as a nationalist, attempts

to naturalize and dignify the revolutionary movement. For a more sober contemporary evaluation of Huang's influence on the revolutionary movements, see Naitō Torajirō, *Shina ron*, pp. 271–73; and for Sun Yat-sen's use of the *MITFL* see Ono Kazuko, "Son Bun."

115. See Li Zhiuran, "Li Ciran 'Mingyi daifang lu' jiumiu chutan" (in Wu Guang, ed., *Huang Zongxi lun*, pp. 338–49). Also Yamanoi, *Kō Sōgi*, p. 297.

116. Hu Shih, "Huang Li-chou lun hsüeh-sheng yün-tung [Peip'ing, 1924]" (Huang Tsung-hsi on the student movement), in *Hu Shih wen-ts'un erh-chi* 3:11–14 (10th ed., 1947).

117. Chang Ping-lin, *T'ai-yen wen-lu* 1:125a.

118. Ibid. 1:128b.

119. Including bribery, "squeeze," extortionate taxation, embezzlement of public funds, and prostitution of their wives (cf. ibid 1:129a).

120. Chang Ping-lin, *T'ai-yen wen-lu* 1:129a.

121. Hsiao Kung-ch'üan, *Chung-kuo cheng-chih ssu-hsiang shih* 2:264.

122. T'an P'i-mo, *Ch'ing-tai ssu-hsiang shih-kang*, pp. 8–20.

123. Hou Wai-lu, *Chin-tai Chung-kuo ssu-hsiang hsüeh-shuo shih*, vol. 1, pp. 104–64.

124. Hou's application of this view to the interpretation of Ch'ing thought is far less rigid and doctrinaire than that of T'an P'i-mo and shows a much closer acquaintance with Huang's writings. Since in other respects Hou's work is done in a conscientious and thoroughgoing manner, with due regard for his source materials, it is unfortunate that he should be burdened with a theory and terminology that tends to obscure, instead of clarify, the real issues. If, for instance, to present Huang in a favorable light he must be characterized as "antifeudal," it becomes difficult to appreciate what he found of value in the Confucian feudal ideal or in what respects he significantly modifies it.

125. Hou Wai-lu, *Chin-tai Chung-kuo ssu-hsiang hsüeh-shuo shih*, vol. 1, p. 119.

126. Ibid., p. 113.

127. Ibid., pp. 108–109, 112–13.

128. Ibid., pp. 120, 122, 124.

129. Ibid., p. 128.

130. See Xie Gang, "Wenci yu," pp. 71–77. For an astute analysis of this three-way conflict in the urban setting, see Richard von Glahn, "Urban Social Conflict in the Late Ming," pp. 280–307. See also Mizoguchi Yūzō, "Iwayuru Tōrinha shinshi shisō."

131. See Ono, "Tōrinha to sono seiji shisō," pp. 258–64; Bettine Birge, *Women and Property in Sung Dynasty China (960–1279: Neo-Confucianism and Social Change in Chien-chou, Fukien.* Ph.D. diss., Columbia University, 1992.

132. John Dardess, *Confucianism and Autocracy* (Berkeley: University of California Press, 1981), p. 84. Although recent Japanese scholars have tended to differentiate among so-called gentry on the basis of the varying degrees to which they manifested Confucian concerns, and whether these concerns were directed toward the state, urban administrative centers, or their home localities, the common denominator among these characterizations appears to be the shared Confu-

cian educational background and professed values of this class. For a summary and assessment of such views, see Mori Masao, "The Gentry in the Ming Period," pp. 39, 43–46.

133. Dardess, *Confucianism and Autocracy*, p. 84.

134. There is an enormous literature on the subject (most of it ephemeral), going back over half a century. For a summary of some recent writings in China, see Foon Ming Liew, "Debates on the Birth of Capitalism in China During the Past Three Decades," pp. 61–66.

135. As an example one might cite the article by Xiong Yüezhi on Huang Tsung-hsi and T'ang Chen in *Shanghai shifan daxue xuebao, zhe xue shehui kexue* (pp. 27–31). Others like Xie Gang, "Wenci yu," p. 73, fundamentally question this "capitalist" interpretation, arguing that Huang spoke for the landlord class in essentially traditional terms.

136. *Quanji* 1:7.

137. *Quanji* 1:9.

138. *Quanji* 1:10–11.

139. *Quanji* 1:12.

140. See, for instance, Xiong Yüezhi, "Lun Huang Zongxi, Tang Zhen," pp. 27–31, who links them to a "progressive, capitalist, intellectual enlightenment."

141. See Wu Guang, ed., *Huang Zongxi lun.*

142. This linkage of classical Confucians, Huang's generation, and the modern reform and revolutionary leaders is not uncommon in recent writing. As an example see the article by Li Jinquan (in Wu Guang, ed., *Huang Zongxi lun*, pp. 322–29).

143. See Naitō Torajirō, *Shina ron*, pp. 113–15, 259–71; and Joshua Fogel, *Politics and Sinology: The Case of Naitō Konan*, pp. 127–28, 174–79, 268–70.

144. Yamanoi, *Min Shin*, p. 296; Mizoguchi, *Zenkindai*, p. 274.

145. Shimada, *Senkusha tachi*, pp. 123–30; Yamanoi, *Kō Sōgi*, pp. 287–94.

146. For example, Mizoguchi, *Zenkindai*, pp. 5–17, 260; Ono, *Kō Sōgi;* Yamanoi, *Kō Sōgi*, pp. 66, 70.

147. Ono, *Kō Sōgi*, pp. 223–24, and Yamanoi, *Min Shin*, pp. 293–96, both affirm that Huang went beyond *mimpon shugi* to a *minshu shugi* that was, however, not the exact equivalent of Western democracy.

148. Ono, *Kō Sōgi*, pp. 213–14.

149. Ibid., pp. 73–76.

150. Yamanoi, *Kō Sōgi*, pp. 75–77.

151. Ren Jiyu, *Zhongguo zhexue shi* 4:13–19.

152. This would seem to be the implication also of the discussion by Li Jinquan (in Wu Guang, ed., *Huang Zonxi lun*, p. 328).

153. Ren Jiyu, *Zhexue shi* 4:14, 19; Chen Shengxi and Liu Guangsheng, "Huang Zongxi sixiang ji chi *Mingyi daifang lu* zheyao," p. 194; Liu Shu-hsien, "Huang Tsung-hsi wan-chieh pu-pao?" pp. 156–59. This is a common theme of the conference papers in Wu Guang, ed., *Huang Zongxi lun*, but it is perhaps most noteworthy in those by such leading scholars as Zhang Dainian (p. 7), Cai Shangsi (p. 242), and Qiu Hansheng (p. 250).

154. Ono, *Kō Sōgi*, pp. 221–22; Struve, "Huang Zongxi in Context," pp. 474–

79. See also Monika Übelhör (in Wu Guang, ed., *Huang Zongxi lun,* pp. 303–309) on Wang Ken as a precursor of Huang's MITFL.

155. These included Ma Tuan-lin, Wang Yang-lin, Chang Huang, and others (as referred to in the notes to the translation of Huang's MITFL, which follows). But even the orthodox Ch'eng-Chu school scholar, Ch'iu Chün (for whom Huang himself had little use), contributed to this "practical learning" and institutional studies as shown by Hung-lam Chu in "Ch'iu Chün's *Ta-hsüeh yen-i pu* and Its Influence," pp. 1–32.

156. For example, Mizoguchi, *Zenkindai,* pp. 5–17, 260; Ono, *Kō Sōgi:* Yamanoi, *Kō Sōgi,* pp. 66, 70, and *Min Shin,* p. 296, 406.

157. See Lin Ch'i-yen, "Yüan-yüan," pp. 42–43.

158. See Koh Byong-ik, "Huang's Expectation," p. 70.

159. For a convenient summary of Ku's political beliefs see Hsiao Kung-ch'üan, *Cheng-chih* 2:269–74; and Matsui Hitoshi, *Shina kinsei seiji shichō,* in Sekai kōbō shiron 15:145–356 and 376–94. See also Chen Zuwu, "Huang Zongxi, Gu Yanwu he lun," pp. 50–55; and Lung-chang Young, "Ku Yen-wu's Views on the Ming Examination System," pp. 48–63.

160. Lü's political ideas are discussed in de Bary, *Learning for One's Self,* pp. 324–45; Jung Chao-tsu, "Lü Liu-liang chi ch'i ssu-hsiang," pp. 1–86; Hu Ch'u-sheng, "Huang Li-chou yü Lü Wan-ts'un," pp. 1–8; Ch'ien Mu, *Chin san-pai-nien hsüeh-shu shih* 1:69–87.

161. For T'ang's political views see his *Chien Shu;* Xiong Yüezhi, "Lun Huang Zongxi, Tang Zhen," pp. 27–31; see also Hsiao Kung-ch'üan, *Cheng-chih* 2:265–68; Ch'en Teng-yüan, "Shu *Ming-i tai-fang lu* hou," which also presents other parallels to Huang Tsung-hsi's thought on specific issues; and Jacques Gernet, trans. and ed., *Ecrits d'un sage encore inconnu* (by T'ang Chen), and "L'Homme ou la paperasse," in Dieter Eikemeier and Herbert Franke, eds., *State and Law in East Asia.*

162. For a similar judgment by Koh Byong-ik, see his "Huang's Expectation," p. 70.

Preface of Huang Tsung-hsi

1. Mencius explains that "a long time has elapsed since this world of men received its being, and there has been along its history now a period of good order, and now a period of confusion" (*Mencius* 3B:9). Earlier, order had been brought out of confusion by Yao and Shun, King Wu and the Duke of Chou successively. Now Mencius considers it his task to reassert the principles of order in a period of confusion.

2. The Hsia, Shang, and Chou dynasties from earliest recorded times to 221 B.C.

3. Hu Han (1307–81): a scholar of the Late Yüan and early Ming periods who participated in the compilation of the official history of the Yüan dynasty (*Ming shih* 285:7310; *Dictionary of Ming Biography,* hereafter DMB, p. 1445).

Hu's cyclical theory of history, based upon the "changes" of the *I Ching* and speculations of Shao Yung, is presented in an essay, "The Calculation of Cycles," in his collected works (*Hu Chung-tzu chi* TSCC ed. 1:1a.) Huang cited this essay in his

own work, the *I-hsüeh hsiang-shu lun* (Kuang-ya ts'ung-shu ed., 6:36b–37a), written in 1661, shortly before the *Ming-i tai-fang lu,* at a time when Huang was deeply
immersed in *I Ching* studies and the "learning of emblems and numbers." Hu
states: "Since the death of Confucius, throughout the dynasties succeeding the
Chou—the Ch'in, Han, Chin, Sui, T'ang, Sung—and on down for two thousand
years, the time has not and will not come for a change." Confucius died in 479 B.C.,
according to tradition. Hu and Huang reckoned from the first year (477 B.C.) of the
sixty-year cycle starting after Confucius' death, added 2,160 years (on the basis of a
more complicated and precise calculation than in the rough figure just quoted) and
got A.D. 1683 as the time after which a change for the better might take place. (For
the theories and calculations of Hu Han, see the extensive and detailed discussions
in Koh Byong-ik, "Huang Tsung-hsi's Expectation of the Coming of a New Era," in
Journal of the Social Sciences and Humanistics 30 (Seoul: Korean Research Center,
June 1969): 43–74.) However, by the time he wrote his later work *P'o-hsieh lun,*
Huang had given up such hopes and indicates that Hu Han's theory is nothing but
groundless speculation. See Shen Shanhong and Wu Guang, eds. *Huang Zhongxi
quanji* (hereafter *Quanji*) 1:195).

4. Great Prosperity (*ta-chuang*): a state of affairs that is the subject of Hexagram
34 of the *Book of Changes.* James Legge summarizes the significance of this symbol
as follows: "It suggested to King Wen a state or condition of things in which there
was abundance of strength and vigor. Was strength alone enough for the conduct of
affairs? No. He saw also in the figure that which suggested to him that strength
should be held in subordination to the idea of right, and exerted in harmony with
it" (Legge, trans., *Yi King,* pp. 129–30).

5. Lan-shui: a village southeast of Yü-yao, Chekiang Province, in the eastern
Ssu-ming mountains. Huang's *Nien-p'u* (31b) speaks of this place as Lan-chi, otherwise known as Lu-chia pu. For Lan-chi see *Yü-yao chih* (1778 ed.), *ts'e* 1:7a. For Lu-
chia pu, see ibid. (1:1b), and *Yü-Yao hsien chih* (1899 ed.), *ts'e* 1 (map section), 6b.

6. Wang Mien (1287–1359): Late Yüan and early Ming scholar and painter. Failing in the examination for the *chin-shih* degree, he secluded himself in a mountain
retreat where he painted, wrote poetry, and composed the treatise upon the model
of the *Chou li* mentioned by Huang. However, it is said that he would show it to no
one, but carried it around with him constantly and read it to himself by lamplight
when everyone else had retired. Since Huang had not seen the book and it is not
listed among Wang's works, it was probably never published. Wang is said to have
served as an adviser to Chu Yüan-chang during the latter's rise to power, but there is
much uncertainty and confusion concerning this and other aspects of his life. See
DMB, p. 1396 (Biography by Chu-tsing Li); and Wang Mien, *Chu-chai shih chi*
4:10a (1525 ed.); *Ming shih* 285:7311.

7. Confucian classic, purportedly an account of the early Chou order, attributed
to the Duke of Chou.

8. I Yin: according to tradition a minister under the first emperor of the Shang
dynasty, known for his wisdom and statesmanship. See James Legge, *Shoo King
(Shu ching)*, in *Chinese Classics* 3:4–6, 191–93; *Shih chi* 3:3a–8b; and E.
Chavannes, *Mémoires Historiques* 1:177–80, 187–89.

9. Lü Shang (also known as T'ai Kung Wang and Chiang T'ai Kung): a high officer of the Shang dynasty who broke with the tyrant Chou Hsin and later aided Wu Wang, as chief councillor, in overthrowing the Shang (*Shih chi* 32:1a; Chavannes, *Memoires Historiques* 4:34–87; Giles, no. 1862).

10. Chi Tzu: a high nobleman under Chou Hsin, last emperor of the Shang dynasty, who was imprisoned for protesting against Chou's decadent and tyrannical ways. Freed by King Wu following the latter's conquest of Chou, Chi Tzu refused to serve under Wu but wrote the "Great Plan" contained in the *Book of History*, which served Wu as a guide to good government (Legge, *Shoo King,* in *Chinese Classics* 3:269, 278, 320ff.; *Shih chi* 38:2a).

11. Here Huang speaks of himself as waiting for a visit from a worthy prince, and in the next line he speaks of the dawn just breaking—hence my short title "Waiting for the Dawn." But in Ku Yen-wu's letter to Huang (see translation, "Letter from Ku Yen-wu to Huang Tsung-hsi"), Ku refers to Huang's work simply as *Tai-fang lu* (Record of waiting for a visit), and the modern scholar Wu Guang believes that the first part of the title "Ming-i," as used in all extant printed editions, was added later by Ch'üan Tsu-wang. See *Quanji* 1:423. I have combined the two meanings in my title and subtitle: *Waiting for the Dawn: A Plan for the Prince.*

12. The text here reads *i chih ch'u tan, ming erh wei jung:* Huang seems deliberately to have striven for ambiguity in this passage in order to hint at what he could not discuss freely. *I* is to be understood in relation to Hexagram 36 of the *Book of Changes,* entitled *Ming-i.* The wording of the passage suggests that it is a variation on a theme from the commentary on the fifth line of this hexagram, which reads: "The darkness cannot be dispelled, [but] the light cannot be extinguished." This signifies that Chi Tzu, whose legend is associated with the *Ming-i* hexagram, can neither dispel the forces of darkness nor be extinguished by them; his integrity, the unquenchable light, prevents him from taking arms against a tyrant with a legal right to rule, yet it endures through all tyranny (SSCCS, *I Ching* 4:36:4b; Legge, *Yi King,* pp. 135, 242, 311). Since *i* as interpreted in this hexagram and its commentaries signifies the principle of darkness or tyranny, Huang's immediate allusion seems to be to "night," just breaking into dawn. As such it may refer back to the period of disorder or decay, which at the beginning of the preface he says is about to give way to a new era of order. However, *i* also has the meaning of "peace" and "well-being," and it might also be understood here with reference to the new era Huang anticipates. Still another meaning of *"i"* is "barbarian," which is the sense commonly understood by Chinese readers who associate *ming* with the Ming dynasty and *i* with the barbarian or Manchu dynasty, but even so Huang's real meaning is veiled. It is possible, however, that having the Manchus and the Ming in mind, he wished the reader to complete for himself the parallel he has subtly suggested with the line of commentary just cited from the *Ming-i* hexagram. Thus, since *an* plainly stands for *i* in this case, the line could be read, "The Manchus cannot be expelled, [but] the Ming cannot be extinguished." At the time Huang wrote, all organized resistance to the Manchus had ended, yet scattered Ming adherents like Huang could hope that the finest Ming traditions would be perpetuated in the persons and writings of its worthy followers, just as had been done for the fallen Shang by Chi-Tzu.

The locus classicus for this expression *"i-chih ch'u-tan, ming erh wei-jung"* is *Hou-Han shu* 67:15b (Biography of Li Ying). The second half appears earlier in the *Tso chuan* (Fifth Year of Duke Shao). See *Ch'un-ch'iu ching-chuan chi-chieh*, SPTK 21:8b; Satō Shinji, *"Min-i taihō roku* no kipon shisō," *Akademia* 30 (1961), Nagoya, Nanzan daigaku, p. 13.

13. Li-chou: a literary name (*hao*) used by Huang Tsung-hsi, who speaks of himself as an old man because he saw his years of official service as being at an end and he writes as if this were his last political will and testament, though in fact he lived on for many years after he first so spoke of himself in 1653. Wu Guang (Wu Kuang), *Huang Tsung-hsi chu-tso hui-k'ao* (hereafter, *Chu-tso*), p. 3.

On the Prince

1. The first character of the title *Yüan chün* has a verbal force: "getting to the source [of something]," which would be lost if the title were simply translated as the "Origin of Princes." Here *yüan* means studying not only the historical origin but also the basis or nature of the prince. Following Legge, I have used "prince" in its primary meaning of *monarch* or *sovereign* to render the Chinese *chün*, which in classical literature applies to any prince or lord entitled to respect, be he emperor, king, duke, or baron.

2. Hsü Yu was a legendary philosopher and ascetic, revered by the Taoists, who is said to have refused the throne when Emperor Yao offered it to him, and to have washed out his ears lest they be contaminated by talk of holding high office (*Shih chi* 61:6a; Huang Fu-mi, *Kao shih chuan*, SPPY ed., A:2b–3a; James Legge, *The Texts of Taoism, Kwang-tze* (hereafter, *Kwang-tze*) 1:169–70; Giles, no. 797). However, the more proximate source of Huang's reference is probably the *Po-ya ch'in* of the Sung Taoist and poet Teng Mu (1247–1306; also, see the introduction).

Wu Kuang was offered the throne by T'ang the Completer, but refused it. Weighing himself down with a stone, he jumped into a river where he remained for over four hundred years. He reappeared in the time of Wu Ting of Shang (c. 1324 B.C.), who likewise offered him the throne. Again Wu Kuang refused and went back to his former seclusion (Liu Hsiang, *Lieh hsien chuan, Shuo-fu* ed., ts'e 59:2b; Legge, *Kwang-tze*, 1:329 and 2:162–63).

These two examples were undoubtedly drawn by Huang from Teng Mu's *Po-ya ch'in*, as explained in the introduction.

3. Yao and Shun were legendary emperors of China's Golden Age (2300–2200 B.C.?). Yao took Shun as his minister, and after a successful partnership in ruling, set aside his own son so that Shun might succeed him as emperor (Legge, *Shoo King,* in *Chinese Classics* 3:16–51; *Shih chi* 1:10a–20a, 20a–31a; Chavannes, *Memoires Historiques* 1:42–96; Giles, nos. 2436, 1741).

4. Yü (or the Great Yü). During the time of the Emperor Shun he saved the empire from a great flood, for which service he was ennobled and made a minister, eventually succeeding Shun on the throne as first emperor of the Hsia dynasty (Legge, *Shoo King,* in *Chinese Classics* 3:52–61; *Shih chi* 2:1a–26a; Chavannes, *Memoires Historiques* 1:79–81, 97–163; Giles, no. 1846).

5. After his conquest of the empire, Han Kao-ti (or Han Kao-tsu), the founder of

the Former Han dynasty, held an audience for all his ministers and vassals at which he drank a toast to his father and said: "At first you, sire, continually thought of me, your servant, as a good-for-nothing, one who could not apply himself to any professional occupation, who was not as industrious as my brother. Now who has achieved the more, I or my elder brother?" H. H. Dubs, *History of the Former Han Dynasty* 1:199; *Shih chi* 8:34a. See also *The Cambridge History of China*, vol. 1 (Denis Twitchett and Michael Loewe, eds.), ch. 2 (esp. pp. 110–28). Previously, Kao-tsu had named his brother King of Tai, but the latter had forsaken his kingdom for fear of a Hsiung-nu invasion.

What Dubs above and Chavannes (*Memoires Historiques* 1:392–93) translate as "achievement" or "task accomplished" (*yeh*) can also be understood as "property acquired," "estate." Huang's use of the word elsewhere in this passage shows that he understands it in the latter sense.

6. For the term *chu*, "master" could also be translated as "host," but in China, as in the West, the relationship between host and guest most often suggests that the former is obliged to accommodate the latter, in accordance with long-standing traditions of hospitality. Yet Huang obviously means that the guest has no rights, being at the mercy of the host's generosity, and thus "master" conveys better the idea of primacy, superiority, or sovereignty as Huang intends it here, and "tenant" the subordination of the people to the ruler.

7. Legge, *Mencius* 4B:3.

8. *Shang shu*, T'ai-shih B, SPTK, 6:5b, and *Mencius* 1B:8 in reference to the last ruler of Shang (see note 10 below).

9. The original quotation is from *Chuang Tzu*, Jen-chien shih, SPTK, *Nan-hua chen-ching* 2:16b. It is also found in the *Surviving Writings of the Ch'eng Brothers* (*Erh Ch'eng i-shu* 5:77 Erh hsien-sheng yü in *Erh Ch'eng chi*, Beijing: 1981), where it has a different meaning (i.e., the constant relation between prince and minister is a mutual commitment to moral principle, not an inescapable obligation to serve). If prince and minister do not agree on principles, according to Ch'eng I and Chu Hsi, the minister should leave the prince's service. See *Ts'ui-yen*, Chün-ch'en pien, 2:1242–1247.

10. T'ang the Completer overthrew the last emperor of the Hsia dynasty, Chieh Kuei, and inaugurated the Shang dynasty. According to traditional accounts, Chieh was a vicious tyrant whose wickedness aroused the people to revolt under T'ang's leadership.

Wu, the first emperor of the Chou dynasty, successfully concluded the war undertaken by his father, King Wen, against the Shang dynasty under the despot Chou Hsin. In Confucian literature Chou Hsin and Chieh Kuei were condemned for their extravagance and cruelty, just as T'ang and Wu were praised for their great virtue and wisdom (Legge, *Shoo King*, in *Chinese Classics* 3:173–90, 268–319; Chavannes, *Memoires Historiques* 1:169–207, 221–24).

11. A story found in Ssu-ma Ch'ien's *Shih chi* (61:1a–6b). Po I and Shu Ch'i went to see King Wen of Chou, hearing of his gracious hospitality toward the old and wise, but before they reached him Wen died. According to this version of the events at that time, the next king, Wu, was in such haste to overthrow the Shang

emperor, Chou Hsin, that he went off to war without observing the proper mourning for his father. Po I and Shu Ch'i criticized him for his lack of filial piety toward his father and lack of good faith in attacking his sovereign. After Wu's successful conquest of Shang, Po I and Shu Ch'i refused to acknowledge Wu's claim to the empire, would not eat the food provided for them by him, and eventually starved to death.

This account has aroused considerable controversy, owing to the fact that the *Analects* and *Mencius* comment favorably upon Po I and Shu Ch'i for their loyalty and purity, while this version puts the Confucian hero, King Wu, in an especially bad light. Among those who questioned the authenticity of the *Shih chi* biography were the Sung statesman Wang An-shih and the Ch'ing scholar Ts'ui Shu 1740–1816 (*Analects* 5:22, 6:14, 15:12, 18:8; *Mencius* 2B:2, 5B:1, 6B:6, 7B:15; Wang An-shih, *Lin-ch'uan hsien-sheng wen-chi,* SPTK 63:9b; Ts'ui Shu (1740–1816), *Feng-hao k'ao-hsin lu,* TSCC 8:145–150).

12. *Chuang Tzu,* Autumn Floods, SPTK *Nan-hua chen-ching* 6:28a; Burton Watson, trans., *The Complete Works of Chuang Tzu,* p. 188.

13. This refers to Mencius' justification of the people's overthrowing of a tyrant. To kill a tyrant is not regicide since a tyrant cannot be considered a king. "King Hsüan of Ch'i asked, saying 'Was it so in the records?' The king said, 'May a minister then put his sovereign to death?' Mencius said, 'He who outrages the benevolence proper to his nature is called a robber; he who outrages righteousness is called a ruffian. The robber and ruffian we call a mere fellow. I have heard of cutting off the fellow Chou, but I have not heard of putting a sovereign to death in his case'" (Legge, *Mencius* 1B:18).

14. This no doubt refers to the expurgation of *Mencius* on the order of Chu Yüan-chang, the first Ming emperor (r. as Hung-wu, 1368–98), who had strong feelings concerning the classics and their Sung interpreters, but especially objected to Mencius' demeaning of the ruler and exalting of the people. In 1394 the Chancellor of the Hanlin Academy, Liu San-wu (1313–99), compiled an expurgated version, *Meng-tzu chieh-wen,* eliminating 85 objectionable passages and presenting the remaining 170-odd passages as the essential and valid teaching of Mencius. This was disseminated for official use, and it was forbidden to use expurgated passages as themes in the examination system (*Wu-shih-wan chüan lou ts'ang-shu mu-lu, ch'u-pien* 3:160b–162a; L. C. Goodrich, trans., "A Study of Literary Persecution During the Ming [by Ku Chieh-kang]," pp. 299–301; *Ming shih* 127:3769, 139:3981; DMB, pp. 381–92, 956–58). An unexpurgated version, in the *Ssu-shu ta-ch'üan* was promulgated for official use by the third Yung-lo emperor (r. 1403–25), but the choice of accompanying commentary, and deletion of Chu Hsi's endorsement of Mencius, greatly softened its effect. See *Meng-tzu chi-chu ta-ch'üan* (Taiwan: Commercial Press *Ssu-k'u ch'üan-shu* chen pen ed.) 8:5b–6a (pp. 205, 298–99), Commentary on *Mencius* 4B:3.

15. *Chuang Tzu,* Ch'ü-ch'ieh p'ien, SPTK 6:15b; Watson, trans., *Complete Works,* p. 107.

16. Quotation from Ssu-ma Kuang's *Tzu-chih t'ung-chien* (SPTK 135:2b) concerning Shun-ti (r. 477–479), last sovereign of the Liu Sung dynasty. Ascending the

throne as a boy, in 477, he was forced to abdicate two years later when Hsiao Tao-ch'eng seized power and founded the Southern Ch'i dynasty (479–482). When the latter's men broke into the palace, the young king asked tearfully, "Are you going to kill me?" He was told, "You must move to another palace, just the way your ancestor once had the Ssu-ma do [the previous reigning house]." The boy sobbed, "I pray that I shall never again, in any life or reincarnation, be born in a royal house" (original quotation from *Nan shih* SPTK 45:3a). Shun-ti was then taken away and finally murdered.

With this simple quotation, Huang is able to suggest all the sordid violence attending the seizure and loss of power by dynasty after dynasty. The fate of Shun-ti—his abdication, house arrest, and murder—duplicates the fate of the last emperor of the Eastern Chin (A.D. 317–420) at the hands of Shun-ti's forebear.

17. I-tsung: one of the canonical names given to the last Ming emperor, Chu Yu-chien (r. 1628–44), by some of the Ming adherents active in South China after his death. When Peking was surrounded by Li Tzu-ch'eng (1605?–45) in April 1644, I-tsung rejected the proposals sent to him by the rebel chief, arranged for the escape, if possible, of his sons, and then killed his wives and daughters to prevent their falling into enemy hands. To his eldest daughter, just fifteen, he cried, "Why were you born into my house!" and then cut her down with his sword. Soon after, he went up Coal Hill and hung himself. Cf. Ch'ien Chih, *Chia-shen ch'üan-hsin lu,* 1883 ed., 6:13a; *Ch'ung-chen shih-lu,* NLWH 8:233; *Ming shih* 121:3677, Kung-chu lieh-chuan; Arthur W. Hummel, ed., *Eminent Chinese of the Ch'ing Period* (hereafter, ECCP), pp. 191–92; *Cambridge History of China,* vol. 7 (*The Ming Dynasty,* ed. Frederick W. Mote and Denis Twitchett), chapter on "The Ch'ung-chen Reign," by William Atwell (New York: Cambridge University Press, 1988).

18. T'ang: another name for the Emperor Yao. His father had invested him with the principalities of T'ao and T'ang, whence he came to be known as T'ao T'ang Shih. Yü is another name for Shun, which derives from his place of origin, Yü-mu in Honan (*Shih chi* 1:10a–15a; Chavannes, *Mémoires Historiques* 1:42 and 52*n*1).

On Ministership

1. A transposition of an expression found in the *Li chi,* Ch'ü-li, SPTK 1:6a, which according to the commentator Cheng Hsüan enjoins upon the filial son a constant attentiveness to the behests of his parents. Legge translates it: "He should be [as if he were] hearing [his parents] when there is no voice from them, and as seeing them when they are not actually there" (*Li Ki* 1:69). Here it cannot be translated as "not actually there," because it is clear from the passage following that this is a question of discerning desires that are actually there but simply unexpressed, unformulated.

2. *Li chi,* Sang-fu ssu chih, 63:22b.

3. *Tso chuan,* 25th Year of Duke Hsiang, *Ch'un-ch'iu ching-chuan chi-chieh,* SPTK 17:11a.

4. Ch'in dynasty (246–207 B.C.): the first imperial dynasty, which collapsed soon after the death of its founder, Ch'in Shih Huang-ti. See *Cambridge History of China,*

vol. 1 (*The Ch'in and Han Empires,* ed. Denis Twitchett and Michael Loewe), ch. 1 (by Derk Bodde). The Mongol or Yüan dynasty (A.D. 1280–1368) was comparatively short-lived and was often looked upon as foreign by Chinese scholars of the Ming period.

5. Kingdoms of the Six Dynasties period, which was fraught with strife and disorder: Chin (A.D. 265–419); Sung (420–479); Ch'i (479–501); Liang (502–556).

6. Legge, *Mencius* 3B:5.

7. *Huai-nan tzu,* SPTK, 1st ser., 12:2a.

8. Reading *kung* "together" for *ch'i* "their" (cf. *Hai-shan hsien-kuan* ed., 5a, 1.8).

9. Shen-tsung: the canonical name of the emperor who ruled during the Wan-li period (1573–1619). See DMB, pp. 324–38 (biography by Charles Hucker); and *Cambridge History of China,* vol. 7 (Mote and Twitchett, eds.), ch. 9 (by Ray Huang).

10. Counselor *shih fu:* refers to those followers of Confucius who served as itinerant advisers to the rulers of various states during the period of the Contending States (403–221 B.C.). According to the *Shih chi,* "After the death of Confucius, his disciples dispersed and visited the various lords, the more important of them serving as counselors and ministers" (*Shih chi* 121:1b).

11. Chang's power rested on an alliance with the eunuch Feng Pao (n.d., active 1530–92). On Chang Chü-cheng, see DMB, pp. 53–61; Robert B. Crawford, "Chang Chü-cheng's Confucian Legalism," pp. 367–413; Ray Huang, *1587—A Year of No Significance* (New Haven: Yale University Press, 1981), pp. 23–26, 59–65; *Cambridge History of China,* vol. 7 (Mote and Twitchett, eds.), ch. 9 (esp. pp. 518–32).

12. In the classics the relation of minister (*ch'en*) to prince, and son to father, are frequently linked together, as in the *Li chi:* "The ceremonies . . . of mourning and sacrifice . . . illustrate the kindly feelings of minister and son" (Legge, *Li Ki* 2:258–59). This usage is akin to the Confucian emphasis on the Five Relations or Five Duties of Universal Obligation; between parent and child, sovereign and minister, husband and wife, elder and younger brothers, and between friends (cf. *Mencius* 2B:2, 3A:4; *Great Learning* 20:8). Mencius, however, insisted on the virtual parity of prince and minister because of their shared commitment to rightness (*i*), and said a minister should leave a prince if they had no such agreement on what is right (2B:5, 14; 4B:3; 5B:9). On the later perversion of this relationship into a more servile one, especially under Ming autocracy, see Sano Kōji, "*Min-i taihō roku* ni okeru eki-sei kakumei shisō," pp. 136–40.

13. *Mencius* 4B:3: "When the prince regards his minister as a mere dog or horse, the minister regards the prince as any other man of the country." Chu Hsi renders "man of the country" as "anyone met on the road" (*lu-jen*), and Huang uses Chu's term, not Mencius.' Cf. *Meng Tzu chi-chu* 4B:3, Chung-kuo tzu-hsüeh ming-chu chi-ch'eng ed. (hereafter, CKTHMCCC), 10:15a, p. 781.

14. Chuang Tzu was often quoted for his attribution to Confucius of the view that the relationship of prince and minister was as unalterable and inescapable as that of parent and child (*Chuang Tzu* 2:16b). Chu Hsi agreed that the principle of a mutual commitment to rightness (*i*) was unalterable, but there was no such relation

based on blind personal loyalty. Further, he agreed with Mencius that if the ruler lacked such a commitment, the minister should leave. In other words the underlying principle was changeless, but the personal relationship was contractual and became void if there were no agreement in principle. Huang agrees with Chu Hsi (*Meng-tzu chi-chu* 4B:3, CKTHMCCC ed., 10:15a, p. 781). See also ibid., 2B:5, 14, and 5B:9; *Chu Tzu wen-chi* 82:9b–10a; Pa Sung chün chung-chia chi and *Erh Ch'eng i-shu* (Chung-hua ed.) 5:76–77, where Ch'eng I and Chu Hsi affirm the invariable principle of being in accord on what is right, but with it the obligation to withdraw if there is no such agreement.

On Law

1. The Two Emperors: Yao and Shun; the Three Kings: Yü of Hsia, T'ang of Shang, and Wen and Wu of Chou together.

2. In the third century B.C., as the Ch'in absorbed other states in their conquest of the empire, they organized them into commanderies (*chün*) and prefectures (*hsien*) under a unified system of administration. The Grand Councillor, Li Ssu, a proponent of this system, was supported by Ch'in Shih Huang-ti in opposing a feudal restoration with domains under the rule of imperial princes. However, they did not actually originate this system of territorial organization. Of the forty commanderies in the Ch'in empire, twelve had previously been established by other states and some prefectures had existed since the Spring and Autumn period (722–481 B.C.). *Shih chi* 6:6a–23a; Chavannes, *Memoires Historiques* 2:131–32; Derk Bodde, *China's First Unifier*, pp. 22–23, 238–46; *Cambridge History of China*, vol. 1 (Twitchett and Loewe, eds.) pp. 54–56 (Bodde chapter).

3. "In the last years of Han Kao-tsu . . . there were nine kingdoms over which reigned kings who were the sons or younger brothers of Kao-tsu, or had the same family name as he." Ssu-ma Ch'ien explains: "When the empire was conquered by Kao-tsu those of the same blood and family as he were not very numerous. That is why he gave vast domains and great power to his sons by wives of second rank, so that they might keep the peace within the Four Seas, and aid and protect the Son of Heaven." *Shih chi* 8:33b; Chavannes, *Memoires Historiques* 3:87–90; *Cambridge History of China* 1:123–27 (Loewe chapter).

4. Military commanderies (*fang-chen* or *fan-chen*): a decentralized system of military control that prevailed in the T'ang dynasty but was abolished by the Sung in favor of centralized control.

5. Huang further elaborates this point in the newly discovered work called *Liu-shu*. See *Huang Tsung-hsi ch'üan-chi* 1:418–20.

6. *Chuang Tzu*, Ta tsung shih, SPTK 3:9a; Watson, trans., *Complete Works of Chuang Tzu*, p. 81.

7. *Yen Tzu ch'ün-ch'iu*, SPTK 6:19b.

8. *Hsien-chang*: means to uphold the laws and institutions established by the founder of the dynasty; it is an expression applied to Confucius, who "elegantly displayed the regulations of Wen and Wu (founders of the Chou dynasty), taking them as his model" (Legge, *Doctrine of the Mean* 30:1, in *Chinese Classics*, vol. 1).

9. *Li chi,* Ch'ü li, SSCCS 2:9a.

10. *Hsün Tzu,* Chün-tao p'ien, SPTK 8:1a.

11. There is a slight variation in the texts here. See Nishida Taichirō, trans., *Min-i taihō roku* (Tokyo: Heibonsha, 1964), p. 29. I follow the *Quanji* version, 1:7.

12. In Hsün Tzu's discussion of the "Way of the Ruler," he says, "It is men that govern, not laws" (Wang Hsien-ch'ien, *Hsün Tzu chi-chieh* 8:1a; Chu Hsi implicitly amended this when he said in his commentary on the *Great Learning* that it is by self-cultivation and self-discipline that the governance of men is accomplished (*Ta-hsüeh chang-chu,* in *Ssu-shu chi-chu,* CKTHMCCC 13:32).

Establishing a Prime Minister

1. *Chih-hsiang:* the term Huang uses most often for prime minister (*tsai-hsiang*) is a common, but not a formal, title in Chinese official history. At times, two or three men were so designated concurrently, in which case "chief councillor" is a more appropriate translation. But to Huang's mind there should be only one such, and therefore it means here "prime minister." He uses *ch'eng-hsiang* occasionally as its equivalent in what follows. Cf. Robert des Rotours, *Traité des Fonctionnaires et Traité de l'Armée* 1:4; Edward A. Kracke, *Civil Service in Early Sung China,* pp. 30–32; Hucker, no. 6819 ("Counsellor in Chief").

2. *Kao Huang-ti:* i.e., the founder of the dynasty, whose canonical name was T'ai-tsu and reign name Hung-wu (r. 1368–98). In 1380, following the execution of the prime minister, Hu Wei-yung, for plotting against the throne, the prime ministership (*ch'eng-hsiang*) was abolished together with its chief agency of administration (the *chung-shu sheng*), and the Six Ministries were made independent of centralized control. By making the heads of the Six Ministries directly responsible to the emperor, T'ai-tsu hoped to keep any one man from obtaining sufficient power to rival the throne. However, this placed a burden of administration upon the emperor too great for him to cope with and led to the exercise of executive functions by members of his cabinet and eunuchs. *Ming shih* 72:1729; DMB, pp. 638–41; Edward L. Farmer, *Early Ming Government: The Evolution of Dual Capitals,* pp. 30–40, 80; *Cambridge History of China,* vol. 7. (Mote and Twitchett, eds.), ch. 3 (by John D. Langlois, Jr.).

3. Part of Mencius' description of the enfeoffment system as he supposed it to have existed during the early Chou dynasty, c. 1000 B.C. (cf. *Mencius* 5B:2).

4. That is, the relationship of the emperor to the enfeoffed nobility ruling outside his own immediate domain but within the empire.

5. That is, the emperor's relationship to the officials of his court administering directly his own domain around the capital. The point of this passage is to show that in ancient times (i.e., ideally) the emperor's power and dignity were not absolute but relative to a gradually ascending hierarchy of rank, both within his own feudal domain and in China as a whole. Cf. Naitō Torajirō, *Shina ron,* pp. 9, 38, 53, 269.

6. Chou Kung: the fourth son of King Wen of Chou and younger brother of King Wu. He served as counselor to the latter and on Wu's death assumed the regency for seven years during the minority of King Ch'eng. He is frequently spoken

of by Confucius as a model statesman of antiquity. Legge, *Shoo King,* in *Chinese Classics* 3:351–75; *Shih chi* 33:1a; Chavannes, *Memoires Historiques* 1:244–47. For *I Yin,* see translation, "Preface of Huang Tsung-hsi," note 8.

7. *Ho-han:* literally, "Milky Way" (an expression in *Chuang Tzu,* SPTK 1:22b, for something that can be laughed off).

8. In *Analects* 16:2, it is said that these functions normally are performed by the emperor; but in *Analects* 14:43, Confucius said that in ancient times the practice was for the new ruler to observe three years of mourning, during which time the prime minister would direct the government.

9. *Li chi,* Yen-i, SSCCS 62:19a.

10. Pan Ku, *Han shu,* SPTK 84:3b. According to Yen Shih-ku's commentary, this was the Han ritual.

11. Hundred Offices: i.e., all the government officials.

12. *ju-ko:* a term indicating the transaction of state business in the Wen-yüan ko where private audiences with the emperor were held for that purpose.

The Wen-yüan ko was one of four original chambers (*tien*) and cabinets (*ko*) established by the Emperor T'ai-tsu in 1382 on the model of similar institutions in the Sung. The Wen-yüan ko of the Ming was staffed with Hanlin scholars, and in keeping with its name "Cabinet of Profound Learning," the original function of these scholars was as private advisers to the emperor in matters of learning, and as editors of classical texts and historical documents. In the absence of a prime minister, however, the advisory functions of this group were gradually expanded, so that in the Yung-lo period (1403–24) their function was spoken of as "deliberating on matters of state in cabinet." After the accession of Jen-tsung (1424), members of the cabinet such as Yang Shih-ch'i (1365–1444) and Yang Jung (1371–1440) were concurrently ministers of state, and by the reign of Ying-tsung (1435) the cabinet had come to perform most of the duties once attaching to the prime ministership. Liao Tao-nan, *Tien-ko tz'u-lin chi,* Hupei hsien-cheng i-shu ed. 9:1a, 1b; 5a–10b; *Ming shih,* 72:1732–34; DMB, p. 1537; and Yamamoto Takayoshi, "Mindai no naikaku" in *Tōyōshi kenkyū* 20, no. 2 (September 1961): 24–42.

13. "Endorsement" is the translation suggested by Fairbank and Teng for *p'i* (an abbreviation of *p'i-ta,* which is used in the present text), but it is to be understood in a sense similar to the signing of a check, not as necessarily indicating approval. The endorsement might consist of any notation as to the action to be taken in response to a memorial, or simply the comment, "Contents noted." After the abolition of the prime ministership by Ming T'ai-tsu, all materials had to be presented to the emperor directly, and then the endorsements were written up by Hanlin scholars on the basis of his expressed desires. In the Hsüan-te period (1426–36), the "grand secretaries" were ordered to make endorsements in black ink and attach them to the face of the memorial, the emperor later signing in red. In cases of extreme urgency and importance, the chief ministers (who were also grand secretaries) were to deliberate and make a decision without waiting for the emperor's personal endorsement. Liao Tao-nan, *Tien-ko tz'u-lin chi* 9:10b–11a; J. K. Fairbank and S. Y. Teng, "On the Types and Uses of Ch'ing Documents," pp. 17–18, 57.

14. Court clerks: the term *k'ai-fu,* translated here as "court," originally meant to open an office and staff it with officials. In the Former Han this was a privilege

reserved to the Three Dukes, who presided over the three courts of the central administration. Later this privilege was extended to top-ranking generals, and still later to military governors. However, Huang probably has the ancient institution in mind and means that the grand secretaries of the Ming cabinets were more like cabinet clerks than prime ministers (Tu Yu, *T'ung-tien* 3:193; Wang Yang-lin, *Yü hai* 120:19a; Ma Tuan-lin, [*Ch'in-ting*] *Wen-hsien t'ung-k'ao*, Commercial Press *Shih-t'ung* ed., 64:575).

15. Literally, "from inside" (i.e., from the eunuchs). See *Ming shih* 72:1730.

16. Vice-premiers (*ts'an-chih cheng shih*): a post originally created during the T'ang and continued by the Sung, Liao, Chin, and Yüan, but abolished during the Hung-wu reform of the early Ming. At times this post was on a par with the prime minister's in actual importance, and at others immediately subordinate to the latter. During the Sung it was generally the rule to have five premiers and vice-premiers in all, either three of one and two of the other or vice versa. Hucker, no. 6872, renders it "assistant administrator," but vice-premier seems more indicative of the level of importance attached to it by Huang. *Yü-hai* 120:21b; *T'ung-k'ao* 49:451ab; *Ming shih* 72:159c; Kracke, *Civil Service in Early Sung China,* pp. 30–32.

17. Supervising secretaries of the Six Offices of Scrutiny (*liu-ko chi-shih-chung*): i.e., the heads of the six sections of the Censorate, which scrutinized the affairs of the Six Ministries (Mayers, no. 188; Hucker, nos. 1587, 3793).

18. *p'i-hung* ("endorse in red"): the context indicates endorsement in red by the emperor's own hand. The term *p'i-hung* was used in the Ch'ing for an endorsement written by members of the Grand Secretariat with imperial approval (Fairbank and Teng, "On the Types and Uses of Ch'ing Documents." pp. 17–18, 57). Huang's use of *p'i-hung* corresponds to the Vermillion Endorsement (*Chu-p'i*) cited by Fairbank and Teng, ibid., p. 49.

19. Hall of State Affairs (*cheng-shih t'ang*): a hall in which the high ministers met each day to deliberate on and decide matters of state during the T'ang. At the beginning of the dynasty it was located in the Department of the Imperial Chancellery (*Men-hsia sheng*) and after 684 in the Department of the Grand Secretariat (*chung-shu sheng*). *Yü-hai* 120:22a; Rotours, *Traité de Fonctionnaires,* pp. 11–12; Hucker, no. 3939.

20. Probationers (*tai-chao*): a term first used during the reign of Han Wu-ti for scholars who had been selected for service at court and were serving a sort of internship in advisory capacities while awaiting official appointment. With the establishment of the Hanlin Imperial Academy in the T'ang, these probationers were assigned to the Hanlin, where they were classified according to their capacities in classical studies and the various arts, and pursued their studies or academic duties while waiting for a post. The Emperor Hsüan-tsung used some of these scholars to perform secretarial and advisory functions in the disposition of memorials, preparation of edicts, and other state papers. Thereafter, the term *tai-chao* was used as a specific title for low-ranking officials in the Sung, Ming, and Ch'ing dynasties who performed such functions. Huang probably uses it in the generic sense, not as a title. *Han shu* 65:1a., 2b, 78:12b, 13a; *Hsin T'ang Shu* 46:2b, 3a; *Yü-hai* 120:22a; *T'ung-k'ao* 49:450c; see also Hucker, no. 6127 ("Expectant Official").

21. Chang Yüeh (667–730): According to the *Hsin T'ang shu,* "When Chang

Yüeh became Prime Minister [in A.D. 723] he reorganized the Hall of State Affairs and called it the Grand Secretariat and Chancellery. He created five offices behind it, etc. [as quoted by Huang]. All affairs were brought together under the control of the prime minister" (*Hsin T'ang shu* 46:2b, 3a; *Yü-hai* 120:22a; *T'ung-k'ao* 49:450c). For biographies of Chang Yüeh, see *Hsin T'ang shu* 125:5a–9a; Rotours, *Traité des Fonctionnaires*, p. 12n2; *Cambridge History of China*, vol. 3 (*Sui and T'ang China*, ed. Denis Twitchett and John K. Fairbank), pp. 376–79.

22. Hucker, no. 5418.
23. Hucker, no. 4672.
24. Hucker, no. 2781.
25. Hucker, no. 2584.

Schools

1. *P'i-yung* (lit., "bright harmony"). During the Chou dynasty following a Shang tradition, "the College of the Son of Heaven was called the [palace of] Bright Harmony." Cf. SSCCS *Li chi* 5:9b; Legge, *Li Ki* 1:219.

2. *Pan-ch'ao*, or "assigning places at court," is the meaning of this expression as found in SSCCS *Li chi* 1:2b (Legge, *Li Ki* 1:64), but where, however, it has no connection with schools. The commentaries of Cheng Hsüan and K'ung Ying-ta (on the passage in the *Li chi* to which Huang refers at the end of this sentence) interpret *pan* as "to debate principles and policies in the schools and put them into effect for men to observe" (SSCCS *Li chi* 15:9b). This sense seems to parallel Huang's coupling of *pan-ch'ao* with *pu-ling* "to publicize decrees."

3. According to the Royal Institutes of the *Li chi*, during the Chou period men "of 50 years received their nourishment in the [schools of the] districts; those of 60, theirs in the smaller school of the state; and those of 70 in the College" (Legge, *Li Ki* 1:240). "The Minister of Instruction defined and set forth the six ceremonial observances: . . . nourished the aged [officials], to secure the completion of filial piety; showed pity to orphans and solitaries, to reach those who had been bereaved" (ibid. 1:230; *Wen-hsien t'ung-k'ao* 40:379a).

4. *Hsin kuo* (lit., to interrogate [prisoners] and cut off the left ears [of the slain). "When the Son of Heaven was about to go forth on a punitive expedition, he . . . received his charge from his ancestors, and the complete plan of executing it in the College. He went forth accordingly, and seized the criminals; and on his return set forth in the College his offerings, and announced [to his ancestors] how he had questioned [his prisoners] and cut off the ears [of the slain]" (Legge, *Li Ki* 1:220).

5. *Ta-shih-lü: Shih-lü* ordinarily refers to a unit of military organization, but here it must mean an event or occasion, especially with the prefix *ta* ("great") indicating the imperial (or princely) presence, reviewing or leading the troops. The probable source for this statement (and for the reference to *"Judicial proceedings"* that follows) is the commentary of K'ung Ying-ta on the song *Pan shin* in the Book of Odes (SSCCS *Shih ching* 21:36b). This song has been traditionally interpreted as describing a military review at the royal college of the state of Lu, accompanied by the presentation of the ears of the vanquished and a judgment of the fate of enemy

leaders taken captive during punitive expeditions. Cf. Edoard Biot, *Essai sur l'histoire d'Instruction Publique en Chine,* pp. 39–40, 43.

6. The foregoing list of functions served by the College is similar to, and may have been taken in part from, one quoted by Ma Tuan-lin from the *Chih-chiang hsien hsin-hsüeh chi* of Hsiang An-shih (c.s. 1175, d. 1208). Hsiang, a Sung dynasty writer, advocated a universal school system reaching down to every village of twenty-five families or more, but entirely independent of the court and central administration. Huang's proposals are similar to this (*T'ung-k'ao* 40:381:C).

7. See note 3 in the section on "Subofficials."

8. With the decline (during the late T'ang, Five Dynasties, and Sung periods) of the official school system devoted to the preparation of men for government service through the examination system, academies grew up around some of the better private libraries, where serious and independent study could be carried on by men whose primary interest was in true learning rather than official advancement. See Thomas H. C. Lee, "Sung Education Before Chu Hsi," in W. T. de Bary and John Chaffee, eds., *Neo-Confucian Education: The Formative Stage* (New York: Columbia University Press, 1989), pp. 105–36.

9. The proscription of the Chu Hsi school at the end of the twelfth century. See Conrad Schirokauer, "Neo-Confucians Under Attack: The Condemnation of Wei-hsüeh," in John Winthrop Haeger, ed., *Crisis and Prosperity in Sung China,* pp. 163–98.

10. During the Ming dynasty three attempts were made to suppress the academies on the charge of heterodox and subversive teaching: in 1537–38, when Chan Jo-shui (1466–1560) was condemned; in 1579 when Chang Chü-cheng attempted unsuccessfully to destroy the academies; and in 1625 when the powerful eunuch Wei Chung-hsien (DMB pp. 856–57) again ordered their destruction, followed by a purge of "subversives" associated with the Tung-lin Academy of Wu-hsi. Huang has the last period in mind here. *Ming shih* 20:266; 22:303; Ch'ien Mu, *Chung-kuo chin san-pai-nien hsüeh-shu shih,* pp. 7–8; John Meskill, *Academies in Ming China,* pp. 66–159, and Meskill, "Academies and Politics in the Late Ming," in Charles O. Hucker, ed., *Chinese Government in Ming Times,* pp. 149–74.

11. Huang himself cites such a case in his account of Chuang Ch'ang (1437–99; c.s. 1466), which repeats the charge in the same language. In 1457 as a Hanlin bachelor, Chuang, together with two colleagues, submitted memorials rebuking the emperor for his preoccupation with sexual pleasures. For this Chuang and colleagues were flogged at court in the emperor's presence, and Chuang was banished to Kuei-yang. Later rehabilitated, for some years he refused to serve and was accused by the scholar and statesman Ch'iu Chün (1420–95) of "leading scholars throughout the land, into defiance of the court" (*Shuai t'ien-hsia shih pei ch'ao-t'ing*). Ch'iu claimed that the Ming founder T'ai-tsu had made refusal to serve a punishable offense. The remainder of Chuang's life was marked by brief periods of service and long periods of "retirement." Huang says that Chuang's learning emphasized the inexpressibility in words of one's own self-realization of the Way (*wu-yen tzu-te*), a silence that did not preclude also speaking out at court! Huang, *Ming-ju hsüeh-an* (hereafter, MJHA) 45:14; *Ming shih* 179:4754; DMB, p. 96.

12. A quotation from the *History of the Latter Han Dynasty,* describing the activity of scholars at the Imperial Academy who met together to discuss measures taken by the court and to express their opposition to the growing influence of eunuchs in the last years of the Emperor Huan (A.D. 147–168). As a result of their meetings this Confucian group, together with similar conferences of scholars elsewhere in the empire, came to be known as "party men" or "oppositionists" (*tang-jen*). In A.D. 167 over two hundred "party men" were brought into the government. A life-and-death struggle with the eunuchs ensued, which ended in the execution or imprisonment of the party men by successive purges in 168, 170, and 172. *Hou-Han shu* 7:17ab, 8:2b and 3a, 96:7a ff.; 97:1a ff.; Biot, *Essai sur l'histoire,* pp. 189–92; Tjan Tjoe-som, *Po-hu t'ung* (Leiden: Brill, 1943), pp. 146–65.

13. Li Kang (1083–1140). During the last year of the Northern Sung (1126) when Chin (Jurchen) armies threatened the capital of K'ai-feng, the peace faction in the government secured the dismissal of Li Kang, leading proponent of a last-ditch fight, as a means of appeasing the Chin and clearing the way for a settlement. Led by Ch'en Tung (1086–1127), an appointee to the Imperial College, thousands of scholars, students, soldiers, and citizens of the capital assembled at the palace gate, beat the drum traditionally placed at the entrance to a *yamen* or court for the use of anyone demanding that his grievance be heard by the authorities, and presented a memorial protesting Li's dismissal. The demonstrators were successful in securing the reinstatement of Li Kang, but Li proved unable to hold back the Chin and a humiliating peace treaty had to be signed (*Sung shih* 23:4b, 358:1a, 359:1a, 455:1a-4a).

14. Ch'ien and Ou. Just after the accession of Kao-tsung (r. 1127–62), first emperor of the Southern Sung, Ch'en Tung (see note 13 above) and Ou-yang Ch'e (1090–1127) protested violently against the abandonment of Li Kang's defense plans by the minister Huang Ch'ien-shan (?–1129), who subsequently silenced their attacks upon him by having them executed together in the marketplace—rather than banished, as Huang's use of *pien-kuan* suggests (*Sung shih* 455:3b, 4ab).

15. I.e., when the state of Ch'in (221–207 B.C.) unified China and abolished the enfeoffment system in the third century B.C.

16. Six Sections: See Hucker, no. 6916, and Huang's proposals concerning local government (see translation, "The Selection of Scholar-Officials, Part 2," section on *Junior Officials in Prefectures and Districts*).

17. Libationer (*t'ai-hsüeh chi-chiu*): i.e., chancellor or rector of the Imperial College. In ancient times at great feasts the honor of offering the first libation of wine was reserved for the oldest man present. Libationer thus became a term of the highest respect and in the Han was applied to the most learned of the court scholars. Between 275–280, under the Western Chin (265–316), the head of the Imperial College was designated libationer, a title that remained in use until the end of the Ch'ing dynasty. *T'ai-p'ing yü-lan* 236:1a, b; *Li-tai chih-kuan piao* 34:1a, 8a–13a; Mayers, no. 249; Hucker, no. 542.

18. *T'ai-hsüeh* (here "Imperial College") is rendered "National University" by Hucker (no. 6168). Since twentieth-century nationalists and republicans took strong exception to the idea that imperial dynasties represented the Chinese nation,

and used *kuo-li ta-hsüeh* to express the idea of a National University, it would seem that an institution (such as *t'ai-hsüeh*) identified with dynastic regimes rather than with a modern nation-state, should be distinguished from the modern one, so different from the *t'ai-hsüeh* in intent, form, and function.

19. Here Huang follows the recommendation of the Ch'eng brothers and Chu Hsi. See Ch'eng Hao and Ch'eng I, *Erh Ch'eng chi, Ming-tao wen-chi* 1:449–50, and *I-ch'uan wen-chi* 3:563; and Chu Hsi; *Ta-hsüeh chang-chü*, preface, p. 1b–3a.

20. *t'i-tu hsüeh-chen:* cf. Brunnert and Hagelstrom, no. 827; Hucker, nos. 6451, 6452.

21. *po-shih ti-tzu:* cf. Brunnert and Hagelstrom, no. 960; Hucker, no. 4754.

22. *ch'in-t'ien chien:* cf. Mayers, no. 249; Brunnert and Hagelstrom, no. 223; Hucker, no. 1185.

23. *t'ai-i-yüan:* cf. Mayers, no. 268; Brunnert and Hagelstrom, no. 233; Hucker, no. 6184.

24. Lit., "community wine-drinking" (*hsiang-yin-chiu*): a type of banquet originating in ancient times, the principal one of which was held every three years to "honor the worthy and nourish the aged" at the principal school of the district (*hsiang*). According to the commentator, K'ung Ying-ta, the worthy men so honored were those who had successfully completed a three-year course of instruction in the local school and were ready to serve in office. During the T'ang dynasty the ceremony was held annually for those who passed the official examinations. In the Ming it was held semiannually in each prefecture, department, and district under the auspices of the local magistrate and educational officer (SSCCS *Li chi* 61:12a; *I li* 8:4b; Seraphin Couvreur, *Li Ki* 2:652; Robert des Rotours, *Le Traité des Examens,* p. 144; *Ming shih* 56:1419–21).

25. Huang understood the "learning of principle" (*li-hsüeh*) to apply broadly to the Neo-Confucian teachings of both mind and principle developed in the Sung and Ming. See W. T. de Bary, *The Message of the Mind in Neo-Confucianism,* pp. 129–30.

26. With the standardization of the eight-legged essay for the Ming examination system, printers quickly exploited the commercial possibilities in the market among thousands of prospective candidates for guides to the composition of examination essays. *Chin-shih* papers from earlier examinations were first printed in the sixteenth century in the Soochow-Hangchow area (Huang's home territory), then in the North and in Fukien. In 1587 this practice became official when local schools were instructed to print the best papers of the period from 1488–1567 as models for candidates to study. Cf. K. T. Wu, "Ming Printing and Printers," p. 250.

27. The *Family Rituals of Chu Hsi (Chu Tzu chia-li),* also referred to as *Wen-kung chia li:* its attribution to Chu Hsi was later questioned (*Ssu-k'u t'i-yao* 22:5a) but subsequently confirmed. See Ueyama Shumpei, "Shushi no *Karei* to 'Girei keiden tsūkai,'" pp. 173–256; and Patricia Ebrey, *Chu Hsi's "Family Rituals".*

The "Family Rituals" contains regulations for the conduct of family ceremonies, including illustrations of clothing and accoutrements to be used in marriages and funerals, hearses, tablets, inscriptions, etc.; it is included in *Hsing-li ta-ch'üan* (Shih-ch'ü ko ed.), ch. 18–21.

28. Gods of Soil and Grain (*t'u-ku*): the most important of these gods were She and Chi (cf. SSCCS *Chou li* 18:6b, Commentary of Cheng Hsüan: "She and Chi were gods of the soil and grain [*t'u-ku*]"). Since She and Chi were associated with the tutelary gods of the Chou dynasty, Ch'u Lung, and Hou Chi (and also because the fertility of the soil and harvest of grain were considered the basis of the welfare of a state), their sacred altars became symbolic of the state itself and the ruling dynasty. In Ming times, following the traditional practice, the principal altars to She and Chi were maintained in the precincts of the Imperial Palace and subsidiary ones in each prefecture and district. Edouard Biot, *Le Tcheou-li ou Rites des Tcheou* 1:262, 421; Couvreur, *Li Ki* 1:83, 1:289; *Ming shih* 49:1265.)

The Selection of Scholar-Officials (Part 1)

1. There is considerable evidence of concern over the dearth of capable officials during the last Ming reign (1628–44) by leading writers, officials, and the emperor himself. An edict of 1633 instructed the Ministries of Rites and Civil Office to expand the processes of official selection in order to find men of ability and bring them into the government (*Ch'ung-chen shih-lu* 6:2b–3a; cf. also *T'u-shu chi-ch'eng* 25:115.4b; Fu Wei-lin, *Ming shu,* KHCPTS 63:1269). Details of the methods adopted and their operation are in some cases lacking, however, and the terms used here by Huang do not always correspond with official usage as known to me.

The term *pa-kung* refers to a Ming system more commonly known as *hsüan-chü* or to a special form derived from the latter, like that perpetuated as the *pa-kung* by the Ch'ing dynasty (cf. *Ch'eng wei-lu* 24:33b, 34a; Hucker, no. 4371). This form of selection provided competitive examinations for all students in official schools. Those selected by the provincial education intendant were sent to the capital, reexamined by the Ministry of Rites, and either assigned to office or sent back to their schools.

2. The term *Guaranteed Recommendation* (*pao-chü*) refers to a type of recommendation for office (*chien-chü*) by senior officials from among their subordinates or men known to them as worthy of office. Nominees were then examined at the capital by the Ministry of Personnel (originally by the Ministry of Rites) and assigned to office. To prevent abuse of this privilege, it was required that the official act as guarantor of the nominee, being punishable if any of the particulars of the recommendation were proved false or if the nominee was guilty of any misdemeanor in office (*Ming shih* 71:1719; *Ming shu* 63:1261–63, 1271, 1280; Hucker, no. 4468).

3. *Chün-kung* and *t'e-shou,* by which Huang refers to the selection of candidates from the supplementary lists of the provincial and metropolitan examinations respectively, are not formal designations used in official sources dealing with this subject. They may not have been considered regular features of the selection system, being exceptions to the regular procedure made in honor of an occasion or in case of special need. Through the general system of selection from official schools (the *kung* system) for those stipendiaries who had failed to advance through the regular examinations, it was possible for men who had taken the provincial examination

and been relegated to the supplementary list to be recommended for office. *Chun-kung* here may thus refer to what was usually called *en-kung*—recommendation of stipendiaries on special authorization of the emperor, since in official language *en* and *chun* were often coupled to signify an imperial dispensation (*Ming shih* 69:1676, 1681; *Ming shu* 64:1271).

4. The *chi-fen* system was used to test the progress of students in the Imperial College. Examinations on the classics were given each month and students rated according to a point system, receiving one point for a superior performance and one-half for an average performance. At the end of each year, those with eight points were promoted to the next class, and after three years they were recommended for office (*Ming shih* 69:1678; *Hsü t'ung-k'ao* 47:3219b).

5. *Huan-shou* generally indicates a method of recommending officials for transfer to other posts for which they might be well-fitted but would not normally be in line (*Sung shih* 437:7ab; *Ming shih* 71:1717, 1721). Huang suggests that this procedure was used to favor imperial clansmen, and Ku Yen-wu also speaks of this as a system adopted in the Ch'ung-chen period (1628–4) to give preferment to members of the royal house who lack a proper education (*Jih chih lu* 9:22). An instance of this may be the appointment of a royal relative, who had become a *chin-shih* through a special examination for members of the royal house, to be a bachelor (*shu-chi-shih*) of the Hanlin Academy, over the objections of the Board of Civil Office (*Ming shih* 70:1707).

6. Because provincial examiners, when permanently appointed to a given locality, were subject to local pressures and given to favoritism, in 1528 it was decided to send court officials (members of the Hanlin Academy or metropolitan graduates of the first class) to conduct provincial examinations. After a brief suspension from 1564 to 1582, this system was revived and remained in effect until the end of the dynasty (*Hsü-t'ung-k'ao* 35:3158c).

7. *i:* a general term for examinations on the meaning of the classics. In the Ming dynasty this would ordinarily involve composition of an eight-legged essay on passages in the Five Classics and the Four Books (*Ming shih* 70:1b).

8. *lun:* an essay form used since the T'ang dynasty to test the candidates' ability in prose composition. See Rotours, *Traité des Examens,* p. 31; *Ming shih* 70:1694.

9. In addition to a list of those who actually passed the examinations and obtained the degree sought for, a supplementary list was published with the names of about forty candidates whose work was not markedly inferior to that of the men accepted. In this way they received a consolation prize in the form of publicity. Mayers, no. 472; *Ming shih* 70:1693–94.

10. *chin-shih* (Hucker, "Presented Scholar," no. 1148): in the T'ang dynasty this degree was only one of many granted by the Ministry of Rites for which examinations were held at the capital. It gradually became the most important of them, however, and alone survived into the Sung, Ming, and Ch'ing dynasties, when the *chin-shih* degree, awarded at metropolitan examinations, was the highest honor attainable in the regular system of official selection. Rotours, *Traité des Examens,* pp. 128, 151.

11. *shih:* a short poem of five or seven characters to a line, composed for the

examinations according to strict rules of tone and rhyme. A *shih* submitted at a T'ang examination by Po Chü-i is translated into French by Rotours in *Traité des Examens,* pp. 343–44.

12. *fu:* a rhymed composition, the lines of which are of variable length and non-metrical construction, with every second line generally paralleling the preceding one. An example by Po Chü-i is given in Rotours, *Traité des Examens,* p. 335.

13. *ming-ching* examination: one of two regular examinations established by the Sui dynasty (A.D. 598–618) and continued by the T'ang as a test of an official candidate's knowledge of the classics. In the T'ang it generally consisted of questions involving recognition of quotations from the classics (*t'ieh*), followed by an oral examination on the general meaning of the classics (*ta-i*) and three dissertations on contemporary problems (*shih-wu ts'e*). Though the quotation questions were not originally part of the *ming-ching* examination, after they were added to it in 681 they tended to become the most crucial part. Of the degrees awarded by the T'ang, this and the *chin-shih* were considered of the most consequence. Many leading figures of the dynasty obtained one or the other and sometimes both. Later, however, especially in the Five Dynasties period, the *ming-ching* examination fell into disrepute because it was confined to recognition of passages or minor details in the classics, involving sheer memory work and no attempt at general interpretation. *T'ung-k'ao* 30:283ac; Teng Ssu-yü, *Chung-kuo k'ao-shih chih-tu k'ao,* p. 103; Rotours, *Traité des Examens,* pp. 28–30, 147–49.

14. *mo-i:* originally an alternative to oral examination on the meaning of the classics. In the *ming-ching* examinations of the T'ang dynasty, both the oral and written form were used at different times for the *ta-i* type of question on the general meaning of the classics. Huang indicates that the term *mo-i* came to designate not only the manner in which the examination was given but also a specific type of question, involving reproduction from memory of the commentaries on a given passage. This formulation is identical to one found in the letter of Liu Mien to Ch'üan Te-yü (see notes 27 and 28, below), which is no doubt Huang's source. Ma Tuan-lin gives the following specimen of a *mo-i* type examination:

> *Question:* It is said. "Those who have done this are seven men." Please answer by giving seven names. *Answer:* The seven names are so and so. [This question is based on *Analects* 14:40; the names of the seven are given by commentary, not the original text.]
>
> *Question:* It is said, "When you see a man who observes the rules of propriety in his conduct to his ruler, behave to him as a dutiful son should do in nourishing his parents." Please give the continuation of this passage. *Answer:* "When you see a man who transgresses these rules towards his master, take him off as an eagle or hawk pursues a small bird." [Question based on *Tso chuan,* eighteenth year of Duke Wen, tenth month; Legge, *Tso Chuen* 1:282.]
>
> *Questions:* Please give the Han and T'ang commentaries (*chu-su*) on the above passage. *Answer:* The commentaries state . . . " [*T'ung-k'ao* 30:283c]

It may be seen from this that the *mo-i* type of examination, originally intended to deal with the general meaning of the texts rather than the letter, had become similar in content to the *t'ieh* type, which required memorization of the classics. Partly for this reason, these two types tended to be regarded as one and were used interchangeably or together. In the late T'ang, Five Dynasties, and early Sung periods, the *mo-i* displaced other types of examination for degrees granted on the basis of a knowledge of the classics. Many Sung scholars, however, scorned this rudimentary display of memory work and preferred the *chin-shih* examinations, which at least gave some scope for displaying one's literary talents. It is this attitude that Huang opposes in the concluding remarks of this section. *Yü-hai* 115:15b; *Sung shih* 155:3b; Teng Ssu-yü, *K'ao-shih*, pp. 82–85, 103–107, 144–45; Rotours, *Traité des Examens*, pp. 31, 180.

15. Specifically, candidates for the *chin-shih* degree. (Cf. *T'ung-k'ao* 30:283b, from which this passage may be taken by Huang, though it appears identically in the slightly later *Sung shih* 155:2ab.)

16. *t'se:* a dissertation written in answer to a question presenting a rather involved political, economic, or philosophical problem. An example is given by Rotours in *Traité des Examens*, pp. 289ff.

17. *t'ieh:* a quotation, generally of three or four characters but sometimes longer, drawn from a classic that the candidate was supposed to have learned by heart. He was expected to provide from memory the preceding and succeeding parts of the passage, and in some cases to write an essay on it. Originally, when examinations were given orally, the passage in the text shown to the candidate was covered over with only the three or four characters in question showing through. Teng Ssu-yu, *K'ao-shih*, p. 103; Rotours, *Traité des Examens*, pp. 30, 141.

18. Nine Classics: the *Book of Odes* (*Shih ching*), *Book of Changes* (*I Ching*), *Book of History* (*Shu ching*), the three books of Rites (*I li, Chou li, Li chi*), and the three commentaries on the Spring and Autumn Annals (*Tso chuan, Ku-liang chuan, Kung-yang chuan*). See *Jih chih lu* 7:58.

19. Five Classics: at first only two texts, the *Li chi* and *Tso chuan*, were prescribed for this examination (the candidates being allowed to choose three more out of the remaining seven listed in note 18 above). Later the traditional Five Classics were prescribed as a group for this examination: the *I Ching, Shu ching, Shih ching, Ch'un ch'iu,* and *Li chi.* Cf. Rotours, *Traité des Examens*, pp. 136–37.

20. The *I li, Chou li,* and *Li chi.*

21. The *Tso chuan, Kung-yang chuan,* and *Ku-liang chuan.*

22. Intensive study (*hsüeh-chiu*): in the early Sung dynasty a candidate was permitted to specialize in the study of the Mao version of the *Shih ching,* but he was examined on other texts as well. Ma Tuan-lin gives the contents of this examination as follows: Intensive Study—on the *Mao shih,* fifty questions of the *mo-i* type; on the *Lun-yü,* ten questions; on the *Ehr-ya* and *Hsiao-ching* together, ten questions; on the *Chou i* and *Shang shu,* each twenty-five questions (*T'ung-k'ao* 30:283b; also in *Sung shih* 155:2b).

The term *hsüeh-chiu* derives from a T'ang prototype called "Intensive Study of One Classic" (*hsüeh-chiu i-ching*). Cf. Rotours, *Traité des Examens*, pp. 29, 130, 150. In the Sung this examination was identified simply as "Intensive Study" probably because of the incorporation of other texts in this examination or because only the *Mao shih* (not just any one classic) was so treated.

23. This conclusion is based on the contents of the examination as listed in *T'ung-k'ao* 30:283b (or *Sung shih* 155:2b), of which the above passage is a paraphrase.

24. Wang An-shih (1021–86): noted Sung statesman and reformer, who in 1069 abolished the *ming-ching* examination, which had stressed memorization of the classics, and drastically revised the *chin-shih* examinations, so as to emphasize practical understanding of the classics and their application to contemporary problems (*T'ung-k'ao* 31:293–94). Li T'ao, *Hsü tzu-chih t'ung-chien* 265:4a, 24b–25a. For further details of these reforms see pp. 38–39; H. R. Williamson, *Wang An-shih* 2:329–43; John W. Chaffee, *The Thorny Gates of Learning in Sung China*, pp. 70–81.

25. The texts promulgated in 1075 were known as the *New Interpretation of the Three Classics* (*San ching hsin-i*), the three being the *Shih ching, Shu ching,* and the *Chou li* (or *Chou kuan*). The idea here was to emphasize the general meaning and spirit of the classics, rather than memorization of text and commentary. See Thomas Lee, *Government Education and Examinations in Sung China*, pp. 239–41; and Chafee, *The Thorny Gates of Learning*, pp. 68–72, 81, 114.

26. While the *mo-i* type was originally intended as a test of the candidates' understanding of the meaning of the classics, as may be seen from the example in note 14 above, it came to deal more in minor details than in general interpretation and favored memory work over critical analysis. However, even as a test of the candidates' memory it was not so exacting as the *t'ieh-ching* type, which required learning whole texts such as the *Analects* word for word. From either standpoint, then, it was considered a superficial examination.

27. Liu Mien: T'ang official of the late eighth century A.D. (*Hsin T'ang shu* 132:18b). Liu Mien's views on reform of the examinations are to be found in a letter to Ch'üan Te-yü, which appears together with Ch'üan's reply in the latter's collected writings (note 14 above). Liu criticizes the T'ang system as having been copied without modification from that of the Sui dynasty (581–618), which exalted worldly success and produced men lacking in humility and self-restraint. The *chin-shih* examinations, he says, put the greatest emphasis on composition of poetry, thereby failing to give the proper precedence to moral philosophy. Of the *ming-ching* examination he says that a man might understand the Way of the Sages and the meaning of the Six Classics and yet fail because he had not memorized the texts. Then he goes on to make the recommendations cited by Huang Tsung-hsi. Cf. Ch'üan Te-yü, *Wen-chi*, SPTK 41:1a–2b.

28. Ch'üan Te-yü (759–818): a statesman during the reigns of T'ang Te-tsung (r. 780–805) and Hsien-tsung (r. 806–820) who as vice president of the Ministry of Rites supervised the metropolitan examinations from 802 to 805, gaining lasting fame for the scrupulous honesty with which he conducted them. It was apparently during this period that the exchange of letters took place between him and Liu Mien, who was then in Foochow, on the subject of the examinations. In his reply to Liu, Ch'üan acknowledges a regrettable tendency in the system to place a premium on memorization at the expense of understanding. Consequently, in his own administration of examinations, Ch'üan asserts he has tried to discourage this by asking only for the essential meaning of the commentaries, not their literal rendition.

Nevertheless, he upholds the continued use of the commentaries, as indicated by the passage quoted from this letter by Huang. *Chiu T'ang shu* 148:13b; *Hsin T'ang shu* 165:17b; Ch'üan Te-yü, *Wen-chi* 41:2b.

29. Sung Ch'i (998–1061): Northern Sung scholar who was largely responsible for the compilation of the New T'ang History, the direction of which he shared with Ou-yang Hsiu. During the Ch'ing-li period (1041–49), when Fan Chung-yen headed the government, Sung Ch'i submitted a memorial on abuses in the examination system and necessary reforms. In place of examinations emphasizing memorization and poetry composition, he would test candidates in the composition of essays dealing with philosophical, political, and economic problems, so that men with literary ability would have to give serious thought to social welfare. He recommended also that the form of the examinations be simplified, so that men of broad learning would have more freedom to demonstrate what they knew, and that questions of general interpretation be asked so that classical studies would not be devoted exclusively to memorization. *Sung shih* 155:11b, 284:13b; *Yü-hai* 116:21b; T'ai Kung-che, *Wang An-shih cheng-lüeh*, p. 129; Chaffee, *The Thorny Gates of Learning*, pp. 54, 67–69.

30. Wang Kuei (1019–85): Sung dynasty official who rose to high posts under three successive emperors—Ying-tsung, Shen-tsung, and Che-tsung. Following the fall of Fan Chung-yen from power at the end of the reign of Jen-tsung (r. 1023–1064), Wang memorialized the throne on the inadequacies of the examination system inherited from the late T'ang. His arguments are similar to those of Sung Ch'i: complaints against the premium put on literary skills and memorization, and also against the small number of men admitted to official service through the examinations. When Wang An-shih came to power, Wang Kuei supported his reforms wholeheartedly while a Grand Councillor. *Sung shih* 155:12b, 312:21a; Williamson, *Wang An-shih* 2:121–22.

31. The translation of this sentence hinges upon the word *liu* (commonly rendered as "type" or "sort" but sometimes used to mean a "degeneration" or "corruption"). From the argument that follows this passage, it is clear that Huang opposes the examination essays of his day and advocates restoring the old *mo-i* type; therefore he cannot have intended to equate the two here. Moreover, though it can correctly be said that the examination essays of the Ming (*pa-ku-wen* or *shih-wen*) were indirectly derived from the *t'ieh-shu mo-i* type, still these types were abolished by Wang An-shih, who revised the examinations on the classics so as to minimize the need for memorization and literary skill. Despite minor differences, the type of essay used in the Ming derived directly from the form prescribed by Wang. Consequently, where a sharp contrast is being drawn between the two earlier types, it can be said only that the Ming essays are a debased form of the *mo-i,* and not properly of the same sort. *Jih chih lu* 16:42–43, 51–52; *Ming shih* 70:1693–94.

32. The Great Compendia (*Ta-ch'üan*) were compiled by Hanlin scholars under the direction of Hu Kuang (1370–1418) on the order of the Emperor Yung-lo (r. 1403–25), who had them promulgated for official use in 1415. One series dealt with the Five Classics and another with the Four Books, presenting what were regarded as the most authoritative commentaries of the Sung school, notably those of Chu Hsi. A third compendium, the *Hsing-li ta-ch'üan* contained important works of

Sung writers on cosmogony, metaphysics, ethics, education, rites, politics, and literature. Of the three, the *Great Compendium of the Four Books (Ssu-shu ta-ch'üan)* became the most influential owing to its adoption as the standard authority for interpretation of the Four Books, of paramount importance in the examination essays of the Ming. According to the editors of the Imperial Library Catalogue, "The thinking of every educated man in the Ming dynasty had its roots in this book."

However, some Ming Neo-Confucians objected to the selections made by the editors of these compendia, which were far from exhaustive or representative of all points of view. Chu Hsi's views endorsing Mencius' resistance to tyranny were in some cases suppressed, and even "orthodox" Ch'eng-Chu school men could object to the fixing of orthodoxy in this form (see de Bary, *Neo-Confucian Orthodoxy and the Learning of the Mind-and-Heart,* pp. 63–64, 164–68).

33. In attempting to reduce the possibilities for favoritism and arbitrary judgment in the conduct of examinations, a limited number of standard questions were authorized to be asked on each classic, and the form of the answer (generally known as the "eight-legged essay") was prescribed in minute detail. As a result it was possible, in fact advisable, for the candidates to enter the examination halls with ready-made answers to a fair share of the questions that might be asked, by memorizing essays written on these subjects by acknowledged masters of the style, either their own tutors or successful candidates in earlier examinations. *Jih chih lu* 16:47.

The Selection of Scholar-Officials (Part 2)

1. *Hsiang-chü li-hsüan:* refers to a system used in the Latter Han dynasty for the selection of court officials upon the recommendation of local prefects *(chün-shou)* and the prime ministers of the various states *(kuo-hsiang).* This system was supposedly based on the method used in the Chou dynasty and described in the classical books of rites. *Hou-Han shu* 3:4b; *T'ung-k'ao* 28:265a, 267b; *Chou li,* SSCCS 10:11b; *Li chi* 13:16b; Couvreur *Li Ki* 1:300; Legge, *Li Ki* 1:232–34.

2. The Royal Institutes *(Wang-chih)* section of the *Record of Rites (Li chi)* was said to have been compiled at the order of the Han Emperor Wen (r. 179–157 B.C.). It was an attempt to give a systematic exposition of the laws and institutions of the Chou dynasty, on the basis of information from earlier sources such as the *Book of History,* the *Mencius,* and the commentaries of Tso Ch'iu-ming and Kung-yang Kao on the Spring and Autumn Annals. The paragraph that follows paraphrases passages from the *Li chi* text. See Legge's introduction, *Li Ki* 1:18–20, 232–34; Couvreur, *Li Ki* 1:300–303.

3. Grand Director of Music *(ta-yüeh cheng):* his title does not adequately indicate the scope of the educational functions said to have been entrusted to him, including the teaching of poetry, history, and ceremony as well as music.

4. Accomplished Scholar *(tsao-shih)* is another name for Eminent Scholar *(chün-shih).*

5. End of quotation from the *Rites of Chou,* Royal Institutes *(Li chi,* SSCCS 13:16b–17b, Wang Chih).

6. Han Yü (A.D. 768–824): famous official, writer, and poet of prose in the T'ang dynasty. Biography in *Hsin T'ang shu* 176:1a–7a. See also Charles Hartman, *Han Yü and the T'ang Search for Unity.*

7. Success in the examinations given by the Ministry of Rites, such as the *ming-ching* or *chin-shih* examinations, only obtained for the candidate a court rank of the eighth or ninth degree and did not insure him of immediate appointment to an official post. Ordinarily, the candidate had to take three further examinations given by the Ministry of Personnel before this latter board would appoint him to office, and frequently there was a long delay in the process. Rotours, *Traité des Examens,* pp. 219*n*3, 220*n*1; Teng Ssu-yü, *K'ao-shih,* pp. 82, 115.

8. Low-ranking subordinates of the district magistrates and prefects. Some of these titles also apply to minor posts in the central administration, but in this case Huang is trying to point up the contrast between Ming appointment of the lowest-ranking graduates to prefectural posts and district magistracies, and Sung appointment of even the highest-ranking graduates to minor offices in the districts and departments. Cf. *Sung shih* 167:27ab; *Li-tai chih-kuan piao* 54:1b, 2a, 13b; Rotours, *Traité des Fonctionnaires* 2:730–33; Kracke, *Civil Service in Early Sung China,* pp. 46–47.

9. *Ch'eng* and *p'an:* abbr. for *hsien-ch'eng* and *t'ung-p'an* (Kracke: "assistant sub-prefect" and "vice-administrator"). Cf. *Sung shih* 167:23a, 26b; *Li-tai chih-kuan piao* 54:1b, 2a, 3b; Kracke, *Civil Service in Early Sung China,* pp. 46–47; Hucker, no. 457, 7497.

10. Ch'ü Yüan (343–277 B.C.): official of the state of Ch'u and author of the classic elegy *Li Sao. Shih-chi* 84:1a–8a; Giles, no. 503; Paul Pelliot, "L'édition collective des oeuvres de Wang Kouo-wei," *T'oung-pao* 26 (1929): 139*n*1; Arthur Waley, trans., *The Nine Songs.*

11. Ssu-ma Ch'ien (c. 145–80 B.C.): Han dynasty official and author of the first great history of China, the *Shih chi. Shih chi* 130: 1a–30a; *Han shu* 62:1a–23a; Giles, no. 1750; Burton Watson, *Records of the Grand Historian of China.*

12. Ssu-ma Hsiang-ju (d. c. 117 B.C.): writer and official of the Former Han dynasty, known especially for his poetry in the *fu* form. *Shih chi* 117:1a; *Han shu* 57:1a; Giles, no. 1753.

13. Tung Chung-shu (c. 176?–104? B.C.): leading thinker of the Former Han, who systematized Confucian doctrine in terms of yin-yang cosmology. *Shih chi* 121:3ab; *Han shu,* SPTK 56:1a–23b; Giles, no. 2092; Fung Yu-lan, *History of Chinese Philosophy* 1:4–5, 16–18, 74–75, 403–405.

14. Yang Hsiung (53 B.C.–A.D. 18): philosopher, poet, philologist, and mathematician of the Han dynasty, known especially for his studies on the *Book of Changes* and Confucius' *Analects. Han shu* 87A:1a; Giles, no. 2379; Wing-tsit Chan, *A Source Book in Chinese Philosophy,* pp. 289–91.

15. The men cited here, besides being known to posterity for their intellectual achievements, were all officials at one time or another. But despite their attainments in various scholarly fields, they might have failed in the type of examination adopted by the Ming dynasty, which emphasized skill in composing the eight-legged essay and made no allowance for talent in other directions. A view similar to

Huang's is expressed by his contemporary Ku Yen-wu: "If Mi Ch'eng [Han poet] and Ssu-ma Hsiang-ju tried to learn the type of classical interpretation required in the examinations today, they certainly would fail to produce the prescribed form of essay. If Kuan Chung and Sun Wu [skilled in administration and war, masters of clever stratagems] studied today's administrative code, they could not possibly practice its subterfuges" (*Jih chih lu* 9:1).

16. *hsiang-kung-che* (lit., "local tribute"): meaning here those who have passed the provincial examinations and obtained the *chü-jen* degree. Originally the term *hsiang-kung* served in the T'ang dynasty to differentiate those who had advanced to the metropolitan examinations through official recommendation on the basis of local examinations, rather than through the official schools, which were limited to only a few. Thus it did not exactly correspond in importance to the *chü-jen* degree of the Ming, but Huang uses the term in a general sense rather than as a specific title. Cf. Rotours, *Traité des Examens*, pp. 128, 143–44; Teng Ssu-yü, *K'ao-shih*, p. 81; Hucker, no. 2333.

17. Chu Hsi's ideas on official examinations are set forth in an essay entitled "Personal Proposals for the Selection of Officials through the Schools," in *Hui-an Chu Wen-kung wen-chi*, SPTK 69:20a–28b. As regards the content of the examinations, Huang's program differs from Chu Hsi's in that the choice of Sung philosophers in the second session is Huang's own, and in the third session the History of the Sung Dynasty and the Court Records of the Ming Dynasty have been substituted for the *Tzu-chih t'ung-chien* of Ssu-ma Kuang as the fourth subject. In other respects, Huang's recommendations for the examinations go far beyond Chu's in both extent and detail.

18. session (*ch'ang*): under the Ming dynasty, examinations were divided into three sessions, each given three days apart (*Ming shih* 70:1694).

19. *Ta Tai li:* a compilation of treatises on ritual drawn from a mass of such material extant in the first century B.C. by Tai Te—elder cousin of Tai Sheng, who reduced the compilation from 85 to 46 chapters to form what is known as the *Record of Rites* (*Li chi*) or Rites of the Younger Tai (*Hsiao Tai-li*). Though considered inferior to the *Li chi* and neglected by later Han scholars, the surviving portions of the Rites of the Elder Tai assumed new importance in the Sung dynasty when some scholars classified it as a classic along with the *Li chi*. Thus Chu Hsi includes it with the traditionally accepted classic on ritual as a subject for the examinations. Legge, *Li Ki* 1:9; Wylie, *Notes on Chinese Literature*, p. 5; *Hui-an Chu wen-kung wen-chi* (Chübun) 69:5073.

20. Chu Hsi specifies the following subjects for this group: (1) astronomy and geography; (2) the Comprehensive Rites and New Ceremonials (*T'ung-li hsin-i*, published in A.D. 1115); (3) edicts pertaining to military, legal, and penal matters; and (4) the General Encyclopedia (*T'ung-tien*) of Tu Yü.

21. Since the T'ang dynasty it had been common to fix in advance the number to be passed at each year's examinations (*Yü-hai* 115:14b, 16a; Teng Ssu-yü, *K'ao-shih*, p. 117).

22. *Shih-chung:* officials of the Ch'in and Han dynasties who stood in personal attendance upon the emperor, having charge of his personal equipage and con-

veyances and assisting in the handling of state business. During the Former Han there were numerous imperial attendants, this being an office held concurrently by members of the royal family, generals, ministers, other high officials, and noted scholars. In the Latter Han particularly, these posts were frequently held by men of great learning and fine character, who acted as the emperor's closest personal advisers. Gradually, they became charged more and more with official responsibilities, and less with personal attendance upon the emperor, until under the Wei and Chin dynasties the imperial attendants served as heads of the Imperial Chancellery (*men-hsia sheng*). *T'ung-k'ao* 50:456c; Hucker, no. 5229.

23. Secretary (*chu-shih*): cf. *Ming shih* 72:1734, 1739, 1745; Mayers, no. 68; Brunnert and Hagelstrom, no. 292, Hucker, no. 1420.

24. Following a practice inaugurated by the Emperor Wen (r. 179–157 B.C.), men of outstanding attainments (known as "Worthies and Scholars") were recommended by the various commanderies and kingdoms of the empire to serve as advisers to the emperor. In 81 B.C. the emperor ordered his high ministers to consult with the Worthies and Scholars concerning the grievances of the people, whereupon the latter, generally representing the Confucian point of view, protested against government involvement in commerce and industry, demanding the abolition of state monopolies in salt, iron, and fermented liquors, as well as the Office of Equalization and Standards through which the government speculated in goods. These monopolies were defended in the ensuing debate by Sang Hung-yang, chief minister responsible for the government program that had been adopted to finance the large military undertakings of the Emperor Wu (140–86 B.C.). A record of the debate was kept by Huan K'uan and written up in the following reign (73–48 B.C.).

The debate has been partly translated into English by Esson M. Gale under the title, *Discourses on Salt and Iron,* and "Discourses on Salt and Iron" by Gale, C. Lin, and H. Boodberg, pp. 73–110. Excerpts are given in de Bary, Chan, and Watson, eds., *Sources of Chinese Tradition.* Cf. H. H. Dubs, *History of the Former Han* 2:160–61; and Nancy Lee Swann, *Food and Money in Ancient China,* p. 320.

25. Wu Yü-pi (1392–1469): the son of an official from Kiangsi, Wu was nineteen when, in the capital (Nanking) with his father, he read a work by Chu Hsi that dealt with the Ch'eng brothers and resolved to become a real scholar rather than embark on an official career. After gaining a great reputation for his learning, Wu was recommended for an imperial appointment but declined. Despite the highest honors being done to him by the emperor, he persisted in his refusal. Wu is known as a key figure in the development of Neo-Confucian thought in the Ming dynasty, and as the teacher of such men as Ch'en Hsien-chang and Hu Chü-jen. In his *Case Studies of Ming Confucians* Huang Tsung-hsi cites Liu Tsung-chou's praise for Wu's steadfast detachment from public office and worldly success. *Ming shih* 282:7240; *Ming-ju hsüeh-an* (*Shih chieh* ed.) Shih-shuo 2:1.1a–2b; DMB, pp. 1497–1501; Julia Ching and Fang Chao-ying, eds., *The Records of Ming Scholars,* pp. 70–76; M. Theresa Kelleher, "Personal Reflections on the Pursuit of Sagehood: The Life and Journal of Wu Yü-pi (1392–1469)," Ph.D. diss., Columbia University, 1982 (Ann Arbor, Mich.: University Microfilms, 1982).

26. Ch'en Hsien-chang (1428–1500): more commonly known by the name of

his native place, Pai-sha near Canton, Ch'en obtained the *chü-jen* degree in 1447 and then, after studying briefly with Wu Yü-pi, secluded himself for several years of intensive study and meditation. Later he visited the Imperial College and, excelling in poetry composition, gained a considerable reputation at the capital. Nevertheless, he returned home to pursue his studies and, although repeatedly recommended for office, was determined to avoid official life. His teachings emphasized quiet sitting and self-realization. Though Ch'en was criticized by some, in his *Case Studies of Ming Confucians,* Huang Tsung-hsi insists that Ch'en's teaching was grounded in the Confucian tradition and upholds his canonization as a Confucian worthy in 1584. *Ming shih* 283:7261; *Ming-ju hsüeh-an,* Shih-shuo 2:5.28–30; DMB, pp. 153–56; Julia Ching and Fang Chao-ying, eds., *Records of Ming Scholars,* pp. 84–90.

27. Stipendiaries (*lin-sheng*): the system of salaried licentiates originated in 1369, when the first Ming emperor ordered official schools established in each prefecture, department, and district with an authorized enrollment of forty, thirty, and twenty students respectively, who were resident in the locality, chosen by examination, exempt from labor service, and given stipends of rice out of land tax collections. Later on, the number of licentiates increased considerably but the quota for those receiving stipends was not correspondingly increased, so that the latter comprised a very limited and select portion of the total. This remained the case until the last years of the Manchu dynasty.

Frequently, stipendiaries were employed as minor officials in their own localities while preparing for the provincial examinations, and generally those who failed to achieve the next degree within a specified period were taken off the rolls of salaried licentiates and employed as local officials, in positions similar to those mentioned here by Huang. Instead of staffing such offices with men whose only avenue of advancement was through the provincial examinations, Huang desires a separate series of reviews and promotions, which would regularly test the competence of local officials and encourage them with the hope of advancement to the Imperial College or court offices. *Hsü T'ung-k'ao* 50:3244–45; *Jih chih lu* 17:56; Hucker, no. 3728.

28. Acting officials (*she-kuan*): there is no office or practice described in such terms in early literature that exactly corresponds to Huang's proposals here, and he probably intends only a rough analogy. The most conspicuous use of *she* in ancient times was in connection with the institution of regency (*she cheng*). In this case a competent member of the royal family acted on behalf of an heir-apparent too young to rule; his exercise of office was therefore temporary, but not on a trial basis as Huang suggests here. The word *she* was also used in the related case of an official temporarily discharging the duties of a certain office (sometimes concurrently with another), but again not, it seems, on a trial basis. *She* is also used for officials "assisting" their superiors, as would be the case here, but it does not indicate a formal title or relationship. Legge, *Tso Chuen,* p. 1, para. 2; p. 3, para. 2; p. 645, para. 2; p. 651, para. 1; see also Legge, *She King,* in *Chinese Classics* 4:477.

29. Liu Fen: a *chin-shih* of 826 known as an authority on the *Tso chuan.* In 828, during a special imperial examination, he condemned the eunuchs who had seized power and held successive emperors as mere puppets, enthroning and deposing

them at will. The examining officials expressed admiration for his reply, but the emperor was powerless to act against the eunuchs, and the latter eventually had Liu accused of certain crimes for which he was deprived of his post as a censor and banished to a minor post in Kwangsi. *Chiu T'ang shu* 190C:16b; *Hsin T'ang shu* 178:1a.

30. Ch'en Liang (1143–94): a Southern Sung scholar, Ch'en memorialized the throne during the Lung-hsing period (1163–65), when the country was enjoying a respite from war with the Chin (Jurchen) in the North, asking that measures be taken to drive the Chin out of their conquered territories, to force the return of the remains of two imperial ancestors who had died in Chin hands at the end of the Northern Sung dynasty, and to redeem the honor of the dynasty. But a war policy was extremely unpopular among people enjoying peace and prosperity for the first time in years, and no action was taken on Ch'en's proposal. *Sung shih* 436:1a; *Sung-Yüan hsüeh-an* 56:1037 (Shih-chieh Shu-chü ed.); and Hoyt Tillman, *Utilitarian Confucianism: Ch'en Liang's Challenge to Chu Hsi.*

31. Lao Hsiu: disciple of Chang Ch'eng, a diviner who had won favor at court and was closely associated with the eunuch faction in its struggle with the "party men" toward the end of the Later Han dynasty (see translation, "Schools," note 12). When Chang Ch'eng was charged with murder and executed by Li Ying, a leader of the party men, the eunuchs prepared and had Lao Hsiu present to the throne a memorial protesting against Li Ying's administration of justice and accusing him of organizing a widespread conspiracy against the court among the scholars of the land. As a result, the emperor ordered the arrest of Li Ying and hundreds of party men in A.D. 166 (*Hou-Han shu* 97:4a).

32. *Shuo-wen ch'ang-chien:* a revision and amplification of the early dictionary, *Shuo-wen,* compiled by the Late Ming antiquarian, philologist, and poet, Chao I-kuang (d. 1625). Ku Yen-wu shared Huang's low opinion of this work and wrote a detailed refutation of its most glaring faults in the *Jih chih lu.* The editors of the Imperial Library Catalogue characterize it as a voluminous but rambling and slipshod work, uncritical as to sources, with many unjustified deletions from and additions to the original. "In the *Jih chih lu,*" they comment, "Ku Yen-wu was not far wrong in calling Chao 'an illiterate blockhead, fond of showing how clever he was.'" *Ssu-k'u t'i yao* 43:3a; *Jih chih lu* 21:77; Ch'en T'ien, *Ming-shih chi-shih,* KHCPTS ed. p. 2646.

33. *Shih-ta-pien:* probably a mistake for the *Shih-ta-lu* of Liu Chen, a late Ming writer from Hsüan-ch'eng in Anhui. This latter work, listed in the Imperial Library Catalogue, contains records of the rulers and ministers of the Ming. For the most part, it is based on the court records (*shih-lu*) but draws additionally on the writings of other men. The Imperial Library Catalogue says of it that the narratives are careless and inaccurate, while the plan of the work is too diffuse (*Ssu-k'u t'i yao* 50:59a).

Choosing a Capital

1. Northern Capital: Peking, in contradistinction to the Southern Capital, Nanking, which had been the sole capital of the Ming until the Yung-lo emperor

moved it north in 1421, and which remained a secondary capital until the end of the dynasty.

2. It took Li Tzu-ch'eng (1605?–45) a little more than two months to conquer Peking, and the actual battle for the city lasted only two days. After establishing his capital at Sian and proclaiming himself first king of the Ta Shun dynasty in February 1644, Li began a northward drive that swept through T'ai-yüan and Ta-t'ung, from which he pressed on to reach Peking on April 23. The capital fell with little opposition on April 25. *Ming shih* 309:7948–68; ECCP, pp. 491–93; James B. Parsons, *Peasant Rebellions of the Late Ming.*

3. The inglorious retreat of the Emperor Hsüan-tsung (r. 713–756) to Szechuan, which ended his reign in A.D. 756, was a consequence of the revolt of An Lu-shan (705–757). It is one of the most celebrated incidents in Chinese history, for during the course of this long march mutinous troops demanded and secured the execution of the emperor's notorious favorite, Yang Kuei-fei. *Chiu T'ang shu* 9:22a-25a; Giles, no. 1172; *Cambridge History of China,* vol. 3 (Twitchett and Fairbank, eds.), pp. 447–63.

4. Shan-chou: the present Shan-hsien in Honan Province, to which the Emperor Tai-tsung (r. 762–779) fled in 763 when the T'u-fan (Tibetans) suddenly swept into Ch'ang-an. His return was made possible shortly afterward by a small band of imperial troops, who panicked the T'u-fan into withdrawal by beating drums and lighting fires to give the impression that a large force was on its way to the relief of the city. *Chiu T'ang shu* 11:7b–8b.

5. Feng-t'ien: in the present Kan-hsien of Shensi. In the beginning of his reign the Emperor Te-tsung (r. 780–805) had strongly fortified Feng-t'ien as a place of refuge in time of trouble. In 783 he repaired there during the mutiny at the capital, and the city underwent a long and bitter siege at the hands of the rebel Chu Tz'u (742–784). The emperor returned to Ch'ang-an the following year after Chu Tz'u had been defeated and driven from the capital by loyal troops under Li Ch'eng. *Chiu T'ang shu* 12:8b, 20b; *Cambridge History of China* 3:505–507 (C. A. Peterson chapter).

6. I-tsung: one of the canonical names given the last Ming emperor by Ming adherents in the South who carried on resistance to the Manchus after his death. He is more commonly known by his reign name, Ch'ung-chen, or his dynastic title, Chuang-lieh-ti, officially conferred on him by the succeeding dynasty. See ECCP. p. 191 (biography of Chu Yu-chien by George A. Kennedy).

7. In April 1644, after a memorial had been presented by the Grand Secretary Li Chien-t'ai urging the emperor to go South to Nanking, I-tsung declared his intention to die if necessary in the capital, where stood the sacred altars to the Gods of the Soil and Grain, symbolic of the dynastic mandate to rule. Writers differ, however, as to whether he attempted to escape before Li Tz'u-ch'eng surrounded the city on April 23. *Ming shih* 24:334–35; *Ch'ung-chen shih-lu* 17:15ab; *Chia-shen ch'uan-hsin lu* 1:13–18; Wen Ping, *Lieh-huang hsiao-shih* 8:228–34; ECCP, p. 192.

8. In 1449 the Emperor Ying-tsung (reign title, Cheng-t'ung; r. 1436–49]), on the advice of the eunuch Wang Chen, personally led his troops to repel an Oirat invasion northwest of the capital. Ambushed at T'u-mu, near the present Huai-lai

in Chahar Province, the emperor was taken prisoner and held for a year by the Oirat chieftain Yeh-hsien (Esen). During this time Ying-tsung's brother was crowned emperor (reign name Ching-t'ai) and negotiated the former's release the following year. It is difficult to see how this incident can be used as evidence to support Huang's argument. The capital itself was not taken, and if Ying-tsung had remained there, instead of taking the field personally against the advice of his state ministers, he would never have been captured. *Ming shih* 10:138–39; D. Pokotilov, *History of the Eastern Mongols,* trans. from the Russian by Rudolph Loewenthal, pp. 44–50; DMB, pp. 289–94; Frederick Mote, "The T'u Mu Incident of 1449," in Frank Kiernan, ed., *Chinese Ways in Warfare,* pp. 267–72; *Cambridge History of China,* vol. 7 (Mote and Twitchett, eds.), pp. 322–25 (Twitchett and Tilemann Grimm chapter).

9. Yang-ho in the present Yang-kao district of Northeast Shansi, near Ta-t'ung. The Emperor Wu-tsung (reign name Cheng-te; r. 1506–21), bored with life at the capital, made frequent excursions to border outposts northwest of Peking. On occasion he would order his eunuchs to guard the pass at Hsüan-fu (the present Hsüan-hua in southeast Chahar Province) and stop all officials coming and going to the capital. Meanwhile, free of the restraints of the court, he lived a riotous and expensive life, entertained by the most beautiful women that could be found. Wu-tsung also loved to hunt and, fancying himself a great general, engaged in frequent skirmishes with the Mongols. Once in 1517, while directing armies for the relief of Ying-chou, then besieged by the Mongols, he was himself attacked by them at Yang-ho, and it was only after a bitter two-day struggle that the enemy was driven off. This incident, like the preceding one, does not well support Huang's argument, since the emperor was not trapped in the capital and would probably have been safe had he remained there. *Ming shih* 16:209; *Ming shu* 12:158; Pokotilov, *History of the Eastern Mongols,* p. 101; DMB, pp. 307–15; *Cambridge History of China* 7:418–23 (James Geiss chapter).

10. After the capture of the Emperor Ying-tsung by Yeh-hsien (see note 8, above), the capital was threatened by the Oirats and removal of the court to Nanking was considered for a time but finally rejected on the urging of the minister Yü Ch'ien (1398–1457), whose determined defense of the city caused the Oirats to withdraw again to the North. While Ying-tsung had already been captured when this siege took place, the Ching-t'ai reign did not officially start until the following year (1450). Therefore, Huang should have dated this event the last year of Cheng-t'ung (late in 1449). *Ming shih* 10:128–29, 11:141–42; Pokotilov, *History of the Eastern Mongols,* pp. 50–51; DMB, pp. 1608–12; *Cambridge History of China* 7:325–30 (Twitchett and Grimm chapter).

11. The siege to which Huang refers must be that of Chia-ching 29 (September 1550), when the Mongol chieftain An-ta (Altan) threatened the city. No siege is recorded for Chia-ching 28 (1549–50). *Ming shih* 18:146–47; Ch'en Hao, *Ming chi,* Shih-chieh shu-chü ed., 33:346b; Pokotilov, *History of the Eastern Mongols,* pp. 112–14; DMB, p. 319; *Cambridge History of China* 7:474–76 (Geiss chapter).

12. No such event is recorded for the 43rd year of Chia-ching (1564–65). Huang probably has in mind the invasion of the capital area by Mongol peoples of the

northeastern border region in reprisal for the treacherous seizure of one of their chieftains by a Chinese commander. This occurred on Chia-ching 42.10.9 (October 25, 1563). *Ming shih* 18:248–49; *Ming chi* 36:371c; Pokotilov, *History of the Eastern Mongols,* p. 123.

13. *Ta-fu:* ancient name for the royal treasury, according to the account of the Celestial Offices (*T'ien kuan*) of the *Rites of Chou* (*Chou li* 1:4a).

14. On the problems and costs of transporting tax grain and tribute items to the capital, see Ray Huang, *Taxation and Governmental Finance in Sixteenth-Century Ming China,* p. 317.

15. Kuan-chung: the region of Ch'ang-an, capital of China for over one thousand years from the Han through the T'ang dynasties; near the present Sian in Shensi province.

16. Wu and Ch'u: ancient states in the Lower and Middle Yangtse Valley regions respectively.

17. K'uai: ancient name for the Eastern Kiangsu–Western Chekiang area. Here Wu and Hui denote the Kiangsu-Chekiang area in general.

Frontier Commanderies

1. Frontier commanderies (*fang-chen*): the term applied by the New T'ang History to the "forces of the imperial commissioners in command [of a region] (*chieh-tu shih*)." Those on the borders of the empire, which were the first of the commanderies to be created during the K'ai-yüan period (713–741), were also known as "frontier commanderies" (*fan-chen*). It is the latter that Huang advocates restoring, not the commanderies of the late T'ang dynasty, which were established at many points in the interior of the empire. *Hsin T'ang shu* 50:6a; Rotours, *Traité de l'Armée,* p. 785, and *Traité des Fonctionnaires,* p. 670n1.; Hucker, nos. 1865, 1895.

2. This statement could be misleading. The system of frontier garrisons out of which the commanderies developed was indeed established at the inception of the T'ang dynasty. But the term *chieh-tu* (*shih*), by which Huang refers to them here, was used unofficially only after the reign of T'ai-tsung (627–649) for the governors-general (*tu-tu*) of the frontier regions. And the system of commanderies commanded by persons with the official title of military commissioner (*chieh-tu shih*), whose commanderies were known as *fang-chen* (the words used by Huang for the title of this section) and which in effect superseded the *tu-tu* system, did not come into being until the year 710 or 711 and after. However, in listing the commanderies established in the period before the revolt of An Lu-shan, the New Tang History concludes as follows: "Such was the organization of the frontier regions from the period Wu-te [618–626] to the period T'ien-pao [742–755]." Actually, the list seems to apply to the system as it existed about 755, after considerable changes had taken place since the reigns of Kao-tsu and T'ai-tsung. In any case, it is clear from the course of Huang's argument that he is speaking of the system of commanderies in the period just prior to the revolt of An Lu-shan in 755. Rotours, *Traité de l'Armée,* pp. 819–21, *Traité des Fonctionnaires,* pp. 656–57, and "Fonctionnaires des provinces," pp. 234–35; Hucker, no. 777; and T'ang Chang-ju, *T'ang-shu ping-chih chien-cheng,* pp. 76-82.

3. At the time of An Lu-shan's revolt (755) there were only nine commanderies: two in Sinkiang (An-hsi and Pei-t'ing); three in Kansu (Ho-hsi, Shuo-fang, and Lung-yu); one at Ch'eng-tu in Szechuan (Chien-nan); one at T'ai-yüan in Shansi (Ho-tung); one at Peking (Fan-yang); and one at Chao-yang in Jehol (P'ing-lu). Most of these commanderies were created during the K'ai-yüan period (713–741).

Huang's figure on troop strength runs high. At about 742 the average number of troops per commandery was approximately 60,000, the largest being the Fan-yang commandery of An Lu-shan, which had 91,000. Cf. Rotours, "Fonctionnaires des provinces," pp. 288–96, and *Traité de l'Armée*, pp. 786–820.

4. An Lu-shan (d. A.D. 757): a general of mixed Chinese and Turkic ancestry who rose to power by his defense of the northeast border against the Uigurs, becoming military commissioner (*chieh-tu shih*) in command of the Fan-yang district around the present Beijing. His revolt in 755, which caused the flight of the emperor Hsüan-tsung to Szechuan was finally suppressed with Uigur help in 763, but An Lu-shan's part in it had already ended in 757, when he was assassinated by his son. *Chiu T'ang shu* 200A:1b–2a; Arthur F. Wright and Denis Twitchett, eds., *Perspectives on the T'ang*, pp. 8–9, 151, 203; Denis Twitchett, *Financial Administration Under the T'ang Dynasty*, pp. 17–18; *Cambridge History of China*, vol. 3 (Twitchett and Fairbank, eds.), pp. 561–71 (Michael Dalby chapter).

5. Chu Tz'u (A.D. 742–784): the son of a lieutenant under An Lu-shan, in 772 he became military commissioner (*chieh-tu shih*) in command of the Lu-lung district in the present Hopei, and was later ennobled as a prince. In 783 mutinous troops forced Emperor Te-tsung to flee to Feng-t'ien and chose Chu Tz'u as their leader. He declared himself emperor but was driven from Ch'ang-an in the following year and slain by one of his own officers while trying to escape to the West. *Chiu T'ang shu* 200B:1a–7a; Giles, no. 473.

6. On this point the "Treatise on the Army" of the New T'ang History says: "When An Lu-shan, Imperial Commissioner in command of the Fan-yang district, revolted and attacked the capital region, the forces of the Son of Heaven, being too weak, were unable to resist him, and in consequence he took both capitals [Lo-yang and Ch'ang-an]. The Emperor Su-tsung then repaired to Ling-wu [southeast of the present Ling-chou] and the forces of all the military commanderies rose up to chastise the rebel." *Hsin T'ang shu* 50:7ab; Rotours, *Traité de l'Armée*, pp. 821–22.

7. Huang Ch'ao (d. 884): a would-be scholar, salt merchant, and adventurer from Shantung, who was fond of harboring fugitives from justice in a time of great economic distress and unrest. He amassed a following, joined the rebel Wang Hsien-chih in 875, and inherited the latter's leadership upon his defeat and execution. Huang's depredations carried him all the way to Kwangtung and back to Ch'ang-an, which he seized in 880. Although he proclaimed himself emperor and inaugurated a new dynasty, in 883 loyal border troops drove him from the capital and forced his suicide. *Chiu T'ang shu* 19B:200B; *Hsin T'ang shu* 9:225B; Wright and Twitchett, eds., *Perspectives on the T'ang*, pp. 220–26; Giles, no. 847; Lionel Giles, "The Lament of the Lady of Ch'in," *T'oung-pao* 24 (1925–26): 309–16; *Cambridge History of China* 3:722–62 (Robert Somers chapter).

8. Chu Wen (852–912): initially a follower of the brigand Huang, Chu submit-

ted to the throne in 882 and was ennobled as Prince of Liang in 893 for his services to the last emperor of the T'ang in rescuing him from the domination of eunuchs. The emperor, however, quickly came under Chu's control and was assassinated by him in 904. The sole surviving representative of the dynasty abdicated in favor of Chu Wen in 907. After founding the Later Liang dynasty, Chu himself was assassinated by his eldest son, who feared that an adopted son would be favored for the succession. *Chiu Wu-tai shih* 1–7; Giles, no. 475; Wright and Twitchett, eds., *Perspectives on the T'ang,* pp. 53, 228; *Cambridge History of China* 3:779–87 (Robert Somers chapter).

9. This list corresponds to the nine frontier areas (*chiu-pien*) of the Ming dynasty, with the exception noted below. They were located as follows:

1. Liao-tung: hq. at Liao-yang, south of Mukden.
2. Chi-chou: hq. at present Chi-hsien, northeast of Beijing.
3. Hsüan-fu: hq. at present Hsüan-hua, in south Chahar.
4. Ta-t'ung: hq. at present Ta-t'ung in north Shansi.
5. Yü-lin: hq. at present Yü-lin in north Shansi.
6. Ning-hsia: hq. at present Ning-hsia in province of that name.
7. Kansu: hq. at Kan-chou (Chang-yeh) in northwest Kansu.
8. Ku-yüan: hq. Ku-yüan in Kansu (then part of Shensi).
9. Yen-sui: name derives from two anchors of defense line running from Yen-an to Sui-te in north Shensi. Actually, this is another, more common name for the Yü-lin commandery and probably represents a duplication. In making out this list, Huang no doubt had the nine frontier areas of the Ming in mind, but he left out the Shensi (or T'ai-yüan) commandery, and carelessly added Yen-sui to fill out the list of nine, without stopping to realize that it would occupy the same area covered by the Yü-lin commandery. *Ming shih* 76:1866–68; 91:2235.

This list follows the same general defense line as the T'ang commanderies of the K'ai-yüan period but does not extend into Sinkiang.

10. The Ming dynasty maintained commanderies in Kuei-chou with headquarters at T'ung-jen fu (present Chiang-k'ou hsien) and in Yünnan, with headquarters at Yünnan-fu (present Künming). *Ming shih* 76:1869.

11. This practice of making regular visits to court, and the terminology used for it here, derive from a feudal practice described in the *Record of Rites* as obtaining in the Chou period (c. 1000 B.C.). "In relation to the Son of Heaven, the feudal princes were required to send every year a minor mission to the court, and every three years a greater one; once in five years they had to appear in person" (Couvreur, *Li Ki* 3:2.12).

12. It is understood here that his successor would not be an appointee of the court but, as was the case in the T'ang system, a member of his own family designated as heir by the incumbent (or, more rarely, a man chosen by the officers and men of the commandery). See Rotours, *Traité de l'Armeé,* p. 825.

13. Hucker, no. 7158.
14. Hucker, no. 2731.
15. Hucker, no. 7146.

16. *pen-ping:* a convenient but misleading form of reference to the head of the Ministry of War, who sometimes took command or conducted investigations in the field. It was not an official title and does not appear in the "Treatises on Officials and on the Army" in the official Ming History. However, the *San-ch'ao liao-shih shih-lu,* a record of campaigns in Liao-tung from 1618 to 1627 written by Wang Tsai-chin, who took part in these operations as Minister of War in 1622, gives numerous examples of the term *pen-ping* being applied to this office (Nanking kuo-hsüeh t'u-shu-kuan ed. of 1931, Colophon 4b; 1:3a, 14a; 3:14a, 18b; 19b). The other titles in this list appear in order of descending importance, with *ching-lüeh* added at the end as an extraordinary command superior to the *tsung-tu.* It would be impossible to fit *pen-ping* into such a logical order unless the term were identified with some rank inferior to or superseded by the *tsung-ping,* such as perhaps the provincial commander *(tu-chih-hui shih)* of the original garrisons and stations system. Yet it is common for Chinese writers to list things as they come to mind rather than in logical order. Moreover, though the term *pen-ping* might have been applied by extension to immediate deputies of the Minister of War, it would probably not have been applied at the same time to a minor officer like the *tu-chih-hui shih* (Hucker, no. 7200).

17. Hucker, no. 1231.

18. Home troops (lit., "host troops": *chu-ping*); also known as "local troops" *(t'u-ping). Ming shih* 91:2249–52; Wang Tsai-chin, *San-ch'ao* 2:2b.

19. Troops from other garrisons (lit., "guest troops": *k'o-ping*). "Troops transferred from other garrisons and sent to the frontier were called 'guest troops'" *(Ming shih* 91:2242–45).

20. In 1620 a call was sent out for Szechuanese troops, considered among the best fighters in the empire, to reinforce the Liao-tung garrison, which was hard-pressed by the Manchus. She Ch'ung-ming, a Lolo chieftain of the Yung-ning region of Szechuan, whose family had held the hereditary title of *hsüan-fu-ssu* for centuries, offered 20,000 infantry and cavalry men for this mission, but apparently had treasonable motives in doing so. The troops were sent to Chungking, where they remained indefinitely, showing no inclination to move to their ostensible destination. In September 1621, when the local governor put pressure on them to leave, She's subordinates in command of the force engineered a revolt over the issue of higher travel pay for their men from the government. The rebels occupied Chungking, executed the governor together with more than a score of other officials, laid siege to Ch'eng-tu and proclaimed a new dynasty, the Great Liang. The siege of Ch'eng-tu was lifted by government troops and Chungking recaptured the following year, but as She was joined in revolt by a powerful tribal chieftain of Western Kueichou, An Pang-yen, it was not until 1623 that the campaign of suppression could finally be brought to a close, thanks largely to the efforts of the able Ming general, Chu Hsieh-yüan (1566–1638), and the female chieftain, Ch'in Liang-yu. *Ming shih-lu,* T'ien-ch'i 9:14a; *Ming shih* 312:8052–56, 22:3a–6a; *Ming chi* 50:500c; DMB, pp. 219, 1077, 1571.

21. In 1631, when the Manchus launched their attack on Ta ling ho (near the present Chin-chou [Jinzhou] in South Liaoning), Manchurian troops in the service

of the Ming were ordered from Shantung to reinforce the garrison of that city. The leader of these troops, K'ung Yu-te (d. 1632), was a native of Liaotung who had earlier served against the Manchus in Korea under the intrepid guerrilla general Mao Wen-lung. When Mao's enemies at court had him arrested and executed in 1629, K'ung refused to serve under his successor and was employed by the cannon expert (Ignatius) Sun Yüan-hua (d. 1632), then governor of Lai-chou (the present Yeh-hsien) and Teng-chou (the present P'eng-lai) in Eastern Shantung, who had a high respect for the fighting ability of Manchurian troops. On their way to Ta ling ho, K'ung's troops were refused entry to Wu-chiao (in South Hopei, near the Shantung border) by fearful townspeople. Without lodgings or food, the troops mutinied and persuaded K'ung to revolt. After pillaging several towns in Western Shantung, K'ung turned eastward and laid siege to Teng-chou and Lai-chou early in 1632. Teng-chou soon fell, partly through the desertion and treachery of other Manchurian troops within the city, but Lai-chou held out for six months until relieved by a large force from the capital. When Teng-chou was retaken early in 1633, K'ung escaped by sea to join the Manchus, later taking a major part in the conquest of China. A detailed account of the siege of Lai-chou was written in 1712 by a resident of the city, Mao Pin, under the title *P'ing-p'an chi,* republished in 1928 in *Yin li-tsai-ssu-t'ang ts'ung-shu. Ch'ung-chen shih-lu* 5:1–7a; *Ming shih* 23:314–15; *Ming chi* 53:540b; ECCP, p. 435 (biography of K'ung Yu-te by George Kennedy); *Cambridge History of China,* vol. 7 (Mote and Twitchett, eds), pp. 617–18 (William Atwell chapter).

22. Those at court (lit., "the inner court"): indicates those officials closest to the throne, especially the eunuchs.

23. Somewhat similar passages appear in the *Huai-nan tzu,* SPTK 16:5b, and *Yen -t'ieh lun,* SPTK 7:3a. In the *History of the Former Han Dynasty:* "When there are wild beasts in the mountains, greens cannot be picked; when the state has loyal ministers, vice does not thrive" (*Han shu* 77:4b). Thus the looseness of the analogy attaches already to the original sources. Huang seems to suggest that the autonomous rulers of the border regions, no one of whom was powerful enough to threaten the dynasty, would collectively serve as a check on the power of unscrupulous ministers and eunuchs at court. Even though the latter might silence all opposition at the capital, the border regions would not be subject to their manipulations and tyranny.

Land System (Part 1)

1. Yü, first emperor of the Hsia dynasty, divided the country into nine provinces and classifed them according to the character of their soil, establishing three major classes having three subclasses each. Then taxes (or tribute) were fixed for each province according to the expected yield from the land. The establishment of this system is the subject of an important section of the *Book of Documents* called "The Tribute of Yü" (*Yü-kung*). Legge, *Shoo King,* in *Chinese Classics* 3:92ff., 141.

2. Otherwise known as the *Rites of Chou (Chou li).*

3. *t'i-kuo ching-yeh:* expressions used in the opening lines of the *Chou li* indicat-

ing the territorial division of the Chou kingdom (c. 1000–700 B.C.). According to the commentaries on this passage by Cheng Hsüan and Chia Kung-yen, *t'i-kuo* means to divide up the capital city into precincts, and *ching-yeh* to fix the number of villages according to the number of inhabitants in each well-field and district in the country outside the capital (SSCCS, *Chou li* 1:1b; Biot, *Tcheou-li* 1:1–2). Huang's use of these terms, especially in the concluding remarks of this paragraph, show that he has the classifying and delimiting of fields in mind, rather than territorial organization. A passage from the Royal Institutes of the *Li chi,* though it does not use precisely these terms, may illustrate this idea better: "In settling the people, the ground was measured for the formation of towns, and then measured again in smaller portions for the allotments of the people. When the division of the ground, the cities and the allotments were thus fixed in adaptation to one another, so that there was no ground unoccupied, and none of the people left to wander about idle, economical arrangements were made about food; and its proper business appointed for each season" (SSCCS, *Li chi* 13:16a; Legge, *Li Ki* 1:13.230).

4. By the Ch'in state, which created the empire later taken over by the Han, during the period c. 350–220 B.C. The *History of the Former Han Dynasty* says: "When the Duke Hsiao [361–338 B.C.] of Ch'in adopted the policy of Prince Yang, Lord of Shang [d. 338 B.C.], he abolished the *ching-t'ien* ancient well-field system of land division, initiated that of dividing the arable lands by crossroads running south-north and east-west [under which individual holdings were allowed and a tithing system of taxes on private fields was practiced], and urged rewards for cultivation of land and for expansion by warfare. Although the methods were contrary to the ancient way, nevertheless because the policy called attention to that which is fundamental [that is, agricultural pursuits], he was able to crush the neighboring feudatories and to make himself leader among the feudal lords. However, kingly institutions then perished" (*Han shu* 24A:7b; trans. adapted from Swann, *Food and Money in Ancient China,* pp. 144–45); see also *Shih chi* 68:1a–9b; *Cambridge History of China,* vol. 1 (Twitchett and Loewe, eds.), pp. 595–601 (Nishijima Sadao chapter).

5. About 205 B.C. (see Swann, *Food and Money,* pp. 149–50; *Han shu* 24A:8a).

6. See Swann, *Food and Money,* pp. 171–72 (*Han shu* 24A:13b).

7. See *Hou-Han shu* IB:2b–3a.

8. I.e., is not necessary to return to the system of adjusted tax grades adopted by Yü (Hsia dynasty) or by the Chou dynasty.

9. Huang means that the tribute, or tax, paid in the earlier period was only equivalent to rent, since the land holder was given the land by his lord. With the institution of private ownership, however, cultivators had to pay for their own land and might well have regarded any additional payment of taxes as excessive.

10. When Mencius was consulted about the operation of the well-field system, he recommended that in the central parts of the state of T'ang, a tribute of one-in-ten should be paid (*Mencius* 3A:3). According to Swann, the first legal tax-in-kind or its commutation to money of one tenth was imposed under the Eastern Han when a change in A.D. 30–31 was made from the Western Han rate of one-thirtieth (*Food and Money,* p. 369n).

11. Even a man on poor land could pay a tax of one-thirtieth without hardship, but a tax of one-tenth results in a greater sacrifice by men on poorer land since they are living on the subsistence level and cannot reduce costs proportionately. Only men on the best land would have a total income large enough to pay a tenth in taxes and yet have a balance sufficient for their needs.

12. *mai-chio:* the purchase of honorary rank is first mentioned during the Han in 178 B.C., but the sale was widely promoted at cut rates during the reign of Emperor Wu and had a serious effect on the competence and integrity of officials. The degree of rank and privileges attaching thereto varied according to the amount of grain contributed. See Swann, *Food and Money,* pp. 33, 166–72, 273.

13. *tai-chia* (originally *tai-pan* or *pan-tai*): in the reign of Han Wu-ti, as part of the general revenue-raising program, a fixed schedule of rates was established by which sentences could be reduced by the payment of such-and-such amounts of money for each degree of remission. See *Shih chi* 30:7a; Nishida Taichirō, trans., *Min-i taihō roku,* p. 102n5.

14. *chio-ku* (or, according to one interpretation, "monopolized liquors"; see Dubs, *History of the Former Han* 2:107n34.6): in 98 B.C. the right to brew and sell liquor was taken away from the people, and this industry was made a government monopoly, the profits going to the state treasury. In 81 B.C., as a consequence of the debate on government monopolies between scholars and government officials in charge (see translation, "The Selection of Scholar-Officials, Part 2," note 24), this monopoly was abolished.

15. *suan min* (lit., "calculating strings of cash"): a tax on the accumulated wealth of merchants and artisans, traditionally reckoned as 120 cash on every two strings of a thousand cash each, this idea was first adopted in 130 B.C. and renewed in 120 B.C. at the suggestion of K'ung Chin and Tung-kuo Hsien-yang. See Dubs, *History of the Former Han,* 2:42, 64–65; Swann, *Food and Money,* pp. 279–81.

16. Established in 117 B.C. on the proposals of K'ung Chin and Tung-kuo Hsien-yang. Revenues were obtained for the state through the licensing of private enterprise for the production of salt, and perhaps by the leasing of government equipment for this use. Swann, *Food and Money,* pp. 63, 275–77.

17. Tung-kuo Hsien-yang, K'ung Chin, and Sang Hung-yang were three financial experts who served as top advisers or heads of the Ministry of Agriculture in the reign of the Emperor Wu. In making this remark, Huang may have had in mind the following account in the "Treatise on Food and Money" from the *History of the Former Han Dynasty:* "Tung-kuo Hsien-yang was a great salt industrialist of Ch'i, and K'ung Chin was a great iron smelter of Nan-yang; and each of the two had accumulated fortunes of a thousand catties of gold. For this reason Cheng Tang-shih [who as Minister of Agriculture also was in charge of commerce and government finance] recommended them to the throne [120 B.C.]. Sang Hung-yang, a son of a merchant of Loyang, was able to make mental calculations [without the use of "counting sticks"]. When he was thirteen years old [140 B.C.] he became *shih-chung* [that is, palace attendant]. And so the three men discussed matters for government revenue in the finest possible detail (lit., 'to the point of splitting an autumn hair')" (trans. adapted from Swann, *Food and Money,* pp. 271–72; *Han shu* 24B:11a).

18. Kiangnan: the region south of the lower Yangtse River, especially in the Nanking-Soochow-Hangchow area.

19. Ch'ien shih: a family that controlled the Kiangsu-Chekiang area in the late T'ang and Five Dynasties periods. The family's rule was inaugurated by a T'ang warlord, Ch'ien Liu (852–932), who was appointed imperial commissioner in this region in 895 by the T'ang Emperor Chao-tsung, and enfeoffed as Prince of Yüeh in 902. In 907 he was made prince of both Wu and Yüeh by the first emperor of the Later Liang and was confirmed in this position by the succeeding Later T'ang dynasty. When Ch'ien Liu died in 932, after forty years of rule, the title passed to his son, and then successively to three of his grandsons. The last of these, Ch'ien Shu, was forced to yield up his domain to the founder of the Sung dynasty in 978 (*Chiu wu-tai shih* 133:10a–18b; *Hsin wu-tai shih* 67:1a–10b). The rapacity with which this family taxed the people of the region, as well as their general unworthiness to rule, is vehemently condemned by the Sung historian Ou-yang Hsiu (*Hsin wu-tai shih* 67:9b–10b).

20. Chang Shih-ch'eng (1321–67): a salt trader from T'ai-chou (present Tai-hsien) in Kiangsu, who together with his brothers revolted in 1353 against the weakening Yüan (Mongol) dynasty and proclaimed himself Prince Ch'eng of the Great Chou dynasty, with his capital first at Kao-yu and then across the Yangtse at P'ing-chiang (now Soochow [Suzhou]). By 1363 he had extended his holdings to include Hangchow and proclaimed himself Prince of Wu. However, for some years he had carried on a bitter rivalry with Chu Yüan-chang, eventual founder of the Ming dynasty, and after a long struggle during which Chang was besieged in his capital at P'ing-chiang, he was defeated and forced to commit suicide. *Ming shih* 123:3692–96; DMB, p. 99–103 (biography by John Dardess).

21. The division of the empire in ancient times into a royal domain surrounded by a region of feudal and tributary domains originated according to tradition with Yü the Great, founder of the Hsia dynasty. The immediate royal domain comprised a square 1,000 *li* in length on each side (a million square *li* in area). The section of the *Book of Documents* entitled "Tribute of Yü" describes this domain and the type of revenue derived from it (as does *Mencius* 5B:2), but does not indicate the type or rate of tax (tribute) from the feudal domains extending 500 *li* beyond the former. It has been commonly held, as Huang holds, that a tax rate of one-tenth was uniformly applied to territories ruled by or tributary to the Son of Heaven. Thus Legge, following the Ch'ing scholar Hu Wei, says: "We have no mention of the payment or revenue in other domains. It was no doubt on some arrangement analogous to that made for this *fu* [the imperial domain]. The princes occupying the several territories received it, and then paid a tithe of their incomes to the Emperor not in kind but in value, in other articles produced" (Legge, *Shoo King,* in *Chinese Classics* 3:144; see also p. 97). The *Chou li* and *Li chi* describe a similar system obtaining in the Chou dynasty (SSCCS, *Chou li* 10:8a; Biot, *Tcheou-li* 1:196–97; *Li chi* 11:4b; Legge, *Li Ki* 1:11.212). Commentators differ, however, on the interpretation of the tribute system referred to in the *Chou li* passages cited, some saying that feudatories forwarded from one-half to one-quarter of their revenues to the Son of Heaven. This interpretation is followed by Chen Huan-chang, *Economic Principles of Confucius and His School,* p. 640.

Land System (Part 2)

1. The memorial of Tung Chung-shu (176?–104? B.C.), one of the foremost Confucian scholars of the Former Han dynasty, advocating limitation of private land ownership (c. 100 B.C.), is recorded in *Han shu* 24A:14b–15b. Tung tells how under the Ch'in dynasty the early well-field system was abandoned, so that land could be privately owned, bought, and sold. "The rich bought up so much land that their fields were connected along both north-south and east-west roads, while the poor had not even enough land into which to stick an awl. . . . When the Han arose, the government followed the institutions of Ch'in without changing them. Although it would be difficult to act precipitately in a return to the ancient land system (*ching-t'ien*), it is proper to make present usage draw somewhat near to the old system. Let people's ownership of land be limited in order to sustain the poor in their insufficiency, and to block the road toward monopoly" (trans. Swann, *Food and Money in Ancient China*, pp. 179–83; also *Shih chi* 121:11a–12b; *Han shu* 56:1a, biography of Tung Chung-shu).

2. The memorial of Tung Chung-shu not having been acted upon, in 7 B.C. Shih Tan, a Minister of War and Grand Secretary during the reign of the Emperor Ai, addressed the throne: "Of the Sage Rulers of antiquity, there was none who did not first establish the well-field land system, and then their government was accordingly able to keep the peace. . . . Now several generations in turn have enjoyed universal peace, wherein the fortunes of overbearing persons of wealth among officers and people have grown to an estimated amount of several hundred millions, while in contrast the poor and weak have become more straitened. Now it is admitted that a ruler honors the practice of traditional methods of government, and considers it a serious matter to make changes, but the reason why changes are made is in order to save the country in times of crisis. However, even though it has not yet been possible to go into details, it is proper to make certain general restrictions." (trans. adapted from Swann, *Food and Money*, pp. 200–201; *Han shu* 24A:18ab, 86:17b–24a, biography of Shih Tan.

3. When Shih Tan's proposal was put up for discussion at court, the minister K'ung Kuang (65 B.C.–A.D. 5) asked that nobles, officials, and people be limited to holdings of thirty *ch'ing* each. "After a period of three years has been completed for the law to be put into effect, let those who disobey these regulations be subjected to penal servitude, and have excess fields or slaves confiscated by the government" (trans. adapted from Swann, *Food and Money*, pp. 202–203). These regulations were promulgated in 7 B.C., but owing to improved economic conditions and the opposition of influential elements at court, they were never put into effect (*Han shu* 24A:18b; 81:14b).

4. Swann, *Food and Money*, p. 202*n*313.

5. *Mencius* 2A:2, where it is said that neither Po-I, I-Yin, nor Confucius, "in order to obtain the empire would have committed one act of unrighteousness, or put to death one innocent person" (Legge, in *Chinese Classics* 2:544).

6. This passage originates with Hsün Yüeh as quoted in *Han chi*, SPTK 8:3b. It is repeated in an essay entitled "The Land System" (*T'ien-chih*) by Su Hsün (see note 68 of the introduction in the present volume), who like Huang disagrees with the point of view expressed (cf. Su Hsün, *Chia-yu chi*, SPTK 5:8a).

7. Su Hsün (1009–1066): father of the famous Su Shih (Tung-p'o) (1036–1101) and Su Ch'e (1039–1112), and widely known as an independent thinker and prose stylist. For his views on well-fields in the essay on "Land Systems" see *Sung shih* 443:2b–7a; *Sung-Yüan hsüeh-an* 99:1851–52.

8. For Hu Han, see note 10 of the introduction in the present volume. His views on restoration of the well-field system are discussed in *Ching-mou (Hu Chung-tzu chi,* TSCC 1:7–11).

9. Fang Hsiao-ju (1357–1402): a native of Chekiang, who became so famous for his prose style that he was nicknamed "the Little Han Yü." For his services as a tutor, he was greatly honored by the second Ming emperor, Hui-ti, and made a minister of state. After the sudden disappearance of Hui-ti, Fang refused to serve his successor, the Yung-lo emperor, out of loyalty to his former master. His stubbornness and outspoken opposition so angered the new ruler that he was ordered to be butchered in the public square and his family exterminated to the tenth degree of relationship. His writings were suppressed and burned, but several collections of his surviving works were brought out later in the Ming dynasty. *Ming shih* 141:4017–21; *Ming-ju hsüeh-an* 43:455–56; DMB, pp. 426–33 (Frederick Mote); John W. Dardess, *Confucianism and Autocracy,* p. 264–89. For his views on the well-fields see Fang Hsiao-ju, *Hsün-chih chai chi,* SPTK 11:14a–17a; Yü yu-jen lun ching-t'ien-shu.

10. Fixed features of the ancient land system, which Su Hsün quotes at length from the *Chou li.* The relevant passage here reads: "Concerning the management of all land, between the lots of each cultivator, there was a trench and alongside this a pathway; around every ten lots there was a large ditch and alongside it a lane; around every hundred lots there was a waterway, and alongside it a roadway; around every thousand lots was a canal and alongside it a road; around every ten thousand lots was a river and alongside it a highway, so as to enable communication throughout the Imperial domain" (SSCCS, *Chou li,* 15:16b; Biot, *Tcheou-li* 1:341–42).

11. *t'un-t'ien* (lit., "camp farms"): farms organized around an encampment or settlement. The *Ming shih* distinguishes three types of camp farms: military, civilian, and commercial. Most general histories of the Ming, like the present text, are apt to refer to any one of these types simply as *t'un-t'ien,* and it is frequently difficult to ascertain which one is intended. However, the military farms were by far the most important in the Ming dynasty, and since Huang plainly has them in mind, I have tried to eliminate misleading connotations by translating *t'un-t'ien* as "military farms" *(chün-t'un).* These farms were located throughout the country at military garrisons and stations, and while they tended to be more numerous in border regions that were more heavily garrisoned, they were not intended primarily for the development of waste land or colonial expansion. The first such farms were established in the rich, well-settled regions of the lower Yangtse, for the direct purpose of supplying Chu Yüan-chang's troops in those areas. This close connection between use of war-ravaged, deserted, or confiscated lands and military supply is accentuated by the fact that these farms were incorporated in the regular system of military administration, not left in civilian hands as was the case with earlier farms intended for colonial development. For these reasons the term "colonial farms" might better

apply to the civilian farms, used for the resettlement of people from overpopulated areas to war-ravaged or underdeveloped regions, or perhaps to the commercial farms, which were operated in border areas by private interests that received salt certificates in exchange for grain supplied to troops. But neither of these types is involved in Huang's discussion. *Ming hui-tien* 18:45b–48a; *Ming shih* 77:1883– 1886; Shimizu Taiji, "Minsho ni okeru gunton no tenkai to sono soshiki" (Development and organization of military farms in the Early Ming), in *Shigaku zasshi* 44, no. 5 (May 1933): 1–3, 33; Wang Yü-quan, *Mingdai te juntun;* Liew Foon Ming, *Tuntian Farming of the Ming Dynasty;* Albert Chan, *The Glory and Fall of the Ming Dynasty,* p. 41.

12. Cf. *Ming hui-tien* 18:45b.

13. This rough calculation is probably based on the belief that the size of the *mou* had doubled since Chou times. It was believed in Huang's time that one Chou *mou* had consisted of 100 square *pu,* and one *pu* of six *ch'ih;* also that in Han times the standard *mou* came to consist of 240 square *pu,* while during the T'ang dynasty the *pu* was standardized at five *ch'ih.* This *mou* of 240 square *pu,* with *pu* of five *ch'ih,* remained standard until the end of the Ch'ing dynasty and appeared to be just double the size of the Chou *mou* (1,200 square *ch'ih* as compared to 600). But according to a modern scholar, Wu Ch'eng-lo, the basic unit of measurement, the *ch'ih,* had itself changed through the centuries, so that the Chou *ch'ih* was actually .64 of the *ch'ih* in Ming times. Other things being equal, the size of the *mou* in Huang's time would have been almost triple that of the Chou *mou.* Wu Ch'eng-lo, *Chung-kuo tu-liang-heng shih* (A history of Chinese lengths, capacities, and weights), pp. 57–58, 63–66, 75–76, 94–97; Nishida Taichirō, trans., *Min-i taihō roku,* p. 111n8.

14. Under the well-field system, on land of the first class, each cultivator was said to receive one hundred *mou.* Cf. *Chou li* 10:9b, 15:16a; Biot, *Tcheou-li* 1:206–207, 340.

15. The regular grain tax was said to be stored in the granaries of the cultivator's own station (*so*) and later reissued to the cultivators in monthly installments, while the additional grain-tax was stored at garrison headquarters (*wei*) and issued to forces on guard duty. This apportionment of military farm produce was necessitated by a division of functions among the soldier-cultivators, whereby a certain portion of them, in peacetime, were assigned to regular guard duty and were supplied through a tax on the others assigned to cultivate the land. This method of taxation became standard in 1402. Huang's account is taken from the *Ming hui-tien* (Wan-li ed.) 18:50a. (Cf. also Shimizu, "Gunton," *Shigaku zasshi* 44, no. 6 [June 1933]: 52.)

16. *hsiang-sui yung kung fa:* according to the *Rites of Chou,* the inner districts (*hsiang*) of the Chou kingdom were within one hundred *li* of the capital, while the outer districts (*sui*) occupied the region from one to two hundred *li* from the capital (*Chou li* 9:1ab; Biot, *Tcheou-li* 1:173). The tribute system referred to here is probably the tithing system mentioned by Mencius in 3A:3: "The sovereign of the Hsia dynasty enacted the fifty *mou* allotment and the payment of tribute. The founder of the Yin enacted the seventy *mou* allotment and the system of mutual aid. The

founder of the Chou enacted the hundred *mou* allotment and the share system. In reality all those were a tithe." Later in the same chapter Mencius recommends that in the outlying districts there be a system of mutual aid for the cultivation of one out of nine squares of land, and in the central districts cultivators contribute one-tenth of their produce. In his notes on these passages, Chu Hsi identifies the tithing system in the central districts by the term Huang uses here (*hsiang-sui yung kung*). Chu Hsi, *Ssu-shu chi-chu, Meng Tzu chi-chu* 5:5a (CKTHMCCC, p. 599) and 7b (CKTHMCCC, p. 604).

Presumably the rate was one-for-ten, and the amount of tax varied according to the productivity of the soil in different localities. Huang plainly does not mean that the military farms were taxed at the same rate, for he points out later in this section that in relation to yield the rate was approximately one-in-four. What he may have meant is that considering the *mou* to have increased 2.4 times in size since Chou times, this would represent a tax of one peck (*tou*) per Chou *mou;* and assuming that the smaller Chou acre, because of higher productivity, had the same yield (one picul) as the acre of military farmland, this would represent a tax rate of one-in-ten.

17. *Ming hui-tien* 17:17ab.

18. Reading *wei wei nan-hsing* for *wei-nan wei-hsing.* Cf. *Hai-shan hsien-kuan* ed., 29a, 1.1.

19. *Ming hui-tien* 19:59b.

20. In other words, the effect of what Huang proposes would be to create minimum subsistence farms for all households, mainly from the redistribution of estate lands and official lands (i.e., estates granted by imperial favor or lands held by the state), without affecting the private lands held by the well-to-do. (See Lynn A. Struve, "Huang Zongxi in Context," p. 477).

21. According to the original system, promulgated in 1368, in peacetime three-tenths of the troops, including the youngest and most able-bodied, were assigned to garrison duty, while seven-tenths, including the older and weaker troops, worked the farms. In practice the proportion varied greatly according to the time and place; in the interior of the country greater security enabled a higher proportion to cultivate. In wartime all were liable for military service. *Ming hui-tien* 18:45b, 47b; *Ming shih* 77:1883–84; Shimizu, "Gunton," *Shigaku zasshi* 44, no. 5 (May 1933): 25–26; Chan, *Ming Dynasty,* pp. 245–49.

22. How are we to reconcile this statement with the favorable comparison made earlier between this tax and the Chou tax rate? The key point is apparently a lower productivity on the Ming military farms. Much of this land was of poor quality to begin with, and it was cultivated under disadvantageous conditions. The soldier-cultivators were not only liable for military service in wartime, which was often enough in the turbulent Ming dynasty, but were also subject to peacetime training, which would take them away from their farm duties. Also, those who did the cultivating were generally not the most able-bodied men, as Huang has already shown. If, as one contemporary source has it (Shimizu, "Gunton," *Shigaku zasshi* 44, no. 6 [June 1933]: 54), the yield varied from one *tou* per *mou* on poor land, to three or four *tou* per *mou* on good land, the rate on the former could well be one-in-four, as Huang has it here, but one-in-ten on better land, as suggested in the earlier case.

Land System (Part 3)

1. Mencius speaks of these as follows: "The Sovereign of the Hsia dynasty enacted the fifty *mou* allotment and the payment of a tax (*kung*). The founder of the Chou enacted the hundred *mou* allotment and the share system (*ch'e*). In reality what was paid in all of these was a tithe. The share system means mutual division. The aid system means mutual dependence" (Legge, *Mencius,* 3A:3).

2. In the Chin the household tax inaugurated under Wu-ti (A.D. 265–290) was payable in silk gauze (*chüan*) and floss (*mien*). The tax adopted about A.D. 484 under Hsiao-wen Ti of the Northern Wei (not the Wei of the earlier Three Kingdoms) was payable in silk cloth (*po*), silk wadding (*hsü*), floss and unhusked grain (*su*). Cf. *Chin shu* 26:13b; *Wei shu* 110:4b; *T'ung-tien* 4:27a, 5:30a.

3. The early T'ang tax system, adopted in the seventh year of Wu-te (A.D. 624–625), is described as follows by the *Hsin T'ang shu:* "Of those who received [one hundred *mou*] of land, each able-bodied male paid an annual tax of two *hu* in unhusked grain and three *hu* in rice, this being called the land tax (*tsu*). According to what the region produced, each year he had to pay two rolls of silk gauze (*chüan*), two *chang* of damask (*ling*) or sarcinet (*shih*), one fifth of the linen (*pu*) [he produced], three *liang* of silk floss (*mien*), or three *chin* of hemp (*ma*); or else fourteen *liang* of silver in lieu of the above in regions without silkworms, this being called the household tax (*tiao*). As for the use of human labor, each able-bodied male gave twenty days labor each year plus two days for each intercalary month, while those who did not perform this labor paid their *ch'ih* of silk gauze , this being called the service tax (*yung*)" (*Hsin T'ang shu* 51:2b; *Chiu T'ang shu* 48:4b).

4. A characterization of the early T'ang tax system drawn from the political writings of the T'ang statesman and scholar, Lu Chih, 754–805. These writings were much admired by later Chinese in the Confucian tradition, and their memorable passages quoted freely without attribution as to source, since readers were expected to recognize them instantly. The simple expressiveness of this passage, however, is lost in translation. Lu Chih, *Lu Hsüan-kung tsou-i,* KHCPTS 4:90–91.

5. Yang Yen (A.D. 727–781): the success of his tax reform program, inaugurated in 780 under the Emperor Te-tsung, brought him high honors and the prime ministership; but Lu Ch'i, with whom he shared power, engineered his banishment in 781 to Kwangtung. Yang committed suicide that year, before reaching his destination. Giles (no. 2417) is incorrect in stating that the Twice-a-year tax system was never actually adopted (see note 7 below). *Chiu T'ang shu* 118:11a–19a; *Hsin T'ang shu* 145:11b–17a; *Cambridge History of China,* vol. 3 (Twitchett and Fairbank, eds.), pp. 580–82 (Michael Dalby chapter).

6. The adoption of the Twice-a-Year tax (*liang-shui,* lit., "two taxes"), proposed by Yang Yen in 780, resulted from the steady deterioration of the earlier T'ang system, which was predicated on a system of equalized land holdings. Taxes had been levied in effect on the assumption that individuals had an equal ability to pay. With the shift in and concentration of land ownership, however, the tax registers no longer served as a realistic account of land ownership and tax potential. Government revenues decreased just at a time when expenditures were expanded enormously by recurrent civil strife and border wars. The Twice-a-year tax, based on property

holdings, attempted to remedy this situation. A survey of land holdings made the previous year (779) was used as the basis for a new tax register whereby men were classified according to the extent of the land or amount of capital in their possession. After estimating the expenses of the local and central governments, the needed funds were prorated according to local conditions. Merchants were taxed one-thirtieth of their capital holdings. All other taxes were abolished, leaving only the one, payable in cash twice a year, in the summer and fall. It remained in effect through the late T'ang and Five Dynasties, and in slightly modified form in the Sung and early Ming dynasties. *T'ung-tien* 6:33a; *Chiu T'ang shu* 43:9a, 118:12b–14b; *Hsin T'ang shu* 52:1ab; S. Balazs, "Beiträge zur Wirtschafts-Geschichte der T'ang-zeit"; Rotours, "Notes, bibliographiques," pp. 358–61; Denis Twitchett, *Financial Administration Under the T'ang Dynasty,* pp. 22–23, 39–48, 59–61, 113–19, 157–64.

7. *ting-shen ch'ien-mi* (also called *shen-ting ch'ien-mi* or *ting k'ou chih fu*): a headtax on able-bodied males (*ting*) between the ages of twenty and fifty-nine and additionally on other members of families (*k'ou*) payable in money, rice, or both. Having appeared in the Five Dynasties period, it was continued by the Sung and levied mostly in the rich southeastern provinces. From North and West China men were called up in great numbers for labor and military service, but it was impracticable to use southeastern labor in the remote areas where it was needed. Consequently, this money and rice tax was paid in lieu of such service. It was regarded at first as a surtax to meet emergency needs, and attempts were made form time to time to limit the amount exacted or eliminate the tax altogether. However, it gradually became a sizable and indispensable source of government revenue, with especially heavy exactions in the Southern Sung. To evade it householders and local officials falsified census returns, with the result that the number of persons per household, as reported in figures for the Southern Sung, fell to an average of one and a half. Ma Tuan-lin comments: "Once such a system is adopted to meet special need, it is difficult to abolish and [if abolished] easy to restore—how much to be dreaded!" *T'ung-k'ao* 11:113a–c. 117b–118c; *Sung shih* 174:4b, 5a, 7a, 10a.

8. *li-ch'ai yin-ch'ai:* under the Equal Service (*chün-yao*) system first tried in the Cheng-t'ung period (1436–49) and adopted for the country at large in 1488, labor services performed for the state were of two kinds—those for which labor was directly supplied and those for which it was more practicable to hire labor. The liability for these services rotated among the ten subdivisions (*chia*) of each village (*li*), normally once every ten years but sometimes every five, three, or two years. For those jobs classed as *li-ch'ai* ("labor service"), labor had to be provided by the households of the *chia* according to a system of apportionment based theoretically on ability to pay. For those jobs classed as *yin-ch'ai,* silver had to be furnished with which to hire the needed labor. *Ming hui-tien* 20:67a–68b; *Hsü T'ung-k'ao* 16:2912c, 2914e–2915c; *Ming shih* 78:1905–1908; Liang Fang-chung, *The Single-Whip Method of Taxation in China,* pp. 6–7.

9. *i-t'iao-pien fa:* a simplified system of tax collection used more and more widely in the late Chia-ching period and formally adopted for the country at large in 1581. The principal drawbacks of the previous system had been: (1) a steady proliferation

of tax items, classifications, and rates; (2) constant changes in rates of commutation into silver; (3) changes in dates and procedure for tax collections, including payments in arrears and in advance; (4) alienation of land from taxation and abuse of labor tax allocations by the local magnates controlling tax records.

The principal features of the new system were: (1) elimination of numerous land classifications, so that land was taxed on a straight average basis; (2) payment of all labor taxes in silver; (3) combination of land and labor taxes, now both paid in silver, so as to eliminate all forms of commutation; (4) the making of land acreage and male manpower the sole basis of labor taxation, eliminating the "household" and other forms of property but land from consideration. The total effect of these measures, adopted progressively in different regions over a period of years, was to combine all other forms of taxation into the land tax. Thus, in the original name for this system, *pien* stood for "combine" (meaning "the system combining all into one item," which was later corrupted by an obvious pun into "whipping all into one item"—that is, the "Single-whip system"). *Ming hui-tien* 20:68b; *Hsü T'ung k'ao* 2:2793, 16:2918b; *Ming shih* 78:1902–1906, 14b; Liang Fang-chung, *"I-t'iao-pien fa"* (A study of the early forms of the single-whip levy system of land taxation), pp. 10–21. The wording of this passage in the text is almost identical with a description of the Single-whip system found in the *T'u-shu pien* compiled by Chang Huang (1527–1608), 1623 ed., 90:36a; see also Leif Littrup, *Sub-bureaucratic Government in Ming Times*, pp. 91–99, 130–51; Ray Huang, *Taxation and Finance*, pp. 112–22, 130–33; *Cambridge History of China*, vol. 7 (Mote and Twitchett, eds.), pp. 489, 525 (James Geiss and Ray Huang chapters).

10. These do not represent separate taxes but simply quotas applying to all taxes, of which part went outside the locality. Before the Single-whip system was introduced, where such taxes were payable in silver the conversion rate was higher for the state quota than for the local quota (i.e., more silver had to be paid in lieu of a given quantity of grain). When the Single-whip system was introduced, this distinction was eliminated and the same rate of conversion was used for all tax collections. Liang Fang-chung, *"I-t'iao-pien fa,"* p. 30, and *The Single-Whip Method of Taxation*, pp. 26, 30–31, 40–44; Littrup, *Sub-bureaucratic Government*, pp. 41–42.

11. *chün-yao:* a reform of the corvée labor system aimed at equalizing the burden of the miscellaneous labor services required in addition to the standard labor service, *li-chia* (see note 12 below). It was first tried in 1436 and adopted generally in 1488. Labor duty was apportioned according to the number of able-bodied adult males per family and also according to the amount of land tax paid, making this in effect a form of land tax too. Families were divided into three classes according to ability to pay, and new tax registers were drawn up in order to make up-to-date assessments. (See also note 8, above.) *Ming hui-tien* 20:67b; *Hsü T'ung k'ao* 16:2914c–2915c; *Ming shih* 78:1892, 1905–1906; Liang Fang-chung, *"I-t'iao-pien fa."* pp. 6–7, and *The Single-Whip Method of Taxation*, pp. 6–7; Littrup, *Sub-bureaucratic Government*, pp. 52, 76–78.

12. *li-chia:* the basic type of labor service in the Ming and an integral part of the system of local government adopted by the founder of the dynasty in 1381–84. The *li* consisted of 110 households, organized into ten *chia* of ten households each, with

the ten largest households each comprising a group of village headmen (*li-chang*), each alternately responsible for labor services one year out of every ten. Similarly, the ten households of each *chia* rotated in service over a ten-year period. The system was based on tax registers (indicating the available manpower and land tax paid by each family), which were to be revised every ten years. The compilation of these registers was one of the services performed under this system, which was designed primarily to handle local functions such as the collection and forwarding of taxes in each unit, education, and social welfare. When additional extralocal services were assigned increasingly to these units by departmental and district officials, the burden was shifted more and more by the larger households managing the system to the poorer ones. This led to the reform and reorganization embodied in the Equal Service (*chün-yao*) system. *Ming Hui-tien* 20:67ab; *Hsü T'ung-k'ao* 16:2912b–2913c; *Ming shih* 78:1893, 1965; Liang Fang-chung, "I-t'iao-p'ien fa," p. 5, and *The Single-Whip Method of Taxation*, pp. 4–5; Ray Huang, *Taxation and Finance*, pp. 34–36; Wang Yuquan, "Some Salient Features of the Ming Labor Service System," pp. 1–44; Littrup, *Sub-bureaucratic Government*, pp. 36–62, 103–27, 187–92; George Der-lang Chang, "The Village Elder System of the Early Ming Dynasty," *Ming Studies* 7 (1978):53–62.

13. Local tribute (*t'u-kung*): tribute sent by territorial officials to the court in the form of wares or products for which the locality was especially known, such as incense, tea, porcelain, metalware, jewelry, ivory, cloth, etc. These were generally sent according to fixed quotas for articles desired for use at court, the first Ming emperor having been especially concerned lest indiscriminate forwarding of such tribute, in order to win favor at court, result in undue hardship on the people. Nevertheless, at times officials outdid each other in sending tribute, while at other times the quotas were not even met, owing to the decline of court power and prestige. *Hsü T'ung-k'ao* 28:3045a, 29:3059a, 3069b–3070c, 3073a; *Ming shih* 82:1991.

14. *ku-mu chia-yin:* the term *ku-mu* indicates the two general kinds of labor service found in Ming tax systems, also called *ku-i* and *li-i* (*Ming shih* 78:1893), by which labor service was performed either directly by the persons liable for it or by persons hired as substitutes. In the management of these systems a certain amount of expense was incurred by local officials in charge, and this was met by a surtax payable in silver. The terms used here are broad enough so as possibly to include silver surtaxes for the furnishing of labor or troops above the normal to meet an emergency in a particular region. *Hsü T'ung-k'ao* 16:2918b; *Ming shih* 78:1904–1906.

15. *tsa-i:* a general term for labor services required outside the regular tax system. They were ordinarily considered nonrecurring charges decreed to meet special need, but as the need often continued they became fixed charges. Here the term is used to denote especially services formerly performed under the *li-chia* and *chün-yao* systems, which were nominally incorporated in the Single-whip collection yet which actually continued to be performed on the old basis. This was owing to the fact that the gentry continued in control of tax collections and succeeded in modifying the new system so as to keep the burden of labor taxes on the poorer families. As one writer of the time put it, "Though the Single-whip was enacted, the

great households were never affected." *Ming shih* 78:1893, 1904–1908; Liang Fang-chung, *The Single-Whip Method of Taxation,* p. 5; Littrup, *Sub-bureaucratic Government,* pp. 75–76.

16. Toward the end of the Ming dynasty, the troops of the principal border garrisons were largely dependent on outside sources of supply, since the military farm system, intended to make them self-sufficient, had degenerated to the point where it contributed only a small part of the grain needed for the increasingly larger forces used on the northern border. The deficiency was made up by allocations from civilian grain-tax collections and salt taxes. Huang's total for annual pay-and-rations in the Wan-li period is probably a rough estimate based on figures of the various commanderies contained in the Wan-li edition (1587) of the *Ming hui-tien* (28:159a–167b), where pay-and-rations deriving from land taxes (*min-yün* and *ching-yün*) total approximately 5,668,184 taels as commuted into silver.

17. These increases were levied to meet the costs of heavy fighting against the Manchus in the northeast and thus were also known as *Liao hsiang,* or "pay-and-rations for the Liao-tung campaign." An increase in the 46th year of Wan-li (1618) added 3,000,000 taels, and two more in the 47th and last years of the period added another 5,200,000 taels to the annual collections for this purpose. *Ming shih* 78:1904; Chao I, *Ehr-shih-erh shih cha-chi* 36:750; Takashima Katsumi, ed., *Shina zeisei no enkaku* (The development of Chinese tax systems), p. 155; Ray Huang, *Taxation and Finance,* p. 163.

18. This tax to supply troops in training in the border commanderies was enacted in the twelfth year of the Ch'ung-chen period (1639–1640). *Ming shih* 78:1904; Takashima, *Shina zeisei no enkaku,* p. 155.

19. Ni Yüan-lu (1594–1644): a scholar, calligrapher, and official from Chekiang, who became Minister of Revenue in the summer of 1643. His proposal for a combined collection of the three pay-and-rations levies was adopted the same year. The following spring, when Li Tzu-ch'eng took the capital, Ni committed suicide rather than fall into enemy hands, an act for which he was honored by the Ming regime in Nanking and later by the Manchus. *Ming shih* 265:6835–41; ECCP, p. 587; Ray Huang, "Ni Yüan-lu: Realism in a Neo-Confucian Scholar-Statesman," pp. 415–49.

20. See translation, "Military System (Part 1)."

21. Wen-chou, T'ai-chou, and Ch'u-chou are in Chekiang; Hui-chou in Anhui.

22. Cf. *Sung shih* 174:20a. This was done for convenience in delivery of taxes, silver being easier to transport.

23. That is, only a small part of the total tax was payable in silver. This figure is for the tenth year of the Hsi-ning period (A.D. 1077), when 31,940 taels were collected in the summer tax and 28,197 taels in the fall (*T'ung-k'ao* 4:59bc).

24. *Ch'ang-p'ing-ts'ang:* during this period of the Sung dynasty the system of "ever-normal granaries," which had appeared in China as early as 54 B.C., was reorganized and extended by Wang An-shih in an attempt to control grain prices more effectively and make crop loans available to the peasantry. Not only were prices supported in the manner Huang describes, but as corollary to this, government-stored grain was offered on the market in order to keep prices down in times of

scarcity. *T'ung-k'ao* 21:207c–211a; Williamson, *Wang An-shih* 1:145, 154; Swann, *Food and Money,* p. 195.

25. That is, after the adoption of the Single-whip system. See Liang Fang-chung, *The Single-Whip Method of Taxation,* pp. 26, 43, 54–55.

26. Quoted from Lu Chih's second essay on "Equalization and Reduction of Taxes in order to Relieve the People's Distress," where he argues in favor of tax payments in cloth rather than cash. The original reads "What is collected" instead of "What is paid." Lu Chih, *Lu Hsüan-kung tsou-i* 4:94.

27. Cf. *Chou li* 10:9b (Biot, *Tcheou-li* 1:206–207), where it is literally "land with no change, land with one change," etc. The change does not mean mere crop rotation, but a year when the land must lie fallow and unproductive. Therefore "fallow period" is used in place of "change" in the translation following.

28. As a result of the Single-whip system, which did away with classifications in order to simplify the tax registers. Cf. Liang fang-chung, *"I-t'iao-pien fa,"* pp. 16–17.

29. *fang-t'ien:* a system of land classification first tried in the reign of Jen-tsung (1023–1064) and readopted in 1072 on the recommendation of Wang An-shih. A land survey was first made dividing all land into tracts 1,000 *pu* square (about one square mile). Each of these was classified according to general topography and fertility into one of five classes, which were used as a basis for tax assessment. The existing tax quota for each district was then reapportioned so as to distribute the burden according to ability to pay as indicated by these classifications. The system was gradually applied beginning in 1074 and remained in effect until repealed by Ssu-ma Kuang in 1085. Revived twice by Ts'ai Ching (1047–1126) toward the end of the Northern Sung, it was repealed for the last time in 1120. *T'ung-k'ao* 4:58c–59a; *Sung shih* 174:1a–4a; Williamson, *Wang An-shih* 1:292, 383, 2:21–23.

30. *yü-lin ts'e* (lit., "fish-scale registers"): these were detailed records of land ownership, including diagrams and descriptions of all property, as well as a history of its ownership. They differed from the tax registers ("yellow registers"), which listed all forms of taxable property as well as the number of adult males, females, children, and aged in each family. Liang Fang-chung, *"I-t'iao-pien fa,"* pp. 6–9, and *The Single-Whip Method of Taxation,* pp. 10–11; *Ming-tai yü-lin t'u-ts'e k'ao* Journal of Land Economics I, p. 8; Ray Huang, *Taxation and Finance,* p. 42; Littrup, *Sub-bureaucratic Government,* pp. 60–62, and "The Yellow Registers of the Ming Dynasty," pp. 67–106.

31. As was the case in the tax registers used as a basis for the *li-chia* labor tax (see note 12 above).

32. Here and in the preceding sentence, reading *shang-t'ien i mou* as in 1985 edition, rather than *tu-t'ien i mou* as in Wu-kuei-lou ed.

Military System (Part 1)

1. The garrisons (*wei*) and stations (*so*) system was developed by the founder of the Ming dynasty, based on an earlier Yüan system, but did not assume what is considered to be its definitive form until the seventh year of his reign (1374–75). Gar-

risons were set up throughout the country, with a rated strength of 5,600 men each, organized in five "thousand-household stations," the troops of which came from hereditary military households settled on public land and obligated perpetually to provide able-bodied men for army service.

These stations (rated strength 1,020 men), were divided into two "general banners" (fifty men) consisting of five "little banners" (ten men). The stations corresponded roughly to the civil prefecture, and the garrisons, combining the troops of several prefectures, were under the administration of a regional military headquarters (*tu-ssu*) for each province. There were also independent stations directly administered by five chief military headquarters (*wu-chün tu-tu-fu*) for the country at large. This chain of command was purely administrative, however; operational command was given to a general sent out from the capital on the occasion of each campaign. At the end of each operation the troops were released from the general's control and reverted to the control of the administrative system outlined above. In this way it was hoped to prevent generals from building up permanent personal armies obedient to themselves rather than to the central government—see "Military System (Part 3)."

In practice, it proved difficult to keep these units up to rated strength, owing to constant desertions and diversion of troops to grain transport or nonmilitary labor projects. Especially after the Yung-lo period (1403–24), the garrisons and stations were no longer adequate fighting forces, and outside troops had to be brought in or local militia raised to cope with uprisings or invasions. Toward the end of the dynasty, its effective fighting forces were almost entirely hired troops. *Ming hui-tien* 124:74b–75b; *Hsü t'ung-k'ao* 122:3889–95, 123:3897–3904; *Ming shih* 90:2193–96; Wu Han, "Ming-tai ti chün-ping" (hereafter, "Chün-ping") (The hereditary and hired armies of the Ming), pp. 148–75; Romeyn Taylor, "The Yüan Origins of the Wei-so System," in Hucker, ed., *Chinese Government in Ming Times*, pp. 23–40; Edward L. Dreyer, *Early Ming China: A Political History, 1355–1435;* Hucker, nos. 7285, 7658, 7758.

2. Mercenaries (*chao-mu*): the first attempts to supplement the weakening garrisons and stations were made with local militia (*min-chuang*) raised in areas affected by uprising or invasion, such as Fukien and Chekiang during the Cheng-t'ung period. In 1489 a general system of militia conscription was adopted. The militia, however, were not suited, trained, or organized for large-scale operations outside their own locality. To suppress brigands operating over wide areas or to repel enemy invasions, full-fledged mercenaries were recruited who performed continuous military service and who depended wholly on their pay for support, since they were not like the militia part-time farmers. The most effective use of mercenaries was made by Ch'i Chi-kuang, who in 1568 hired mercenaries from Chekiang to create a model border garrison at Chi-chou, and by Yü Ta-yu in combating coastal pirates off Chekiang and Fukien. Their success inspired the extension of the mercenary system to other border areas and even to the capital garrison. *Hsü t'ung- k'ao* 122:3895a, 123:3902a, 128:3941c–3945c, 129:3949b–3955b; *Ming shih* 91:2249–51, 17a–20b; Wu Han, "Chün-ping," pp. 182–89; Liang Fang-chung, "Ming-tai ti min-ping," pp. 201–34; Hucker, no. 298. .

3. *ta-chiang chih t'un-ping* (lit.. "the settler-soldiers of the great generals," better known as *chia-ting,* "family troops"): the earlier policy of permitting generals only temporary operational command of armies had been abandoned when mercenaries were hired, trained, and led by regional commanders (*tsung-ping kuan*). The government's control over these armies was further loosened when the commanding generals, no longer assured of supplies from the court for their troops, took to trading military support for financial support, and wringing what they could directly from the land they occupied.

Lands were seized and granted as rewards to the troops of the army commanders, with the court generally sanctioning it as a substitute for payment and supply from tax revenues. Waste land was also reclaimed and used for this purpose. These lands were usually not worked by the troops themselves, as had been the case under the earlier military farms cultivated by hereditary military households; the troops simply drew the proceeds from them. Thus, at the same time that the troops came more completely under the control of their own generals, the generals acquired financial control over what became their own private domains. This development, which followed a natural course in the last two reigns (1621–44), reached a climax after the fall of Peking with full recognition of the real state of affairs by the regime of Prince Fu in Nanking (1644–55). On the recommendation of Shih K'o-fa, four leading generals were enfeoffed as rulers over domains north of the lower Yangtse, with the vain hope that putting them on their own would stiffen their resistance to the Manchus. *Hsü t'ung-k'ao* 5:2824–26; *Ming-chi nan-lüeh* 3:48–50; *Ming-shih chi-shih pen-mo* 72:31; Wu Han, "Chün-ping," pp. 149, 189–90; T'ang Ch'i-yü, *Li-tai t'un-ken yen-chiu,* pp. 14–15, 127–29.

4. This figure runs close to the rated strength of the garrisons and stations when at their peak, during the Yung-lo period, at which time there were 493 garrisons rated at 5,600 men each and 359 independent stations rated at 1,120 mean each, for a total of 3,161,880. However, by the time the garrisons and stations became largely dependent on pay and supplies from tax revenues (rather than on the produce of military farms), it is unlikely that this large a number was involved. *Ming hui-tien* 124:75a; Wu Han, "Chün-ping," pp. 151, 173–75.

5. The Northwest border troops were not diverted to grain transport duty, like the garrisons of the Southeast, and their general readiness for battle was a more constant concern of the court. The first need for militia and mercenary reinforcement did not therefore arise in this region, but in the Southeast (see note 2 above and note 11 below). Wu Han, "Chün-ping," pp. 182–83.

6. I.e., those on active duty and those working the farms supporting them.

7. The original Ming armies consisted of hereditary troops drawn from households classed as "military" and placed under the administration of the chief military commission (*tu-tu fu*), whereas civilian and artisan households, registered under the Ministries of Revenue and of Works, respectively, were subject to the regular state administration. There was a fixed number of military households, with fixed residence on military farms, obligated to provide able-bodied males in succession for military service. The hired armies, however, were drawn from those households classed as civilian and returned to civil life when no longer needed. They were paid

and supplied through extra taxes on the civil population. Wu Han, "Chün-ping," pp. 147–48; Hucker, no. 7314.

8. *tung shih* (also known as *tung-cheng*—"Punitive Expedition to the East"): the seven-year campaign against the forces of Toyotomi Hideyoshi, which invaded Korea in 1592. Successive expeditionary forces, recruited throughout the country by offering large inducements and rewards to the men participating, were defeated by the Japanese, who finally withdrew from Korea in 1598 owing to the death of Hideyoshi in Japan. Estimates of the expense incurred in the hiring of mercenaries for this campaign ran from six to almost eight million taels. *Ming shih* 20:275–76, 21:279–91; *Ming shih chi-shih pen-mo* 62:44ff, 57; Wu Han, "Chün-ping, p. 197.

9. Instances of this type of conduct by generals of the late Ch'ung-chen (1628–44) and Hung-kuang (1645) periods may be found in their biographies in ECCP (see especially Kao Chieh, p. 410; Liu Tse-ch'ing, p. 531; Liu Liang-tso, p. 524; Tso Liang-yü and Tso Meng-keng, p. 761).

10. This was the amount set in 1472–73 and considered fixed thereafter. *Ming hui-tien* 27:127b.

11. After the removal of the capital to Peking in 1403, the duty of guarding tax rice that had to be transported north each year was assigned alternately to the various garrisons and stations of the empire. It was found uneconomical, however, to use troops normally stationed at a considerable distance from the transport route, and after the accession of the Hsüan-te emperor (1426) the duties of the garrisons in north and south were divided—the former being charged with defense of the capital and the border regions, while southern garrisons, organized under twelve tax transport leaders (*pa-tsung*) and a general commander of grain transport (*ts'ao-yün tsung-lu*), assumed the full responsibilities of escorting tax grain. This proved a great burden and expense for the people of the Southeast and left them without adequate forces to control endemic uprisings and banditry, so that additional troops had to be raised for this purpose. *Ming hui-tien* 27:129a–131b; *Hsü t'ung-k'ao* 31:3095, 31:3097a–3099a; *Ming shih* 79:1916–1917, 153:4206–4209; Wu Han, "Chün-ping," pp. 182–83; Hucker. nos. 4384, 6935.

12. Troops called upon to serve at a distance from their home stations, such as grain escorts and those sent to the capital for periodic defense duty, received a special subsistence allowance because their regular pay-and-rations were barely sufficient, if at all, for their families at home. *Ming hui-tien* 27:124a–127a; *Hsü t'ung-k'ao* 31:3096c–3098b.

13. Chung-tu: a commandery established at Feng-yang in Anhui province, from which city had come the founder of the Ming dynasty, Chu Yüan-chang. *Ming shih* 90:2200, 2213.

14. Ta-ning: a commandery in the region of modern P'ing-ch'üan in southern Jehol. *Ming shih* 40:906, 90:2203, 2219.

15. In 1415, during the Yung-lo reign with the capital at Peking, the practice was inaugurated of bringing in troops from garrisons around the capital for regular periods of training and defense duty. These troops were considered a part of the capital garrison and were call *pan-chün* ("periodic troops"). However, these troops were more and more diverted to work on construction projects such as the building of

palaces and tombs, and as the work was thoroughly detested, those liable for it hired substitutes. Thus by the end of the dynasty, the *pan-chün* had become a mercenary force devoted almost exclusively to labor service. *Ming hui-tien* 134:150a; *Ming shih* 90:2229–2232; Wu Han, "Chün-ping," pp. 161–64.

16. The "new rations" (*hsin-hsiang*) represented the proceeds from additional taxes levied during the late Wan-li period (1618–20) for the payment and supply of troops in excess of the regular standing army. They were issued to such troops by the officials of the region in which they were stationed.

17. The armies of the Ming originally consisted of two main types: those who had served in Chu Yüan-chang's armies during his conquest of the empire, and those who had submitted to the former and been reorganized. A third type was created by an edict of 1394, which ordered the Ministry of War to conscript criminals who were called "Troops of the Imperial Pardon" (*en-chün*). Since not only the criminal himself but also his descendants were condemned to perpetual military service, they were also called "Everlasting Troops" (*ch'ang-sheng chün*). In some cases, as a result of one man's crime, so many of his kin were held responsible that whole communities were sent to serve in distant regions. *Ming shih* 90:2194; Wu Han, "Chüm-ping," p. 160.

18. See note 15 above.

19. Cf. *Ming hui-tien* 19:59b.

20. In 1502 the population of Nanking, including the fourteen prefectures and four departments under its jurisdiction, was 10,179,242, according to figures from tax registers in the *T'u-shu pien,* compiled by Chang Huang (1527–1608). In 1542, according to the same source, it had risen to 10,402,198 (1623 ed., 90:6ab). In 1578 the census for the sixth year of Wan-li, recorded in the *Ming hui-tien* (19:60ab) of that period, gave results for the fourteen prefectures and four departments which total 9,332,651. This is the last regional census listed for the Ming dynasty in such sources as the *Hsü t'ung-k'ao* (13:2895c), *Ming shih* (40:910–32), *Chiang-nan t'ung-chih* (74:3a), and *T'u-shu chi-ch'eng* (ching-chi hui-pien, shih-huo 17). Not only is it thus commonly referred to, but Huang himself has used it for most of his current statistics, though he is writing eighty years later. It is possible he had some other source for his figure of 10,502,651, but it is more likely that this is an erroneous total for the figures given in the *Ming hui-tien* for the various prefectures and departments of the Nanking jurisdiction. The *Chiang-nan t'ung-chih* arrives at a total of 10,903,651 for the same figures (taken from the *Hsü t'ung-k'ao*). The fact that the last three digits of Huang's total are identical with those of the *T'ung-chih* and the last four digits with the total 9,322,651 would seem to indicate that he was working with the same set of figures but added incorrectly (as did the *T'ung-chih*). Such mistakes are not unusual; even the *Ming shih* has errors in this set of figures; those given for Feng-yang and Yang-chou fu do not agree with those appearing in the *Ming hui-tien* (presumed original source), *Hsü t'ung-k'ao,* and *T'u-shu chi-ch'eng.*

Military System (Part 2)

1. From a description by Han Yü of the ceremonial honors due to the imperial commissioner for Lingnan on the part of lesser prefectural commanders whenever

passing through his seat. Cf. Han Yü, [*Chu Wen-kung chiao*] *Ch'ang-li hsien-sheng chi,* SPTK 21:8a.

2. The independence of the army commanders, who in the late Ch'ung-chen period were comparable to the warlords of the early Republican period (1911–27), was probably due more to the weakness of the court than to any deliberate policy of favoring military over civil administration. Judging from the chronological "Table of Regional Commanders" (*Ming tu-fu nien-piao*) in *Erh-shih-wu shih pu-pien,* vol. 4, it appears that civil officials continued to hold supervisory posts throughout this period, though their authority (especially in the last few years) was undoubtedly more nominal than real.

3. *san fu* ("The Three Protectors"): referred originally in the Han to governors in the areas surrounding the capital and from that came to refer to the capital vicinity itself. *Han shu* 5:10b.

4. Chin-chou [Jinzhou] and Ch'i-chou in Shantung Province.

5. For this expression see Hsiao T'ung, *Wen-hsüan,* SPTK 5:18b (Tso Ssu, "Wu tu fu"). Here it must refer to the capital city.

6. In April, just before the fall of Peking, Wu San-kuei (1612–78), commander of the Liao-tung garrison, was ennobled as "Earl Who Pacifies the West" (*p'ing-hsi po*); the rebel-pacifying General Tso Liang-yü (1598–1645) as "Earl Who Pacifies the South" (*ning-nan po*); T'ang T'ung, the commander of the Chi-chou garrison, as "Earl Who Regulates the West" (*ting-hsi po*); and Huang Te-kung (d. 1645), the commander of the Feng-yang garrison, as "Earl Who Quells the South" (*ching-nan po*). At the same time, many other generals were raised one grade in rank. After the fall of Peking, Liu Tse-ch'ing (d. 1648) was ennobled as "Earl Pacifying the East" (*tung-p'ing po*). *Ch'ung-chen shih-lu* 17:8b–9a, 12b–13b; *Ming shih* 24:334; Mao Nai-yung, *Chi-ming feng-chüeh piao* 1b; ECCP, p. 532; Angela Hsi, "Wu San-kuei in 1644: A Reappraisal," pp. 443–53.

7. That is, their generals were also great statesmen.

8. In the *Tso chuan* (Legge, *Tso Chuen,* in *Chinese Classics* 1:351, 353), it is recorded that Chin, one of the states of the Spring and Autumn period, created six armies and their generals were made high ministers in recognition of their services in war.

9. In the early years of the Ming dynasty, the regional commanders (*tsung-ping kuan*) had actual control of military operations, being sent out on occasion of each campaign and relinquishing command of the troops upon the conclusion of the campaign. Since operations were frequently prolonged, however, these commanders tended to become indefinitely established in many areas, and, owing to their power and position, exercised considerable control over civil affairs as well as military. In the Cheng-t'ung period (1436–49) and after, civil ministers were in the ascendancy at court and asserted their control over military affairs by appointing censors to investigate and supervise provincial affairs with military as well as civil powers. These officials, known as *hsün-fu,* were not supposed to have had permanent posts, but like the regional commanders they in time assumed all the functions of provincial governors. Again, after 1540, civil officials known as *tsung-tu* were sent out by the court to coordinate and supervise the forces in several commanderies or provinces. These two tended to become permanent posts, superimposed

upon the existing military and civil administration. They were held by high civil officials, who frequently were designated grand coordinators (*hsün-fu*) of a province and supreme commander (*tsung-tu*) of a larger region at the same time. In the last years of the dynasty still another type of command, the *ching-lüeh* or military commissioner, was created to direct operations over a wide area; it was usually filled by a civil minister of state such as the president of the Ministry of War, who had supreme authority in the field. *Ming shih* 73:1767, 1773–1780; 76:1866–1867; *Ming tu-fu nien-piao* (in *Erh-shih-wu shih pu-pien*, vol. 4); Wu Han, "Chün-ping," pp. 155–57; Hucker, nos. 1231, 2731, 7227.

10. A special section in the official Ming History is devoted to the biographies of twenty-one loyal ministers who committed suicide when Peking was taken in April 1644, rather than fall into the hands of the brigand Li Tzu-ch'eng. They were honored for their loyalty by the court of Prince Fu in Nanking and also by the Manchus. *Ming shih* 265, 266.

11. An example of this is the guerrilla warfare conducted by civilians like Huang Tsung-hsi in Kiangsu, Chekiang, and Fukien against Manchu forces frequently led by turncoat Ming generals.

12. *Lü-shih ch'un-ch'iu*, SPTK 8:5b (Chien hsüan).

13. *Hou-Han shu* 67:24a (biography of Fan P'ang).

14. Pao Yung (d. A.D. 27): an able general in the period of the changeover from the Former to the Later Han dynasty, who prized learning and virtue over military success. Upon the accession of the Emperor Kuang-wu (A.D. 25), he disbanded his forces and refused to serve the new ruler on the grounds that, having served the preceding emperor, he would be ashamed to use the forces entrusted to him in order to win rank and wealth for himself under a new master. *Hou-Han shu* 29:7b–12a.

15. P'eng Yüeh (d. 196 B.C.): a brigand from Shantung who assembled a large band of fighting men in the last years of the Ch'in dynasty and became a general under T'ien Jung in 206 B.C. A year later he joined Han Kao-tsu (or Han Kao-ti), but was liquidated by the latter after his conquest of the empire. *Shih chi* 90:2b–5b; Watson, *Records* 1:191–95; *Han shu* 34:13b–16a; Chavannes, *Memoires Historiques* 2:294–95, 306–15, 370–81, 393–95; Dubs, *History of the Former Han* 1:7–10, 61–78.

16. Ch'ing P'u (d. 195 B.C.): a general of the state of Ch'u who served as commander-in-chief under Hsiang Yü toward the end of the Ch'in dynasty, but was persuaded to rebel against him in 204 B.C. by Han Kao-tsu. When he later rebelled against Kao-tsu in 196 B.C., Ch'ing P'u was defeated and killed after a bitter struggle. *Shih chi* 91:1a–10a; Watson, *Records* 1:196–207; Chavannes, *Memoires Historiques* 2:254, 351–57, 366–70, 393–400; *Han shu* 34:16a–25b; Dubs, *History of the Former Han* 1:10, 60, 80–83, 126–28.

17. That is, Kao-tsu would not presumably have made these men generals out of free choice. They were already powerful generals when he began the conquest of the empire, and the best he could do was to win them to his side. Thus his use of these "warlords" does not support the argument that professional fighting men make better generals than do scholars trained in the service of the state.

18. *Wu-hui* (aconite) and *li-lu* (hellebore): highly poisonous plant roots that

were used, in small quantities and after soaking to diminish their poisonous properties, to treat a wide variety of human ailments. F. P. Smith, *Materia Medica of China,* pp. 3, 110 (1871 ed.); G. A. Stuart, *Chinese Materia Medica,* pp. 7–12, 452 (1928 ed.).

19. Tu Mu, *Fan-ch'uan wen-chi,* SPTK 5:6a–b.

20. Shu-sun T'ung: a scholar who had first served the second emperor of the Ch'in dynasty, then Hsiang Yü, and finally Han Kao-tsu after 205 B.C. He was largely responsible for drawing up the ceremonial procedures adopted by Kao-tsu to give his court an air of legitimacy and gentility. The incident Huang refers to occurred shortly after Shu-sun T'ung's employment as an adviser by Kao-tsu, when over a hundred disciples and scholars in Shu-sun's following became dissatisfied because he had not provided them with good jobs under their new master. Instead Shu-sun had recommended for important assignments only rough and ready fighters, freebooters and mobsters. When informed of his disciples' grumbling over his preference for clever ruffians, Shu-sun explained to them, "The King of Han is fighting to win the world in a time fraught with strife and danger. But what do you scholars know of hurly-burly warfare? Therefore I have had to call for warriors who could cut down generals to capture the enemy flag. Yet those scholars who continue to serve me will not be forgotten [when the right time comes to use them]." *Shih chi* 99:6a; Watson, *Records* 1:291–98; *Han shu* 43:15a; Dubs, *History of the Former Han* 1:20–21.

21. *Shih chi* 99:6b; *Han shu* 43:15b.

22. Han Hsin (d. 196 B.C.): a peasant-soldier who became general-in-chief of Han Kao-tsu's forces in 206 B.C. upon the recommendation of Hsiao Ho, who told Kao-tsu, "If you really wish to contest for control of the world, except for Han Hsin there is no one else who can plan for you." After the conquest of the empire, he was one of the first generals to be liquidated by Kao-tsu in order to consolidate his own power. J. de Francis, "Biography of the Marquis of Huai-yin," *Harvard Journal of Asiatic Studies* 10 (1947): 179–215; *Shih chi* 93:1a–10a; Watson, *Records* 1:208–32; Chavannes, *Mémoires Historiques* 1:306, 314–15, 359–95; *Han shu* 34:1a–13b; Dubs, *History of the Former Han,* pp. 8–10, 12, 68–70.

23. *Chou li* 40:12a (K'ao kung chi): the translation of these terms may well be subject to improvement by someone with a technical knowledge of Chinese weapons, but the essential meaning is clear: there are certain qualities appropriate to different weapons, and in the same way there are different qualities appropriate to soldiers and generals.

Military System (Part 3)

1. "The civil and military were differentiated along two separate paths." This refers to the holding of separate examinations for civil and military officials in the T'ang and after, the former being tested for their literary abilities by the Ministries of Rites or Personnel and advanced in office accordingly, while the latter were tested in military arts to qualify for army posts. Rotours, *Traité des Examens,* pp. 49, 235.

2. When military men were constituted as an hereditary class during the first Ming reign (1368–98).

3. That is, the regional commanders (*tsung-ping kuan*), who were mostly military men, remained in direct command of the troops. However, according to Hucker, in the last Ming reign civil officials and even eunuchs sometimes served as commanding generals. Hucker, no. 7146, 7227.

4. Tu Mu (803–852): T'ang official and poet, known as the "lesser Tu" to distinguish him from Tu Fu. Possessing a rare combination of scholarly and military attainments, his official career was marked by frequent assignment to posts of military importance, as well as by his unceasing exposures of incompetence and maladministration in high places. His prose works contain many treatises on military policy and tactics, emphasizing the importance of topography and the use of men of education and fine character in war. The quotation is from *Fan-ch'uan wen-chi*, SPTK 10:4b (Chu Sun Tzu hsü); see also 5:1a–7b, 11:1a–6a, 16:1a–3b; *Hsin T'ang shu* 166:11b–15b.

5. This represents the standard military organization of the empire during the Yung-lo period (1403–24) and after. Previously, the standard table of organization (adopted in 1393) contained 17 regional commands, 329 garrisons, and 65 independent stations. The regional command (*tu-ssu*) generally corresponded to a province. *Ming hui-tien* 124:75a; *Ming shih* 90:2196–2205; Hucker, no. 7134.

6. That is, attached to the chief commissioners and regional commissioners, as well as the garrison commanders. Cf. *Ming shih* 76:1866–1870; Hucker, nos. 7199, 7311.

7. These commands were purely nonoperational, charged with the maintenance and supply of the standing military organization and administration of military households. Cf. *Ming hui-tien* 124:75a, *Hsü t'ung-k'ao* 122:3890b; *Ming shih* 76:1856–1857, 1873, 90:2193–96; Hucker, no. 374.

8. Standard operational commands of the Ming (cf. *Ming shih* 76:1866). The same ranks were perpetuated by the Ch'ing dynasty, but the last two had dropped in the scale owing to the insertion of two additional ranks above them. Cf. Mayers, no. 441–448; Brunnert and Hagelstrom, no. 751–752; Hucker, nos. 927, 2041, 4384, 6870, 8036.

9. Shen Hsi-i (d. ca. 1547): a general from Kuei-hsien in Kwangsi who, coming from a military family, began a career of bandit suppression in 1517 and by 1526 had risen to the rank of deputy provincial commander (*tu-chih-hui t'ung-chih*). He played a prominent part in the suppression of the revolt at T'ien-chou in Kwangsi during the year 1526–27, assisting the celebrated Wang Yang-ming and rising to the rank of assistant general. Stationed at Liu-chou in the same province, he maintained strict order and wiped out banditry. Before his death he was raised to the rank of deputy grand commander and commanding general of the Kueichou garrison. Shen was especially known for his expert handling of troops and the intense loyalty he inspired in them (*Ming shih* 211:5991–95). This and the other three cases cited are of professional soldiers who demonstrated a capacity for high office without having the education or other qualifications required of civil officials.

10. Wan Piao (1498–1556): of an old military family in Ningpo, Wan started

early upon a military career and by the age of seventeen was already an assistant garrison commander. He was determined, however, to rise above his class, and after training himself in the arts of war each day, he would spend the night studying classical literature. In 1520 he obtained the military *chin-shih* degree and thereafter rose rapidly to vice-commander of the Kwangsi garrison and then commanding general of grain transport, which post he held for many years with distinction. The last years of his life, after 1554, were devoted to raising troops, largely at his own expense, and leading them to repel Japanese pirates harassing the East China coast. During this busy and successful military career, Wan also found time to take an active part in the intellectual life of his time, as a follower of the Wang Yang-ming school, and left numerous writings on military and philosophical questions. *Ming-ju hsüeh-an* 15:124; *Ming shih kao* 175:8a–9a; DMB, pp. 1337–39.

11. Yü Ta-yu (1503–80): a native of Fukien who as a boy was fond of both literary and soldierly arts, but owing to poverty gave up his studies to become a military officer of the lowest rank. In 1535, however, he passed the metropolitan military examinations and thereafter rose rapidly in the ranks. After 1549 he distinguished himself as provincial commander for pirate defense in Fukien. His personal army, combining land and naval forces effectively, became famous as a result of his numerous campaigns against Japanese pirates, and Yü became commanding general in Kwangtung and Fukien successively. He was known for his careful, long-range planning and his unquestioned loyalty to the throne. *Ming shih* 212:5601–1510; DMB, 1616–18.

12. Ch'i Chi-kuang (1528–88): one of the most famous generals of the late Ming, Ch'i came from a military family stationed for generations at Teng-chou in Shantung. He achieved his greatest fame in campaigns against Japanese pirates in Chekiang and Fukien, and is known especially for his advocacy of improved methods in the recruiting, training, and use of troops, concerning which he left many writings. His own force of 3,000 hand-picked Chekiang troops, outfitted with naval craft and firearms, became a model of its kind, and when Ch'i was called to command garrisons on the Northern border after 1567, he extended and intensified this training program over a wide area. In sixteen years of service he largely pacified the Northeast border area, and enjoyed the fullest confidence of Chang Chü-cheng, but when the latter died his enemies had Ch'i exiled to Kwangtung and finally discharged from service. A temple was erected in his honor in Foochow and, when the Japanese attacked China in the 1930s, was refurbished as a symbol of resistance to aggression. *Ming shih* 212:5610–22; DMB, pp. 220–24.

Finance (Part 1)

1. *Mencius* 7B:27.

2. "With a handful of grain I go out and divine" (*Shih ching* 196; Legge, *She King,* in *Chinese Classics* 4:334; B. Karlgren, *Book of Odes,* p. 145). Legge, following the standard commentaries, says that this refers to a custom "of spreading finely ground rice on the ground, in connection with divination, as an offering to the spirits," But Ku Yen-wu, the great classicist and Huang's contemporary, interprets this

practice as a form of payment, like the latter. "In ancient times money was not widely used; neither the Odes nor the *Book of Documents* mentions currency or coins. And so the person seeking divination used grain. The same was true in early Han; the biographies of diviners in the *Shih chi* say 'if the diviner gives an erroneous answer, he is not allowed to keep the grain'" (*Shih chi,* SPTK 127:6a; *Jih chih lu* 3:17). But see Y. C. Wang, "The Distribution of Coin Types in Early China," *American Numismatic Society Museum Notes* 3 (1942): 131.

3. From a celebrated passage in which Mencius refutes those who argue that scholars should grow their own food: "If you do not have intercommunication of the productions of labor and an interchange of men's services, so that one from his surplus may supply the deficiency of another, then husbandmen will have a superfluity of grain and women will have a superfluity of cloth. If you have such interchange, carpenters and carriage-wrights may all get their food from you. Here, now, is a man who at home is filial, and abroad respectful to his elders; and watches over the principles of the ancient kings, awaiting the rise of future learners—and yet you will refuse to support him. How is it that you give honor to the carpenter and carriage-wright, and slight him who practices benevolence and righteousness?" (Legge, *Mencius* 3:B4).

4. Apparently Huang means that cash was used as an alternative to supplement grain and cloth as a ready means of exchange and maintain a balanced supply. Nishida Taichirō, trans. *Min-i taihō roku,* p. 147, translates *heng* here as standard of value, but this would not be too compatible with Huang's further statement that "cash was inversely proportionate to grain and cloth in value."

5. *Hou-Han shu* 43:3b–4b; *Cambridge History of China,* vol. 1 (Twitchett and Loewe, eds.), pp. 585–90 (Nishijima Sadao chapter).

6. Cf. *T'ung-k'ao* 8:86b, which reports the opposite—namely, that the use of cash was restored. According to *Chin shu* 16:3a, it was Wei Wen-ti who in 221 banned the use of cash, and Wei Ming-ti who restored it, as confirmed by *T'ung-tien* 8:47c.

7. Huan Hsüan's dates are 369–404: a proposal made in A.D. 402, during the reign of An-ti of the Eastern Chin, but not put into effect (*Chin shu* 16:11a; *T'ung-k'ao* 8:86c). For the most part, as a source for the pre-Sung Chinese economy, Huang seems to have relied on the *T'ung-k'ao.*

8. Quoted from the memorial of K'ung Lin-chih (369–423) in opposition to the proposal of Huan Hsüan to abolish the use of cash in A.D. 402. K'ung, whose views prevailed at court, argued that the diversion of grain and cloth to serve as media of exchange would reduce the available supply of these goods for actual use. Citing the failure of the abolition of cash during the Wei dynasty (mentioned above by Huang), K'ung favored rectifying the evils of the cash system without abolishing it altogether. *T'ung-k'ao* 8:86c–87a.

9. San-wu: the region of South Kiangsu and North Chekiang provinces. *Ku-chin ti-ming ta-tz'u-tien* (hereafter, KCTMTTT), pp. 29, 107, 370, 1019.

10. Ching: region including Hunan, Hupeh, and parts of Kueichou, Kwangsi, and Kwangtung. KCTMTTT, p. 940.

11. Ying: Wu-ch'ang in Hupei province. KCTMTTT, p. 757.

12. Chiang: Kiukiang in Kiangsi province. KCTMTTT, p. 325.
13. Hsiang: Ch'angsha in Hunan province. KCTMTTT, p. 916.
14. Liang: Nan-cheng in Southwest Shensi province. KCTMTTT, p. 814.
15. I: Ch'eng-tu in Szechuan province. KCTMTTT, pp. 738d–739a.
16. Chiao and Kuang: Kwangtung, Kwangsi, and Northern Annam.
17. *T'ung-k'ao* 8:88a.
18. *T'ung-k'ao* 8:88b.
19. Ch'i-chou: Ch'i-hsien in Southwest Hopei province. KCTMTTT, p. 1212.
20. Cf. *T'ung-k'ao* 8:89b.
21. The commentary on this passage in *T'ung-k'ao* 8:89c, citing the "Account of the Western Regions" in the *History of the Former Han Dynasty,* identifies this type of currency as coming from the regions of Chi-pin (Kashmir) and Wu-i-shan-(yen?) (southeast Iran and Baluchistan). Cf. *Tz'u-hai,* ssu 196.
22. Cf. *T'ung-k'ao* 8:89b.
23. Cf. *Hsin T'ang shu* 54:12b–13a.
24. Wu-ling: mountainous region at the intersection of south Hunan, eastern Kwangsi, and northwest Kwangtung. KCTMTTT, p. 118.
25. Cf. *Hsin T'ang shu* 54:13a; *T'ung k'ao* 8:92a.
26. *Hsin T'ang shu* 54:13a; *T'ung k'ao* 8:92a.
27. Cf. *Hsin T'ang shu* 54:14b.
28. Ibid.
29. There was no twelfth year of Yüan-feng, this period lasting from only 1078 to 1086. Moreover, Ts'ai Ching had not yet risen to power at this time. This error undoubtedly arises from a misreading of the passage in the "Treatise on Economics in the Sung History" (*Sung shih* 180:19a–20a) describing the measures taken by Ts'ai Ching in the Cheng-ho period (1111–17):

> In the first year of Cheng-ho cash was cheap and goods expensive, so that the people were hard up for food. It was decreed that the places for casting iron cash should be put in operation as before in Shensi and reproduce the large iron cash of the Yüan-feng period, which were worth two ordinary cash. . . .
> At that time in Kuan-chung cash was very cheap (light) and tin was added to it in order to make it heavier (worth more). Actually this cash was worth no more than iron cash; the price of goods rose daily, and the resulting evils were worse than with [the cash supposed to be] worth ten [ordinary cash]. In the second year (A.D.;1112) Ts'ai Ching returned to power.

Then follows the passage quoted by Huang. Huang Tsung-hsi seems to have punctuated this so as to read the ten and two together, giving "the twelfth year." Then he apparently looked back through the text to find out which period was in question and, seeing the reference to the Yüan-feng period, accepted it without realizing that it was mentioned retrospectively. The correct date is the second year of Cheng-ho, or A.D. 1112.

30. This should be understood as trading in gold and silver, not their use as currency (contrary to the impression given by Huang). See Nishida Taichirō, trans. *Min-i taihō roku,* p. 155*n*10.

31. Here again Huang gives the wrong date: this decree was handed down in the 29th year of the Shao-hsing period (1159), after the changeover to the Southern Sung (not in the Ch'ung-ho period [1118] of the Northern Sung). Cf. *Sung shih* 180:21b.

32. *Sung shih* 180:22a.

33. In favor of a system of paper money (*Yüan shih* 93:20b): translated into English by C. S. Gardner in Robert P. Blake, "The Circulation of Silver in the Moslem East Down to the Mongol Epoch," pp. 317–21.

34. Lit., "gold and silver became the mother and paper money the child." This passage generally follows the wording of the *Yüan shih* 93:20: "The system uses goods of value as security (mother) and paper notes as its representative (child), the paper and reserve standing in proper relation to each other" (Gardner, trans., in Blake, "The Circulation of Silver," p. 317). The terminology used here derives from such early works as the *Kuo-yü* and *Han shu,* where "mother" was applied to heavy coins and "child" to light ones. Thus: "In ancient times upon Heaven sending down calamities and tribulations, the rulers thereupon measured their wealth and currencies and balanced the light and heavy coins in order to relieve the people. Whenever in times of misfortune people suffered from money being too tight, then the rulers made a heavier currency (of higher value) and put it into circulation. And thus there was mother (or heavy coin) to balance child (or light coin) for circulation. The people all greatly benefited from this" (*Han shu* 24B:2b; Swann, *Food and Money,* pp. 225–27). In the present case paper money, though of higher denominations than the coins, is referred to as "child" and its reserve in gold or silver is called "mother." The balance between them is therefore of a different sort from the earlier case involving a balanced supply of complimentary circulating media. For other uses of these terms see Lien-sheng Yang, *Money and Credit in China,* pp. 33–34; Katō Shigeshi, *Chūgoku kaheishi kenkyū,* p. 218.

35. *tzu-mu hsiang ch'üan erh hsing:* (cf. Gardner, in Blake, "The Circulation of Silver": "Paper and reserve standing in proper relation to each other." My use of "balance" for *ch'üan* follows Swann and the commentary on *Han shu* 24B:2b.

36. *Ming shih* 81:1962–1963.

37. Supervisorates (*t'i-chü-ssu*): offices set up throughout the empire to develop and control the production of natural resources as well as a wide variety of other industrial and commercial enterprises. This system of controls was developed under the Sung dynasty and maintained on a wide scale by the Mongols. The chief resources controlled were salt, tea, iron, gold, silver, copper, lead, tin, and jade. In some cases these were operated as government monopolies, but generally control was exercised through the licensing of private producers who turned a certain quota or percentage of production over to the state. *Yüan shih* 88:9b ff., 84:2b, 10a; *Sung shih* 167:16a–20a, 176:29a, 182:18b, 184:21b.

38. Cf. *Yüan shih* 94:2b.

39. Policy adopted by the founder of the Ming dynasty and continued by most of his successors. *Ming shih* 81:1973.

40. Cf. *Ming shih* 81:1973–1974.

Finance (Part 2)

1. This was a recurrent evil in the casting or minting of Chinese coins. The value of coins was determined primarily by the weight of metal they contained, but also by the cost of coining. The issuing agent was frequently tempted to cut his costs both in the metal and labor used to produce the coins. Usually, however, people learned quickly that such issues were not worth their face value and discounted them on the exchange. The government often fixed heavy penalties for refusal to accept these issues at face value, but such measures generally did not avail to support artificially a debased coinage. Thus the stability of the currency was sacrificed in favor of short-sighted profiteering. Cf. Wilhelm Vissering, *On Chinese Currency,* pp. 155–57.

2. These denominations were used throughout the Ming dynasty, but their actual value in metal did not generally correspond to their face value. Illustrations of these taken from rubbings may be found in *Li-tai ku-ch'ien t'u-shuo,* compiled by Ting Fu-pao, pp. 151–72. The present text refers to these denominations by the characters cast on the face, viz., *che erh,* "worth two" (cash), *tang wu* "worth five" (cash), etc. Cf. *Ming shih* 81:1961–1962.

3. The result was a shortage of copper cash and price deflation, so that producers could not get enough return on their goods to meet taxes fixed at a comparatively inflated rate.

4. The different issues of each reign were not of uniform cast or value. This not only involved greater expense in production, but resulted in wide fluctuation of cash values, encouraged counterfeiting, and lowered confidence in the currency generally. Cf. *Ming shih* 81:1965–1969.

5. I.e., of earlier dynasties. For details of these weaknesses or abuses, see Vissering, *On Chinese Currency,* ch. 2–5; and Harry Glathe, "The Origin and Development of Chinese Money," pp. 158–60, 210–14, 278; Yang, *Money and Credit,* pp. 30–34, 37–38. On the failure of the Ming to work out a consistent monetary policy, see Ray Huang, *Taxation and Finance,* p. 317.

6. That is, the value of copper cash fluctuated in terms of its silver equivalent.

7. After the adoption of the Single-whip system in the Chia-ching period (formalized in 1581), all taxes were paid in silver (see translation, "Land System Part 3)." Generally in the latter part of the dynasty salaries were paid in copper cash not up to par value, but occasionally protests secured part payment in silver. *Ming shih* 81:1967–1968.

8. I.e., in the Ming dynasty.

9. A total of one hundred ounces, the catty (*chin*) being reckoned as sixteen ounces on the Chinese scale.

10. Paper notes were issued in the early reigns of the dynasty but were abandoned after the Hung-chih and Cheng-te periods (1488–1521). They had been printed in great quantity without sufficient reserve, and people discounted them heavily in favor of silver or copper cash, which had real value. *Ming shih* 81:1964–1965, 1969; Yang, *Money and Credit,* pp. 66–67; Chan, *Ming Dynasty,* pp. 131–33; Ray Huang, *Taxation and Finance,* pp. 69–74, 232, 261.

11. Chiang Ch'en: a native of T'ung-ch'eng in Anhui province, Chiang became a

licentiate and a member of the Fu-she society. As a protégé of Fan Ching-wen (1587–1644; ECCP, p. 229) and Ni Yüan-lu (1594–1644), he was given a special appointment to the Ministry of Revenue while Ni was president in 1643. In the summer of that year he made his celebrated proposals for the issue of paper money, which were unsuccessfully inaugurated early the following year. Though Huang identifies him only as a licentiate, the *Ch'ung-chen shih-lu* (16:8b) and *Ch'ung-chen ch'ang-pien* (1:13) identify him as an office manager (*ssu-wu*) of the ministry, and the *Ming shih* (251:6501–6502) and *Ming shih kao* 235:23a) as a secretary (*chu-shih*). His eight-point program for paper currency as an alternative to heavier taxation to meet military needs is presented in *Ch'ung-chen ch'ang-pien* 1:13–16. Cf. also *Ming-shih chi-shih* 22:3151; Chu I-tsun, *Ming shih tsung* 70:9a; *Ming-chi pei-lüeh* 19:14b; Hucker, no. 5817.

12. Equivalent to 1,000 copper cash (ten strings) or one tael of silver.

13. The *Erh lao ko* text reads "gold" here but other sources listed in preceding and following notes indicate that silver is meant. See Sun Ch'eng-tse (1593–1675), *Ch'un-ming meng yü lu* 38:30ab.

14. Wang Ao-yung (d. 1644): a *chin-shih* graduate of 1625–26 from Tzu-ch'uan in Shantung, Wang served under Ni Yüan-li as vice president of the Ministry of Revenue and was responsible for the operation of the paper currency scheme he had adopted from Chiang Ch'en. Following its failure and the fall of Peking to Li Tzu-ch'eng in April 1644, Wang remained in the capital and, after being subjected to a "shakedown" imprisonment by the brigand chief, purchased his freedom and continued in office during Li's transitory regime. When the Manchus came, Wang again switched sides. Serving the conquerors in their campaign against the forces of the Ming regime, Wang was captured and killed in November 1644, whereupon he was honored posthumously with the rank of Minister of Revenue. The character Ao in his given name sometimes appears as 鰲 instead of 鼇 (e.g., the Kuang-hsü edition of *Erh ch'en chuan* by the Ch'ing Historiographical Board, 1:14a) and has been changed to this reading in the MITFL as found in MITFL 20b:1.4 in Huang's *Li-chou i-chu hui-k'an* (Collected works) (hereafter LCICHK). However, the character used in the Ch'ien-lung edition (42b:1.7) is also used by the *Ming shih* 251:6501–6502, *Ming shih kao* 235:23a, *Ch'ing-shih lieh-chuan* (1928) 78:5a–6a, and the Harvard-Yenching indices of Ming and Ch'ing biography; therefore it is taken as standard. Cf. also *Ch'ung-chen ch'ang-pien* 2:72, 90; Hsü Tzu, *Hsiao-t'ien chi-nien fu-k'ao,* 1861 ed., 2:6b, 4:42a.

15. This figure does not make sense and consequently has been changed to 30 million in the LCICHK version of the text (MITFL 20b). However, a fuller account of this incident contained in Sun Ch'eng-tse, *Ch'un-ming meng yü lu* 38:30ab, indicates that the error is not simply a misprint of the figure. This account runs: "In the sixth month of the sixteenth year of Ch'ung-chen [1643], the licentiate from T'ung-ch'eng, Chiang Ch'en, was summoned to court and stated 'It is feasible to operate a system of paper money. If in one year 30 million *kuan* of paper money is printed, with one *kuan* equal to one tael of silver, in a year 30 million taels of silver could be obtained.' The vice president of the Ministry of Revenue, Wang Ao-yung also said: 'If 30 million *kuan* are printed the first year, *they can be used in place of the silver*

surtax amounting to more than 20 million taels, as a means of lightening the tax burden on the poor people. In succeeding years if 50 million kuan is printed, it will bring in 50 million taels of silver. Since so much would be brought in, silver would be as cheap as dirt. Not only could the silver surtax be remitted, but each province could issue one million *kuan* to provide stipends for "nourishing the honesty" of officials [i.e. supplement official salaries to lessen the temptation to graft].' So the emperor established a Paper Currency Office in the Imperial Treasury, which printed money night and day. Then the government rounded up the merchants and called upon them to sell it [float the issue] at a rate of one *kuan* for one tael of silver, but none was willing to do so. The merchants of the capital abruptly packed up their bags and walked out." Then follow objections to this raised by Chiang Te-ching, differently worded from those recounted by Huang.

Accounts of this incident in the *Ming shih* (251:6501–6502) and *Ming shih kao* (235:23a) are worded identically to Huang's, except that Wang Ao-yung's remarks are omitted and it is merely stated that he approved the plan. However the 50 million figures cited in the above account from the *Ch'un-ming meng-yü lu* are supported by another account in the *Ch'ung-chen ch'ang-pien* 1:13, where the Ministry of Revenue, with Wang Ao-yung in charge of the paper currency program (2:72, 90), recommended an issue of 50 million.

From the great similarity of wording, it is likely that the MITFL, *Ming shih kao, Ming shih,* and *Hsiao-t'ien chi-nien* all drew upon the same original source, and that in abstracting from it Huang left out the lines underlined above (one column of type in the *Ch'un-ming meng yü lu* version.

16. Chiang Te-ching: a *chin-shih* graduate of 1622 from Chin-chiang in Fukien. In March 1642, he became Minister of Rites and Grand Secretary, in which posts he devoted himself especially to investigating the actual strength of the armed forces and the wasteful use of public funds for their support. He advocated a reduction of field commands in order to unify and simplify administration, and asked for a return to the original Ming military system, abolishing the expensive mercenaries and reducing the great number of surtaxes imposed on the people. By his strenuous opposition to new taxes and to Ni Yüan-lu's program of paper currency financing, he incurred the emperor's displeasure and was discharged shortly before the fall of Peking to Li Tzu-ch'eng. Subsequently, he refused to serve in the Nanking regime of Prince Fu but did take office briefly in the court of Prince T'ang in Fukien in 1645. Resigning the following year on account of illness, he died in October 1646. *Ming shih* 251:6500–6503; *Ming shih kao* 235:21b; *Hsiao-t'ien chi-nien* 2:6b–8b; DMB, p. 5; Hucker, no. 5963.

17. In 1375. *Ming shih* 81:1961–1962; Yang, *Money and Credit,* pp. 66–67.

18. *Shen-tao shih chiao:* an expression from the *I Ching* (3:20b): "When we contemplate the spirit-like way of Heaven, we see how the four seasons proceed without error. The sages, *in accordance with this spirit-like way of Heaven, laid down their instructions* and all under heaven yield submission to them" (Legge, *Yi King,* p. 230; emphasis added). Here the reasoning seems to be: "The Founder of the dynasty ruled as if with divine power and was able to do things lesser rulers could not. Yet even he did not attempt to use paper money except for rewards and official salaries."

19. A form of paper note that made its appearance during the reign of the Emperor Hsien-tsung (c. A.D. 807), when there was a dire shortage of copper cash. Traveling merchants and officials deposited their cash at government offices and received in return negotiable notes called "flying money," which could be carried readily to any part of the empire. This helped to relieve the cash shortage, and at the same time proved a great convenience to travelers since copper cash in any quantity was bulky and heavy to carry. It seems likely that "flying money," instead of being a printed note, was a written receipt sealed with the imperial seal and identifiable by fitting the torn edge with the torn edge of a stub kept at the Imperial Treasury. Therefore, it served as a draft for the transfer of credit but did not circulate as money. Cf. *Chiu T'ang shu* 49:9a; *Hsin T'ang shu* 54:13ab; Vissering, *On Chinese Currency,* pp. 120–21; T. F. Carter and L. C. Goodrich, *The Invention of Printing in China and Its Spread Westward* (rev. ed., 1955), pp. 103–12.

20. *hui-p'iao:* bills of exchange circulated privately in the absence of more convenient legal tender. Presumably they were similar to the *hui-tzu* of the Southern Sung dynasty, which originally were circulated locally in exchange for tea, salt, and iron, and then were adopted as legal tender after they had taken the place of cash in commercial transactions. The term *hui-p'iao* was later used for private drafts in Huang's time and throughout the Ch'ing dynasty. *T'ung-k'ao* 9:98b; *Sung shih* 181:1a; Chang Chia-hsiang, *Chung-kuo pi-chih shih,* p. 11; Vissering, *On Chinese Currency,* pp. 165, 183, 207; Yang, *Money and Credit,* pp. 56, 68, 92; Katō Shigeshi. *Kaheishi,* pp. 460–62.

21. In 970, during the first Sung reign, so-called "convenient money," similar to the "flying money" of the T'ang, was issued at the capital for the use of merchants and officials traveling to the provinces. Like their predecessors, however, these notes were not real currency and did not displace cash in common use, but simply served as letters of credit or bank drafts. The first real paper money was printed and circulated privately in Szechuan during the reign of Chen-tsung (998–1022). Owing to the widespread use of these bills of exchange (*chiao-tzu*) and their indispensability to commerce in this region, the government opened up banks to issue them as legal tender in 1023–24 during the reign of Jen-tsung. It is this type of currency that became the standard paper money of the Northern Sung, not the "convenient money," as Carter erroneously suggests. It is also this type, having a definite term of redemption, that Huang discusses in what follows. *T'ung k'ao* 9:94a, 97a; *Sung shih* 181:1a; Chang Chia-hsing, *Chung-kuo pi-chih shih,* pp. 10–11; Chu Hsieh, *Chung-kuo hsin-yung huo-pi fa-chan shih,* pp. 14–16, 27–32; Vissering, *On Chinese Currency,* pp. 167–77; Carter / Goodrich, *The Invention of Printing in China,* pp. 71–72; Yang, *Money and Credit,* pp. 52–53.

22. *chieh:* this was a limit in regard to both quantity of issue and time of redemption. Though these notes were not freely convertible, the government did guarantee that at prescribed intervals they could be exchanged for specie or new notes. This was generally reckoned as every three years, but Yang (*Money and Credit,* p. 53) estimates that new notes were actually issued every other year. The amount of each issue was supposedly limited by reserve requirements, yet this was not always the case. *T'ung-kao* 9:97a; Vissering, *On Chinese Currency,* pp. 170–72.

23. *T'ung-k'ao* 9:97b; Vissering, *On Chinese Currency,* p. 176.

24. Actually, the cash reserve was about 30 percent of the total note issue. See Yang, *Money and Credit,* p. 53.

25. *ch'eng-t'i ch'ao-fa:* lit., "system for maintaining the value of paper currency" by keeping reserves of hard metal or enforcing an official rate of exchange with other forms of currency. Vissering, *On Chinese Currency,* pp. 164, 180–182; Yang, *Money and Credit,* p. 66.

26. Huang's wording follows the *Yüan shih* account of a new issue in 1287, but the original system was adopted in 1260. Cf. *Yüan shih* 93:21a; Blake, "The Circulation of Silver," pp. 318–20; Yang, *Money and Credit,* pp. 63–64.

27. The issuance of paper currency in the early Ming was not governed by the limits (*chieh*) set upon the quantity of note issued or term of redemption. Instead, in 1374 a system was set up for the redeeming of worn, torn, or soiled bills for which new notes were issued. Since it was comparatively easy to counterfeit damaged and frayed bills, and to get them redeemed by new notes, the total issue expanded out of all proportion to actual reserves. Cf. *Hsü T'ung-k'ao* 10:2859bc; *Ming shih* 81:1962–1963; Chu Hsieh, *Huo-pi,* p. 139.

28. I.e., jumping to conclusions. A simile drawn from *Chuang Tzu* 1:2.16. "You are going too fast. You see your egg and expect to hear it crow. You look at your cross-bow and expect to have broiled pigeon in front of you" (trans. Giles, *Chuang Tzu,* p. 45; cf. Watson, trans., *Complete Works of Chuang Tzu,* p. 47).

29. *yen-yin:* a certificate representing the payment of money for salt at a government office, which could then be exchanged for the salt itself when presented at the salt factories. This was done so that merchants who had to travel a great distance to obtain salt would not have to carry heavy loads of specie with them in order to make payment. This practice was begun in the Sung and continued by later dynasties. Cf. *T'ung-k'ao* 9:97a, 98b; 16:161a; *Hsü T'ung-k'ao* 20:2955b; *Sung shih* 182:15b; Vissering, *On Chinese Currency,* pp. 169, 173.

Finance (Part 3)

1. *chi-hsiung chih li:* two of the five general types of rites performed during the Chou period under the direction of the Grand Master of Sacred Ceremonies. The rites of celebration consisted chiefly of sacrifices to the Lord of Heaven, heavenly bodies, earthly spirits, and royal ancestors. The rites of mourning were held in connection with deaths, natural calamities, famines, epidemics, military defeats, revolts, and disorders. *Chou li* 18:5b–8a (Biot, *Tcheou-li* 1:418–24).

2. *k'uang fei:* baskets of bamboo used in ancient times as containers for offerings of fine cloth, gems, food, and wine cups (*Shu ching* 6:2b, 3ab, 4a, 5a; Legge, *Shoo King,* in *Chinese Classics* 3:99, 102, 107, 111, 116, 119). The *k'uang* is mentioned many times in the *Shih ching* as a container for gifts or offerings, usually in connection with courtship or betrothal (Mao, nos. 3, 20, 154, 161, 222, 291: see Legge, in *Chinese Classics* 4:8, 30–31, 228–29, 245, 401, 604, and Karlgren, *Book of Odes,* pp. 3, 12, 97–98, 104, 175–76, 250; see also Arthur Waley, *The Analects of Confucius,* pp. 30, 45, 164–165, 163, 186, 192). The *fei,* a square covered basket, is mentioned in the *I li* as a container for wine cups used during the marriage ceremony

(5:14b, 6:30a; John Steele, *The I li,* pp. 22, 35). Here Huang probably refers to wedding gifts in general, not necessarily to the use of these particular types of basket.

3. Given by the groom's family to the family of the bride. E. T. C. Werner, *Descriptive Sociology: Chinese,* 27ac, 29c, 30a.

4. *han lien:* the first of these characters refers to an age-old custom of placing precious stones or metals, especially jade, in the mouth of the deceased when dressing the corpse for burial. The extraordinary properties of these objects were supposed to exert a preservative influence on both the body and spirit of the dead. In the *Chou li* this practice is described as of great importance in royal burials, but presumably was restricted to the nobility. Huang probably condemns its adoption by the people at large as not in keeping with common station and a needless extravagance for the poorer classes. *Chou li* 6:11a (Biot, *Tcheou-li* 1:124); Werner, *Descriptive Sociology,* pp. 148a, 159c, 160c, 164a; Henri S. Dore, *Researches into Chinese Superstitions* 1:47.

5. To the deceased in order to provide them with sustenance, and to Gods of the Soil in order to obtain safe passage for the soul through the underworld. Cf. Werner, *Descriptive Sociology,* pp. 153b, 160a, 164a; Dore, *Researches* 1:111.

6. *ch'u-ling* (lit., "straw spirits"): buried with the dead to accompany and serve them. According to the *Li chi* (9:24a; Legge, *Li Ki* 1:173), Confucius approved the use of these but condemned wooden images as inhumane, since they might lead to the use of living victims. Werner, *Descriptive Sociology,* pp. 152c, 157b, 159c, 162a.

7. *wu:* practices originally deriving from shamanism, but here indicating indigenous superstitions in general, including some associated with Taoism and assimilated into Buddhism.

8. Originally a substitute for the coins and other valuable objects buried with the dead for their use in the afterlife, but later burned to propitiate the spirits. Dore, *Researches* 1:117–23.

9. *chai chan ch'i-sai* (*chan,* "to dip," should read *chiao,* "sacrifice and thanksgiving"): refers to such ceremonies as the Buddhist one for securing safe passage or release from Hell (*tso chai*) and the Taoist sacrifice of thanksgiving for the rescue of departed souls (*ta chiao*). Cf. Dore, *Researches* 1:151.

10. Including actors and prostitutes.

11. *chi-fang* (lit., "loom factories"): not a common term but one used to designate at least some of the imperial textile factories (also known as *chih tsao* or *chi fang*) established by the Ming dynasty to supply the needs of the imperial household and the government. These factories, generally under the management of eunuchs, were established in Nanking, Soochow, Hangchow, Shao-hsing, etc., Huang's home region being a center of the silk-weaving industry. Whether Huang has in mind private or state-run factories is not clear, but it is probably both. *Ming hui-tien* 201:108b; *Ming shih* 82:1997–1998.

12. *chih chih i pen:* according to Confucian teaching, there is a proper order in all things. As it is said in the *Great Learning:* "Things have their root [or trunk: *pen*] and their branches [*mo*]. To know what is first and what is last leads one near to the Way. . . . It cannot be, when the root is neglected, that what should spring from it

will be well-ordered." The terms *pen* and *mo* are used in a variety of related senses and may be translated variously as "primary and secondary," "original and derivative," "essential and nonessential," etc.

13. I.e., according to the three classical books of rites—*Chou li, I li* and *Li chi*— or, as Huang indicates elsewhere, such modifications of them as Chu Hsi's *Family Rituals.*

14. See Huang's chapter on education, wherein he asserts that all such observances among the people should follow strictly the prescriptions of the so-called *Family Rituals of Chu Hsi (Chu Tzu chia-li).*

15. *mo* (lit., 末 "branch"): inevitable consequences of the basic error, which was abandonment of the ancient ritual.

16. *ch'ung-pen i-mo:* in my earlier translation, I asserted that this expression itself was first used by Ssu-ma Chih, an official of the state of Wei (220–265), who in a memorial upheld the importance of agricultural production and urged a policy of discouraging commerce. See de Bary, "Plan for the Prince," Ph.D. diss., Columbia University, (Ann Arbor, Mich.: University Microfilms, 1953), pp. 1–50 (cf. *San kuo chih, Wei chih* 12:20b). Professor Yü Ying-shih offers the following on this point:

> These four characters [崇本抑末] first appear in Wang Fu's (c. 90–165) *Ch'ien-fu lun* (ch. 2: "Wu-pen," last para.). [See *Ch'ien-fu lun chien chiao-cheng,* p. 23.] But the idea is much older. In the *Yen-t'ieh lun* (ch. 1: "Pen-i"), we find the expression *Ch'ung-pen t'ui-mo* 崇本推末, which means the same thing [*Yen-t'ieh lun,* p. 2]. However, we have good reason to believe that Huang may have been directly influenced by the arguments in the *Ch'ien-fu lun* because his other important point about both industry and commerce being 'essential' *(kung-shang chieh pen* 公商皆本) seems to have been also a further development from Wang Fu's notion that both industry and commerce have, respectively, their "essentials" and "non-essentials" [*Ch'ien-fu lun chien chiao-cheng,* pp. 15–16].

17. *The Mean (Chung yung)* 20 speaks of the wise ruler as receptive to all kinds of artisans and tradesmen.

18. A paraphrase of Mencius, who was an advocate of *laissez-faire* economic policies: "If, in the market place of his capital, the ruler levies a ground rent on the shops but does not tax the goods, or enforces the proper regulations without levying a ground rent . . . then all the traders of the empire will be pleased, and wish to store their goods in his market place.

"If at his frontier passes there is an inspection of persons but no taxes charged on goods or other articles, then all the travelers of the empire will be pleased and wish to make their tours on his roads" (Legge, *Mencius* 2A:5).

Subofficials

1. *hsü-li:* a general term for persons performing minor and subordinate official functions, more commonly rendered *li-hsü* or simply *li.* Though originally employees of almost menial status, the *li-hsü* came to represent a class of subofficials or subbureaucracy corresponding to the "clerical, administrative and fiscal" classification of the United States Civil Service. They were not full-fledged officials (*kuan*),

since they did not enter through the examination system, but many occupied key administrative positions and were rewarded for "meritorious" service by appointment to lesser official posts (*kuan*). Because Huang takes a dim view of the excessive importance and power enjoyed by these subofficials in his time, the term has for him the sense of "petty bureaucrat." On this issue see also Ku Yen-wu, *Jih chih lu chi-shih*, Chūbun ed., 8:187–90, David Kornbluth, "Ku Yen-wu and the Reform of Local Administration"; and Chan, *Ming Dynasty*, pp. 305–10. On subofficials in the Sung, see James T. C. Liu, "Sung Views on the Control of Government Clerks," *Journal of the Economic and Social History of the Orient* 10, no. 2 (1967): 3.

2. According to the *Chou li*, these titles constituted the last four out of eight ranks of civil officials serving in the ministries or territorial divisions; as such they were considered trained career officials, not mere local employees. The custodian (*fu*) was responsible for the safe-keeping and maintenance of official property; the scribes (*shih*) kept the records; the aides (*hsü*) served as personnel supervisors, having charge of ten orderlies (*t'u*), who handled the transmission of orders. Cf. *Chou li* 1:2b, 3:15a,; Biot, *Tcheou-li* 1:4, 60.

3. *pu-shu ch'i-hui: hui* refers to an annual inspection to which the subordinate officials were summoned by their supervisor, who examined their records and inquired into their conduct of office. Cf. *Chou li* 3:13b, 14b, 16b; Biot, *Tcheou-li* 1:53, 56, 63.

4. The System of Rotational Draft Services (*ch'ai-i-fa*), which had obtained under previous dynasties and was maintained under the first reigns of the Sung dynasty, secured the performance of essential labor services by conscripting manpower from the households in each locality. Theoretically, peasants were liable for this duty only a few days each year, and the burden was supposed to fall most heavily on the more well-to-do families. Throughout the early period, however, there were complaints that the system was being abused and the burden being shifted more and more upon the poorer peasantry, who thus had insufficient time to work their own fields. In 1071 Wang An-shih attempted to remedy this by hiring professional labor, paid for by a new system of money taxation graduated to soak the rich landowner and city merchant. This was called the System of Hired Services (*ku-i* or *mu-i;* see *T'ung-k'ao* 12:427). But subsequently protests were made that tax collectors were raising inordinate sums of money, far more than needed to pay for the required services, and that both rich and poor were suffering from these excessive exactions. After Wang's fall from power, Ssu-ma Kuang abolished the hiring system and restored the old draft services in 1086. By 1094, however, the hiring system was reinstated in modified form and remained to a greater or lesser extent the system until the end of the Manchu dynasty. A lengthy discussion of this question is given in Williamson, *Wang An-shih* 1, ch. 15, and further in James T. C. Liu, *Reform in Sung China,* pp. 99–109.

5. I.e., of having uneducated, untrained men serving as full-time officials.

6. Hucker, no. 7846.

7. Hucker, no. 4925.

8. Hucker, no. 480.

9. *hu-chang:* since *hu* stands for "households" and by extension "taxation upon

households," this title could also be translated "chief of taxation," which was actually his function.

10. Hucker, no. 1510.

11. Cf. *T'ung-k'ao* 12:127c, or *Sung shih* 177:1a, from which Huang adapts the descriptions of official functions in this section.

12. Storekeeper services performed under the *chün-yao* system of the Ming dynasty. This duty was among those payable directly in labor, not in silver, and was generally rotated among the households once every ten years, but sometimes more frequently. *Ming shih* 78:1905–1906; Liang Fang-chung, *"I-t'iao-pien fa,"* p. 6; Hucker, nos. 3258, 763.

13. These were the key men in the *li-chia* system for performing local services, the chief one of which was the collection and forwarding of taxes. Established in 1381–82 by the founder of the Ming dynasty, this system was based on administrative units of 110 households, which in cities were called *fang* and in the country were called *li*. The ten most prosperous families in each unit were designated district or village headmen (*fang chang* or *li chang*), each responsible one year in ten for the performing of these services. Since the official charged with tax collections was financially responsible for turning over the local tax quota to territorial officials, only the wealthier families were in a position to guarantee satisfaction of this demand. However, each such leader had at his disposal ten families (a *chia*) to supply the labor involved. *Ming hui-tien* 20:67ab; *Hsü t'ung-k'ao* 16:2913a; *Ming shih* 78:1905; Liang Fang-chung, *"I-t'iao-pien fa,"* 6; Chang, "Village Elder System," pp. 53–62.

14. Hucker, no. 4803.

15. *tsao-li, k'uai-shou,* and *ch'eng-ch'ai:* Hucker, no. 459.

16. I.e., "silver services" under the *chün-yao* system. Cf. *Ming hui-tien* 20:70a; *Ming shih* 78:1904–1905.

17. *tsa-i:* the *li-chia* system was considered the regular service (*cheng-i*), while all others including the *chün-yao* were called miscellaneous services (Liang Fang-chung, *"I-t'iao-pien fa,"* p. 8). The effect of Huang's proposal would have been to incorporate these miscellaneous services into the regular *li-chia* system.

18. Chiefly by Ssu-ma Kuang. Cf. Williamson, *Wang An-shih* 1:235–43.

19. The duties of the supply master (or official agent) included the obtaining of transport, labor, and general supplies, the supervision of markets, and collecting of excise taxes. Since this assignment generally involved greater expense to the individual charged with it than he could realize from excise collections, it was considered a great burden and sometimes bankrupted the individual. This was particularly true of farmers without business experience, who often sustained great losses in official dealings with shrewd merchants. Though this job was supposed to be assigned to the well-to-do, it was so hated that those who could tried to avoid being classed in the higher brackets, with the result that the responsibility fell upon those less able to sustain such losses. Both Ssu-ma Kuang and Wang An-shih were in agreement on the evil effects of this system. Cf. Williamson, *Wang An-shih* 1:214–20, 223, 231.

20. The amount collected under the hiring system was a fixed charge, and the

same sum had to be contributed each year regardless of the actual need for such services or the varying ability of the people to pay for them. Under the old system the numbers of men and amount of service varied according to economic conditions, sometimes being remitted in times of famine. While the hiring system was in effect (1080–86) many memorials complained that the amount of money raised was in excess of the need and was constantly increasing. Cf. Williamson 1:227–35.

21. *kuan-cheng che:* lit., "those who are observing the workings of the government," having passed the final examination and qualified for office. This and the two other types of eligibility just following refer to the system of selecting officials set forth by Huang in the section "Selection of Officials (Part 2)" (see translation).

22. A proposal made earlier by Yeh Shih (1150–1223). See *Shui-hsin wen-chi,* SPTK 3:24a (Li-hsü).

23. That is, this type of employment is to replace the stipendiary system. See translation, "The Selection of Scholar-Officials (Part 2)."

24. Registrar (*ching-li*), record keeper (*chao-mo*), clerk (*chih-shih*). Cf. *Ming hui-tien* 4:19b; Mayers, nos. 295, 296, 300; Hucker, nos. 1227, 291, 1050.

25. Assistant magistrate (*ch'eng* or *hsien-ch'eng*), deputy assistant (*pu* or *chu-pu*), warden (*tien-shih*). Cf. *Ming hui-tien* 4:20a; Mayers, nos. 291, 292, 294; Hucker, nos. 457, 4762, 6638.

26. *Mencius* 5B:5: "He who takes office on account of his poverty must decline an honorable situation and occupy a low one. . . . What office will be in harmony with this . . . declining of riches and preferring to be poor? That of guarding the gates or beating the watchman's stick. Confucius was once keeper of stores, and said 'My calculations must all be right. That is all I have to care about.'" These are traditionally accounted the first offices Confucius held. The moral is that one should concern himself with the duties proper to his station and not overreach himself.

27. A pun on *ch'üan-pu* (an old term for the Ministry of Personnel) and *ch'ien-pu* (referring to a practice that developed in the Wan-li period of choosing candidates by drawing lots).

28. *ting-shou:* the supplement to the dictionary *Tz'u-yüan* cites this passage in the *Ming-i tai-fang lu* to illustrate the use of this term, meaning "to purchase the rights of succession to another man's job or property."

29. In the words of the Sung scholar Yeh Shih (*Shui-hsin hsien-sheng wen-chi,* SPTK 3:23a), which were also paraphrased by Ku Yen-wu in his "Essay on Prefectures and Districts" (*T'ing-lin wen-chi* 1:11b–12a; Chün-hsien-lun 8). See also Miao Ch'üan-chi, *Ming-tai hsü-li;* and Kornbluth, "Ku Yen-wu and the Reform of Local Administration." On subofficials in the Ming, see Littrup, *Sub-bureaucratic Government.*

30. On this point see Littrup, *Sub-bureaucratic Government,* p. 92.

31. *shou-ling kuan:* the top administrative assistants to the regular civil service officials in the various offices of the central government. Cf. *Ming hui-tien* 2:5a–14a; Hucker, no. 5388.

32. Section clerk (*ts'ao-yüan*): employees performing clerical and administrative duties in the offices of the central government and of the provincial governors and

county prefects during the Han dynasties. In the latter case they were procured locally, and appointed or discharged at the pleasure of the local official, not the court. As a result they were men who knew local conditions and were chosen on the basis of recognized abilities. Later, when the appointive power was centralized in the court, it became more difficult to ascertain the qualifications of these subofficials, who were drawn from any locality, not necessarily from the one to which they were appointed. *Hou-Han shu* 34:3b–4a; *T'ung-tien* 20:116b, 32:184c, 33:188c–191b; *Jih chih lu* 8:74–77; Hucker, no. 6931.

33. In the Sui dynasty (590–618). *T'ung-tien* 33:181a, 191:a; *Jih chih lu* 8:75.

34. In other words, Huang would return to a system resembling that of the Han dynasty, with the minor governmental employees serving the provincial governors, prefects, and magistrates being appointed by them from among qualified graduates of local schools. See translation, "The Selection of Scholar-Officials (Part 2)," where Huang's system of local administration generally follows the Han system (*Hou-Han shu* 34:4a; *T'ung-tien* 33:189–91a).

Eunuchs (Part 1)

1. Concerning the power of eunuchs in the Former Han, see Yü-ch'üan Wang, "An Outline of the Central Government of the Former Han Dynasty," pp. 171–73, which does not, however, cover the worst period of eunuch domination during the Latter Han. For the role of eunuchs in the T'ang, see J. K. Rideout, "The Rise of Eunuchs in the T'ang Dynasty," *Asia Major*, n.s. 1, pt. 1 (1949): 53–72; 3d ser., pt. 1 (1952): 42–58. For the Sung dynasty, see Ch'ai Te-keng, "Sung huan-kuan ts'an-yü chün-shih k'ao," pp. 181–225. For the Ming, see Chao I, *Erh-shih erh shih cha-chi* 35; and Charles O. Hucker, *The Ming Dynasty: Its Origins and Evolving Institutions,* pp. 53–54, 92–96.

2. Consultation in the emperor's private chambers, where eunuchs could influence imperial decisions. See translation, "Establishing a Prime Minister," and Robert B. Crawford, "Eunuch Power in the Ming Dynasty," pp. 117–47.

3. *nei-k'u:* there were six storehouses attached to the Ministry of Revenue and known collectively as *nei-k'u.* However, the one Huang has in mind is the *nei ch'eng-yün k'u,* in which silver and gold were kept. Up until the Cheng-t'ung period (1436–49) tax collections were mostly in grain, but thereafter when taxes were commuted into silver, a total of one million taels was stored in this latter treasury. A little over 10 percent of this was used to pay the military, and the remainder was all reserved for imperial use. In the Cheng-te period (1506–21) and after, this treasury was under the control of eunuchs who succeeded in diverting a major part of silver collections to the *nei ch'eng-yün k'u.* Cf. *Hsü T'ung-k'ao* 30:3083a–3088b; *Ming shih* 74:1818–1826, 79:1926.

4. *T'ai ts'ang:* established in 1442 to serve as the silver depository for the Ministry of Revenue, and therefore known also as the "silver treasury" (*yin-k'u*). Here were stored tax collections commuted into silver and used by the civil administration to defray state expenses. Toward the end of the Ming dynasty the eunuchs successfully drew upon these reserves to meet expenses of the imperial household,

despite the strong objections raised by ministry officials. Huang means that the demands of the imperial household were satisfied first and state needs came second, not that the funds were first deposited in the Imperial Treasury and then transferred to the State Treasury. Cf. *Hsü T'ung-k'ao* 30:3083a–3088b; *Ming shih* 79:1927–1929; Hucker, no. 6227.

5. *tung-ch'ang:* one of the most hated and feared institutions of the Ming dynasty, established by the Emperor Yung-lo (1403–24). Having risen to power through the assistance of eunuchs who had served as his spies in the entourage of the preceding emperor, Yung-lo established a special secret service agency near the Eastern Gate of the capital, and entrusted its direction to his faithful and intimate followers among the eunuchs. It was closely interrelated with the imperial guards (*chin-i-wei*), which had been made responsible for the security of the court by the founder of the dynasty, and guard officers served as constables and wardens of the Eastern Yard. For this reason they were collectively termed the" Yard-Guard" (*ch'ang-wei*).

The Eastern Yard served as headquarters for an elaborate spy network maintained throughout the capital, to report on the doings and utterances of all who might be suspected of treasonable or scandalous conduct. Once arrested, the accused frequently were beaten or left to languish and die in prison without being brought to trial, or else they had to pay large sums to the eunuchs for their release. This proved such a lucrative business and potent weapon for silencing opposition that rival factions at times had competing Yards established (e.g., Western Yard and Inner Yard), but the Eastern Yard outlasted these others. It reached the height of its power and brutality during the T'ien-chi period (1621–27), when the powerful eunuch Wei Chung-hsien (1568–1627) used it as a means of liquidating great numbers of his critics in the civil administration. Huang Tsung-hsi's father was among those who died at his hands. The power of the Eastern Yard was curbed briefly after the accession of the last emperor and the fall of Wei Chung-hsien, but had been largely regained by the last years of that reign when the dynasty fell. Cf. *Hsü T'ung-k'ao* 56:3313c, 136:4020bc; *Ming shih* 74:1821, 1826, 95:2329, 2331–35ff.; Hucker, ed., *Chinese Government in Ming Times,* pp. 47–48, 57, 61–62, 98, 113.

6. *fa-ssu:* i.e., the Ministry of Justice (*hsing-pu*), Censorate (*tu-ch'a yüan*), and the Censorate Court of Judicial Review (*ta-li-ssu*). Cf. *Ming shih* 94:2305.

7. I.e., after the creation of the Ch'in empire, 221 B.C.

8. Control over the production of all goods for imperial use was maintained by special offices in the imperial household staffed by eunuchs, who supervised the purchase, requisition, or making of clothes, textiles, food, liquor, medicines, palace furnishings, arms, metalwork, ivory, gems, trinkets, games, etc. Cf. *Hsü T'ung-k'ao* 56:3313a; *Ming shih* 74:1819–1820.

9. The court was divided into the imperial household, also known as the "inner court" (*nei-t'ing*) and the state administration or "outer court" (*wai-t'ing*). The former was staffed with eunuchs directly responsible to the emperor, while the latter was staffed by civil officials and administered by the Grand Secretariat and Six Ministries. Both of these "courts" maintained offices to procure the goods each required, those of the state administration being run by the Ministry of Works. Un-

der the founder of the Ming dynasty the number of eunuchs was kept to a minimum and their activities strictly limited to the imperial household. Under the Emperor Yung-lo, however, the eunuchs were greatly increased in numbers and power, being charged with many supervisory and investigative duties normally performed by officers of the state administration. The purpose of this was to bring key military, legal, and financial functions more directly under the emperor's control, so that he would be less bound by established precedent and the remonstrances of civil officials. In the case of the procurement of goods, the eunuchs extended their control to enterprises nominally administered by the Ministry of Works, on the ground that the imperial household required increased amounts of the goods they produced or procured. The power of eunuchs in this sphere was especially strong in the Hsüante and Cheng-te periods (1426–36, 1506–21) and generally during the latter part of the dynasty (when eunuchs were dominant). The imperial textile factories mentioned in "Finance (Part 3)" (see translation) are an example of eunuch encroachment upon the jurisdiction of the Ministry of Works in the production of silk. Cf. *Hsü T'ung-k'ao* 56:3313a–3314c; *Ming shih* 74:1826–1827, 82:1997–1998; *Jih chih lu* 9:33–38; Chan, *Ming Dynasty*, pp. 175–83.

10. After I-tsung (reign name: Ch'ung-chen) ascended the throne in 1628, the eunuch Wei Chung-hsien was soon stripped of his powers and sent into retirement, where he was finally forced to commit suicide to avoid arrest. Many of his followers were likewise eliminated from the government, and opponents of his who had survived Wei's ruthless purges were restored to office. Strict curbs were put upon the eunuchs' activities to prevent them from interfering in state affairs. Nevertheless, in the course of his reign I-tsung lapsed steadily into the habit of dependence upon eunuchs into which so many of his imperial predecessors had fallen. In particular, eunuchs were prominent in military affairs, and the fall of Peking to Li Tzu-ch'eng was due in no small part to the treachery of eunuch generals who yielded key fortresses and opened the gates of the capital to the enemy. *Ming shih* 23:309–10, 24:320–21; *Ch'ung-chen shih-lu* 17; Wen Ping, *Lieh-huang hsiao-shih* 1:13–18; *Jih chih lu* 9:38; ECCP, pp. 191, 846.

11. On the last day of I-tsung's life the bell was struck in the palace to summon his officials for the morning audience, but no one appeared. Thereupon the emperor, accompanied by his faithful eunuch Wang Ch'eng-en, went to Coal Hill where both committed suicide. His inability to see his ministers would seem to have been due to the prevailing confusion, not to any attempt by eunuchs to hold him incommunicado. But Huang's meaning is perhaps simply that an emperor should have scholar-officials as his close companions in constant attendance, so that he would spend his last hours and die in better company than that of a eunuch. Cf. *Ming-chi pei-lüeh* 20:33b; *Hsiao-t'ien chi-nien* 4:5b.

12. *nei-ch'en:* according to tradition, in the Chou period there was no separate class of palace official, since palace affairs were handled by regular scholar-officials (*shih*), under the supervision of the prime minister. Under the Ch'in and Han empires, however, eunuchs became imperial household officials, and the term *nei-ch'en* is found applied to the eunuch Shih Hsien, who controlled the government under the Emperor Yüan from 47–32 B.C. Nevertheless, though eunuchs held of-

fice in the imperial household increasingly during the Former or Latter Han, scholar-officials also held such posts, and it was not until the first reign of the T'ang dynasty (A.D. 618–626) that the imperial household was staffed exclusively by eunuchs. Thereafter, a clear distinction was drawn between the "inner ministers" (*nei-ch'en* or *nei-kuan*), who were eunuchs serving in the palace, and the outer ministers (*wai-ch'en* or *wai-kuan*), who were scholar-officials serving in the state administration but excluded from palace posts. Cf. *Han shu* 27A:16b, 24b; *T'ung-tien* 27:159ab; *Jih chih lu* 5:78, 9:32; Rotours, *Traité des Fonctionnaires* 1:240; Yü-ch'üan Wang, "Central Government of the Former Han Dynasty," p. 172.

Eunuchs (Part 2)

1. Reading *tse* "to blame" for *kuei* "to esteem," as corrected in LCICHK ed., 23b:1.5.

2. Cheng Hsüan (A.D. 127–200): a leading scholar of the Latter Han and outstanding authority of his time on ancient ritual, whose commentary on the three classical books of rites is still standard. At the time Huang was writing (1662–63), the name Hsüan was taboo, being part of the reigning emperor's given name (Hsüan-yeh), and so the commentator's name was customarily rendered Cheng Yüan. Huang does not, however, conform to conventional usage. *Hou-Han shu* 65; Giles, no. 274; *Ssu-k'u tsung-mu* 19:1a.

3. The original text of the *Chou li*, purporting to explain how the Chou court was organized, describes the functions of the wives of second rank (*chiu pin*) in training and directing the imperial concubines, nine of which were assigned to each. "Each directed those assigned to her, and at the appointed times went with her charges to the emperor's chamber [to spend the night with him]." The classical books of rites abound with precise numerical arrangements such as this: nine wives each directing nine concubines. Cheng Hsüan fills out the arrangement by the neat scheme Huang cites, explaining that in this way one whole series would be completed in fifteen nights preceding the full moon and would repeat itself in the fifteen nights following. Thus the activities of the bed chamber are made to correspond with heavenly cycles. But the *Chou li* itself does not specify the frequency with which these ladies attended the emperor, and Huang can question the accuracy of the commentary where he could not the scripture. SSCCS, *Chou li* 8:18b; Biot, *Tcheou-li* 1:154.

4. "Mencius said, 'Those who give counsel to the great should despise them and not look at their pomp and display. . . . Food spread before me over ten cubits square and attendant girls to the amount of hundreds—these, though my wishes were realized, I would not have. . . . What they [princes] esteem I would have nothing to do with; what I esteem are the rules of the ancients. Why should I stand in awe of them?'" (Legge, *Mencius* 7B:34). The "rules [or system] of the ancients" would in the traditional view refer to Chou dynasty practice, with which current usage was not in conformity.

5. Reading *kung* for *ch'i*. Cf. Hai-shan hsien-kuan ed., 52b:line 3.

6. Criticized by Mencius for their extravagance. Cf. *Mencius* 1A:4, 1B:1, 1B:2.

7. Meaning: Since the Duke of Chou and Mencius could not have been wrong, it must be Cheng Hsüan who is wrong in attributing such a system to the Duke of Chou.

8. *Chung-tsai:* in ancient times the prime minister was also the chief of official personnel. Later, when a separate Ministry of Personnel was established, this became an honorific title for the Minister of Personnel (*li-pu shang-shu*). In this case the Chou system is referred to and *chung-tsai* therefore means "prime minister," here representing the civil administration as opposed to the imperial household under the emperor. Cf. SSCCS, *Chou li* 1:1a; Biot, *Tcheou-li* 1:1–2; Brunnert and Hagelstrom, no. 333A; Hucker, no. 1632.

9. In Huang's own time Chiang Te-ching as vice-minister of the Rites memorialized the throne to place eunuchs under the civil administration, citing the *Chou li* as authority. The system outlined in the *Chou li* was believed to have been created by the Duke of Chou, who was the leading statesman at the founding of the Chou dynasty. Ku Yen-wu also cited the *Chou li* as authority in advocating the adoption of this system. Cf. *Jih chih lu,* KHCPTS ed. (Hun-jen ssu jen), 9:32, 38 and 5:78.

10. *hsing yü* (roughly, "criminal amputees"): in early times criminals liable to the death penalty were sometimes castrated instead and used as eunuchs. Huang insinuates that eunuchs are an untrustworthy and vicious lot, not as a result of castration but because they were recruited from among capital offenders, in particular those guilty of treason. However, about A.D. 581 the first emperor of the Sui dynasty abolished castration as a form of punishment, and thereafter eunuchs were obtained from among captives and persons sold into slavery. *Han shu* 27A:24b, 77:4a; Rideout, "The Rise of Eunuchs in the T'ang Dynasty," p. 54.

11. *san-kung:* the precise meaning of this term here is unclear, but Huang certainly intends a drastic reduction of imperial wives. In the *Li chi* and *Chou li, kung* is used as a form of indirect reference to imperial or noble wives, identifying them by the palaces or pavilions they occupied. *San-kung* then might simply mean three wives, which seems the most likely interpretation. But in the *Li chi* the term *san-kung* itself is applied to the wife of a feudal noble (18:22ab; Legge, *Li Ki* 1:223; Couvreur, *Li Ki* 2:294), and the commentary explains that this is because the noble's wife had half the number of pavilions the empress had—the empress herself being referred to as *liu-kung* or "Six Pavilions" (*Li chi* 61:11b, and Legge, *Li Ki* 2:432; *Chou li* 7:15b, and Biot, *Tcheou-li* 1:142).

If Huang uses *san-kung* in this sense, it would mean reducing the emperor's harems to three but not necessarily reducing his wives to that number, since each pavilion had a normal complement of thirteen wives of various ranks, augmented whenever the empress was in residence there by thirty-nine wives or concubines personally in attendance upon her. This would not seem to reduce the number of wives substantially even if the number of pavilions were halved, so it would not serve Huang's purpose. A third possibility arises from the application of the term *san-kung* in later times to the palaces of the emperor, empress, and empress dowager (*Han shu* 86:12a), each of which would have eunuchs in attendance. If *san-kung* is used in this sense, it would presumably mean limiting the emperor to one consort. Matsui Hitoshi (*Shina kinsei seiji shichō,* in Sekai kōbō shiron 15:92) suggests that *san-kung* refers to the first three ranks of wives (*hou, fun-jen,* and *chiu-pin*), of which there would be thirteen in all according to the Chou system.

12. See translation, "On the Prince," note 5.

13. Hui-tsung (A.D. 1082–1135): last emperor of the Northern Sung, who was defeated by the Chin (Jurchen) and abdicated in favor of his son, Ch'in-tsung, in 1125. When the Chin took the capital, K'ai-feng, in 1127, Hui-tsung and Ch'in-tsung were captured along with most of the imperial family and were sent to Manchuria, where they died in captivity. Hui-tsung's ninth son escaped the Chin, however, and founded the Southern Sung dynasty at Nanking. *Sung shih* 22:13b; 23:17b; Giles, nos. 145, 159, 166.

Letter from Ku Yen-wu to Huang Tsung-hsi

1. This letter is prefixed to the *Ming-i tai-fang lu* in the Ehr-lao-ko edition and in many subsequent editions. It also appears, with the emendation noted below, in an appendix to the *Nan-lei wen-ting* (LCICHK, *ts'e* 8, *Fu-lu* 2a), and in the text of the *Ssu-chiu lu* (LCICHK, *ts'e* 16:17b). The life chronologies of both Huang and Ku state that it was written in 1676 (LCICHK 1, *Nien-p'u* 35b; Chang Mu, *Ku T'ing-lin hsien-sheng nien-p'u* 35b (*Chia-yeh t'ang ts'ung-shu* ed., pp. 66–67). In his preface to the *P'o-hsieh-lun,* Huang says Ku Yen-wu "saw the MITFL and 'thought it not bad.'" This could well be a reference to the present letter, but is not certainly so.

The historian and Huang's intellectual heir Ch'üan Tsu-wang (1705–55) accepted the letter's authenticity, as is indicated in his colophon to the *Ming-i tai-feng lu* (immediately following this letter). More recently, both the authenticity and date of the letter have been disputed. Of those who have gone into the matter in some detail, the most recent (1985) contributor to the debate, Zhao Gang, affirms the authenticity of the letter and dates it 1677. See Zhao Gang, "Gu Yanwu 'Yu Huang Taizhong shu' xinzheng," pp. 17–18. I have not gone into the matter myself; for me the main interest of the letter is Ku's general endorsement of the MITFL and his statement that the *Jih chih lu* agrees with six- or seven-tenths of what Huang says in the *Tai-fang lu.* This is verifiable from the contents of the *Jih chih lu,* independent of the letter, and also in part from Huang's preface to the *P'o-hsieh-lun,* which was written after 1691. The latter is included in *Nan-lei wen-ting* and in *Quanji* 1:192–207.

2. Wu-lin: old name for Hangchow in Chekiang province and which derives from mountains of that name just west of the city (KCTMTTT 505a; *Ku T'ing-lin nien-p'u* 67ab).

3. O-Chiang (the Ts'ao-o chiang): a river in Eastern Chekiang, thirty miles west of Yü-yao, hometown of Huang Tsung-hsi (KCTMTTT 809d; *Ku T'ing-lin nien-p'u* 67a).

4. *ts'ang-fu* (lit., "addle-pated father"): a deprecatory term used by men of the Wu region (Ku and Huang were such) in speaking of men from what is now the Honan region, especially if the latter had any pretensions to learning (cf. T'ang Ch'iu, *Chin yang ch'iu,* Kuang-ya shih ed., 2:11a; Liu I-ch'ing, *Shih-shuo hsin-yü,* SPTK, 1st ser., 2A:28b).

5. Ku was sixty-four years old when this letter was presumably written (in K'ang-hsi 16 [1677], according to the chronology of Zhao Gang); see note 1 above.

6. Quoting Han Yü, *Ch'ang-li hsien-sheng wen-chi,* SPTK 6:4a.

7. *Li chi* 37:23b (Hsüeh chi).

8. *Analects* 9:19.

9. Chi-men: district just outside the Te-sheng Men, westernmost gate in the north wall of Peking. Here it is used to denote Peking in general (cf. *Ku-t'ing-lin nien-p'u* 66b).

10. This letter as contained in the *Ssu-chiu lu* and appended to the *Nan-lei wen-ting* gives the names of these disciples as "the Messrs. Ch'en and Wan." The compiler of Ku's *Life Chronology (Nien-p'u),* Chang Mu, identified these two gentleman as Ch'en Hsi-ku (1634–87) of Ting-hai in Chekiang province, who passed the *chin-shih* examination the year this letter was written (1676) and then entered the Hanlin Academy; and Wan Ssu-t'ung, who was at that time in Peking as guest of the noted official and scholar, Hsü Ch'ien-hsüeh (1631–94). Ch'en and Wan had studied together under Huang at Ningpo in the spring of 1665 (*Ku T'ing-lin nien-p'u* 67a; Ch'üan Tsu-wang, *Hsü yung-shang ch'i-chiu shih,* 1918 ed.) However, more recent research by Zhao Gang (see note 1 above) indicates that Wan Yen (1637–1705; ECCP, p. 804), not Wan Ssu-t'ung or Wan Ssu-ta, was the member of the Wan family referred to.

11. A quotation from the *Book of Changes:* "After the death of Shen-nung, there arose Hwang Ti, Yao and Shun. They carried through the [necessarily occurring] changes, so that people did [what was required of them] without being wearied; yea, they exerted such a spirit-like transformation that the people felt constrained to approve [their ordinance] as right. When a series of changes has run its course, another change ensues. When it obtains free course, it will continue long. Hence it was that these sovereigns were helped by Heaven" (Legge, *Yi King,* p. 383).

12. An often quoted line from *Mencius* 3 B:9.

13. The question of changing the location of the capital was a delicate one. Sensitive or suspicious quarters might interpret it as suggesting a change of rulers, since dynastic interests were closely associated with ancestral shrines and palaces. Therefore, Ku cryptically alludes to the subject by using the title *"feng-ch'ün,"* a name that had been awarded by Kao-tsu, founder of the Han dynasty, to Lou Ching, in appreciation of the latter's having persuaded Kao-tsu to establish his capital at Ch'ang-an (Kuan-chung) instead of at Loyang. Put in this way, there would be less ground for suspecting subversive intent. *Han shu* 43:10b–13b (biography of Lou Ching); Chavannes, *Memoires Historiques* 2:384; Dubs, *History of the Former Han* 1:108.

14. Kuan-chung: ancient Ch'ang-an region (Sian in Shensi province).

15. Huang had been to Nanking many times, but probably not to Kuan-chung. Ku, as this letter implies, had traveled extensively in the latter region.

16. *Ch'ien-liang lun:* an essay on the injustice of requiring taxes to be paid in money rather than in kind, a practice adopted during the Ming dynasty. Earlier it had been possible to pay taxes in grain or some other goods produced by the landholders themselves. Ku's views are similar to those expressed by Huang in his "Finance (Part 1)" and " Land System (Part 3)" (*T'ing-lin-wen-chi,* SPTK, 1st. ser., 1:13a–17a).

17. Huang was three years older by Chinese count, a little less than three by Western reckoning.

Ch'üan Tsu-wang: Colophon

1. This colophon is contained in the collected short works of Ch'üan Tsu-wang (1705–55) (*Chi-ch'i t'ing chi wai-pien* 31, KHCPTS 5:1109) and appears following the present text in Huang, *Li-chou i-chu hui-k'an, ts'e* 12.

2. *Cheng-chün* (lit., "summoned lord"): an honorific term used of a man invited to serve at court, who for lofty reasons declines the honor (cf. *Hou-Han shu* 83:52). Out of loyalty to the Ming, Huang Tsung-hsi had several times refused invitations to serve at the Manchu court.

3. *T'ai-ch'ung* is a courtesy name or style (*tzu*) of Huang Tsung-hsi.

4. Yao-chiang: a river running through Huang Tsung-hsi's home district, Yü-yao in Eastern Chekiang province. This name was sometimes used to identify a local school of thought originating with the famous Ming philosopher, Wang Yang-ming, who was a native of Yü-yao.

5. He was actually fifty-three years old.

6. Wan Hsi-kuo, the literary name of Wan Ch'eng-hsün (1670–c. 1730): a grandson-in-law of Huang Tsung-hsi. His father, grandfather, and seven granduncles, including the historian Wan Ssu-t'ung were all pupils of Huang (ECCP, p. 804, biography of Wan Yen by Tu Lien-che).

7. The Prince of Lu died on the island of Chin-men, off Amoy, late in 1662. As a survivor of the ruling house of the Ming, he had led remnant Ming forces in the Chekiang area from 1645 to 1653. Huang Tsung-hsi had served under him while the temporary court was at Shao-hsing and then in the Chusan Islands off the eastern tip of Chekiang (see ECCP, p. 180, under the Prince's personal name of Chu I-hai, biography by J. C. Yang). See Lynn Struve, *The Southern Ming*, pp. 79–94, 111–20.

Chüan's reference to the Prince of Lu is veiled in a pun, *lu-yang chih wang,* which suggests the Prince of Lu (Lu-wang) by sound association and also recalls the dauntless spirit of a Lu-yang mentioned in the *Huai-nan Tzu*. Fearing that evening would fall before he had defeated his enemies, Lu-yang shook his spear at the declining sun, which straightaway rose back in the sky to the extent of three zodiacal signs. At the time Ch'üan is speaking of, the fortunes of the Ming had declined so low that their only hope lay in some such unlikely feat as this (*Huai-nan Tzu,* SPTK, 1st ser., 6:1b).

8. This refers to the death of Prince Kuei (also called Prince Yung-ming), a survivor of the Ming royal house who carried on resistance to the Manchus in southwest China. After the collapse of his armies, he had taken refuge in Burma in 1659, and was held a virtual prisoner there until turned over to Manchu forces in January 1662. Brought back a captive to Yünnan, he and his son were strangled to death in June of the same year (ECCP, p. 193, biography of Chu Yu-lang by J. C. Yang), Struve, *The Southern Ming*, pp. 99–100.

9. *shih-chin tai-chin*: a quotation from *Hou-Han shu* 62:21b (biography of Ch'en Shih) where, however, the last character is *chung* (lit., "Wearing the headband, he

awaited his end." The distinctive headdress of scholars during the Ming dynasty is here a symbol of resistance to the Manchus, who required the Chinese to shave their heads, wear queues, and adopt Manchu dress. Huang Tsung-hsi is shown wearing Ming headdress in a portrait facing p. xxiii of the *Nan-lei hsüeh-an* by Huang Ssu-ai (1947 ed.).

10. Ch'üan Tsu-wang (1705–55): a native of Chekiang, whose forebears had remained loyal to the Ming dynasty and served the regime of the Prince of Lu during the last years of the struggle against the Manchus. Although a *chin-shih* graduate of 1736, Ch'üan forsook official life the following year, when as a result of intrigue he was disqualified for a post in the Hanlin Academy. He devoted the rest of his life to study and teaching and is best known as a historian of the Ming resistance movement in the South as well as a biographer of many leading figures in the early Ch'ing period. An admirer of Huang Tsung-hsi, he aided the latter's descendants in editing and supplementing the *Sung-Yüan hsüeh-an,* which Huang had left unfinished at his death. See ECCP, pp. 203–205 (biography by Fang Chao-ying); Lynn Struve, "The Early Ch'ing Legacy of Huang Tsung-hsi," pp. 106–21.

Glossary of
Names and Terms

an (darkness) 闇
An-hsi 安西
An Lu-shan 安祿山
An-ti (Eastern Chin) 安帝
An-ta (Altan) 俺答

chai chan ch'i-sai 齋醮祈賽
ch'ai-i 差役
ch'ai-i fa 差役法
Chan Jo-shui 湛若水
chang (piece) 丈
Chang (emperor) 章
ch'ang (session) 場
Ch'ang-an 長安
Chang Ch'eng 張誠
Chang Chü-cheng 張居正
Chang Huang 章潢
Chang Lin 張林

Chang Mu 張穆
Chang Ping-lin 章炳麟
ch'ang-p'ing ts'ang 常平倉
ch'ang-sheng chün 常生軍
Chang Shih-ch'eng 張士誠
Chang Tsai 張載
ch'ang-wei 廠衛
Chang-yeh 張掖
Chang Yüeh 張說
Chao I-kuang 趙宧光
chao-mo (record keeper) 照磨
chao-mu 召募
Chao-tsung (T'ang) 昭宗
ch'e (tax) 徹
che erh 折二
ch'en (minister) 臣
chen-fu 鎮撫
Ch'en Hsi-ku 陳錫嘏
Ch'en Hsien-chang 陳獻章
Ch'en Liang 陳亮
Chen Te-hsiu 真德秀
Ch'en Tung 陳東
Chen-yüan (reign) 貞元
Ch'eng (prince) 誠
ch'eng-ch'ai 承差
Ch'eng-Chu 程朱
cheng-chün 徵君
ch'eng-fu 承符
Ch'eng Hao 程顥
ch'eng-hsiang 丞相
Cheng Hsüan 鄭玄
Ch'eng I 程頤
cheng-i (regular service) 正役
cheng-shih t'ang 政事堂
Cheng Tang-shih 鄭當時
Cheng-te (reign) 正德
ch'eng-t'i ch'ao fa 稱提鈔法
Ch'eng-tu 成都
Cheng-t'ung (reign) 正統
Ch'i (dynasty) 齊
Ch'i (state) 齊

ch'i (their) 其
ch'i-chang 耆長
Ch'i Chi-kuang 戚繼光
Chi-chou 薊州
Chi-chou 冀州
Ch'i-chou 齊州
chi-fang 機坊
chi-fen 積分
chi-hsien 薊縣
chi-hsiung chih li 吉凶之禮
chi-men 薊門
Chi-pin (Kashmir) 罽賓
Chi Tzu 箕子
chia (family) 家
Chia-ching (reign) 嘉靖
chia-ting 家丁
Chiang Ch'en 蔣臣
chiang-hsüeh 講學
Chiang-k'ou hsien 江口縣
Chiang Te-ching 蔣德璟
Chiao (region) 交
chiao-tzu 交子
chieh (limit) 界
Chieh (tyrant) 桀
chieh-hu 解戶
Chieh Kuei (Hsia) 桀癸
chieh-tu 節度
chieh-tu shih 節度使
chien-chü 薦舉
Ch'ien Han shu 前漢書
Ch'ien-liang lun 錢糧論
Ch'ien Liu 錢鏐
ch'ien-pu 鐵部
Ch'ien Shih 錢氏
ch'ien-shih 僉事
Ch'ien Shu 錢俶
ch'ien-tsung 千總
ch'ih 尺
Chih-chiang hsin hsien-hsüeh chi 枝江新縣學記
chih-hsiang 置相
chih-shih (clerk) 知事

chih tsao 織造
chin (catty) 斤
Chin (dynasty) 晉
Chin (state) 晉
Chin (Jurchen) 金
Ch'in (dynasty) 秦
Chin-chiang (Fukien) 晉江
Chin-chou (Liaoning) 錦州
chin-i wei 錦衣衛
Chin-ling 金陵
Ch'in Shih Huang-ti 秦始皇帝
Chin shu 晉書
ch'in-t'ien chien 欽天監
Ch'in-tsung (emperor, Sung) 欽宗
Ching 荊
Ching (emperor) 景
ch'ing (acre) 頃
Ching-chi hui-pien 經濟彙編
Ch'ing-chou 青州
ching-li 經歷
Ch'ing-li (reign) 慶曆
ching-lüeh 經略
Ching-mou 井牧
Ching-nan po 靖南伯
Ching Pu 黥布
ching-shih chih-yung 經世致用
Ching-t'ai (reign) 景泰
ching-t'ien 井田
chio-ku 榷酤
Ch'iu Chün 邱濬
Chiu T'ang shu 舊唐書
chiu-pien 九邊
chiu-pin 九嬪
Chou (dynasty) 周
Chou (tyrant) 紂
Chou Hsin 紂辛
Chou kuan 周官
Chou Kung (Duke of Chou) 周公
Chou li 周禮
Chou Tun-i 周敦頤
chu (master) 主

chu (tax) 助
Ch'u (state) 楚
Ch'u-chou 處州
Chu Hsi 朱熹
Chu I-hai 朱以海
chü-jen 舉人
Ch'ü li 曲禮
ch'u-ling 芻靈
chu-p'i 朱批
chu-ping 主兵
chu-pu 主簿
chu-shih (secretary) 主事
Chu Tz'u 朱泚
Chu Wen 朱溫
Chu Yu-lang 朱由榔
Ch'ü Yüan 屈原
Chu Yüan-chang 朱元璋
chüan 卷
chüan (silk gauze) 絹
chüan-pu 絹布
ch'üan-pu 銓部
Ch'üan Te-yü 權德輿
Ch'üan Tsu-wang 全祖望
Chuang Ch'ang 莊昶
Chuang-lieh-ti (I-tsung) 莊烈帝 (毅宗)
chuang-ting 壯丁
Chuang Tzu 莊子
chüeh-hsüeh 絕學
chün (commandery) 郡
Chün-ch'en p'ien 君臣篇
Ch'un-ch'iu 春秋
Chün-hsien lun 郡縣論
chün-hsien tso 郡縣佐
chun-kung 准貢
chün-kung 郡公
chün-shih 俊士
chün-shou 郡守
chün-tao (prince, ruler) 君道
chün-t'un 軍屯
chün-tzu 君子
chün-yao 均徭

Ch'ung-chen (reign) 崇禎
Ch'ung-ho (reign) 重和
ch'ung-pen i-mo 崇本抑末
chung-shu sheng 中書省
chung-tsai 冢宰
Chung-tu 中都
Chung yung 中庸

en-chün 恩軍
en-kung 恩貢
Erh hsien-sheng yü 二先生語
Erh-shih-wu shih pu-pien 二十五史補編
Erh-ya 爾雅

fa (law) 法
fa-ssu 法司
fan-chen 藩鎮
Fan Ching-wen 范景文
Fan Chung-yen 范仲淹
Fan P'ang 范滂
Fan-yang 范陽
fang-chen 方鎮
Fang Hsiao-ju 方孝孺
fang-li chang 坊里長
fang-t'ien 方田
feng-chien 封建
Feng-ch'un 奉春
Feng Pao 馮保
Feng-t'ien 奉天
Feng-yang 奉陽
fu (custodian) 府
fu (capital region) 輔
fu (poetic exposition) 賦
Fu (prince) 福
fu-chiang 副將
fu-jen (lady) 夫人
fu-min 富民
Fu-she 復社

Hai-shan hsien-kuan 海山仙館
Han (dynasty) 漢

Han Fei Tzu 韓非子
Han Hsin 韓信
Han Kao-ti 漢高帝
han lien 含殮
Han Wu-ti 漢武帝
Han Yü 韓愈
Hanlin 翰林
hao 號
ho erh pu t'ung 和而不同
ho-han 河漢
Ho Hsin-yin 何心隱
Ho-tung 河東
Honan 河南
hou (queen) 后
Hou Chi 后稷
Hou-Han shu 後漢書
Hou Wai-lu 侯外廬
Hsi-ning (reign) 熙寧
hsiang (army rations) 餉
hsiang (community) 鄉
Hsiang (Duke) 襄
Hsiang (region) 湘
Hsiang An-shih 項安世
hsiang-chü li-hsüan 鄉舉里選
hsiang-kung-che 鄉貢者
hsiang-sui yung kung fa 鄉遂用貢法
hsiang-yin-chiu 鄉飲酒
Hsiang Yü 項羽
hsiang-yüeh 鄉約
Hsiao-ching 孝經
Hsiao Kung-ch'üan 蕭公權
Hsiao Tai li 小戴禮
Hsiao Tao-ch'eng 蕭道成
hsien (district) 縣
hsien-chang 憲章
hsien-ch'eng 縣丞
Hsien-tsung 憲宗
hsien-wei 縣尉
Hsin ching 心經
hsin-hsiang (new rations) 新餉
hsin-hsüeh 心學

hsin-kuo 訊讞
Hsin T'ang shu 新唐書
hsing-li fang 刑禮房
Hsing-li ta-ch'üan 性理大全
hsing-pu 刑部
hsing-yü 刑餘
hsiu-chi chih-jen 修己治人
hsiu-shih 秀士
hsü (aide) 胥
hsü (silk wadding) 絮
Hsü Ch'ien-hsüeh 徐乾學
Hsü Heng 許衡
hsü-li 胥吏
Hsü Yu 許由
Hsüan (king) 宣
hsüan-chü 選舉
Hsüan-fu 宣府
hsüan-fu shih 宣撫使
Hsüan-hua 宣化
hsüan-shih 選士
Hsüan-te (emperor) 宣德
Hsüan-te (reign) 宣德
Hsüan-tsung 玄宗
Hsüan-yeh 玄燁
hsüeh-chiu i-ching 學究一經
hsüeh-kuan 學官
hsün-fu 巡撫
hu (measurement) 斛
hu-chang 戶長
Hu Chü-jen 胡居仁
hu fang 戶房
Hu Han 胡翰
Hu Kuang 胡廣
Hu Shih 胡適
hu-tiao 戶調
Hu Wei 胡渭
Hu Wei-yung 胡惟庸
Huai-lai (Chahar) 懷來
Huan (emperor) 桓
Huan K'uan 桓寬
huan-shou 換授

Huang Ch'ao   黃巢
Huang Ch'ien-shan   黃潛善
Huang Te-kung   黃得功
Huang Tsung-hsi (Huang Zongxi)   黃宗羲
Hui-chou   徽州
hui-p'iao   會票
Hui-tsung   徽宗
Hung-chih (reign)   弘治
Hung-wu (reign)   洪武

I   益
i (question)   義
i (righteousness)   義
i chih ch'u tan, ming erh wei jung   曵之初旦明而未融
I Ching   易經
I li   儀禮
i-t'iao-pien fa   一條鞭法
I-tsung, Chu Yu-chien   毅宗朱由檢
I Yin   伊尹

Jen-tsung   仁宗
jen-tzu   任子
Jih chih lu   日知錄
ju (scholar)   儒
ju-ko   入閣

K'ai-feng   開封
k'ai-fu   開府
K'ai-yüan (reign)   開元
Kan-chou   甘州
Kan-hsien (Shensi)   乾縣
K'ang-hsi   康熙
Kansu   甘肅
Kao Huang-ti   高皇帝
Kao-tsung   高宗
Kao-yu   高郵
ko (cabinet)   閣
k'o-chü   科舉
k'o-ping   客兵
ku-i   顧役
Ku-liang chuan   穀梁傳

ku-mu chia-yin 顧慕加銀
Ku T'ing-lin 顧亭林
k'u-tzu 庫子
Ku Yen-wu 顧炎武
Ku-yüan 固原
k'uai-shou 快手
kuan (official) 官
kuan (string of cash) 貫
kuan-cheng 官政
kuan-cheng che 觀政者
Kuan Tzu 管子
Kuang (region) 廣
k'uang fei 筐籃
Kuang-hsü (reign) 光緒
Kuang-wu 光武
kuei (esteem) 貴
Kuei-yang 貴陽
K'un-ming 昆明
kung (tax) 貢
kung (together) 共
kung ch'i shih-fei yü hsüeh-hsiao 公其是非於學校
K'ung Chin 孔僅
Kung-chu lieh-chuan 公主列傳
kung-i 公議
K'ung Kuang 孔光
K'ung Lin-chih 孔琳之
kung-ping 弓兵
kung-shou 弓手
Kung-yang Kao 公羊高
Kung-yang chuan 公羊傳
K'ung Ying-ta 孔穎達
K'ung Yu-te 孔有德
kuo-hsiang 國相
kuo-li ta-hsüeh 國立大學
Kuo-yü 國語

Lai-chou (Shantung) 萊州
Lan-ch'i 藍溪
Lan-shui 藍水
Lao Hsiu 牢修
Lao Tzu 老子

li (mile) 里
li-ch'ai 力差
li-chang (village leader) 里長
Li chi 禮記
Li Chien-t'ai 李建泰
Li-chou 梨洲
li fang 吏房
li-hsü 吏胥
li-hsüeh 理學
li-i 力役
Li Kang 李綱
li-lu 藜蘆
li-pu shang-shu 吏部尚書
Li sao 離騷
Li Ssu 李斯
Li Tzu-ch'eng 李自成
Li Ying 李膺
li yün 禮運
liang (tael) 兩
Liang (dynasty) 梁
Liang (region) 梁
Liang Ch'i-ch'ao 梁啓超
liang-shui 兩稅
Liao 遼
Liao-hsiang 遼餉
Liao-tung 遼東
Liao-yang 遼陽
lien-hsiang 練餉
lin-sheng 廩生
ling (damask) 綾
Ling-chou 靈州
ling-lo 綾羅
ling-shih 令史
Ling-wu 靈武
liu (type) 流
Liu Chen 劉振
Liu-chou 柳州
Liu Fen 劉蕡
liu-k'o chi-shih chung 六科給事中
liu-kung 六宮
Liu Mien 柳冕

Liu Shao-ch'i 劉少奇
Liu shu 留書
Liu Tsung-chou 劉宗周
Liu San-wu 劉三吾
Liu Tse-ch'ing 劉澤清
Lou Ching 婁敬
lu (circuit) 路
Lu (state) 魯
Lu Ch'i 盧杞
Lu Chih 陸贄
Lu-chia pu 陸家埠
Lu Hsiang-shan 陸象山
lu-jen 路人
Lü Liu-liang 呂留良
Lü Shang (Chiang T'ai Kung, T'ai Kung Wang) 呂尚姜太公太公望
lu-shih 錄士
lu-yang chih wang 魯陽之望
lun 論
Lun-yü 論語
Lung-hsing (reign) 隆興
Lung-yu 隴右

ma (hemp) 麻
Ma Tuan-lin 馬端臨
Mai Ch'en 買臣
mai-chüeh 賣爵
Mao shih 毛詩
Mao Tse-tung 毛澤東
men-hsia sheng 門下省
Meng Tzu chieh-wen 孟子節文
mien (floss) 綿
min (people) 民
min-chu chu-i 民主主義
min-pen chu-i 民本主義
min-yün 民運
Ming (dynasty) 明
ming-ching 明經
Ming hui-tien 明會典
Ming-i (hexagram) 明夷
Ming-i tai-fang lu 明夷待訪錄
ming-ju 名儒

ming-shih 名士
Ming shih-lu 明實錄
Ming tu-fu nien-piao 明都府年表
minpon shugi 民本主義
minshu shugi 民主主義
mo (branch) 末
mo-i 墨義
Mo-ling 秣陵
mou (acre) 畝
mu-i 募役

Naitō Konan 内藤湖南
Nan-pei shih 南北史
Nan-yang 南陽
nei-ch'en 内臣
nei ch'eng-yün k'u 内承運庫
nei-k'u 内庫
nei-kuan 内官
nei-t'ing 内庭
Ni Yüan-lu 倪元璐
nien-p'u 年譜
Ning-hsia 寧夏
Ning-nan po 寧南伯
Ningpo 寧波

O-chiang (river) 娥江
Ou-yang Ch'e 歐陽澈
Ou-yang Hsiu 歐陽修

pa-ku wen 八股文
pa-kung 拔貢
pa-tsung 把總
pan-ch'ao 班朝
pan-chün 班軍
pao-chü 保舉
Pao Yung 鮑永
Pei-t'ing 北庭
pen (root, trunk) 本
pen-ping 本兵
P'eng-lai 彭萊
P'eng Yüeh 彭越

p'i 批
p'i-chao 辟召
pi-fu 秘府
p'i-hung 批紅
p'i-ta 批答
p'i-yung 辟雍
pien-kuan 編管
P'ing-chiang 平江
P'ing-ch'üan 平泉
ping fang 兵房
P'ing-hsi po 平西伯
P'ing-lu 平盧
P'ing-p'an chi 平叛記
po (silk cloth) 帛
Po Chü-i 白居易
P'o-hsieh lun 破邪論
Po I 伯夷
po-shih ti-tzu 博士弟子
po-shih ti-tzu yüan 博士弟子員
Po-ya ch'in 伯牙琴
pu (linen) 布
pu (measurement) 步
pu-ling 布令
pu-shu ch'i-hui 簿書期會
pu-tao 捕盜

san-fu 三輔
san-kung 三宮
San-kuo chih 三國志
san-ts'ung 散從
San-wu 三吳
Sang-fu ssu chih 喪服四制
Sang Hung-yang 桑弘羊
Shan-chou (Honan) 陝州
Shan-hsien 陝縣
Shang (dynasty) 商
Shang shu 尚書
shang-shu (memorialize) 上書
shang-t'ien i-mou 上田一畝
Shantung 山東
Shao-hsing (reign) 紹興

she cheng 攝政
she chi (gods) 社稷
She Ch'ung-ming 奢崇明
she-kuan 攝官
Shen Hsi-i 沈希儀
Shen-nung 神農
shen-tao shih chiao 神道施教
shen-ting ch'ien-mi 身丁錢米
Shen-tsung 神宗
sheng (pint) 升
shi minshu shugi 士民主主義
shih (poetry) 詩
shih (scholar-official) 士
shih (scribe) 史
Shih chi 史記
shih-chin tai-chin 飾巾待盡
Shih ching 詩經
shih-chung (palace attendant) 侍中
shih-fu 師傅
shih-huo 食貨
shih-jen 士人
Shih K'o-fa 史可法
Shih-shuo 師說
shih-ta-fu 士大夫
Shih-ta lu 識大錄
Shih-ta pien 識大編
Shih Tan 師丹
shih-wen 時文
shih-wu ts'e 時務策
shitaifu minshu shugi 士大夫民主主義
shou-ling kuan 首領官
Shu Ch'i 叔齊
shu-chi fang 樞機房
shu-chi-shih 庶吉士
Shu ching 書經
Shu-sun T'ung 叔孫通
shu-yüan 書院
Shun (sage-king) 舜
Shun-ti (Liu Sung dynasty) 順帝
Shuo-fang 朔方

Shuo-fu 說郛
Shuo-wen ch'ang-chien 說文長箋
so (station) 所
ssu (court) 寺
ssu (silk) 絲
ssu-ma 司馬
Ssu-ma Ch'ien 司馬遷
Ssu-ma Chih 司馬芝
Ssu-ma Hsiang-ju 司馬相如
Ssu-ma Kuang 司馬光
Ssu-shu ta-ch'üan 四書大全
ssu-t'u 司徒
su (grain) 粟
Su Ch'e 蘇轍
Su Hsün 蘇洵
Su Shih (Tung-p'o) 蘇軾東坡
suan min 算緡
Sui (dynasty) 隋
Sui-te 綏德
Sun Wu 孫吳
Sun Yat-sen 孫逸仙
Sun Yüan-hua 孫元化
Sung (dynasty) 宋
Sung Ch'i 宋祁

ta-chiang chih t'un-ping 大將之屯兵
ta chiao 打醮
Ta-ch'üan 大全
ta-chuang 大壯
ta-fa 大法
ta-fu (treasury) 大府
Ta-hsüeh yen-i pu 大學衍義補
ta-li ssu 大理寺
Ta-ning 大寧
Ta-shih-lü 大師旅
Ta shun (dynasty) 大順
ta ssu-t'u 大司徒
Ta Tai li 大戴禮
Ta-t'ung 大同
ta-yüeh cheng 大樂正
tai-chao 待詔
tai-chia 貸假

Tai-fang lu　待訪錄
T'ai-chou　泰州
T'ai-ho (reign)　太和
T'ai-hsien　泰縣
t'ai-hsüeh　太學
t'ai-hsüeh chi-chiu　太學祭酒
t'ai-i yüan　太醫院
T'ai-shih　泰誓
T'ai-ts'ang　太倉
Tai-tsung (T'ang)　代宗
T'ai-tsung (T'ang)　太宗
T'ai-yüan　太原
T'an Ssu-t'ung　譚嗣同
T'ang (dynasty)　唐
T'ang (founder of Shang)　湯
T'ang Chen　唐甄
tang-jen　黨人
tang wu　當五
tao-shih (Taoist)　道士
T'ao T'ang shih　陶唐氏
te-sheng men　德勝門
t'e-shou　特授
Te-tsung (T'ang)　德宗
Teng-chou (Shantung)　登州
Teng Mu　鄧牧
ti-chu chieh-chi tsai-yeh p'ai　地主階級在野派
t'i-chü ssu　提舉司
t'i-kuo ching yeh　體國經野
t'i-tu hsüeh-cheng　提督學政
ti-tzu yüan　弟子員
ti-wang chih hsin-hsüeh　帝王之心學
t'ieh (quotation, question)　帖
t'ieh-ching　帖經
t'ieh-shu　帖書
t'ieh-shu mo-i　帖書墨義
tien (chamber)　殿
T'ien-ch'i (reign)　天啓
t'ien-chih　田制
t'ien-hsia　天下
t'ien-hsia chih jen　天下之人
t'ien-hsia wei-kung　天下為公

T'ien-kuan 天官

T'ien-pao (reign) 天寶

tien-shih 典史

Ting-hsi po 定西伯

ting k'ou chih fu 丁口之賦

ting-shen (tax) 丁身

ting-shen ch'ien-mi 丁身錢米

ting-shou 頂首

tou (peck) 斗

Toyotomi Hideyoshi 豐臣秀吉

tsa-i 雜役

tsai-hsiang 宰相

Ts'ai Ching 蔡京

ts'an-chiang 參將

ts'an-chih cheng-shih 參知政事

ts'ang-fu 傖父

tsao-li 皂隸

Ts'ao-o chiang 曹娥江

tsao-shih 造士

ts'ao-yüan 曹掾

ts'ao-yün tsung-ping 漕運總兵

ts'e 册

tse (blame) 責

ts'e (essay) 策

tso chai 做齋

Tso Ch'iu-ming 左丘明

Tso chuan 左傳

Tso Liang-yü 左良玉

Tso Meng-kung 左孟琪

Tso Ssu 左思

tso-yu tu-tu 左右都督

tsu (tax) 租

Ts'ui-yen 粹言

tsung-ping 總兵

tsung-ping kuan 總兵官

tsung-tu 總督

t'u (orderly) 徒

tu-ch'a yüan 都察院

tu chih-hui shih 都指揮使

tu-chih-hui t'ung-chih 都指揮同知

T'u-fan 吐蕃

t'u-ku 土穀
t'u-kung 土貢
Tu Mu 杜牧
T'u-mu 土木
t'u-ping 土兵
Tu-shu pien 讀書編
tu-ssu 都司
tu-t'ien i-mou 土田一畝
tu-tu 都督
tu-tu fu 都督府
Tu Yu 杜祐
Tu Yü 杜預
tung-ch'ang 東廠
tung-cheng 東征
Tung Chung-shu 董仲舒
Tung-kuo Hsien-yang 東郭咸陽
Tung-lin 東林
Tung-ping po 東平伯
tung shih 東事
tzu (master) 子
tzu (style) 字
tzu-mu hsiang ch'üan erh hsing 子母相權而行

wai-kuan 外官
wai-t'ing 外庭
Wan Ch'eng-hsün 萬成勳
Wan Hsi-kuo 萬西郭
Wan-li (reign) 萬曆
wan-min 萬民
Wan Piao 萬表
Wan Ssu-t'ung 萬斯同
Wan Yen 萬言
Wang An-shih 王安石
Wang Ao-yung 王鰲永
Wang Ch'eng-en 王承恩
Wang Ch'i 王圻
Wang-chih 王制
Wang Fu-chih 王夫之
Wang Hsien-chih 王仙芝
Wang Ken 王艮
Wang Kuei 王珪

Wang Mien 王冕
Wang Tsai-chin 王在晉
Wang Yang-ming 王陽明
wei (garrison) 衛
Wei Chung-hsien 魏忠賢
Wei Ming-ti 魏明帝
wei-nan wei-hsing 未難為行
wei-wei nan-hsing 未為難行
Wei Wen-ti 魏文帝
Wen-chou 溫州
Wen Chung Tzu 文中子
Wen-hsien t'ung-k'ao 文獻通考
Wen-yüan ko 文淵閣
Wu (King) 武
Wu (region) 吳
wu (shaman) 巫
Wu Ch'i 吳起
Wu-ch'iao (Hopei) 吳橋
Wu-Ch'u 吳楚
wu-chün tu-tu-fu 五軍都督府
Wu Guang 吳光
Wu-hsi 吳錫
Wu-k'uai 吳會
Wu Kuang (recluse) 務光
Wu-lin 武林
Wu-ling 五嶺
Wu San-kuei 吳三桂
Wu-tai shih 五代史
Wu-tsung 武宗
Wu-tu fu 吳都賦
Wu Wang (King Wu) 武王
wu-yen tzu-te 無言自得
Wu Yü-pi 吳與弼

ya-ch'ien 衙前
Yamanoi Yū 山井湧
Yang-ho 陽和
Yang Hsiung 揚雄
Yang Jung 楊榮
Yang Shih-ch'i 楊士奇
Yang Yen 楊炎

Yao (sage-king) 堯
Yao-chiang 姚江
yeh (estate) 業
Yeh-hsien (Esen) 也先
Yen-an 延安
Yen Shih-ku 顏師古
Yen-sui 延綏
yen-yin 鹽引
Yenching 燕京
yin-ch'ai 銀差
yin-k'u 銀庫
Ying 郢
Ying-chou 應州
Ying-tsung 英宗
Yü (sage-king) 禹
yu-chi 遊擊
Yü Ch'ien 于謙
Yü-lin 榆林
yü-lin ts'e 魚鱗冊
Yü Ta-yu 俞大猷
Yü-yao 餘姚
yüan (department) 院
Yüan (dynasty) 元
Yüan chün 原君
Yüan-feng (reign) 元封
Yüan-ho (reign) 元和
Yüeh (region) 越
yung (service tax) 庸
Yung-lo (reign) 永樂
Yung-ming (Kuei) (prince) 永明(桂)
yung-tiao 庸調
Yünnan-fu 雲南府

Abbreviations

The following sinological abbreviations are used:

CKTHMCCC   Chung-kuo tzu-hsüeh ming-chu chi-ch'eng 中國子學名
         著集成
CKTMTTT   Chung kuo ti-ming ta-tz'u tien 中國地名大辭典
DMB   *Dictionary of Ming Biography*
ECCP   *Eminent Chinese of the Ching Period*
KHCPTS   *Kuo-hsüeh chi-pen ts'ung-shu* 國學基本叢書
KSKSSK   Kinsei kanseki sôkan 近世漢籍叢刊
KCTMTTT   *Ku-chin ti-ming ta-tz'u-tien* 古今地名大辭典
LCICHK   *Li-chou i-chu hui-k'an* 梨洲遺著彙刊
MCB   *Mélanges Chinois et Buddhique*
MITFL   *Ming-i tai-fang lu* 明夷待訪錄
MJCCTLSY   Ming-jen chuan-chi tzu-liao so-yin 明人傳記資料索引
MJHA   *Ming-ju hsüeh-an* 明儒學案
MS   Ming shih 明史
NLWH   Chung-kuo nei-luan wai-huo li-shih ts'ung-shu [中國]
         內亂外禍歷史叢書

SKCS   Ssu-k'u ch'üan-shu 四庫全書
SKCSCP   Ssu-k'u ch'üan-shu chen-pen 四庫全書珍本
SPPY   Ssu-pu pei-yao 四部備要
SPTK   Ssu-pu ts'ung-k'an 四部叢刊
SSCCS   *Sung-pen shih-san ching chu-su fu chiao-k'an chi* 宋本十三經
            注疏附校勘記
SSGTK   Shushigaku taikei 朱子學大系
SYHA   Sung-Yüan hsüeh-an 宋元學案
TSCC   Ts'ung-shu chi-ch'eng 叢書集成
WMSCK   Wan Ming shih-chi k'ao (Hsieh Kuo-chen) 晚明史籍考
            (謝國楨)

Principal Editions of the Ming-i tai fang lu

The present translation was first undertaken in 1947–48 on the basis of the *Erh-lao ko* text (see number 1 below) and then collated with editions numbered 2 and 3 below. This translation was first made available in 1953 through University Microfilms, Ann Arbor, Michigan. It has now been checked with the text as it appears in volume 1 of *Huang Zongxi quanji* (number 4 below). A detailed discussion of the history of the text, and variant versions, may be found on pages 421–27 of the last-named text.

1. *Erh-lao ko* 二老閣, woodblock edition, was edited by Cheng Hsing 鄭性, who built the Erh-lao ko library to house the collections of his own family and that part of Huang Tsung-hsi's collection which survived a fire at Huang's house in 1717. The extensive researches of Wu Guang give 1736 as the date of this edition (see his *Huang Tsung-hsi chu-tso hui-k'ao*—hereafter *Chu-tso*—pp. 7–9). Printed with the *Ming-i tai-fang lu* in this edition was Huang's *Ssu-chiu lu* 思舊錄 and the letter of Ku Yen-wu, which served as an introduction. This edition is quite rare, and the author is indebted to the late Professor Teng Chih-ch'eng of Yenching University for permitting him to consult a personal copy.

As noted above, the present translation is based on the *Erh-lao ko* edition and collated with those listed below. There is no great divergence among the texts, but there are minor printing errors.

2. *Hai-shan hsien-kuan ts'ung-shu* 海山仙館叢書, woodblock edition, was edited by T'an Ying 譚瑩 and published by P'an Shih-ch'eng in Canton in 1849. There is no indication as to the original source of the text published in this edition, but presumably it is a revised version of the *Erh-lao ko* edition. Several of the textual corrections made in it have been incorporated in the LCICHK edition, and these have been followed in the present translation. The name of the author, however, is incorrectly given as Huang Tsung-yen, Li-chou 黃宗炎, 梨洲; Li-chou is Huang Tsung-hsi's *hao*, but Tsung-yen is the name of his younger brother.

3. *Wu-kuei lou* 五桂樓 edition, edited by Huang Ch'eng-i 黃承乙, a descendant of the author, was published by Fu Huai-tsu 傅懷祖, of Shao-hsing, Chekiang, in 1879. A colophon by the editor states: "Formerly there was the wood-block edition of the *Erh-lao ko*, and later on this work was included in the *Hai-shan hsien-kuan ts'ung-shu*. The blocks of the *Erh-lao ko* edition have long since been lost, while the *ts'ung-shu*, published in Canton, contains a great many volumes and is extremely hard to buy.... To this work in the *Erh-lao ko* edition was added the *Ssu-chiu lu*.... In the collected writings of Ch'üan Hsieh-shan [Tsu-wang] there is a prefatory note. These are included in the present edition."

The text of this edition, published under the general title "Surviving works of Huang Li-chou" (*Huang Li-chou i-shu*) is identical with the *Ehr-lao ko* edition page for page and line for line. It has appeared in several printings, but none of these to my knowledge contains the colophon of Ch'üan Tsu-wang, supposedly included by Huang Ch'eng-i. One copy in the National Library of Beijing contains Fu's preface, the letter of Ku Yen-wu, and Huang's colophon; another in the writer's possession has only the letter of Ku Yen-wu. A more recent movable-type edition by the *Pei-yang kuan pao-chü* 北洋官報局, based on the *Wu kuei-lou* edition, is similar to the NLB version but also contains a list of errata for the *Erh-lao ko–Wu-kuei lou* editions.

The general title of this edition, *Huang Li-chou hsien-sheng i-shu*, should not be confused with the later *Huang Li-chou i-shu, shih chung* 黃梨洲遺書, 十種, published in Hangchow in 1905 (see under Huang Tsung-hsi below).

4. Huang Zongxi quanji (*Huang Tsung-hsi ch'üan-chi: The complete works of Huang Tsung-hsi*, 黃宗羲全集) was published in Hangzhou by the Zhejiang guji chuban she in two volumes in 1985 under the auspices of the Zhejiang Academy of Social Sciences and the editorial direction of Shen Shanhong and Wu Guang. The volume includes two brief texts, "Wen-chih" (Refine-

ment and substance) and "Feng-chien" (The enfeoffment system), pp. 416–20, said to have once been a part of the *Ming-i tai-fang lu* but never published as such; they are not translated herein.

Chinese and Japanese Sources

References in the text and notes are by chapter (chüan) *number followed by page number in the edition cited.*

Bu Jinzhi 步近智. "Ming mo donglin xuepai de sixiang tezheng" 明末東林學派的思想特征. In *Wenshizhe* 文史哲 5 (1985): 17–24.

Cai Shangsi 蔡尚思. "Cong Zhongguo sixiang shi kan Huang Zongxi de fanjunquan sixiang" 從中國思想史看黃宗義的反君權思想. In Wu Guang, ed., *Huang Zongxi lun*, pp. 242–49.

Ch'ai Te-keng 柴德賡. "Sung huan-kuan ts'an-yü chün-shih kao" 宋宦官參預軍事考. In *Fu-jen hsüeh-chih* 10 (1941): 181–225.

Chang Chia-hsiang 張家驤. *Chung-kuo pi-chih shih* 中國幣制史. Peking: Min-kuo ta-hsüeh, 1925.

Chang Hsüeh-ch'eng 章學誠. *Wen-shih t'ung-i* 文史通義. *Chang shih i-shu* 章氏遺書. Shanghai: Commercial Press, 1936.

Chang Huang 章潢. *T'u-shu pien* 圖書編. 1623 ed.

Chang Mu 張穆. *Ku T'ing-lin hsien-sheng nien-p'u* 顧亭林先生年譜. Chia-yeh t'ang ed. 嘉業堂叢書.

Chang Ping-lin 章炳麟. *T'ai-yen wen-lu* 太炎文錄. Chang-shih ts'ung-shu ed.

Chao Er-hsün 趙爾巽, ed. *Ch'ing shih kao* 清史稿, 486.4a (biography of Huang Tsung-hsi). Peking: Chung-hua shu-chü, 1927–28.

Chao I 趙翼. *Ehr-shih erh shih cha-chi* 二十二史劄記. TSCC ed.

Ch'en Hao 陳鶴 and Ch'en K'o-chia 陳克家. *Ming chi* 明紀. Shih-chieh shu-chü ed. Shanghai: Commercial Press, 1935.

Chen Shengxi 陳生璽 and Liu Guangsheng 劉光生. "Huang Zongxi sixiang ji qi *Mingyi daifang lu* zheyao" 黃宗義思想及其明夷待訪錄折要. *Nankai shi-xue* 南開史學 1 (1983): 177–95.

———. "Mingyi daifang lu shu-ming jie" 明夷待訪錄書名解. In *Zhongguo zhexue yan-jiu* 2 (1984): 100.

Ch'en Teng-yüan 陳登原. "Shu *Ming-i tai-fang lu* hou" 書明夷待訪錄後. *Nanking Journal* 4, no. 2 (1934): 277. Notes on the principal themes of the *Ming-i tai-fang lu*, with background information from historical sources on certain problems and excerpts from contemporary writers with similar views.

Ch'en T'ien 陳田. *Ming-shih chi-shih* 明詩紀事. Shanghai: Commercial Press KHCPTS ed.

Chen Zuwu 陳祖武. "Huang Zongxi, Gu Yanwu he lun" 黃宗義顧炎武合論. In *Guizhou shehui kexue* 貴州社會科學 56, no. 5 (1985): 50–55.

Ch'eng Hao 程顥 and Ch'eng I 程頤. *Erh Ch'eng wen-chi* 二程文集 (TSCC ed). *Erh Ch'eng i-shu*, in *Erh Ch'eng chi*. Beijing: Zhonghua shuju, 1981.

Ch'eng-wei lu. See Liang Chang-chü.

Chi-ch'i t'ing chi. See Ch'üan Tsu-wang.

Chi Liu-ch'i 計六奇. *Ming-chi nan-lüeh* 明季南略 (in KHCPTS ed.).

——. *Ming-chi pei-lüeh* 明季北略 (1671 ed.).

Chi Wan-hsien 齋婉先. *Huang Tsung-hsi chih ching-shih ssu-hsiang yen chiu* 黃宗義之經世思想研究. Taipei: Cheng-chih ta-hsüeh, 1991.

Chi Wen-fu 嵇文甫. *Wan-ming ssu-hsiang shih lun* 晚明思想史論. Chungking: Commercial Press, 1944.

Chi Yün 紀昀. [*Ch'in-ting*] *Li-tai chih-kuan piao* 欽定歷代職官表. SPPY ed. Shanghai: Chung hua, 1935.

Chi Yün. [*Ch'in-ting*] *Ssu-k'u chüan-shu chen-pen* 四庫全書珍本 (SKCSCP). Taiwan: Commercial Press, 1977.

——. *Ssu-k'u ch'üan-shu tsung-mu* 四庫全書總目. Shanghai: Ta-tung shu-chü ed., 1930.

Chiang Fan 江藩. *Han-hsüeh shih-ch'eng chi* 漢學師承記. Shanghai: Commercial Press, 1934. Includes notes of Chou Yü-t'ung 周予同.

Chiang-nan t'ung-chih. See Yin Chi-shan.

Chiang T'ing-hsi 蔣廷錫, ed. [*Ku chin*] *T'u-shu chi-ch'eng* 古今圖書集成. Shanghai, 1884–88.

Ch'ien Chih 錢軹. *Chia-shen ch'üan-hsin lu* 甲申傳信錄. 1883 ed.

Ch'ien I-chi 錢儀吉. *Pei-chuan chi* 碑傳集. 1893 ed. Biography of Huang Tsung-hsi (131:1a).

Ch'ien Lin 錢林. *Wen-hsien cheng-ts'un lu* 文獻徵存錄. Yu-chia shu 有嘉樹 ed. of 1858.

Ch'ien Mu 錢穆. *Chung-kuo chin san-pai-nien hsüeh-shu shih* 中國近三百年學術史. 2 vols. Shanghai: Commercial Press, 1937.

——. *Wang Shou-jen* 王守仁. Shanghai: Commercial Press, 1934.

Chin shu. See *Erh-shih-ssu shih.*

Ch'ing shih lieh-chuan 清史列傳. Ch'ing Historiographical Board 清史館. Peking: Chung-hua shu-chü, 1928.

Chiu T'ang shu. See *Erh-shih-ssu shih.*

Chiu wu-tai shih. See *Ehr-shih-ssu shih.*

Chou li. See [*Sung pen*] *Shih-san ching.*

Chou Ping-lin 周炳麟, ed. *Yü-yao hsien-chih* 餘姚縣志. 1889 ed. Biography of Huang Tsung-hsi (23:1a).

Chu Hsi 朱熹. *Chu-tzu ch'üan-shu* 朱子全書. 1714 ed.

——. *Chu-tzu wen chi* 朱子文集. TSCC ed.

——. *Hui-an Chu Wen-kung hsien-sheng wen-chi* 晦庵朱文公先生文集. Ssu-pu ts'ung-k'an (hereafter, SPTK) ed. Also in edition of Chūbun shuppan-sha, Kyoto, 1977.

——. *Meng Tzu chi-chu* 孟子集注. See *Ssu-shu chi-chu*, Chung-kuo tzu-hsüeh ming-chu chi-ch'eng ed.

——. *Pai-lu tung shu-yüan chiao-kuei* 白鹿洞書院教規. TSCC ed.

——. *Ssu-shu chi-chu* 四書集注. Chung-kuo tzu-hsüeh ming-chu chi-ch'eng (hereafter, CKTHMCCC) ed.

——. *Ta-hsüeh chang-chü*, in *Ssu-shu chi-chu*, CKTHMCCC ed.

——. [*Yü-p'i*] *T'ung-chien kang-mu* 御批通鑑綱目. 1887 reprint of K'ang-hsi ed.

Chu Hsieh 朱偰. *Chung-kuo hsin-yung huo-pi fa-chan shih* 中國信用貨幣發展史. Chungking: Commercial Press, 1943.

Chu I-tsun 朱彝尊. *Ming shih tsung* 明詩綜. Liu-chiang ko 六絳閣, K'ang-hsi ed.

——. *P'u-shu-t'ing chi* 曝書亭集. SPTK, 1st ser.

Chu Wen-chüan 褚閒鵑. *Huang Li-chou hsüeh-shu ssu-hsiang yen-chiu* 黃梨洲學術思想研究. Taipei: Chung-yung t'u-shu ch'u-pan-she, 1976.

Ch'üan Te-yü 權德輿. *Ch'üan Ts'ai-chih wen-chi* 權載之文集. SPTK, 1st ser.

Ch'üan Tsu-wang 全祖望. *Chi-ch'i t'ing chi* 鮚埼亭集 and *Wai-pien* 外編. KHCPTS ed. (Shanghai: Commercial Press, 1936).

——. *Hsü Yung-shang ch'i-chiu shih* 續甬上耆舊詩. Ningpo: Ssu-ming wen-hsien she, 1918.

——. *Li-chou hsien-sheng shen-tao-pei wen* 梨洲先生神道碑文. *Chi-ch'i t'ing-chi* 11:131. Biography of Huang Tsung-hsi (written c. 1740).

Chuang Tzu. Harvard-Yenching Index Series ed. For translations, see H. A. Giles, A. C. Graham, and Burton Watson.

Chuang Tzu 莊子. (Nan-hua chen-ching), SPTK ed.

Chung-kuo tzu-hsüeh ming-chu chi ch'eng. See Hsiao T'ien-shih.

Ch'un-ch'iu ching-chuan chi-chieh 春秋經傳集解. SPTK ed.

Ch'ung-chen ch'ang-pien 崇禎長編. Author unknown. NLWH ed. See *Wan Ming shih-chi k'ao* (hereafter, WMSCK) 4:32.

Ch'ung-chen shih-lu 崇禎實錄. Author unknown. Nanking: 1940. Photolithographic reprint of *Chia yeh t'ang* MS in Kiangsu Provincial Library. See WMSCK 4:31a.

Erh ch'en chuan 貳臣傳. Ch'ing Historiographical Board. Kuang-hsü ed.

Ehr-shih-ssu shih [*Ch'in-ting*] 二十四史 [欽定]. Han-fen lou 涵芬樓. Facsimile reprint of the Palace ed. of 1739: Shanghai, 1916.

Erh-shih-wu shih pu-pien 二十五史補編. 6 vols. Shanghai: K'ai-ming ed. 1936–37.

Fan Yeh 范曄. *Hou-Han shu* 後漢書. SPTK ed.

Fang Hsiao-ju 方孝孺. *Hsün-chih chai chi* 遜志齋集. SPTK, 1st ser.

Fu Wei-lin 傅維鱗. *Ming shu* 明書. Ch'ang sha: Commercial Press, 1938. KHCPTS ed.

Fukumoto Masakazu 福本雅一. "Kō Sōgi no bungaku kan" 黃宗羲の文學觀. In *Shisen* 史泉 *Kansai daigaku shigakkai*, nos. 23–24 (March 1962): 49–66.

Guo Houan 郭厚安. "Mingyi daifang lu du hou" 明夷待訪錄讀后. In *Xibei shifan daxue xuepao* 3, no. 45 (1985): 73–81.

Hai-tung i-shih 海東逸史 by Weng-chou lao-jen 翁州老人 (author unknown). See WMSCK 12:3b. *Ssu-ming ts'ung-shu*, 2d ser. Biography of Huang Tsung-hsi dealing mainly with period 1644–49.

Han shu. See *Erh-shih-ssu shih*, or under Fan Yeh, for SPTK ed..

Han Yü 韓愈. *Chu Wen-kung chiao Ch'ang-li hsien-sheng chi* 朱文公校昌黎先生集. SPTK, 1st ser.

Hou-Han shu. See *Erh-shih-ssu shih*.

Hou Wai-lu 侯外廬. *Chin-tai Chung-kuo ssu-hsiang hsüeh-shuo shih* 近代中國思想學說史. 2 vols. Shanghai: Sheng-huo shu-chü, 1947.

Hsiao Kung-ch'üan 蕭公權. *Chung-kuo cheng-chih ssu-hsing shih* 中國政治思想史. Shanghai: Commercial Press, 1947.

Hsiao T'ien-shih, gen. ed. *Chung-kuo tzu-hsüeh ming-chu chi ch'eng* 中國子學名著集成. Taipei: National Central Library, 1978–79.

Hsiao T'ung 蕭統. *Wen-hsüan* 文選. SPTK ed.

Hsiao-t'ien chi-chuan. See Hsü Tzu.

Hsiao-t'ien chi-nien. See Hsü Tzu.

Hsieh Kuo-chen 謝國楨. *Huang Li-chou hsüeh-p'u* 黃梨洲學譜 (abbr. *Hsüeh-p'u*). *Kuo-hsüeh hsiao ts'ung shu*, Shanghai: Commercial Press, 1932. The best all-round study of Huang Tsung-hsi's life, his thought in general (though his political thought is dealt with only briefly), his writings, intellectual associations, and disciples.

——. *Ming-Ch'ing chih chi tang-she yün-tung k'ao* 明清之際黨社運動考. Shanghai: Commercial Press, 1935.

——. *Wan Ming shih-chi k'ao* 晚明史籍考 (WMSCK). Peking: National Library, 1933.

Hsin T'ang shu. See *Ehr-shih-ssu shih*.

Hsin wu-tai shih. See *Ehr-shih-ssu shih*.

Hsing-li ta-ch'üan. See Hu Kuang.

Hsiung Kung-che 熊公哲. *Wang An-shih cheng-lüeh* 王安石政略. Shanghai: Commercial Press, 1937.

Hsü Hsien 許獻, ed. [*Chung-hsiu*] *Tung-lin shu-yüan chih* 重修東林書院志. 1881 ed.

Hsü Tzu 徐鼒. *Hsiao-t'ien chi-chuan* 小腆紀傳. Chinling ed. of 1887–88.

——. *Hsiao-t'ien chi-nien fu-k'ao* 小腆紀年附攷. 1861 ed.

Hsüeh-p'u. See Hsieh Kuo-chen.

Hsün Tzu. Harvard-Yenching Index ed., 1949 (reprint, Taipei: Chinese Research Materials Center, 1966); also in SPTK ed.

Hsün Yüeh 荀悅. *Han Chi* 漢紀. SPTK, 1st ser.

Hu Ch'u-sheng 胡楚生. "Huang Li-chou yu Lü Wan-ts'un" 黃梨洲與呂晚村. In *Wen-shih hsüeh-pao* 文史學報 14 (June 1984): 1–8.

Hu Han 胡翰. *Hu Chung-tzu chi* 胡仲子集. TSCC ed.

Hu Kuang 胡廣 et al., eds. *Hsing-li ta-ch'üan* 性理大全. Shih ch'ü ko ed. 石渠閣.

—— et al., eds. *Meng Tzu chi-chu ta-ch'üan* 孟子集注大全. Ssu-k'u ch'üan-shu chen-pen 胡適的日記 ed.

Hu Shih 胡適. *Hu Shih te jih-chi* 胡適的日記. Taipei: Yüan-liu ch'u-pan kung-ssu, 1990.

——. "Huang Li-chou lun hsüeh-sheng yün-tung" 黃梨洲論學生運動 (Huang Tsung-hsi on the student movement). In *Hu Shih wen-ts'un erh-chi* 胡適文存二集 3:1–14. Shanghai: Yüan-tung t'u-shu kung-she, 1924; 10th ed., 1947.

Hu Wei 胡渭. *I-t'u ming-pien* 易圖明辨. Shou-shan ko ts'ung-shu ed. 守山閣叢書.

Huai-nan tzu 淮南子. SPTK, 1st ser.

Huan Kuan 桓寬. *Yen-t'ieh lun* 鹽鐵論. SPTK ed.

Huang Chih-chüan 黃之寯. *Chiang-nan t'ung-chih* 江南通志. 1736 ed.

Huang Fu-mi 皇甫謐. *Kao shih chuan* 高士傳. SPPY ed.

Huang Ping-hou 黃炳垕. *Huang Li-chou hsien-sheng nien-p'u* 黃梨洲先生年譜 (abbr. *Nien-p'u*). In Huang Tsung-hsi, *Li-chou i-chu hui-k'an* (Collected works; hereafter, LCICHK), 19a. Compiled in 1873 by a seventh-generation descendent of Huang Tsung-hsi, but not very complete for the years of Huang's participation in the Ming resistance movement (1644–50). Cf. *Hsüeh-p'u*, p. 91.

Huang Ssu-ai 黃嗣艾. *Nan-lei hsüeh-an* 南雷學案. Kuo-hsüeh ts'ung-shu, Cheng-chung shu-chü 正中書局, 1936; reprint, Shanghai: Cheng-chu shu-chü, 1947. A lengthy study of Huang Tsung-hsi's life and thought, this work nevertheless contains only a brief biography, a list of works attributed to Huang with no bibliographical data and some excerpts from his writings following the original *hsüeh-an* form. For the most part it is devoted to numerous brief biographies of Huang's intellectual predecessors, members of his family, colleagues, disciples, etc.

Huang Tsung-hsi 黃宗羲. *Chin shui ching* 今水經. 1 ch., LCICHK ed.

——. *Hai-wai t'ung-k'u chi* 海外慟哭記. 1 ch., LCICHK ed. Questionably attributed to Huang Tsung-hsi. Cf. *Hsüeh-p'u*, p. 68; Ishihara Michihiro, *Nihon kisshi no kenkyū*, p. 521.

———. *Hsing ch'ao lu* 行朝錄. According to Huang, this collection originally consisted of "several tens" of titles dealing with Ming resistance in the South, but extant editions contain considerably less than that, including some of doubtful authenticity. LCICHK contains the following individual titles of which the first nine are identified as part of the *Hsing ch'ao lu*:

> *Lung-wu chi-nien* 隆武紀年. 1 ch.
> *Kan-chou shih-shih chi* 贛州失事記. 1 ch.
> *Shao-wu cheng-li chi* 紹武爭立紀. 1 ch.
> *Lu chi-nien* 魯紀年. 2 ch.
> *Chou-shan hsing-fei* 舟山興廢. 1 ch.
> *Jih-pen ch'i-shih chi* 日本乞師記. 1 ch. Cf.

also text as collated by Ishihara Michihiro, *Nihon kisshi no kenkyū*, p. 522.

> *Ssu-ming shan chai chi* 四明山寨記. 1 ch.
> *Yung-li chi-nien* 永歷紀年. 1 ch.
> *Sha-ting chou chi luan* 沙定洲紀亂. 1 ch.

In addition the following titles contained in LCICHK, though not identified as part of the *Hsing ch'ao lu*, do appear as such in other editions:

> *Tz'u-hsing shih-mo* 賜姓始末. 1 ch.

Cheng Ch'eng-kung chuan 鄭成功傳. 1 ch. Probably not the work of Huang Tsung-hsi, since it duplicates unnecessarily the preceding title and deals with some events occurring after Huang's death. See *Hsüeh-p'u*, pp. 63–66.

Chang Yüan [Hsüan] chu hsien-sheng shih-lüeh 張元(玄)著先生事略. 1 ch.

Concerning additional titles sometimes listed as part of the *Hsing-ch'ao lu*, as well as on questions of authorship, see *Hsüeh-p'u*, pp. 63–66; Ma T'ai-hsüan, "Chu-tso," pp. 72–74; Ch'üan Tsu-wang, *Chi-ch'i t'ing chi, wai-pien*, 29:1072 (Pa Li-chou hsien-sheng, *Hsing ch'ao lu*).

———. *Huang Li-chou i-shu, shih chung* 黃梨洲遺書,十種. Compiled by Chiang Lin-chen 蔣廖振. Hangchow, 1905. Containes ten titles by Huang Tsung-hsi, including the *Ming-i tai-fang lu* and a considerably abridged version of the *Ming-ju hsüeh-an*.

———. *Huang Li-chou wen-chi* 黃梨洲文集. Ch'en Nai-ch'ien 陳乃乾, ed. Beijing: Zhonghua shuju, 1959.

———. *Huang Zongxi quanji* 黃宗羲全集. Compiled by Shen Shanhong 沈善洪. 2 vols. Hangzhou: Zhejiang guji chubanshe, vol. 1, 1985; vol. 2, 1986.

——. *I-hsüeh hsiang-shu lun* 易學象數論. 6 ch. Kuang-ya ts'ung-shu ed.

——. *Li-chou i-chu hui-k'an* 梨洲遺著彙刊 (LCICHK). Compiled by Hsieh Feng-ch'ang 薛鳳昌. Shanghai, 1910. Though not a complete collection of Huang Tsung-hsi's works, it is the largest available one, containing thirty-three titles. Long works such as the *Ming-ju hsüeh-an* and *Sung-Yüan hsüeh-an* are not included.

——. *Meng Tzu shih-shuo* 孟子師說. Huang's version of his teacher Liu Tsung-chou's comments on passages in Mencius. LCICHK ed. and *Ch'üan-chi*, vol. 1, pp. 48–166.

——. *Ming wen an* 明文案. 217 ch. Manuscript edition in National Library of Beijing.

——. *Ming wen hai* 明文海. 482 ch. *Ssu-k'u ch'üan-shu* ed., National Library of Beijing. Manuscript edition in Zhejiang Provincial Library.

——. *Ming-ju hsüeh-an* 明儒學案. 62 ch. The edition cited in this study is that contained in the *Ssu-ch'ao hsüeh-an* 四朝學案 (Shanghai: Shih-chieh shu-chü, 1936), a reprint of the 1739 edition of Cheng Hsing 鄭性. Also contained in the *Wan-yu wen-k'u.*

An earlier edition by Chia Jun 賈潤 (Tzu yün chai 紫筠齋 ed., printed by Chia's son in 1707) is still extant and was copied into the Imperial Manuscript Library. It is an abridged version, however, and Cheng Hsing states in the preface to his own edition that Chia censored the original to make it conform more to his own views (cf. *Ssu-k'u tsung-mu* 58:5a; *Hsüeh-p'u*, p. 54).

——. *Ming-ju hsüeh-an* 明儒學案. Beijing: Zhong-hua shujü, 1985.

——. *Nan-lei shih-li* 南雷詩歷. 4 ch. LCICHK ed. Also contained in *Nan-lei chi*, SPTK, 1st ser.

——. *Nan-lei wen-an* 南雷文案, 10 ch.; *wai-chi* 外集, 2 ch. LCICHK ed. Also in *Nan-lei chi*, SPTK, 1st ser.

——. *Nan-lei wen-ting* 南雷文定; *ch'ien-chi* 前集, 11 ch.; *hou-chi* 後集, 4 ch.; *san-chi* 四集, 3 ch.; *ssu-chi* 三集, 3 ch. LCICHK ed. Also in Commercial Press, KHCPTS, TSCC, SPPY; also Taipei: Shih-chieh shu-chü, 1964.

——. *Nan-lei wen-yüeh* 南雷文約. 4 ch. LCICHK ed. Also extant in *Erh-lao ko* ed.

——. *P'o-hsieh lun* 破邪論. 1 ch. LCICHK ed. Also in *Huang Zongxi quanji* 1:191–207.

——. *Ssu-chiu lu* 思舊錄. 1 ch. LCICHK ed.

——. *Sung-Yüan hsüeh-an* 宋元學案. 100 ch. *Ssu-ch'ao hsüeh-an*, Shih-chieh shu-chü ed. Completed by Huang Po-chia 黃百家 and Ch'üan Tsu-wang 全祖望. This edition is a reprint of the 1838 edition of Feng Yün-hao 馮雲濠 and Wang Tzu-ts'ai 王梓材.

Concerning the history of this and other editions, see *Hsüeh-p'u,* pp. 56–57, and Ma T'ai-hsüan, "Chu-tso," p. 7. On the 100 ch. supplement (*pu-i* 補遺) by Wang Tzu-ts'ai, see *Hsüeh-p'u*, pp. 56–57, and Hu Shih, "Sung-Yüan hsüeh-an pu-i ssu-shih-erh chüan-pen pa," 宋元學案補遺四十二卷本跋 *Library Science Quarterly* 1, no. 3 (September 1926): 473–77.

    Above are listed only the principal writings of Huang Tsung-hsi and titles cited in the present study. Concerning other works by Huang or attributed to him, as well as for other editions of the works listed here, see *Hsüeh-p'u*, pp. 53–91; Ma T'ai-hsüan, "Chu-tso," pp. 69–80.

Imazeki Hisamaro (Toshimaro?) 今關壽麿. *Nihon ryūgū no Min-matsu shoshi* 日本流寓の明末諸士. Part 6: *Kō Rishū no Nihon kisshi ni tsuite* 黄梨洲の日本乞師に就いて. In *Kindai Shina no gakugei* 近世支那の学芸. Tokyo: Minyūsha, 1931. Originally published as separate title in 1928.

Ishihara Michihiro 石原道博 or Dōsaku 道作. *Nihon kisshi no kenkyū* 日本乞師の研究. Tokyo: Fuzambō, 1945. A study of Ming missions to Japan in the 1640s and 1650s by a lifelong student of the subject.

Inaba Iwakichi 稻葉岩吉. *Min-matsu Shin-sho kisshi Nihon shimatsu* 明末清初乞師日本始末. *Nihon oyobi Nihonjin*, nos. 572, 574.

Jih-chih lu. See Ku Yen-wu.

Jih-pen ch'i-shih chi. See Huang Tsung-hsi, *Hsing ch'ao lu.*

Juan Yüan 阮元 *Ch'ou-jen chuan* 疇人傳. LCICHK, *ts'e* 1. Also in *Huang-Ch'ing ching-chieh* ed. Biography of Huang Tsung-hsi dealing principally with his work as a mathematician and astronomer.

Jung Chao-tsu 容肇祖. "Lü Liu-liang chi ch'i ssu-hsiang" 呂留良及其思想. In *Fu-jen hsüeh-chih* 5, nos. 1–2 (December 1926): 1–86. Includes an extensive discussion of Huang's relations with Lü Liu-liang.

——. *Ming-tai ssu-hsiang shih* 明代思想史. Shanghai: K'ai-ming shu tien, 1941. An excellent survey of Ming thought, especially valuable for Huang's intellectual heritage from the Wang Yang-ming school, the Tung-lin, and Liu Tsung-chou.

Kao Chun 高準. *Huang Li-chou cheng-chih ssu-hsiang yen-chiu* 黄梨洲政治思想研究. Taipei: Chung-kuo wen-hua hsüeh-yüan, 1967.

——. "Huang Li-chou chih chih-kuo fang-lüeh lun" 黄梨洲之治國方略論. In *Hua-hsüeh yüeh-k'an* 121 (January 1982): 8013.

Katō Shigeshi 加藤繁. *Chūgoku kaheishi kenkyū* 中國貨幣史研究. Tokyo: Tōyō bunko, 1992.

Ku Ch'ing-mei 古清美. *Huang Li-chou chih sheng-p'ing chi ch'i hsüeh-shu ssu-hsiang* 黄梨洲之生平及其學術思想. Taipei: Kuo-li Taiwan ta-hsüeh wen-hsüeh yüan, 1978.

Ku T'ing-lin nien-p'u. See Chang Mu.

Ku Yen-wu 顧炎武. *Jih-chih lu* 日知錄. Shanghai: Commercial Press, 1934. KHCPTS ed.

———. *Jih-chih lu chi-shih*. Kyoto: Chūbun shuppansha, 1978.

———. *T'ing-lin wen-chi* 亭林文集. In *T'ing-lin i-shu* 亭林遺書, Sui-ch'u t'ang ed. 遂初堂; also Beijing: Zhong hua ed., 1983; and SPTK ed.

Ku Ying-t'ai 谷應泰. *Ming shih chi-shih pen-mo* 明史紀事本末. Commercial Press, KHCPTS ed.

Kuribayashi Nobuo 栗林宣夫. *Rikōsei no kenkyū* 里甲制の研究, p. 418. Tokyo: Bunri Shoin, 1971.

Kuruhara Keisuke 來原慶助. *Kinsei Shina seiji ronsaku* 近世支那政治論策. *Min-i taihō roku* 明夷待訪錄. Tokyo: 1916. Contains the original text of the *Ming-i tai-fang lu* as found in the *Wu-kuei lou* edition of Huang Ch'eng-i, a brief biography of Huang Tsung-hsi, and a translation into Japanese of the text. Both the translation and annotations are frequently in error. Lent to me through the kindness of Professor Kaizuka Shigeki of Kyoto University.

Lao Ssu-kuang 勞思光. *Hsin-pien Chung-kuo che-hsüeh shih* 新編中國哲學史. 5 vols. T'aipei: San-min shu-chü, 1981, 1987.

Li-chi. See *Sung-pen shih-san ching*.

Li Fang 李昉, ed.. *T'ai-p'ing yü-lan* 太平御覽. Hsi-hsien Pao shih ed. 歙縣包氏, 1807.

Li Huan 李桓. *Kuo-ch'ao ch'i-hsien lei-cheng* 國朝耆獻類徵. Hsiang-yin Li shih ed. 湘陰李氏. Biography of Huang Tsung-hsi (404:1a).

Li Jinquan 李錦全. "Cong 'Yuan' 'liu' guanxi kan Huang Zongxi minzhu qimeng sixiang de lishi diwei" 從源流關係看黃宗羲民主啓蒙思想的歷史地位. In Wu Guang, ed., *Huang Zongxi lun*, pp. 322–29.

Li-tai chih-kuan piao. See Chi Yün.

Li T'ao 李燾. *Hsü tzu-chih t'ung-chien ch'ang-pien* 續資治通鑑長編. Chia-ching 24 (1545). Hai-yu Chang shih ed.

Li Tzu-jan 李滋然 (Li Ziran). *Ming-i tai fang lu chiu-miu* 明夷待訪錄糾謬. Ching-hua yin-shu chü 京華印書局, 1909.

Li Yen-shou 李延壽. *Nan Shih* 南史. SPTK ed.

Li Yüan-tu 李元度. *Kuo-ch'ao hsien-cheng shih-lüeh* 國朝先正事略. SPPY ed. Biography of Huang Tsung-hsi (27:4a–8b).

Li Zhuoran 李焯然 (Li Cho-jan). "Li Ziran 'Mingyi daifang lu' jiumiu chutan" 李滋然明夷待訪錄糾謬初探. In Wu Guang, ed., *Huang Zongxi lun*, pp. 338–49.

Liang Chang-chü 梁章鉅. *Ch'eng-wei lu* 稱謂錄. 1884 ed.

Liang Ch'i-ch'ao 梁啓超. *Ch'ing-tai hsüeh-shu kai-lün* 清代學術概論. Tokyo: Bunkyudō, 1938.

———. *Chung-kuo chin san-pai nien hsüeh-shu shih* 中國近三百年學術史. In *Yin-ping shih ch'üan-chi* 飲冰室全集. Chung-hua shu-chü ed., 17:75.4. A survey of Chinese thought in the last three centuries by a prominent scholar who was largely responsible for drawing popular attention to Huang Tsung-hsi in recent times.

——. *Huang Li-chou Chu Shun-shui ch'i-shih Jih-pen pien* 黃梨洲朱舜水乞師日本辯. *Yinping shih wen-chi* 飲冰室文集. Shanghai: 1925. A discussion of the probable date of Huang's mission to Japan, favoring the year 1644.

Liang Fang-chung 梁方仲. "*I-t'iao-pien fa*" 一條鞭法 (A study of the early forms of the single-whip levy system of land taxation). *Chung-kuo chin-tai ching-chi shih yen-chiu* 4, no. 1 (Special Issue: May 1936).

——. "Ming-tai ti min-ping" 明代的民兵. *Chung-kuo she-hui ching-chi shih chi-k'an* 5, no. 2 (June 1937).

——. *Ming-tai yü-lin t'u-ts'e k'ao* 明代魚鱗圖冊考. In *Ti-cheng yüeh-k'an* 地政月刊, 1, no. 8 (1933).

Liao Tao-nan 廖道南. *Tien-ko tz'u-lin chi* 殿閣詞林記. *Hupei hsien-cheng i-shu* ed. 湖北先正遺書.

Lin Ch'i-yen 林啓彥. "Tsung *Ming-i tai-fang lu* lun Huang Tsung-hsi cheng-chih ssu-hsiang ti yüan-yüan" 從明夷待訪錄論黃宗羲政治思想的淵源. In *Feng Ping-shan t'u-shu-kuan jin hsi chi nien lun-wen chi*. Hong Kong: University of Hong Kong Press, 1985; also in Japanese: *Hiroshima daigaku tōyōshi kenkyūshitsu hōkoku* 広島大学東洋史研究室報告, 6 (September 1984): 34–48.

Liu Hsiang 劉向. *Lieh hsien chuan* 列仙傳. *Shuo-fu* ed.

Liu I-cheng 柳詒徵. *Chung-kuo wen-hua shih* 中國文化史. Nanking, 1932.

Liu I-ch'ing 劉義慶. *Shih-shuo hsin-yü* 世説新語. SPTK, 1st ser.

Liu Shu-hsien 劉述先. *Huang Tsung-hsi hsin-hsüeh chih ting-wei* 黃宗羲心學之定位. Taipei: Yün-ch'en wen-hua shih-yeh kung-ssu, 1987.

——. "Huang Tsung-hsi wan chieh pu-pao?" 黃宗羲晚節不保. *Wen-hsing* 106, no. 4 (1987): 156–59.

Liu Tsung-chou 劉宗周. *Cheng-jen she-yüeh* 證人社約. SPTK, 1st ser.

——. *Liu Tzu ch'uan-shu* 劉子全書. 1822 ed.

Lu Chih 陸贄. *Lu Hsüan-kung tsou-i* 陸宣公奏議. Taipei: Commercial Press, 1965, KHCPTS ed.; Shanghai: Commercial Press, SPTK ed.

Lü Liu-liang 呂留良. *Lü Wan-ts'un hsien-sheng wen-chi* 呂晚村先生文集. Ch'ing movable-type edition (undated); reprint, Shanghai: Commercial Press, 1973.

——. *Ssu-shu chiang-i* 四書講義. 43 ch. 1686 ed.

Lü-shih ch'un-ch'iu 呂氏春秋. SPTK, 1st ser.

Lu Shih-i 陸世儀, *Fu-she chi-lüeh* 復社紀略 WHNL ed.

Luo Huaching 罗华庆. "Lue lun Huang Zongxi gong qi shifei yu xuexiao de sixiang" 略論黃宗羲公其是非于學校的思想. In *Huazhong shiyuan xuebao* (September 1984): 55–60.

Ma T'ai-hsüan 馬太玄. "Huang Tsung-hsi chih sheng-p'ing chi ch'i chu-tso" 黃宗羲之生平及其著作. In *Sun Yat-sen University Bulletin of Institute of*

History and Languages 2, no. 15 (February 1928): p. 66. A brief survey of Huang's life and work with some bibliographical information.

Ma Tuan-lin 馬端臨. [*Ch'in-ting*] *Wen-hsien t'ung-k'ao* 欽定文獻通考. Shanghai: Commercial Press, *Shih-t'ung* ed., 1935–36.; SPTK ed.

Mao Nai-yung 毛乃庸. *Chi-ming feng-chüeh piao* 季明封爵表. Nanking: N.p., 1933.

Mao Pin 毛霦. *P'ing-pan chi* 平判記. In *Yin-li tsai ssu t'ang ts'ung-shu* 殷禮在斯堂叢書.

Matsui Hitoshi 松井等. *Shina kinsei seiji shichō* 支那近世政治思潮. Vol. 15 in the series Sekai kōbō shiron 世界興亡史論. Tokyo: Heibonsha, 1931. Contains a Japanese translation of the *Ming-i tai-fang lu*, apparently from the LCICHK ed., with brief interlinear notes. The translation is generally superior to Kuruhara's, but owing to the retention of whole phrases from the Chinese original, many passages obscure in the Chinese remain so in this translation.

Mei shih-shih. See Lu Shih-i.

Miao Ch'üan-chi 繆全吉. *Ming-tai hsü-li* 明代胥史. Wen-hua chi-chin ts'ung-shu (series). Taipei: Chia-hsin shui-ni kung-ssu, 1969.

Ming chi. See Ch'en Hao.

Ming-chi nan-lüeh, pei-lüeh. See Chi Liu-ch'i.

Ming hui-tien. See Shen Shih-hsing.

Ming-ju hsüeh-an. See Huang Tsung-hsi.

Ming shih (see also *Erh-shih-ssu shih*). Beijing: Zhonghua shuju, 1974.

Ming shih chi-shih pen-mo. See Ku Ying-t'ai.

Ming shih kao. See Wang Hung-hsü.

Ming shih lu 明實錄. Photolithographic reprint of the *Ming shih* formerly in the Kiangsu Provincial Library, Nanking: 1940.

Ming shu. See Fu Wei-lin.

Miyazaki Ichisada 宮崎一定. "Min-i taihō roku tōsakushū" 明夷待訪錄當作集. In *Tōyōshi kenkyū* 24, no. 2 (1965): 211–14, and 25, no. 2 (1966): 216–22. Also in *Ajia shi kenkyū* 5 (Kyoto: Dōbōsha, 1978): 315–29.

Mizoguchi Yūzō 溝口雄三. *Chūgoku zenkindai shisō no kussetsu to tenkai* 中国前近代思想の屈折と展開. Tokyo: Tokyo University Press, 1980.

———. "Iwayuru Tōrinha shinshi no shisō" 所謂東林派紳士の思想. *Tōyō bunka kenkyūjo kiyō* 75 (1978): 111–341.

———. "Min-i taihō roku no rekishiteki ichi" 明夷待訪錄の歴史的位置. *Hitotsubashi ronsō* 81, no. 3 (March 1979): 342–59.

Mo Po-chi 莫伯驥. *Wu-shih-wan chüan lou ts'ang-shu mu-lu, ch'u-pien* 五十萬卷樓藏書目錄初編. 1931 ed.

Naitō Torajirō (Konan) 内藤虎次郎. *Shina ron* 支那論. Tokyo: Bunkaidō,

1914. Includes a general discussion of Huang's political thought in relation to the problems of early Republican China.

——. *Shina shigaku shi* 支那史學史. Tokyo: Kobundō, 1949. Based on lecture notes by students of Naitō and edited by his son Kenkichi 乾吉, assisted by Kanda Kiichirō 神田喜一郎. Includes a brief section on Huang's importance as an historian and on the Eastern Chekiang School.

Nakayama Kyūshirō 中山久四郎. *Min-matsu no Nihon kisshi oyobi kisshi* 明末の日本乞師及乞資. In *Shigaku zasshi* 26, no. 5 (May 1915).

——. *Min-matsu no Nihon kisshi hokō* 補考. In *Shigaku zasshi* 29, no. 9 (September 1918). This and the preceeding item include a discussion of the missions to Japan of Feng Ching-ti and Huang Tsung-hsi, supporting the view that the latter did make such a trip.

Nan Bingwen 南炳文. "Huang Zongxi kending fengjian junzhu zhuanzhi zhidu de sixiang" 黃宗羲肯定封建君主專制制度的思想. In Wu Guang, ed., *Huang Zongxi lun*, pp. 350–57.

Nan-lei wen-an. See Huang Tsung-hsi.

Nan-lei wen-ting. See Huang Tsung-hsi.

Nan-lei wen-yüeh. See Huang Tsung-hsi.

Nan-shih. See *Erh-shih-ssu shih.*

Nien-p'u. See Huang Ping-hou.

Nishi Junzō 西順藏. *Min-i taihō roku* 明夷待訪錄. Tokyo: Mainichi Library (Tōyō no meicho), 1956.

Nishida Taichirō 西田太一郎, trans. *Min-i taihō roku* 明夷待訪錄. Tokyo: Heibonsha, 1964.

Ojima Sukema 小島祐馬. "Kō Sōgi no seiji keizai shisō" 黃宗羲の政治経済思想. In *Keizai ronsō* 7, nos. 1 (July 1918): 68–76, and 2 (August 1918): 213–24; and in *Chūgoku shakai shisō* 中国社会思想, Tokyo: Chikuma shobō, 1967.

Ono Kazuko 小野和子. "'Fu Zōshō kyūzō Kō Rishū sensei *Ryū sho*' ni tsuite" 傅增湘旧藏黃梨洲先生留書について. In *Shinchō chika no minzoku mondai to kokusai kankei* 清朝治下の民族問題と国際關系, pp. 42–52. Tokyo: Nihon gakujutsu shinkōkai, 1991.

——. *Kō Sōgi* 黃宗羲. In *Chūgoku jimbutsu sōsho*, 2d ser., no. 9. Tokyo: Jimbutsu ōraisha, 1967.

——. "Kō Sōgi no zen hansei: Toku ni *Min-i taihō roku* no seiritsu katei to shite" 黃宗羲の前半生：特に明夷待訪錄の成立過程として. *Tōhō gakuhō* 34 (1964): 135–98.

——. "Ryūsho no shisō" 留書の思想. In Iwami Hiroshi 岩見宏 and Taniguchi Kikuo 谷口規矩夫, eds., *Minmatsu Shinsho no kenkyū* 明末清初の研究, pp. 503–45. Kyoto: Kyōto daigaku jimbun kagaku kenkyūjo, 1989.

——. "Son Bun ga Minakata Kumagusu ni okutta 'Genkun, Genshin' ni tsuite 孫文が南方熊楠に贈つた「原君原臣」について." In *Son Bun kenkyū* 14 (April 1992): 19–24.

——. "Tōrinha to sono seiji shisō" 東林派とその政治思想. *Tōhō gakuhō* 28 (1958): 249–82.

——. "Torintō kō 東林黨考. *Tōhō gakuhō* 52 (1980): 563–94; 54 (1983): 259–323.

Ou-yang Hsiu, Sung Ch'i 歐陽修, 宋祁 *Hsin T'ang shu* 新唐書. SPTK ed.

——. *Ou-yang Wen-chung kung chi* 歐陽文忠公集. SPTK, 1st ser.

Pan Ku 班固. *Han shu*, SPTK ed.

Qin Peiheng 秦佩珩. "Huang Lizhou jingji sixiang gouzhen" 黃梨洲經濟思想鈎沉. In *Qiushi xuegan* 求是學刊 29 (August 1982): 68–71.

Qiu Hansheng 邱漢生. "Du *Mingyi daifang lu* zaji" 讀明夷待訪錄雜記. In Wu Guang, ed., *Huang Zongxi lun*, pp. 250–62.

Ren Jiyu 任繼愈. *Zhongguo zhexue shi* 中國哲學史. Vol. 4. Beijing: Renmin, 1979.

San-kuo chih. See *Erh-shih-ssu shih*.

Sano Kōji 佐野公治. "*Min-i taihō roku* ni okeru eki-sei kakumei shisō" 明夷待訪錄における易姓革命思想. In *Nihon Chūgoku gakkai hō* 17 (1965): 136–40.

Satō Shinji 佐藤震二. "*Hakugakin no shisō to Min-i taihō roku*" 伯牙琴の思想と明夷待訪錄. In *Tōhō gakuhō* 23 (1962): 80–94.

——. "*Min-i taihō roku* no kihon shisō." 明夷待訪錄の基本思想 *Akademia* 30 (1960): 1–28.

Shang shu 尚書. SPTK ed.

Shen Shanhong 沈善洪, ed. *Huang Zongxi quanji* 黃宗羲全集. 2 vols. Hangzhou: Zhejiang guji chubanshe 浙江古籍出版社, v.1 1985; v.2. 1986.

Shen Shih-hsing 申時行. *Ta-Ming hui-tien* 大明會典. Palace ed. of 1587 in 228 ch.

Shen-tao pei. See Ch'üan Tsu-wang.

Shih-ch'eng-chi. See Chiang Fan.

Shih chi. See *Erh-shih-ssu shih*.

Shih-p'u. See Wan Ssu-ta.

Shih-t'ung 十通. Shanghai: Commercial Press, 1935–36.

Shimada Kenji 島田虔次. *Chūgoku ni okeru kindai shii no zasetsu* 中国における近代思惟の挫折. Rev. ed. Tokyo: Chikuma shobō, 1970.

——. "Chūgoku no Rousseau" 中国のルソー. In *Shisō*, no. 435 (September 1960): 66–85. Also in *Chūgoku kakumei no senkusha tachi* 中国革命の先駆たち. Tokyo: Chikuma shobō, 1965.

——. *Shushigaku to Yōmeigaku* 朱子学と陽明学. Tokyo: Iwanami, 1967.

Shimizu Taiji 清水泰次. "Minsho ni okeru gunton no tenkai to sono so-shiki" 明初に於ける軍屯の展開とその組織 (Development and organization of military farms in the Early Ming). In *Shigaku zasshi* 44, nos. 5 and 6 (May–June 1933).

Ssu-ma Ch'ien 司馬遷. *Shih chi* 史記. SPTK ed.

Ssu-ma Kuang 司馬光. *Tzu-chih t'ung-chien* 資治通鑑. SPTK, 1st ser.

Ssu-k'u. See Chi Yün.

Su Hsün 蘇洵. *Chia-yu chi* 嘉祐集. SPTK, 1st ser.

Su Te-yung 蘇德用, comp. *Liu Chi-shan, Huang Li-chou hsüeh-an ho-chi* 劉蕺山, 黄梨洲學案合輯. Taipei: Cheng-chung shu-chü, 1954.

Sun Ch'eng-tse 孫承澤. *Ch'un-ming meng yü lu* 春明夢餘錄. In Ssu-k'u ch'üan-shu chen-pen ed.

[*Sung-pen*] *Shih-san ching chu-su fu chiao-k'an-chi* 宋本十三經注疏校勘記 (SSCCS, *Mai-wang hsien kuan* ed. 脈望仙館, 1987).

Sung shih. See *Erh-shih-ssu shih.*

Sung-Yüan hsüeh-an. See Huang Tsung-hsi.

T'ai-p'ing yü-lan. See Li Fang.

Takashima Katsumi 貴島克己, ed. *Shina zeisei no enkaku* (The development of Chinese tax systems) 支那税制の沿革. Dairen: South Manchurian Railway, 1933.

Takeuchi Yoshio 武内義雄. *Sōgaku no yurai oyobi sono tokushusei* 宋學の由來及び其特殊性. In *Tōyō shichō*. Tokyo: Iwanami kōza, 1934.

T'an P'i-mo 譚丕謨. *Ch'ing-tai ssu-hsiang shih-kang* 清代思想史綱. 3d ed. Shanghai: K'ai-ming shu-chü, 1947.

T'ang Chang-ju 唐長孺. *T'ang-shu ping-chih chien-cheng* 唐書兵志箋正. Beijing: Science Press, 1975.

T'ang Chen 唐甄. *Ch'ien shu* 潛書. Shanghai: Guji chubanshe, 1955.

——. *Ch'ien shu chu* 潛書注. Chengdu: Chengdu sichuan jenmin chubanshe, 1984.

T'ang Ch'iu 湯球. *Chin yang ch'iu* 晉陽秋. Kuang-ya shih ed.

T'ang Ch'i-yü 唐啓宇. *Li-tai t'un-ken yen-chiu* 歷代屯墾研究. Shanghai: Commercial Press, 1947.

T'ang Jo-ying 唐若瀛, ed. *Yü-yao chih* 餘姚志. 1778 ed.

Tang-she yün-tung. See Hsieh Kuo-chen.

Tang Zhen 唐甄. *Chien shu* 潛書. Shanghai: Guji chubanshe, 1955.

Teng Mu 鄧牧. *Po-ya ch'in* 伯牙琴. In *Chih-pu-tsu chai ts'ung-shu* 知不足齋叢書.

Teng Shih 鄧實. "Teng Mu-hsin *Po-ya ch'in* chi pa." 鄧牧心伯牙琴集跋. In *Kuo-ts'ui hsüeh-pao*, wen pien 36 國粹學報, 文篇 (n.d.: late Ch'ing).

Teng Ssu-yü 鄧嗣禹. *Chung-kuo k'ao-shih chih-tu k'ao* 中國考試制度考. Shanghai: Commercial Press, 1936.

Ting Fu-pao 丁福保. *Li-tai ku-ch'ien t'u-shuo* 歷代古錢圖説. Shanghai: I-hsüeh shu-chü, 1940.

Tso chuan. In *Ch'un-ch'iu ching-chuan chi-chieh* 春秋經傳集解. SPTK ed.

Ts'ui Shu 崔述. *Feng-hao k'ao-hsin lu* 豐鎬考信錄. TSCC ed.

Tu Mu 杜牧. *Fan-ch'uan wen-chi* 樊川集. SPTK ed.

T'u-shu chi-ch'eng. See Chiang T'ing-hsi.

Tu Yu 杜佑. *T'ung-tien* 通典. Shanghai: Commercial Press, *Shih-t'ung* ed., 1935–36.

T'ung k'ao. See Ma Tuan-lin.

T'ung tien. See Tu Yu.

Übelhör, Monika. "*Mingyi daifang-lu* de xian-ju Wang Gen 'yi tianxia zhi tienxia' de sixiang." In Wu Guang, ed., *Huang Zongxi lun,* pp. 303–309.

Ueyama Shumpei 上山春平. "Shushi no *Karei* to 'Girei keiden tsūkai'" 朱子 の家礼と儀礼経伝道解. In *Tōhō gakuhō* 54 (1982): 173–256.

Wan Ming shih-chi k'ao (WMSCK). See Hsieh Kuo-chen.

Wan Ssu-ta 萬斯大. *Hsüeh Ch'un-ch'iu sui-pi* 學春秋隨筆. *Huang-Ch'ing ching-chieh* ed.

——. *Li-chou hsien-sheng shih-p'u* 梨洲先生世譜 (abbr. *Shih-p'u*). LCICHK, *ts'e* 1:1a–2b. A brief account of the leading members of Huang's family up to his time, by one of the latter's outstanding disciples.

Wang An-shih 王安石. *Chou-kuan hsin-i* 周官新義. TSCC ed.

——. *Lin-ch'uan hsien-sheng wen-chi* 臨川先生文集. SPTK, 1st ser.

Wang Ch'i 王圻. *Hsü wen-hsien t'ung-k'ao* 續文獻通考. 1603 blockprint ed.; also *Ch'in-ting* ed. (in Commercial Press *Shih-t'ung*; see Ma Tuan-lin).

Wang Ching-yün 王慶雲. *Shih-ch'ü yü-chi* 石渠餘記. 1888 ed.

Wang Fu 王符. *Ch'ien-fu lun chien chiao-cheng* 潛夫論箋校正. Beijing: Chung hua shu chü, 1985.

Wang Hung-hsü 王鴻緒. *Ming shih kao* 明史稿. *Ching-shen t'ang* ed. 敬慎堂.

Wang Kuang-fu 汪光復. *Hang-hsieh i-wen* 航澥遺聞. In *Ch'ing-t'o i-shih* 荊駝逸史. Compiled by Ch'en Hu i-shih 陳湖逸士. Cf. WMSCK 2:2b, 12:4b.

Wang Mien 王冕. *Chu-chai shih-chi* 竹齋詩集. 1525 ed.

Wang Shou-jen 王守仁 (Yang-ming 陽明). *Wang Wen-ch'eng kung ch'üan-chi* 王文成公全集. SPPY ed., entitled *Yang-ming ch'üan-shu.*

Wang Tsai-chin 王在晉. *San-ch'ao liao-shih shih-lu* 三朝遼事實錄. Nanking: Kuo-hsüeh t'u-shu-kuan, 1931.

Wang Ying-lin 王應麟. *Yü-hai* 玉海. Chekiang shu-chü ed., 1883.

Wang Yü-quan 王毓銓. *Mingdai de juntun* 明代的軍屯. Beijing: 1965.

Wei-shu. See *Erh-shih-ssu shih.*

Wen-hsien t'ung-k'ao. See Ma Tuan-lin.

Wen Ping 文秉. *Lieh-huang hsiao-shih* 烈皇小識. NLWH ed.

Wu Chao-hsin 吳兆莘. *Chung-kuo shui-chih shih* 中國稅制史 (History of Chinese tax systems). Shanghai: Commercial Press, 1937.

Wu Ch'eng-lo 吳承洛. *Chung-kuo tu-liang-heng shih* 中國度量衡史 (A history of

Chinese lengths, capacities, and weights). Shanghai: Commercial Press, 1936.

Wu Guang 吳光 (Wu Kuang). *Huang Tsung-hsi chu-tso hui-k'ao* 黃宗羲著作彙考. Taipei: Hsüeh-sheng shu-chü Student Book Co., 1990.

——. "Huang Zongxi yizhu kao" 黃宗羲遺著考. In Shen Shanhong and Wu Guang, eds., *Huang Zongxi Quanji* 1:421–48; 2:550–84.

——, ed. *Huang Zongxi lun* 黃宗羲論. Hangzhou: Zhejiang guji chubanshe, 1987.

Wu Han 吳晗. *Chu Yüan-chang chuan* 朱元璋傳. Kirin: 1949.

——. "Ming-tai ti chün-ping" 明代的軍兵 (The hereditary and hired armies of the Ming). *Chung-kuo she-hui ching-chi shih chi-k'an* 中國社會經濟史集刊 (Chinese social and economic review) 5, no. 22 (June 1937): 148–75.

Wu Kuang 吳光 (Wu Guang). *Huang Tsung-hsi chu-tso hui-k'ao* 黃宗羲著作彙考. Taipei: Hsüeh-sheng shu-chü, 1990.

Wu-shih-wan chuan lou ts'ang-shu mu-lu, ch'u pien. See Mo Po-chi.

Wu Wenhan 吳文翰. "Huang Zongxi te falu sixiang" 黃宗羲的法律思想. In *Xibei shiyuan xuepao, shehui kexue* 西北師院學報社會科學 2, no. 32 (June 1982): 96–100.

Xie Gang 謝剛. "Mingyi daifang lu yu Qingchu wenci yu" 明夷待訪錄與清初文字獄. In *Zhonguo shi yanjiu* 3 (August 1983): 71–84.

Xiong Yüezhi 熊月之. "Lun Huang Zongxi, Tang Zhen fantui fengjian zhuanzhi zhuyi de minzhu sixiang" 論黃宗羲唐甄反對封建專制主義的民主思想. In *Shanghai shifan daxue xuebao, zhe xue shehui kexue* 3 (1973): 27–31.

Yamanoi Yū 山井湧. *Kō Sōgi* 黃宗羲. Tokyo: Kōdansha, 1983.

——. *Min-i taihō roku* 明夷待訪錄. In *Chūgoku no meicho* 中国の名著. Tokyo: Keisō shobō 勁草, 1969.

—— et. al. (comp.). *Minmatsu Shinsho seiji hyōron shū* 明末清初政治評論集. Tokyo: Heibonsha 平凡社, 1971.

—— *Min Shin shisōshi no kenkyū* 明清思想史の研究. Tokyo: Tokyo University Press, 1980.

Yang Yenfu 楊廷福. *Mingmo san da sixiang jia: Huang Zongxi, Gu Yanwu, Wang Fuzhi* 明末三大思想家:黃宗羲, 顧炎武, 王夫之. Shanghai: Silian Chubanshe, 1955.

Yao Ming-ta 姚名達. *Liu Tsung-chou nien-p'u* 劉宗周年譜. Shanghai: Commercial Press, 1934.

Yao Yujie 姚郁杰. "Guan yu Yuan-jun de zhongxin lundian" 關于原君的中心論點. *Ningxia daxue xuebao* 3 (1982): 80–83.

Ye Shichang 葉世昌. "Guan yu Huang Zongxi de gongshang jie ben lun" 關于黃宗羲的工商皆本論. In *Fudan xuebao* 復旦學報 (July 1983): 108–10.

Yeh Shih 葉適. *Shui-hsin wen-chi* 水心文集. SPTK, 1st ser.

Yen-t'ieh lun 鹽鐵論. Kuo hsüeh chi-pen ts'ung-shu. Shanghai: Commercial Press, 1936.

Yen Tzu ch'ün-chiu 晏子春秋. SPTK, 1st ser.

Yin Chi-shan 尹繼善. *Chiang-nan t'ung-chih* 江南通志. 1736 ed.

Yokota Terutoshi 横田輝俊. "Minmatsu no bunjin kessha ni tsuite" 明末の文人結社について. *Shigaku kenkyū* 88 (1963): 61–80.

Yü-hai. See Wang Ying-lin.

Yü-yao chih. See T'ang Jo-ying.

Yü-yao hsien chih. See Chou Ping-lin.

Yüan-shih. See *Erh-shih-ssu shih*.

Zhang Dainian 張岱年. "Huang Lizhou yü Zhongguo de minzhu sixiang" 黃梨洲與中國民主思想. In Wu Guang, *Huang Zongxi lun*, pp. 1–7.

Zhao Gang 趙剛. "Gu Yanwu 'Yu Huang Taichong shu' xinzheng" 顧炎武與黃太沖書新証. In *Lanzhou daxue xuebao, shehui kexue* 蘭州大學學報社會科學 34, no. 4 (October 1985): 17–18.

Zhong Erju 衷尔鉅. "Lun *Mingyi daifang lu* de zhexue sixiang" 論明夷待訪錄的哲學思想. In *Gansu sheng shehui kexue yuan, Shehui kexue*, no. 34 (1985–86): pp. 6–10.

Zhou Jizhi 周繼旨. "Shixi Huang Zongxi de junhai lun yu xianqin rujia zhengzhi sixiang de yuanyuan guanxi" 試析黃宗羲的君害論與先秦儒家政治思想的淵源關係. In Wu Guang, *Huang Zongxi lun*, pp. 310–21.

Works Cited in Western Languages

References in the text and notes are by volume number followed by chapter and/or page number.

Andrew, Anita M. "The Local Community in the Early Ming Social Legislation." *Ming Studies* 20 (1985): 57–67.

Atwell, William S. "From Education to Politics: The Fu she." In W. T. de Bary, ed., *The Unfolding of Neo-Confucianism.* New York: Columbia University Press, 1975.

Backhouse, E., and J. O. P. Bland. *Annals and Memoirs of the Court of Peking.* Boston: Houghton Mifflin, 1914; reprint, New York: AMS Press, 1970.

Balazs, Stefan. *Beiträge zur Wirtschafts-Geschichte der T'ang-zeit.* In Mitteilungen des Seminars für Orientalische Sprachen. Berlin: 1931.

Bernard, Henri, S.J. *Matteo Ricci's Scientific Contributions to China.* Trans. by E. T. C. Werner. Shanghai: Henri Vetch, 1935.

Biot, Edouard. *Essai sur l'histoire de l'instruction publique en Chine.* Paris: B. Duprat, 1847.

——. *Le Tcheou-li ou Rites des Tcheou.* 3 vols. Paris: Imprimerie Nationale, 1851.

Blake, Robert P. "The Circulation of Silver in the Moslem East Down to the Mongol Epoch." *Harvard Journal of Asiatic Studies* 2, no. 3 (December 1937): 291–328.

Bodde, Derk. *China's First Unifier.* Leiden: E. J. Brill, 1938; reprint, Hong Kong: Hong Kong University Press, 1967.

Bruce, J. P. *Chu Hsi and His Masters.* London: Probsthain, 1923; reprint, New York: AMS Press, 1973.

——. *The Philosophy of Human Nature.* London: Probsthain, 1922; reprint, New York: AMS Press, 1973.

Brunnert, H. S., and V. V. Hagelstrom. *Present-Day Political Organization of China.* Revised by N. J. Kolessoff. Trans. by A. Beltchenko and E. E. Moran. Shanghai: Kelly and Walsh, 1912; Taipei: Ch'eng Wen, 1971.

Busch, Heinrich. "The Tung-lin Academy and Its Political and Philosophical Significance." *Monumenta Serica* 14 (1949–55): 1–163.

Carter, Thomas Francis. *The Invention of Printing in China and Its Spread Westward.* New York: Columbia University Press, 1925; 2d rev. ed. edited by L. C. Goodrich, New York: Ronald Press, 1955.

Chaffee, John W. *The Thorny Gates of Learning in Sung China: A Social History of Examinations.* Cambridge: Cambridge University Press, 1985.

Chan, Albert. *The Glory and Fall of the Ming Dynasty.* Norman: University of Oklahoma Press, 1982.

Chan, Wing-tsit. *A Source Book in Chinese Philosophy.* Princeton: Princeton University Press, 1963; paperback, 1969.

Chang, George Der-lang. "The Village Elder System of the Early Ming Dynasty." *Ming Studies* 7 (1978): 53–62.

Chavannes, Edouard. *Les Memoires Historiques.* 5 vols. Paris: Ernest Leroux, 1895.

Ch'en, Huan-chang. *Economic Principles of Confucius and His School: Studies in History, Economics and Law.* New York: Columbia University Press, 1911.

Ch'ien, Tuan-sheng. *The Government and Politics of China.* Cambridge: Harvard University Press, 1950.

Ching, Julia, and Fang Chao-ying, eds. *The Records of Ming Scholars.* Honolulu: University of Hawaii Press, 1987.

Chu, Hung-lam. "Ch'iu Chün's *Ta-hsueh yen-i pu* and Its Influence in the Sixteenth and Seventeenth Centuries." *Ming Studies* 22 (Fall 1986): 1–32.

Chu, Shih-chia. "Chang Hsüeh-ch'eng: His Contributions to Chinese Local Historiography." Ph.D. diss., Columbia University, 1950. Brief discussion of relation to Huang, Wan Ssu-t'ung, and Ch'üan Tsu-wang.

Couvreur, Seraphin. *Li Ki.* 2 vols. Ho Kien Fou: Imprimerie de la Mission Catholique, 1913.

Crawford, Robert B. "Chang Chü-cheng's Confucian Legalism." In W. T. de Bary, ed., *Self and Society in Ming Thought,* pp. 367–413. New York: Columbia University Press, 1970.

——. "Eunuch Power in the Ming Dynasty." *T'oung Pao* 49, no. 3 (1961): 117–47.

Crawford, Robert B., Harry M. Lamley, and Albert B. Mann. "Fang Hsiao-ju in the Light of Early Ming Society." *Monumenta Serica* 15, no. 2 (1956): 303–27.

Dardess, John W. *Confucianism and Autocracy.* Berkeley: University of California Press, 1983.

de Bary, Wm. Theodore. *East Asian Civilizations: A Dialogue in Five Stages.* Cambridge: Harvard University Press, 1988.

———. *The Message of the Mind in Neo-Confucianism*. New York: Columbia University Press, 1989.

———. *Neo-Confucian Orthodoxy and the Learning of the Mind-and-Heart*. New York: Columbia University Press, 1981.

———. *The Trouble with Confucianism*. Cambridge: Harvard University Press, 1991.

de Bary, Wm. Theodore, ed. *Self and Society in Ming Thought*. New York: Columbia University Press, 1970.

———, and John Chaffee, eds. *Neo-Confucian Education: The Formative Stage*. Berkeley: University of California Press, 1989.

———, Wing-tsit Chan, and Burton Watson, eds. *Sources of Chinese Tradition*. 2 vols. New York: Columbia University Press, 1960; paperback, 1964.

Dennerline, Jerry. *The Chia-ting Loyalists: Confucian Leadership and Social Change in Seventeenth Century China*. New Haven: Yale University Press, 1981.

———. "Fiscal Reform and Local Control: The Gentry-Bureaucratic Alliance Survives the Conquest." In Frederic Wakeman, Jr., and Carolyn Grant, eds., *Conflict and Control in Late Imperial China*. Berkeley: University of California Press, 1975.

Dore, Henri, S.J. *Researches into Chinese Superstitions*. 13 vols. Translated by M. Kennelly. Shanghai: Tusewei Press, 1913–38.

Dreyer, Edward L. *Early Ming China: A Political History, 1355–1435*. Stanford: Stanford University Press, 1982.

Dubs, Homer H. "Han Yü and the Buddha's Relic: An Episode in Medieval Chinese Religion." *Review of Religion* 11, no. 1 (November 1946): 5–17.

———. *History of the Former Han Dynasty*. 2 vols. Baltimore: Waverly Press, vol. 1, 1938; vol. 2, 1944.

———. *The Works of Hsüntze*. London: Probsthain, 1928; reprint, New York: AMS Press, 1977.

Ebrey, Patricia. *Chu Hsi's "Family Rituals": A Twelfth-Century Chinese Manual for the Performance of Cappings, Weddings, Funerals, and Ancestral Rites*. Princeton: Princeton University Press, 1991.

ECCP. See Hummel.

Fairbank, J. K., and S. Y. Teng. "On the Types and Uses of Ch'ing Documents." *Harvard Journal of Asiatic Studies* 5, no. 1 (January 1940): 1–71.

———. *The United States and China*. Cambridge: Harvard University Press, 1948.

Farmer, Edward L. *Early Ming Government: The Evolution of Dual Capitals*. Cambridge: Harvard University Press, 1976.

Ferguson, J. C. "Political Parties of the Northern Sung." *Journal of the North China Branch, Royal Asiatic Society* (1927): 36–56.

Fogel, Joshua. *Politics and Sinology: The Case of Naitō Konan (1866–1934)*. Harvard Committee on East Asian Studies. Cambridge: Harvard University Press, 1984.

Franke, Wolfgang. "Preliminary Notes on the Important Chinese Literary Sources for the Study of the Ming Dynasty." *Studia Serica*. Monograph Series A, no. 2. Ch'engtu: West China Union University, 1948.

Fu, Lo-shu. *Teng Mu: A Forgotten Chinese Philosopher.* Leiden: E. J. Brill, 1965. Reprint from *T'oung Pao* 53: 1–3 (1965).

Fung Yu-lan and Derk Bodde, trans. *History of Chinese Philosophy.* 2 vols. Princeton: Princeton University Press, 1952–53.

——, trans. "The Rise of Neo-Confucianism and Its Borrowings from Buddhism and Taoism." *Harvard Journal of Asiatic Studies* 7, no. 2 (July 1942): 89–125.

——, trans. *A Short History of Chinese Philosophy.* New York: Macmillan, 1948; New York: Free Press, 1966.

Gale, Esson M. *Discourses on Salt and Iron: A Debate on State Control of Commerce and Industry in Ancient China.* Leiden: E. J. Brill, 1931.

Gale, Esson M., C. Lin, and P. Boodberg, trans. "Discourses on Salt and Iron." *Journal of the North China Branch, Royal Asiatic Society* 65 (1934): 73–110.

Gernet, Jacques. *Ecrits d'un sage encore inconnu* (a translation of T'ang Chen's *Ch'ien shu*). Paris: Gallimard/UNESCO, 1991.

——. "L'Homme ou la paperasse: Aperçu sur les conceptions politiques de T'ang Chen." In Dieter Eikemeier and Herbert Franke, eds., *State and Law in East Asia.* Weisbaden: Harrassowitz, 1981.

Giles, H. A. *Chuang Tzu: Mystic, Moralist, and Social Reformer.* London: Quaritch, 1899; reprint, London: Allen and Unwin, 1936; Taipei: Ch'eng Wen, 1969.

Giles, Lionel. "The Lament of the Lady of Ch'in." *T'oung-pao* 24 (1925–26): 305–80.

Glathe, Harry. "The Origin and Development of Chinese Money." *China Journal* 30 (1939): 97–107, 158–67, 210–18, 278–88.

Goodrich, L. C. *Invention of Printing in China.* Revised from original work by Thomas Francis Carter. New York: Ronald Press, 1955.

——. *The Literary Inquisition of Ch'ien-lung.* Baltimore: Waverly Press, 1935.

——, trans. "A Study of Literary Persecution During the Ming [by Ku Chieh-kang]." *Harvard Journal of Asiatic Studies* 30, no. 3 (December 1938): 254–311."

Goodrich, L. Carrington, and Fang Chao-ying, eds. *Dictionary of Ming Biography.* New York: Columbia University Press, 1976.

Graham, A. C. *Chuang Tzu: The Inner Chapters.* London: Allen and Unwin, 1981.

Grimm, Tilemann. "Das Neiko der Ming Zeit, von Anfangen bis 1506." *Oriens Extremus* 1 (1954): 139–77.

Haeger, John Winthrop, ed. *Crisis and Prosperity in Sung China.* Tucson: University of Arizona Press, 1975.

Handlin, Joanna. *Action in Late Ming Thought: The Reorientation of Lü K'un.* Berkeley: University of California Press, 1983.

Hartman, Charles. *Han Yü and the T'ang Search for Unity.* Princeton: Princeton University Press, 1986.

Henke, F. G. *The Philosophy of Wang Yang-ming.* Chicago: Open Court, 1916.

Hightower, James R. *Topics in Chinese Literature.* Harvard-Yenching Institute Studies. Vol. 3. Cambridge: Harvard-Yenching Institute, 1950.

Hsi, Angela. "Wu San-kuei in 1644: A Reappraisal." *Journal of Asian Studies* 34, no. 2 (February 1975): 443–53.

Hsiao, K. C. "Li Chih: An Iconoclast of the Sixteenth Century." *Tien Hsia Monthly* 6 (April 1938): 317–41.

Hsu, P. C. *Ethical Realism in Neo-Confucian Thought.* New York: Columbia University Press, 1933.

Hu Shih. "The Chinese Renaissance." *China Year Book: 1924,* pp. 633–51. T'ientsin: T'ien-tsin Press, 1924; reprint, Chicago: University of Chicago Press, 1934.

Huang, Ray. "Ni Yüan-lu: Realism in a Neo-Confucian Scholar-Statesman." In W. T. de Bary, ed., *Self and Society in Ming Thought,* pp. 415–49. New York: Columbia University Press, 1970.

——. *Taxation and Governmental Finance in Sixteenth-Century Ming China.* Cambridge: Cambridge University Press, 1974.

Huang Siu-chi. *Lu Hsiang-shan: A Twelfth-Century Chinese Idealist Philosopher.* American Oriental Series, vol. 27. New Haven: Yale University Press, 1944; reprint, Westport, Conn.: Hyperion Press, 1977.

Hucker, Charles O. *A Dictionary of Official Titles in Imperial China.* Stanford: Stanford University Press, 1985.

——. *The Ming Dynasty: Its Origins and Evolving Institutions.* Michigan Papers in Chinese Studies, no. 34. Ann Arbor: University of Michigan Center for Chinese Studies, 1978.

Hucker, Charles O., ed. *Chinese Government in Ming Times: Seven Studies.* New York: Columbia University Press, 1969.

Hughes, E. R. *The Great Learning and the Mean-in-Action.* London: Dent, 1942; New York: E. P. Dutton, 1943.

Hummel, Arthur W., ed. *Eminent Chinese of the Ch'ing Period (1644–1912)* (abbr. ECCP). Washington, D.C.: GPO, 1943–44.

Karlgren, B. *Book of Odes.* Stockholm: Museum of Far Eastern Antiquities, 1950.

Keene, Donald. *The Japanese Discovery of Europe.* London: Routledge and Kegan Paul, 1952; rev. ed., Stanford: Stanford University Press, 1969.

Kornbluth, David. "Ku Yen-wu and the Reform of Local Administration." *Select Papers from the Center for Far Eastern Studies,* no. 1 (1975–76). Chicago: University of Chicago, 1975–76.

Kracke, Edward A. *Civil Service in Early Sung China.* Cambridge: Harvard University Press, 1953.

Lee, Thomas H. C. *Government Education and Examinations in Sung China.* Hong Kong: Chinese University Press, 1985.

Legge, James, trans. *The Chinese Classics.* 5 vols. Oxford: Clarendon Press, 1865–1895; reprint, Hong Kong: Hong Kong University Press, 1961.

——, trans. *Li Ki, Book of Rites.* 2 vols. In Max Müller, ed., *Sacred Books of the East,* vols. 27 and 28, Oxford: Oxford University Press, 1891; reprint, New York: University Books, 1967.

——, trans. *The Texts of Taoism: Kwang Tze.* 2 vols. In *Sacred Books of the East,* vols. 39 and 40. Oxford: Oxford University Press, 1891.

——, trans. *Yi King.* In *Sacred Books of the East,* vol. 16. Oxford: Clarendon Press, 1899.

Liang Fang-chung. *The Single-Whip Method of Taxation in China.* Translated by Wang Yü-chuan (partial translation of Liang's *"I-t'iao pien fa";* see listing for Liang in preceding section). Chinese Economic and Political Studies. Cambridge: Harvard University Press, 1956.

Liao, W. K. *Complete Works of Han Fei Tzu.* 2 vols. London: Probsthain, 1939.

Liew Foon Ming. "Debates on the Birth of Capitalism in China During the Past Three Decades." *Ming Studies* 26 (Fall 1988): 61–76.

——. *Tuntian Farming of the Ming Dynasty (1368–1644).* Hamburg: Geselschaft fur Natur und Völkerkunde Ostasiens, 1984.

Lin Mou-sheng. *Men and Ideas.* New York: John Day, 1942.

Lin Yutang. *The Gay Genius: The Life and Times of Su Tungpo.* New York: John Day, 1947.

Lin Yutang, ed. *The Wisdom of Confucius.* New York: Random House, Modern Library, 1938.

Littrup, Leif. *Sub-bureaucratic Government in China in Ming Times: A Study of Shandong Province in the Sixteenth Century.* Oslo: Institute for Comparative Research in Human Culture, 1981.

——. "The Yellow Registers of the Ming Dynasty: A Translation from the Wan-li Da-ming Hui-dian." *Papers on Far Eastern History,* no. 16: pp. 67–106. Canberra: Australia National University, 1977.

Liu, James T. C. *Reform in Sung China.* Cambridge: Harvard University Press, 1959.

Margoulies, George. *Anthologie Raisonnée de la Litterature Chinoise.* Paris: Payot, 1946.

——. *Le Kou-wen Chinois.* Paris: P. Geuthner, 1946.

Mayers, William F. *The Chinese Government.* Shanghai: Kelly and Walsh, 1896; 3d ed., rev. by G. M. H. Playfair, Taipei: Ch'eng Wen, 1970.

McKnight, Brian. *Village and Bureaucracy in Southern Sung China.* Chicago: University of Chicago Press, 1971.

Mei, Yi-pao. *The Ethical and Political Works of Motse.* London: Probsthain, 1929.

Meskill, John. *Academies in Ming China: A Historical Essay.* Tucson: University of Arizona Press, 1982.

Mote, Frederick. "The T'u Mu Incident of 1449." In Frank Kierman, Jr., and John K. Fairbank, eds., *Chinese Ways in Warfare.* Harvard East Asian Series, no. 74. Cambridge: Harvard University Press, 1974.

Mote, Frederick, and Denis Twitchett, eds. *The Ming Dynasty.* Vol. 7 of *The Cambridge History of China.* New York: Cambridge University Press, 1988.

Parsons, James B. *Peasant Rebellions of the Late Ming.* Tucson: University of Arizona Press, 1970.

Pokotilov, D. *History of the Eastern Mongols During the Ming Dynasty from 1368 to 1634* (Part I). Translated from the Russian by Rudolph Loewenthal. *Studia Serica,* Monograph Series A, no. 1 (Ch'engtu: West China Union University, 1947).

Report of the Librarian of Congress (1929–30), esp. pp. 351–53. Washington, D. C.: Library of Congress, 1931.

Rideout, J. K. "The Rise of Eunuchs in the T'ang Dynasty." *Asia Minor,* n.s. 1, pt. 1 (January 1949): 53–72; continued in 3d ser., pt. 1 (October 1952): 42–58.

——. "The Context of the Yüan Tao and Yüan Hsing." *Bulletin of the School of Oriental and African Studies* 30, no. 2 (London: University of London).

Rotours, Robert des. *Le Traité des Examens.* Paris: Ernest Leroux, 1932.

——. *Traité des Fonctionnaires et Traité de l'Armée.* Leiden: E. J. Brill, vol. 1, 1947; vol. 2, 1948.

——. "Les grands fonctionnaires des provinces en Chine sous la dynastie de T'ang," *T'oung Pao,* 2d ser., vol. 25 (1927): 219–332.

——. "Notes, bibliographiques sur les ouvrages de sinologie parus depuis 1929." In *Mélanges Chinois et Bouddhiques* 2 (Brussels, 1932–33): 358–61.

Sansom, G. B. *The Western World and Japan.* New York: Knopf, 1950.

Schirokauer, Conrad. "Neo-Confucians Under Attack: The Condemnation of Wei-hsüeh." In John Winthrop Haeger, ed., *Crisis and Prosperity in Sung China,* pp. 163–98. Tucson: University of Arizona Press, 1975.

Shaw Kinn Wei. *Democracy and Finance in China.* New York: Columbia University Press, 1926.

Smith, F. P. *Materia Medica of China.* London: 1871; 2d rev. ed., Taipei: Ku-t'ing Book House, 1969.

Steele, John, trans. *The I-li.* London: Probsthain, 1917.

Struve, Lynn A. "Ch'en Ch'ueh and Huang Tsung-hsi: Confucianism and Modern Times in the Seventeenth Century." In Ch'en Li-fu, ed., *International Symposium on Confucianism in the Modern World,* pp. 1441–58; and *Journal of Chinese Philosophy* 18, no. 4 (March 1991): 5–23.

——. "The Concept of Mind in the Scholarship of Huang Tsung-hsi (1610–1695)." *Journal of Chinese Philosophy* 9, no. 1 (1982): 107–29.

——. "The Early Ch'ing Legacy of Huang Tsung-hsi: A Reexamination." *Asia Major* 1, no. 1, 3d ser. (1988): 83–121.

——. "Huang Zongxi [Tsung Hsi] in Context: A Reappraisal of His Major Writings." *Journal of Asian Studies* 47, no. 3 (August 1988): 474–502.

——. *The Southern Ming.* New Haven: Yale University Press, 1984.

Stuart, George A. *Chinese Materia Medica.* Shanghai: 1928; 2d rev. ed., Taipei: Ku-t'ing Book House, 1969.

Swann, Nancy Lee. *Food and Money in Ancient China.* Princeton: Princeton University Press, 1950.

T'ang Leang-li. *The Inner History of the Chinese Revolution.* London: Rutledge, 1930; New York: Dutton, 1930.

T'ao, L. K. "A Chinese Political Theorist of the 17th Century." *Chinese Social and Political Science Review* 2, no. 1 (1927): 71–78. Sections 1 and 3 of the *Ming-i tai-fang lu* (entitled "On Kingship" and "On Law"), translated into English with a brief introduction.

Taylor, Romeyn. *Basic Annals of Ming T'ai-tsu.* San Francisco: Chinese Materials Center, 1975.

——. "The Yüan Origins of the Wei-so System." In Charles Hucker, ed., *Chinese Government in Ming Times,* pp 23–40. New York: Columbia University Press, 1969.

Teng, S. Y., and K. Biggerstaff. *An Annotated Bibliography of Selected Chinese Reference Works.* Peiping: Yenching, 1936; reprint, Harvard-Yenching Institute, 1950; 3d ed., Cambridge: Harvard University Press, 1971.

Tillman, Hoyt Cleveland. *Utilitarian Confucianism: Ch'en Liang's Challenge to Chu Hsi.* Cambridge: Harvard University Press, 1982.

Tjan Tjoe-som. *Po Hu t'ung: The Comprehensive Discussions in the White Tiger Hall.* 2 vols. Leiden: E. J. Brill, 1949–52.

Twitchett, Denis. *Financial Administration Under the T'ang Dynasty.* Cambridge: Cambridge University Press, 1963.

Twitchett, Denis, and John K. Fairbank, gen. eds. *The Cambridge History of China.* New York and Cambridge: Cambridge University Press. Vol. 1, *The Ch'in and Han Empires,* ed. Denis Twitchett and Michael Loewe (1986); vol. 3, *Sui and T'ang China,* ed. Denis Twitchett and John K. Fairbank (1979); vol. 7, *The Ming Dynasty,* ed. Frederick Mote and Denis Twitchett (1988).

Van Glahn, Richard. "Urban Social Conflict in the Late Ming." *Journal of Asian Studies* 50, no. 2 (May 1991): 280–307.

Vissering, Wilhelm. *On Chinese Currency: Coin and Paper Money.* Leiden: E. J. Brill, 1877; Taipei: Ch'eng Wen, 1968.

Wakeman, Frederic. "The Price of Autonomy." *Daedaelus* (Spring 1972): 35–70.

Waley, Arthur. *The Analects of Confucius.* London: Allen and Unwin, 1938.

———, trans. *The Nine Songs.* London: Allen and Unwin, 1956.

Wang, Tch'ang-tche, S.J. *La Philosophie Morale de Wang Yang Ming.* Paris: P. Geuthner, 1936; Shanghai: T'ou-se-we, 1936.

Wang, Yü-ch'üan. "An Outline of the Central Government of the Former Han Dynasty." *Harvard Journal of Asiatic Studies* 12, nos. 1 and 2 (June 1949): 134–87.

Wang Yuquan. "Some Salient Features of the Ming Labor Service System." *Ming Studies* 21 (Spring 1986): 1–44.

Watson, Burton, trans. *The Complete Works of Chuang Tzu.* New York: Columbia University Press, 1968.

———, trans. *Records of the Grand Historian of China.* 2 vols. New York: Columbia University Press, 1961.

Werner, E. T. C. *Descriptive Sociology: Chinese.* Edited by H. R. Tedder. London: 1910.

Wieger, L. *Textes Historiques.* 3 vols. Hsien hsien: Imprimerie de la Mission Catholique, 1903.

Wilhelm, Hellmut. *Gu Ting-lin der Ethiker.* Darmstadt: L. C. Wittich, 1932.

———. "The Po-hsüeh hung-ju Examination of 1679." *Journal of the American Oriental Society,* nos. 7–11 (1951): 60–66.

Williamson, H. R. *Wang An-shih.* 2 vols. London: Probsthain, 1935.

Woodbridge, S. I. *China's Only Hope.* New York: Ravell, 1900; reprint, Westport, Conn.: Hyperion Press, 1975.

Wright, Arthur F., and Denis Twitchett, eds. *Perspectives on the T'ang.* New Haven: Yale University Press, 1973.

Wu, K. T. "Ming Printing and Printers." *Harvard Journal of Asiatic Studies* 7, no. 3 (February 1943): 203–60.

Wylie, Alexander. *Notes on Chinese Literature.* Shanghai: Presbyterian Mission Press, 1922.

Yang, Lien-sheng. "Ming Local Administration." In Charles O. Hucker, ed., *Chinese Government in Ming Times: Seven Studies.* New York: Columbia University Press, 1962.

——. *Money and Credit in China: A Short History.* Cambridge: Harvard University Press, 1952.

——. *Topics in Chinese History.* Harvard-Yenching Institute Studies. Vol. 4. Cambridge: Harvard-Yenching Institute, 1950.

Young, Lung-chang. "Ku Yen-wu's Views on the Ming Examination System." *Ming Studies* 23 (Spring 1982): 48–63.

Index

Other Works in the
Columbia Asian Studies Series

Love Song of the Dark Lord: Jayadeva's Gītagovinda, tr. Barbara Stoler
Miller. Also in paperback ed. Cloth ed. includes critical text of the
Sanskrit. 1977; rev. ed.   1997

Ryōkan: Zen Monk-Poet of Japan, tr. Burton Watson   1977

*Calming the Mind and Discerning the Real: From the Lam rim chen mo
of Tson-kha-pa*, tr. Alex Wayman   1978

*The Hermit and the Love-Thief: Sanskrit Poems of Bhartrihari and
Bilhaṇa*, tr. Barbara Stoler Miller   1978

The Lute: Kao Ming's P'i-p'a chi, tr. Jean Mulligan. Also in paperback ed.   1980

*A Chronicle of Gods and Sovereigns: Jinnō Shōtōki of Kitabatake
Chikafusa*, tr. H. Paul Varley   1980

Among the Flowers: The Hua-chien chi, tr. Lois Fusek   1982

Grass Hill: Poems and Prose by the Japanese Monk Gensei, tr. Burton
Watson   1983

*Doctors, Diviners, and Magicians of Ancient China: Biographies of
Fang-shih*, tr. Kenneth J. DeWoskin. Also in paperback ed.   1983

Theater of Memory: The Plays of Kālidāsa, ed. Barbara Stoler Miller.
Also in paperback ed.   1984

*The Columbia Book of Chinese Poetry: From Early Times to the Thirteenth
Century*, ed. and tr. Burton Watson. Also in paperback ed.   1984

*Poems of Love and War: From the Eight Anthologies and the Ten Long
Poems of Classical Tamil*, tr. A. K. Ramanujan. Also in paperback ed.   1985

The Bhagavad Gita: Krishna's Counsel in Time of War, tr. Barbara
Stoler Miller   1986

The Columbia Book of Later Chinese Poetry, ed. and tr. Jonathan
Chaves. Also in paperback ed.   1986

The Tso Chuan: Selections from China's Oldest Narrative History, tr.
Burton Watson   1989

Waiting for the Wind: Thirty-six Poets of Japan's Late Medieval Age,
tr. Steven Carter   1989

Selected Writings of Nichiren, ed. Philip B. Yampolsky   1990

Saigyō, Poems of a Mountain Home, tr. Burton Watson   1990

The Book of Lieh Tzu: A Classic of the Tao, tr. A. C. Graham.
Morningside ed.   1990

*The Tale of an Anklet: An Epic of South India—The Cilappatikāram
of Iḷaṅkō Aṭikaḷ*, tr. R. Parthasarathy 1993

Waiting for the Dawn: A Plan for the Prince, tr. and introduction by
Wm. Theodore de Bary   1993

STUDIES IN ASIAN CULTURE

COMPANIONS TO ASIAN STUDIES

INTRODUCTION TO ASIAN CIVILIZATIONS
Wm. Theodore de Bary, General Editor

NEO-CONFUCIAN STUDIES

Neo-Confucian Terms Explained: Pei-hsi tzu-i, by Ch'en Ch'un, ed.
and tr. Wing-tsit Chan   1986
Knowledge Painfully Acquired: K'un-chih chi, by Lo Ch'in-shun, ed.
and tr. Irene Bloom   1987
To Become a Sage: The Ten Diagrams on Sage Learning, by Yi T'oegye,
ed. and tr. Michael C. Kalton   1988
The Message of the Mind in Neo-Confucian Thought, by Wm. Theodore
de Bary   1989

9 780231 080972

About the Authors

M. H. Abrams, Class of 1916 Professor of English, Emeritus, at Cornell University, is a distinguished scholar who has written prize-winning books on eighteenth- and nineteenth-century literature, literary theory and criticism, European Romanticism, and Western intellectual history. He inaugurated *A Glossary of Literary Terms* in 1957 as a series of succinct essays on the chief terms and concepts used in discussing literature, literary history and movements, and literary criticism. Since its initial publication, the *Glossary* has become an indispensable handbook for all students of English and other literatures.

Geoffrey Galt Harpham has been a co-author of the *Glossary* since the eighth edition in 2005. He is president and director of the National Humanities Center in North Carolina and has written extensively in the fields of critical theory and intellectual history. Among his books are *The Character of Criticism, Shadows of Ethics: Criticism and the Just Society, Language Alone: The Critical Fetish of Modernity,* and *The Humanities and the Dream of America.*